Bitter-
sweet
Destiny

DEL THIESSEN

Bitter-sweet Destiny

The Stormy Evolution of Human Behavior

TRANSACTION PUBLISHERS
New Brunswick (U.S.A.) and London (U.K.)

Copyright © 1996 by Transaction Publishers, New Brunswick, New Jersey 08903.

All rights reserved under International and Pan-American Copyright Conventions. No part of this book may be reproduced or transmitted in any form or by any means, electronic or mechanical, including photocopy, recording, or any information storage and retrieval system, without prior permission in writing from the publisher. All inquiries should be addressed to Transaction Publishers, Rutgers—The State University, New Brunswick, New Jersey 08903.

This book is printed on acid-free paper that meets the American National Standard for Permanence of Paper for Printed Library Materials.

Library of Congress Catalog Number: 95-25116
ISBN: 1-56000-245-X
Printed in the United States of America

Library of Congress Cataloging-in-Publication Data

Thiessen, Delbert D.
    Bittersweet destiny : the stormy evolution of human behavior / Del Thiessen.
        p. cm.
    Includes bibliographical references and index.
    ISBN 1-56000-245-X (alk. paper)
    1. Genetic psychology. 2. Behavior evolution. 3. Human behavior. I. Title.
BF701.T44 1995
155.7—dc20   95-25116
                                                                        CIP

Contents

Part V   Into the Mountains

Acknowledgements

Many people gave me suggestions on parts of this book, some of which I took, some of which I did not. I am especially grateful to Dr. David Cohen who convinced me that the undertaking was worth it. Other tough but always helpful critics included Drs. Robert Cocke, Devendra Singh, Jan Bruell, Lee Willerman, Peter MacNeilage, Joe Horn, Larry Parsons, Daniel Gilbert, Phillip Gough, Walt Wilczynski, Michel Domjan, David Buss, and Joseph Lopreato. I am also grateful to Wesley Wynne and Veronica Henderson who read some of the earlier chapters, Susana Douglas who did the original illustrations, Joyce Bagwell who typed many of the tables, and Susan Martin who for years has supported my efforts. I would also like to thank Mr. Laurence Mintz for his valuable advice and editorial assistance. Not least, I thank my wife, Denise, for her encouragement, and my son, Trevor, to whom this book is dedicated.

A Short Note to the Reader

This is not an ordinary book. It combines a discourse on the evolution of human behavior with a philosophical perspective—not a stilted thesis on life, but a contemporary and controversial interpretation of our bittersweet destiny. Material is presented against the broad background of everyday life, allowing the reader to see the theory of evolution shaping his or her own behavior. In this manner the reader can judge the evidence and ideas against one's own philosophical ideas.

The book is also a story of our beginnings, our striving for life and reproduction, and our hopes for the future. The story begins with the heroic efforts of the naturalists Charles Darwin and Alfred Wallace to unlock the secrets of evolution, continuing on with a vivid description of our fossil history and our chance origin. From there the story implicates disease processes in evolution, highlights our irrational and rational nature, focuses on those characteristics of brain evolution and language that make us distinctive, and illustrates our most basic survival and reproductive mechanisms. But the story is only completed by inspecting our darker side, our "selfish genes," as biologist Richard Dawkins called them, and our "savage genes," as we sometimes see them, that cause us to murder, rape, and go to war.

When evolutionary theory is aimed at human behavior the controversies begin. Critics allow the extrapolation of evolutionary theory to a wide range of animal species, and even human morphology and physiology, but when the same perspective is applied to human behavior there is a stirring of dissent as strong as the desert sands. Even some of those who have contributed the most to evolutionary theory, and thus indirectly to the understanding of human behavior, are the harshest dissenters. To them, evolutionary hypotheses do not cross the threshold separating other animals from humans—humans somehow have escaped the regularities of the universe.

Instead of the critics openly insisting on the inapplicability of evolutionary principles to human behavior, which would reflect on their scientific integrity, they suggest that theories and methodologies applied to humans are naive at best and malevolent at worst. While in good conscience they cannot separate humans from other species, they can on personal, political, and religious grounds deflect the efforts to place humans in a common evolutionary framework.

What the *judges of appropriateness* fear, it seems, is that accepting evolutionary notions about human behavior strikes at the heart of free will, self-determination, and social equality. In response to these concerns two things should be said. The first is most obvious: things are as they are no matter what we might wish. We ignore facts and avoid controversy at our own risk. The second response is that there is nothing inherently malevolent about evolutionary theory as it is applied to humans. True, history provides the horrific examples of the consequence of viewing cultural differences as genetic. But just as gene theory can be misapplied for political reasons, so can environmental and ideological theories. Indeed, more genocide and social harm have been committed for religious, moralistic, political, and ideological reasons, than for any "evolutionary" argument. Even when genetic arguments have been used for human discrimination or extermination, the rationalizations only act as a cover for political motivations. The misapplication of cultural imperatives is just as potentially dangerous and ill-advised as the misapplication of genetic imperatives.

One last word about the controversies surrounding the investigation of human behavior. Those who would bury the evidence of human evolution in the sands of time seem fearful that knowledge is dangerous and that most individuals cannot be trusted with the truth. Moralists would rather have people live with a benevolent lie than confront the implications of their evolutionary history. But in a true democracy people should have access to the deep arguments of science, allowing them to judge the worth of the matter. To this end, *Bittersweet Destiny* draws out the evolutionary argument to its logical end—no holds barred.

The picture of human behavior painted is not always pretty because our background is one of conflict and selfish longing. We are not here entirely because of our altruistic nature, but because of our aggressive determination. Still, at the end of our story we see our own emergence as an evolutionary success without precedence—the human story that is still unfolding, still changing, still evolving.

The author does not attempt to document each and every statement, but instead presents the evolutionary logic within a wider and sometimes personalized philosophy. Neither is speculation eschewed; it is the theoretical glue that unites facts. It cannot be eliminated in any broad theorizing. One can therefore legitimately take issue with many of the arguments, and arrive at different conclusions. The book is fashioned so that can happen. Readers who want more can pursue the general references at the end of each chapter. There they can find more specific information and counter arguments than are in the text; extending their own thinking in several directions.

Preface

Nothing in our lives makes sense unless we look though a biological lens. Peering deeply, we understand our origin, our affiliation with all animals and plants, our complexity, and our cultural destination. There's a beauty in this as great as Albert Einstein's theory of relativity, the plays of William Shakespeare, the sculptures of Michelangelo. Our being is all one whole cloth, cut out by natural selection, woven together by neural networks, spun out in adaptive behaviors. The sweetness is in knowing the legacy of our triumph, the integrity of the mind, and the carefully structured messages of survival and reproduction.

Ah, but there is more—we see also through the biological lens darkly. The fabric of our evolution sweeps wider than our enchanting complexities, our reaching for the stars. It includes our favoritism toward relatives who share our own genes, our incredible ability to deceive ourselves and others, our careful choice of mates to fulfill our genetic needs, our extreme passions of murder, rape, and abuse. It's all there, our striving for success, the terror of the "selfish gene," the indifference to the hurt of others. Good, bad, and indifferent, we serve the replication of our DNA.

The stormy history of our past is upon us. The Darwinian revolution, begun nearly one hundred and fifty years ago, has finally swirled into our daily lives, showcasing the magnificence of our existence, and impressing us with its cold reality. We are now at the cusp, where an old millennium ends and a new one begins. Survival and extinction are at issue. If we are to overcome old politics, unsound ideologies, and the fragmentation of civilization, we must react. Part of that reaction is to admit our tie to the selfish gene, thereafter building a moral system that makes evolutionary sense. Knowing our origin, we must face our bittersweet destiny.

Introduction

*The Stickman pushed the dice in front of me, announcing
"New shooter coming out." Three of my $100 black chips
shined vividly on the green and white pass line, adding fuel to
my pounding heart. The crowd was a blur, yelling, clicking
multicolored chips, downing house drinks and blowing white
smoke to the Boxman at the center. The table was hot, showing
a trend—giving life to probability, adding to the feeling of
destiny. Could the run of luck hold? I saw differing opinions,
with chips on both the "pass line," and the "no pass line"—
different hopes and strategies. The "bones," cold in my hand,
seemed to wink in the overhead light. I slammed them hard
against the far end of the table, praying to the gods of chance.
"Seven, a lucky seven," sang the Stickman. Yells and moans
penetrated my consciousness as lightning struck and luck
found its level around the table. I grabbed my booty, scurrying
away, knowing that I had missed disaster by a crazy bounce.*

—A Las Vegas Bum

In the Balance: An Uncertain Journey

The entire tapestry of life, our own and that around us, has the distinctive quality of uncertainty. But for a horseshoe nail, a war lost; but for an island retreat, a species gone. The English dramatist, Samuel Foote, himself somewhat of a gambler, caught the sense of this when he remarked that "Death and dice level all distinctions." There is no biological game of life and death where only predictability and rationality play out the rolls. The quirky qualities of life are there, our bittersweet destiny. We must attend to them, as we do in this book.

Our Daily Bread

Before his death, Isaac Asimov, that great popularizer of science, estimated our odds of dying from events large and small. The least likely death is from freezing into an ice cube billions of years from now. The

1

most likely death is from heart failure or cancer. Asimov rolled for himself one of the small numbers. Somewhere between the extremes lies the texture of daily uncertainty.

Here are some of your odds—the probabilities of success and failure: winning a major lottery (1 in 16,000,000), having intercourse during the next year (1 in 5), graduating from high school (7.5 in 10), never reproducing (1 in 5), catching malaria in the tropics (1 in 5,800), coming down with schizophrenia (1 in 167), dying from heart disease (1 in 3) or cancer (1 in 5), getting hit by lightning (1 in 9,100). Everything we do or is done to us carries a probability estimate.

We do what we can to rearrange the odds in little ways. We take care of our health, drive carefully, and stay away from mobs. We also strive for certainty in big ways. Religion helps structure our existence, providing us with solace from chance and misfortune. Science, too, helps manage disease and death, shifting the odds in our favor. And, with theory and philosophy, we explain the unknown and rationalize our plight. The temptation is to agree with Omar Khayyám that uncertain life takes precedence over a certain death: "Drink! for you know not whence you came, nor why: Drink! for you know not why you go, nor where." If the conclusion of life is dark and inevitable, at least we smooth the way and play the game of life to the hilt.

What of Our Biology?

Chance and circumstance envelop our biological history as tightly as our daily life. How could it be otherwise—uncertainty today but certainty yesterday? The novelist J.B. Priestley defined our psychic dilemma: "Although we talk so much about coincidence we do not really believe in it. In our heart of hearts we think better of the universe, we are secretly convinced that it is not such a slipshod, haphazard affair, that everything in it has meaning." Consider human evolution: it seems miraculous—a planned certainty, an undeniable fate. But does nature play the harp of destiny for man, or is it just another dice game? If destiny, then why did man appear so late on the evolutionary scene, and why are his fortunes unknowable? If a dice game, are we a fluke, a product of uncertainty and low-level predictability. What if God really does play dice with the Universe, and the "seven" that we see today on this felt table of life becomes the "snake-eyes" of tomorrow?

What then? What use are our grand philosophies, our momentary pleasures?

No doubt about it, the evolution of man is strange—it's taken some bumps, curves, and crooked paths along the way. But evolution is not random, and herein lies a critical distinction. Chance and happenstance are natural processes of unrecognized impulses—modes of acting that harbor unpredictable outcomes but that still operate within the constraints of biology and physics—not random, only *contingent*. By contingent, we mean unforeseen interaction between events—the sequence of which is unpredictable. The eighteenth-century philosopher, Voltaire, was absolutely correct when he said that, "Chance is a word that does not make sense. Nothing happens without a cause." Our lives may be bitter, or sweet, but they are destiny played out by causes of the past. We can agree with that, yet still view the world as as decidedly unpredictable. Cause is still king, just difficult to pin down.

The meaning is clear. We arrived in today's world because of the contingencies of our past. We are here because of the survival of a unique and fragile vertebrate species that first appeared about 525 million years ago in the Cambrian Period. We evolved in response to environmental demands for specific adaptations but also because we escaped some major catastrophes, temporarily winning the game of probabilities. In every sense we are an improbable—nearly miraculous—species, one with a checkered past.

The Journey

There are two themes in this book. The first is that there is something happenstantial about our existence. We could have been different; we could have been nothing at all. Figuratively, we are the product of "stormy evolution"—contingent lightning strikes of the environment that drove our evolution. The second theme is that evolution has produced human strategies that limit negative contingencies, even turning these events into assets. We are not passive products of contingent evolution, bouncing off the walls of life like dice; we are dynamic players in the game of life, displaying behaviors that tend to match the contingent features that surround us. Stated philosophically, *we do not walk through nature; nature walks through us*: we were formed by contingencies, carrying reflections of those contingencies in our structures and behaviors. Just as a tree bows in direction with the wind, our nature reflects the forces of history.

Contingency on the High Seas

Our history is remindful of the true adventure story, *Sink the Bismarck*, written by C.S. Forester, who also wrote *The African Queen* and the Hornblower sea tales. At the outset of World War II, the British heroically sank the seemingly invincible German battleship, *Bismarck*. It's a story of contingency and improbability, much like our own evolution. The important event came early. A sixteen-inch shell from the cruiser HMS *Prince of Wales* hit the *Bismarck*, causing an oil leak which slowed the huge ship, allowing other British ships and torpedo planes to close in on the warship and eventually send her to the bottom of the Atlantic. The author, as part of this story, traces the key sixteen-inch shell from the munitions factory in England to the *Prince of Wales*, finally causing the crucial damage of the *Bismarck*. The first shell striking the well-fortified Bismarck seemed minimally significant at the time, but as Edmund Burke reminds us, "By gnawing through a dike, even a rat may drown a nation." The greatest weights sometimes hang on the finest wires.

There are two ways of interpreting the outcome: the first is to work backward from the sinking of the *Bismarck* to the manufacturing of the pivotal shell. The second is to work forward from the manufacturing process to the fatal hit. The backward look leads us to a fateful shell, manufactured by a particular company of men for the HMS *Prince of Wales*; with the backward look, the sinking seems inevitable. But when we rerun the events from the point of the shell's manufacture, with the forward look, the outcome seems anything but inevitable. Thousands of sixteen-inch shells were manufactured by platoons of workers, some shells remained in storage, some loaded on the cruisers HMS *Norfolk*, HMS *Stafford*, and HMS *Prince of Wales*, all of which took part in the action. Only a few of the shells were ever fired, one of which hit a vulnerable point on the battleship *Bismarck*. The contingencies leading to a single shell in a particular ship at a critical juncture in time are endless in number. No one could have predicted any of these events. Couple these unlikely circumstances with the low probability that the *Prince of Wales* was able to get into firing range and deliver the deadly shell, plus the fact that the *Bismarck* had to slow her speed, allowing other ships and planes to converge on the action. Viewed from this perspective, the contingencies of this epic event jump out all over the place. Great happenings like this are not trifles, but they spring from trifles—nothing is inevitable until it happens.

The lesson for understanding the evolution of ourselves is clear from Forester's story. We look at humans from the same two perspectives, backward and forward, leaving us with different impressions. The backward look is often how we explain ourselves, tracing our existence back to earlier fossil forms of *Homo erectus* and *Homo habilis*. When we do, the events are logical, entirely rational, smelling heavily of predestination. But, when we begin with those same fossil forms and try to extrapolate forward to *Homo sapiens*, it's virtually impossible. So many things were going on three to four millions years ago, none of which specifically illuminated the track of evolution, or its eventuality.

What Can We Understand About Ourselves?

We conclude that human evolution is a dark continent of uncertainty—a lucky outcome of chance and necessity—an unexpected breath of life constrained by biology and physics, advancing toward nothing in particular. But, however formed, man is special, a complex distillation of nature, a unique product of natural selection, and a quirky roll of the biological dice. We made it through the labyrinth of improbabilities, avoiding the catastrophes that killed 99 percent of our brethren species, taking on adaptive traits both strange and stunning.

In this book we examine man's improbable development and present circumstances, beginning with the history of evolutionary thought and the contribution of Charles Darwin's and Alfred Wallace's grand theory of natural selection. Here are the personal stories that anchored the entire structure of evolutionary theory. These great historical developments are then contrasted with chance events that constrain natural selection, often sending evolution in unpredictable directions. Our early discussions will focus on the contingencies—historical extinctions of most species, fossil evidence for the multiple possibilities of man's evolution, the molding influences of disease and changing environments—those stormy hits of improbability and unpredictability that impress their character on our behavior and consciousness.

Beyond these primary attributes of life, we explore how humans manage to survive, function in society, find love, and have offspring—how we play out our seven decades. Our emphases are always on our biological legacy, the historical improbabilities and imperatives that shout out their demands on a daily basis. The questions we most want answered are these. How are our evolutionary characteristics expressed in matters of love and hate? What is the origin and substance of mind and consciousness, the deep-seated motivations that move us to heights of glory and depths of despair? Do we carry a general purpose calculator on our shoulders, or is it a mix of specific adaptations? Are culture and civilization new adaptations that elevate humans beyond their evolutionary origins, or are they simply new ways in which old instincts are expressed? And what is the historical composition of man's moral fabric—the good, the bad, and the ugly? How can it all be put together into a fresh theory of human behavior and contingent evolution? And, finally, do we have the strength and courage to face what we may be—is there anything but biology and death?

Future Tense

We are some distance from a complete understanding of human nature, but like a ghost rising from the mist, a form is emerging, the one that we pursue here. That form is biological, but also seemingly spiritual and oftentimes paradoxical. Man is both ennobled and debased almost beyond description through the evolutionary process. There always seem to be two sides of the biological coin, as the writer Robert Willmott emphasized: "Joy and grief are never far apart. In the same street the shutters of one house are closed while the curtains of the next are brushed by the shadows of the dance. A wedding party returns from the church; and a funeral winds to its door. The smiles and sadness of life are the tragicomedy of Shakespeare. Gladness and sighs brighten the dim mirror he beholds."

The Deep Message of the Past

Human behavior is the outcome of millions of years of adjusting to an unsteady world, a genetic barometer of the past, an expression of designs for survival and reproduction. Our tormented history is reflected among the fossils lifted from the dry creek beds of Ethiopia, and in our evolutionary response to climate, predators, prey, disease, and others of our genus hominid. Most of what we were—our myriad ancestors—is dead, the unsuccessful reactions to a killing field of unpredictable imperatives. Only a rare number escaped, those who happened to carry the traits of reproduction.

Thus, our behaviors harbor the harsh messages of the past. No behavior, attitude, or emotion is exempt—none untried in the grand drama of survival. An endless stream of adaptations parade through our lives: sexual desire, parental love, lust, the sense of beauty, altruism, courage, the awe of creation, also fear, guilt, anxiety, jealousy, selfishness, and impulses toward abuse, rape, murder, and war. All were carved out during our evolution, universally etched into the molecules of the cellular DNA, and set as instincts in the neural nets of the brain.

There is no escaping the conclusion: good and bad mix freely in our being. More startling is the recent understanding that even the good serves a selfish purpose, just another mode of adaptation that draws us toward reproduction. Our genes carry the script of love, cooperation, and conflict, not because social systems mold our personality, but because our personality finds a haven in the cloak of culture. As the French playwright insightfully said long ago: "No society has been able to abolish human sadness, no political system can deliver us from the pain of living, from our fear of death, our thirst for the absolute. It is the human condition that directs the social condition, no vice versa."

We cannot view love, loyalty, and altruism without also seeing hate, abandonment, and selfishness. If parental care can be explained through evolutionary principles and contingencies of history, so can infanticide and abortion. If marital bonding and incest taboos are imprints of our genetic past, so are child abuse, rape, and murder. "Even mother's milk nourishes murderers as well as heroes," observed the sardonic playwright George Bernard Shaw. We may wish for better, but when we accept one of our sides, we accept the other. *This is our bittersweet destiny*, to be noble, debased. It is in this interplay of opposites where we see the scientific perspective of good and evil, life and death.

The good and bad of human behavior, the self-centeredness spelled out in love and hate, reflect the trials by fire of ancient time. Love or hate, all sorts of deep compulsions, and the costs of those acts turn on the past. Reluctantly we stare at our own image and see the sharp edges of destiny. Philosophy and gods be damned, the hand of destiny writes on.

Our great loss of innocence began with a vengeance with the heroic efforts of the body and mind by Charles Darwin and Alfred Russel Wallace.

References

Cited in the Introduction

Asimov, I. (1979). *A Choice of Catastrophes*. New York: Simon and Schuster.
Forester, C.S. (19). *Sink the Bismark*.
Krantz, L. (1992). *What the Odds Are*. New York: Harper Perennial.

General References

Fitzgerald, E. (1966). *The Rubáiyát of Omar Khayyám*. Greenwich, CT: New York Graphic Society.
Forester, C.S. (1954). *The Nightmare,* including, *Last Nine Days of the Bismarck.* Boston: Boston, Little, Brown.
Gould, S.J. (1994). "The Evolution of Life on the Earth." *Scientific American*, 63–69, 271.
Monod, J. (1971). *Chance and Necessity*. New York: Knopf.

I

Truth in the Marble

Would you that spangle of Existence spend
About THE SECRET—quick about it, Friend!
*   A Hair, they say, divides the False and True—*
And upon what, prithee, does Life depend?

                    —Omar Khayyám

Man's destiny is to recapture the saga of life.

1

Arrow of Destiny

One grand master metaphor dominated, perverted, and
obstructed European efforts to discover man's place in
nature. This was the simple notion of a Great Chain of
Being. The whole universe, European scientists and
philosophers explained, consists of an ordered series of
beings, from the lowest, simplest, and tiniest at the
bottom to the highest and most complex at the top. To the
question, "What is man, that thou art mindful of him?"
the Psalmist answered (and natural philosophers
agreed), "thou hast made him a little lower than the
angels, and hast crowned him with glory and honour."

—Daniel J. Boorstin

A fateful day in retrospect, September 7, 1832. HMS *Beagle*, under the command of Robert Fitzroy, sailed into the small garrison port of Bahia Blanca, a godless place on the edge of Patagonia, some 400 miles south of Buenos Aires. The shallow bay, clogged with mud and colorless reeds, swarmed with thousands of crabs. Hot winds off the Argentinean sea swept across the dreary Patagonian plain. Desolate. Forbiding. Could there be anything of interest here?

Charles Darwin, the ship's naturalist and companion to Fitzroy, jammed two pistols in his belt, grabbed his rock hammer, and walked off the *Beagle* into history. Near the area of Punta Alta, thousands of miles from his English home of Shrewsbury, Charles Darwin made his greatest discoveries—prehistoric bones of ancient animals buried within the cliffs of Patagonia. Immense bones. These were not the first fossils ever found, far from it, but they were some of the most amazing. Darwin had uncovered the cold white bones of the giant sloth, *Megatherium*; the closely related *Megalonyx* and *Scelidotherium*; the hippopotamus-

11

like animal, *Toxodon*; an extinct species of the elephant family, *Mylodon*; a llama as large as a camel; and a giant armadillo that would be the envy of all Texans. He also found skeletons of horses that had been extinct for thousands of years. All this at twenty-two years of age; all this in a rocky cliff no more than 200 yards square. We can sense Darwin's elation and puzzlement. He was confronting extinct creatures that were virtually unknown to the world. These bones alone would assure his fame as a naturalist.

But he was at a loss to explain their origin. The discovery of the bones of horse-like species at a geological time when they were unknown in the Western Hemisphere was just as mysterious as the presence of the extinct giants. Was this proof that horses browsed the South American savanna long before the Spanish conquistadors arrived in the sixteenth century? Could it be that all of these species were echoes of past existences, perhaps modified over time or gone extinct never to reappear? Even the gravesite was strange, for the strata of muddy reddish clay in which these bones appeared was peppered with the fossils of marine shells, as if the land had risen out of the sea before the great extinction of animals.

At this moment Darwin had no great insight about the origin of the bones—no clearly formulated law of evolution. After all, Darwin accepted a monotheistic God who could do anything, create unusual species and pull mountains out of the sea. And he was still able to embrace the sentiment of the English poet Andrew Marvell who asked, "Who can foretell for what high cause this darling of the Gods was born?" In fact, Darwin was on the *Beagle* as a companion and, later, a naturalist to Captain Fitzroy. Fitzroy, who was commissioned to survey the rugged coast of South America, hoped that Darwin would help prove the Book of Genesis and verify the Great Flood described in the Bible. Darwin had no reason to doubt the Great Flood, but time and experience do wonders. Later, the impress of Patagonia would cause him to reflect: "The wonderful relationship between the dead and living animals on the same continent will later shed more light on explaining the appearance of organic creatures on earth and their disappearance than any other body of facts, and I have no doubt that such a relationship truly exists."

The implications of Darwin's observations would leave him little peace; they would affect his relationship with Fitzroy. Darwin may have used Fitzroy as a sounding board for his new ideas. In any case, problems festered, some philosophical. Captain Fitzroy was a respected and competent captain; in many ways he exhibited an unequaled magnanimity. But he had a sharp temper, explosive in nature. According to Darwin, "He was also somewhat suspicious and occasionally in very low spirits, on one occasion bordering on insanity." Once he ejected Darwin from his cabin because of a disagreement over slavery—in contrast to Fitzroy, Darwin abhorred slavery in any form. Shortly after this argument Fitzroy apologized through his officer and allowed Darwin to return. Quarrels became common, some of the worst about Genesis and the creation of man—a new thought was forming in Darwin's mind. The bones of Patagonia weighed heavily.

As his relationship with Captain Fitzroy worsened Darwin was more inclined to stay on land while Fitzroy sailed up and down the South American coast, surveying and mapping the periphery of the continent. Fitzroy was sinking into despair, a moody road he traveled until he cut his throat in 1865. There was madness in his family—a generation earlier his uncle Viscount Castlereagh, foreign minister of England, had cut his own throat. There was also a haunting madness on board: the previous captain of the *Beagle* had committed suicide in Fitzroy's cabin in 1829. Darwin must have felt a kind of freedom away from the depressive confines of the *Beagle* and her deteriorating captain. How remarkable that the origin of Darwin's notions of evolution, later to be detailed in his theory of natural selection, depended on happenstance— on the chancy events that led Darwin inland to his greatest thoughts. The irony was that Fitzroy, wanting Darwin to prove the Book of Genesis, provided the setting for the destruction of the religious interpretation of creation.

Arguably, Darwin gave birth to the world's most important idea. Perhaps more significantly, he took something away—the belief in a deity. God was replaced by causal law. On reflection we were left swinging in the causal wind of time, which James Thomson in his "City of Dreadful Night" graphically described : "I find no hint throughout the Universe of good or ill, of blessing or of curse, I find alone Necessity Supreme; with infinite mystery, abysmal, dark unlighted ever by the faintest spark for us the flittering shadows of a dream." People moaned with sadness that "The Great Companion is dead." The only consolation was that if Darwin killed God, he also in the same blow slew the Devil. Thus the news was not all bad.

Conception and Gestation

Darwin did not jump to the conclusion that nature built man out of the distant forms—he did not immediately see the lawful connections between man and beast. But he was compelled by the facts, led inexorably through discovery and happenstance, to the conclusion that man shares a biological blueprint with every other species.

Bones, bones, bones—the dead thermometer of early body heat. They spoke of a distant past, another world, other beings. But all could not be read through the bones; there was the sheer diversity of life. Why? Why the uncommon natives of Tierra Del Fuego, who shaved their eyebrows, went mostly naked and coated their copper-colored skin with grease— able to withstand the stinging cold and piercing winds at the very southern tip of South America? Why the ostrich-like bird of Patagonia, now honored with Darwin's name, *Rhea darwini*, when, if disturbed in the nest, would chase a man on horseback riding full tilt? How can anyone explain the Chilean Andes, 7,000 feet in altitude, where trees were found that once grew 700 miles away on the shores of the Atlantic Ocean? Again the fossils and rocks, definitely out of place, reflected the dynamic nature of the earth; the earth, that had sunk beneath the sea, now stood elevated 7,000 feet. Were the answers embedded in old theological notions, or in the dynamic nature of the earth?

In Chile Darwin experienced an earthquake that wrecked dozens of great ships in the port of Talcahuano, killed animals by the hundreds, uprooted trees, and tossed about great masses of earth and rock. That day Darwin looked into the wild eye of the forces that broke apart lands, caused others to sink, and forced huge rocks up by thousands of feet. Imagine the impression. God or Geology?

The *Beagle* arrived at St. Stephen's Harbor in the Galapagos Islands, September 15, 1835, exactly three hundred years after the islands were discovered by Fray Tomas de Berlanga, Bishop of Panama. Five hundred miles off the coast of Ecuador, and now owned by that country, was this baker's dozen of strange islands, inhabited by the most unusual creatures assembled by the hands of fate.

Darwin had been gone from England nearly four years; his confidence was growing—his experiences showing in his face. Yet, the mystery and sheer diversity of the Galapagos Islands would shake Darwin's way of thinking about the world. Giant tortoises moved like primeval creatures, weighing up to, and even more than, 500 pounds, large enough to ride—gentle as kittens. There were marine lizards several feet long, looking like miniature scaly dragons. By the thousands, these giant iguanas swarmed over the land, using their long flat tails to balance themselves and navigate between the rocks. Expert swimmers, they could remain under water for an hour, eating mostly seaweed. There were scarlet crabs that moved over the lizards' backs hunting ticks. Birds groomed the tortoises of parasites that the large animals could not reach. On James Island alone Darwin counted twenty-six species of land birds—hawks, turtle doves, and finches, all so tame that they would literally alight on his rifle. It was enough to upset any preconceptions of life.

The finches were especially revealing, as they had diversified across the island groups, forming unique species, clearly adapted for particular habitats. Some had heavy plier-like beaks used to break large nuts. Others had smaller, longer beaks to probe cactuses for unsuspecting insects. Still others had medium-sized beaks suitable for eating small seeds and nuts. In appearance and behavior of the variegated groups matched the environment in which they lived.

Darwin might have concluded from these observations that species arise and diversify under the pressure of environmental demands. Surprisingly, he did not—the critical information was there. At this point Darwin simply observed, collected specimens, and thought. He would not shape the final form of his theory of natural selection for another twenty-three years. He worked incessantly at geological and biological problems, as focused as leaf-cutting ants building a birthing nest for new larva. He may have had preliminary insights into evolutionary processes, but he cautiously avoided the final step. The ideas gestated.

The Belief in Good Luck and Personal Immortality

What kind of man would leave the comforts of England, knowingly exposing himself to the risks of exploration? And many risks there were. By rough count Charles Darwin faced near-death seven times during his five years on the *Beagle*. One of these incidents occurred while sailing the *Beagle* through the icy straits of Tierra del Fuego. Darwin and Fitzroy had left the *Beagle* in small boats to explore the land around a gigantic glacier. As they stared into its cold beauty, a huge chunk of glacial ice split off, falling into the sea with a terrible crash. The resulting tide hurled the boats on the beach like so much flotsam. First one, then two, finally three great waves nearly swept the boats and men away. Darwin, appreciating the potential disaster of being stranded miles from the *Beagle*, sprinted down the beach with a couple of sailors to secure the boats. Fitzroy was so grateful that he named a nearby peak, Mount Darwin, the name it carries today.

Over and over again, Darwin and the intrepid *Beagle* crew subjected themselves to nearly unmanageable dangers. For weeks, in an attempt to round Cape Horn at the tip of South America, the little ship battled the mountainous seas. Once a great wave engulfed and nearly capsized the *Beagle*, carrying away one of her small boats. The ship would have floundered had the crew not in the nick of time opened the ports, letting the sea water rush out. In another winter passage through these same straits the rigging froze and the decks were covered with snow. For days at a time hurricane winds buffeted the *Beagle*, with the battle continuing for a month before the *Beagle*, surviving the fury of nature, emerged into the calm beauty of the Pacific Ocean.

Darwin also faced great dangers in the interior of South America. Natives were always a threat. The *Beagle's* camp was once overrun by irritated Fuegians seeking the captain. Fortunately Fitzroy and Darwin were out exploring when that happened. Rowing inland on the Rio Santa Cruz, the wind and tide failed them and every man, including Darwin, took turns towing the boats upstream with ropes fitted with collars. The nights were bitterly cold, yet they were still in danger of Indian attacks. In order to conserve food, Captain Fitzroy kept the crew on short rations for days. Their luck held until they returned safely to the *Beagle*.

Why would anyone go into disease-infested areas where there were no immunizations or vaccinations for any tropical diseases—malaria, yellow fever, cholera, dysentery? Darwin had his first attack of fever during his early encounter with South America. Not long after, during a horseback trip onto the Northern Pampas near Buenos Aires, he took sick with malaria. The most dangerous encounter was in Chile when Darwin was bitten by an Andean Benchuga bug, an attractive inch-long beetle with soft black wings. A carrier of Chagas's disease, it may have been responsible for Darwin's life-long maladies.

Darwin never spared himself despite the dangers. Caught in an earthquake off the coastal town of Valdivia in Chile, Darwin ignored the devastation and moved into the mountains, crossing the Andes by the highest and most dangerous route, over the Portillo Pass to Mendoza— it was no easy task, considering the rarefied air of high altitude and approaching winter. Yet Darwin later remarked: "Never did I more deeply enjoy an equal space of time."

Just being there, anywhere on or near the *Beagle*, was courageous. The 242-ton, ninety-foot sailing vessel, small by today's standards, was a creaky wooden-frame ten-gun brig. It carried seventy-four persons, about 1.2 linear feet per person. Darwin wrote his friend Henslow in England: "The absolute want of room is an evil that nothing can surmount." Worse, Darwin was constantly seasick, which may have been a blessing in disguise. Possibly he would not have made his monumental discoveries during the many weeks spent in the interior of South America had he been more comfortable on the *Beagle*. Our good luck.

Why did Charles Darwin knowingly subject himself to great dangers; why does anyone? At twenty-two Darwin had just received his B.A. at Cambridge. He had opportunities in medicine and the clergy, though he was indifferent to both. His father had a successful medical practice in Shrewsbury, lived in a fine house, had a comfortable income, and was highly respected. Charles was smart, a tall, slim figure, blond haired, with a tendency toward baldness—a well-formed head with a broad brow, brown eyes—pleasant good looks. He was already well-connected in the social and scientific gentry of England. In short, Charles did not have to take chances; his future was assured in England. But he did, over and over again.

In his Pulitzer Prize winning book, *The Denial of Death*, Ernest Becker offers a concept of courage that applies to Darwin. Man is selfish, he says, and narcissistically believes that he possesses unique immortality. He believes in his own luck. As Aristotle put it somewhere, luck is when the guy next to you gets hit with the arrow. Accordingly, this narcissism is what keeps a man marching point-blank into a hail of rifle fire—only the man next to him will get the bullet. This same selfish force propelled Darwin across the plains of Patagonia and over the mountains of Chile. It is the force of life that overcomes dangers, leading to some of the greatest discoveries of the world. Ironically, the very genetic forces of narcissism that lift men to staggering heights of courage are the same that Darwin uncovered with this theory. Darwin's narcissistic gene found itself.

Darwin Held the Pieces of the Puzzle

The puzzle Darwin pondered was how do species arise and change? Not a simple puzzle, but one of which he held the pieces. In his seabag Darwin carried a well-thumbed copy of Sir Charles Lyell's *The Principles of Geology*, dated 1830—the first piece of the puzzle. In this masterpiece that would forever change the view of the earth, Lyell concluded that the present slow pace of geological events was simply a continuation of an enduring process that had gone before. No longer could the earth be thought of as having been created at 9 A.M., October 23, 4,004 B.C. as Archbishop James Usher of Armagh had calculated in 1581. If mountains and oceans had been formed at the present rate of change, the earth had to be millions of years old. Lyell's view of continuous change was called *uniformationism*, meaning that the steady, uniform action of the forces of nature could account for its present condition. As we know today, the earth is about 4.8 billion years old, plenty of time for change to occur, whatever its nature. Darwin later argued that evolution needed great amounts of time for species to evolve: important biological modifications required countless generations. Lyell, the geological benefactor, gave Darwin the needed time.

Darwin also had another piece of the puzzle, the influential paper, *First Essay on Population*, written in 1798 by Thomas Malthus, the first economic demographer from Scotland. In this essay he pointed out that populations grow geometrically, whereas food supplies increase only arithmetically. Geometrical growth is like a small flame igniting a sudden bonfire; arithmetic growth is like the flame of a cigarette moving steadily toward the end. The implication is that population density is destined to outstrip food supplies, just as mice will reproduce themselves out of house and home. Under these harsh realities not all individuals have equal abilities to survive and reproduce. "Famine, war, pestilence and vice," the four horsemen of the Apocalypse, visit the many as the few survive. Darwin would later stress that the natural variation of traits within populations, subjected to environmental stresses, always marching to the hoofbeats of the four horsemen, allows the most adapted individuals to survive. Over generations the process of differential success repeats itself until new species arise.

Darwin's third puzzle piece he had for many years before launching his theory. It was the many observations whereby animal breeders deliberately selected animals for reproduction because of valued traits—egg laying in chickens, milk production in cows, wool production in sheep. Artificial selection quickly established new levels of animal production. Later Darwin would explain that the same process occurred in nature; selection by natural forces was analogous to selection by artificial means.

Several other pieces to the puzzle were falling into place. Darwin had seen many instances of related species sharing similar geographical areas, looking as if they were modified forms of each other. He was well aware of similarities among animals; he knew that the famous Carolus Linnaeus (1707-1778) had classified animals and plants on the basis of similarities into species, genera, family, class, and order. The classification offered by Linnaeus suggested inherited relations among species. Even the fossils sometimes spoke of things to be. Also, the sheer diversity of life forms, their distribution on islands and continents, and their similarities and differences hinted at evolutionary descent with modification. Depending on how one counts these related observations, Darwin held about seven critical pieces to the puzzle of evolution—certainly the outline of the final form was there.

Our adventurer knew a lot more. His grandfather, Erasmus Darwin had published an extensive speculative theory of evolution. The problem with this theory, the same problem that Charles faced, was that the intermediate forms that connected species were not apparent. Jean-Baptiste de Lamarck (1744-1829), the French naturalist, had said that the apparent gaps between species were merely illusory, that the intermediate forms were somewhere on earth yet to be found. Darwin believed that. Lamarck was responsible for the concept of "use" and "disuse," the transmission of acquired characteristics from generation to generation: rats running a maze each generation would eventually master the maze upon the first exposure, so the theory goes. Charles Darwin included Lamarck's ideas of use and disuse in his theorizing, although present-day biologists ignore Darwin's "non-genetic" approach. As late as 1871, in his classic book, *The Descent of Man and Selection in Relation to Sex*, Darwin thought that environmental effects could be inherited.

One piece of the puzzle he would deny, that related to other naturalists. Alfred Russell Wallace was close to the grand theory of evolution before Darwin put his pen to paper. Darwin knew of this work, and the related work of other naturalists, yet years later he would assert that "evolution was not in the wind." Here is what he said in his autobiography in 1887. "It has sometimes been said that the success of the *Origin* proved 'that the subject was in the air,' or 'that men's minds were prepared for it.' I do not think that this is strictly true, for I occasionally sounded not a few naturalists, and never happened to come across a single one who seemed to doubt about the permanence of species."

Darwin was clearly wrong: [the idea of] evolution by natural selection was not only in the air, but its birth was inevitable. If not Darwin, someone else would have claimed credit. The question remains: if Darwin had the major pieces to the puzzle, even as he left the Galapagos Islands for his home in England, why didn't he put them together? We will return to this question, but first let's examine why the theory of evolutionary change through descent and modification, the theory of natural selection, was an inevitable outgrowth of history.

The Historical March Toward Evolutionary Theory

Scientific knowledge depends in great measure on the development of appropriate tools: there can be no mature science of astronomy without a telescope, nor a science of cellular biology without a microscope. Nevertheless, it is eerie how ideas can exist for a long time before becoming verified through technology or improved methodologies. Johannes Kepler was seeking laws governing planetary motion long before the telescope was made available by Galileo: after attempting to fill gaps with hypothetical planets, Kepler finally hit upon a scheme that satisfied him; that was 1596, about fifteen years before the telescope was used to confirm his first two planetary laws. Similarly, the first clear description of the cell by Anthony von Leeuwenhoek in 1679 was anticipated by Robert Boyle, who in 1666 believed that individual "atoms" cluster together to form complex units like cells with particular shapes. It appears that objective truths are sometimes grasped intuitively before they can be crystalized with measurement—ideas first, resolutions second.

When intuition is verified, or people think it is, alternative explanations shrink in importance—strong ideas take center stage. Ill-formed opinions, along with their speculators, quickly slip back into the dusty rooms of history. Much like Michelangelo sculpting David in white marble, once David took form, other possibilities fell away. "The truth was in the marble."

Our current view of evolution is the same. Early intuitions and speculation pointed us in the right direction—some eerily, indeed. Slowly we validated a range of ideas; the rest became less compelling. The result is a theory of evolution shaped by universal truth, intuitively grasped by visionaries—the truth emerging from the white marble.

Early Light

Let there be no mistake. Biological evolution is so real, so evident, that its discovery was inevitable. "There are no new truths, but only truths that have not been recognized by those who have perceived them without noticing," said the novelist, Mary McCarthy. Evolution is one of those mighty truths, like planetary motion or organized cells. Arguably, our appreciation of the theory of evolution depends on social history, blended with our own ideology. But as the form emerges, considered from every angle, the aggregate perception becomes more like the truth it represents. In the short run, truth is obscured by social values; in the long run it emerges pure as David.

The story of evolution shows us why Darwin was driven to the theory of natural selection, why Alfred Russell Wallace arrived at the same point in the same critical moment of history, why others would have etched their names into scientific history had Darwin and Wallace never existed. The story also anticipates why there will eventually be a "final theory of man." The truth is there, to be drawn out of the marble.

In the bone pile of history are the intellectual giants who gave us the powerful ideas about life forces and evolution. Nearly every major advance in knowledge carries a specific name, a real person, suggesting, as Thomas Carlyle mused: "History is the essence of innumerable biographies." Many early notions proved absolutely wrong, but it is surprising how accurate some were. The Grecian philosophers and scientists of the sixth century B.C. boldly proposed a self-organizing explanation for the earth, eschewing a distinction between living and nonliving matter. Thales of Miletus (640–584 B.C.) thought that all matter originated from water. According to this "water-origin" theory, creation required no external impetus—it was self-actualized. Thales's student, Anaximandos (611–546 B.C.), believed that water was derived from a more primeval and impersonal building substance. Empedocles of Akragas (490–430 B.C.) proposed that living matter stemmed from nonliving matter. He added that living organisms arose initially in water and later developed into terrestrial organisms. The elements from which life came were earth, water, air, and fire. For centuries this view was held to be true. Anaximandos was even more specific about the origin of man. Man arose from shark-like fish, reflecting, perhaps, his pessimism about humans. Wrong, all wrong, you say. But notions that will later arise from these early ideas are that complex geological and organismic forms can self-organize; structured forms are produced from simpler elements—one thing can turn into another.

From these ancient Ionic sages came other ideas, some showing a startling intuitive grasp of the evolutionary process. Heraclitus, around 500 B.C., boldly asserted that species were not immutable; they could change—an ungodly thought at the time. Anaximander of Miletus in 570 B.C. actually used the verb "to evolve" to refer to species change. The unique aspect of Empedocles's idea about the formation of life was that nonliving matter gave rise to parts of living organisms, such as heads, hands, and feet, which were later joined together to form whole organisms. Only viable combinations continued to exist; the nonviable assortments died off. The scheme is strangely modern: natural selection, taking advantage of existing variation, resulting in combinations of traits that are viable, ultimately influencing reproduction.

Evolutionary dogma began to crystalize about the fifth century B.C. with powerhouse philosophers Plato (428–348) and his student Aristotle (384–322 B.C.). Plato taught that the observable world is no more than a shadow of the truth. Species are variable reflections of some ideal essence. Thus, a moscovy duck, reproducing its type each generation, is merely a fuzzy reflection of "duckdom." The true nature of ducks is an idealized form, unblemished, an essence that is unknowable except in abstraction. One wonders if Plato would have settled for a statistical average as an explanation of "essence," had he known much about averages and variations around them?

Both Plato and Aristotle realized that some animal species are more similar than others, graduated in degree. Plato declared that there was an unbroken gradation from the lowest to the highest living forms—from water fleas to divinity. Aristotle elevated this idea to an extreme in his great work, *Historia Animalium*, by setting forth a chainlike series of forms, beginning with inanimate matter and simple plants, moving up the chain to marine organisms, birds and mammals. There were fourteen steps with humans representing the highest point on his "Scale of Nature." As part of this chain Aristotle distinguished between animals with blood, those that we generally refer to as vertebrates, and those that he thought had no blood, worms, shellfish, and insects. Hundreds of years later, Europeans, including the leading protagonists of evolutionary processes, adopted this hierarchical model of life, sometimes referring to it as the *Ladder of Nature* or the *Great Chain of Being.*

Neither Plato or Aristotle thought of the Scale of Nature as an evolutionary record of species changing from simple to complex, from inanimate material to humans, or from primitive to recent. Instead, the staircase depicted "the order of things," mirroring a hierarchy of perfection. The underlying force, according to the supreme historians, Will and Ariel Durant, is entelechy, the inner drive toward perfection. Accordingly, Aristotle, "rejects the natural selection of accidental mutations; there is no fortuity in evolution; the lines of development are determined by the inherent urge of each form, species, and genus to develop itself to its fullest realization of its nature. There is design, but it is less a guidance from without than an inner drive for 'entelechy' by which each thing is drawn to its natural fulfillment." Humans were most perfect in this scheme, blessed by the gods. The hierarchical scheme quickly became religious dogma. Right or wrong, the Scale of Nature was psychologically beneficial for mankind; providing an order of things, a philosophical tranquilizer to calm existential insecurity in a confusing world of things living and dead. Man is an ordering species and looks for his place in nature.

The religious interpretation of species differences prevailed for centuries. Species had an inviolable essence, an immutability, all created by the gods. Had we been gods on Mount Olympus, creating or watching the creation of life, there would have been no need to devise a Great Chain of Being, with its implication of low to high, old to new, simple to complex. All species would have been equally formed and unchangeable. Nevertheless, subsequent philosophers and naturalists could not easily ignore that the steps in Aristotle's staircase looked like a ladder of progressive evolution. As it was, man stood in a sea of doubt. God was mythical; nature was real. Reproduction and death surrounded the thoughtful individual as he pressed for knowledge of his own beginning and ultimate end. God was not enough—man sought explanations that might very well come through the categorization of organisms and the unification of things in nature.

And so men speculated. Could it be that species are not immutable, after all? Is it possible that the order in which species march across the stage of life varies according to complexity? Do species change from one form into another? All inevitable questions; all challenges to godly interpretations. Perhaps it is historically accurate, as George Bernard Shaw asserted: "All great truths begin as blasphemies."

Lying beneath the ground was the biggest blasphemy of all—petrified life—fossils. Even before Aristotle, ancient Greek thinkers knew about fossils. Xenophanes, for one, and Herodotus, for another, had seen marine fossils in the most unlikely places, mountains. Herodotus suggested that they could have gotten there only by a shifting of land and water, an incredible idea when people believed that the world and life were immutable. Talk about intuition! Xenophanes of Colophone in about 540 B.C. observed fossils in differing earth strata, concluding that each layer represented a universal extinction of all plants and animals. Each event was followed by a recreation of the living world. This idea was later elaborated on by France's most famous naturalist, Baron Georges Cuvier (1769–1832). We will meet Cuvier again.

Even mammalian bones, such as those of primitive elephants and cave bears, were found deep in the rocks. In keeping with the times, the bones were thought to be the remains of dragons, giants, and other mythical creatures. The Grecian artifacts were not then called fossils; it was only in the 1500's that the term fossil was coined by the German geologist, Georg Agricola, coming from the Latin words *fodere*, meaning to dig, and *fossa*, referring to a trench or depression. The term came into current use only in 1809, with the French zoologist Jean-Baptiste Lamarck.

So, the shells and bones unearthed by the Greeks told a story of lost organisms from distant times and other worlds—*changing* worlds. The apparent repositioning of the lands and seas—the presence of strange dead forms—suggested long periods of earthly change. Aristotle, for example, said, "The whole vital process of the earth takes place so gradually and in periods of time which are so immense compared with the length of our life, that these changes are not observed: and before their course can be recorded from the beginning to end, whole nations perish and are destroyed." Again, the seed of knowledge is planted for later harvest by Lyell, Darwin, Wallace, and others.

The Internal Ring of Truth

No doubt the ideas of the ancient Greeks were strange and often wrong. Yet they were sometimes very close to the "big picture of evolution." They did it with little historical knowledge, and no technology—no telescopes, microscopes or brain scanners—nothing, that is, except intuition about how the cosmos is structured. That may have been enough. We will see that it was enough for Charles Darwin as well.

Intuition is an unconscious strategy, a powerful source of knowledge. We don't know much about it, but it appears that we use it during times of uncertainty, times when we have no specific information but still must make a judgment. How does it work? Picture yourself driving down a lonely road at night. It has been raining; the foreign smells of dampness reach you even through the closed windows of the car. You see nothing out of the ordinary, but increasingly you sense that something is wrong. The shadows crowd in, the darkness becomes blackness, and the road seems to narrow within the space for your myopic headlights. Sensing danger, you slow the car, and just in time, too, for around the next curve the road is completely washed out: twenty feet of canyon right across the road. Had you hit that washout—curtains. That's intuition. Now how did you know something was wrong? Well, you might have been tired, making you feel more vulnerable. Maybe you thought that the recent rains had been particularly hard. Or, perhaps the most significant, you realized unconsciously that absolutely no traffic had passed going in the opposite direction. Who knows exactly how your unconscious worked? Whatever, your brain took in information, mulled it over, did some mental correlations, and came up with a solution.

As with fear and longing, both of which motivate problem-solving behavior, intuition sets the psychic parameters, giving the mind force and clarity. Our best bet is that intuition is part of our survival ingenuity, pounded into our DNA by the environment of the past, just like neurosensory abilities and reproductive behaviors. The errors and successes of genetic history dog our trail. Hominids—able to sense danger, determine probabilities, deal with inconsistencies, or make use of convergent information—were more likely to survive, passing those traits on to offspring. Intuition, the unconscious reflection of those abilities, can prevent automobile accidents; it can also reach out into the cosmos for insights about the world and ourselves.

Like babes in the woods, the Greeks looked at nature, and began to organize, correlate, and synthesize information. In retrospect we see in their intuitive observations the birth of a scientific method, a process that Sir Francis Bacon in 1623 referred to as *induction*. Induction is the attempt to observe raw data and logically interconnect those data into meaningful arrangements—a stamp collector's delight. John Stuart Mill, a philosopher and contemporary of Charles Darwin, explained in his *System of Logic* of 1843 that induction is the process of inference that "proceeds from the known to the unknown," or, perhaps more accurately proceeds from the known to a new synthesis of knowledge. And yet, isn't induction really a kind of intuition in action? And didn't the Greeks use it effectively?

From Greeks to the Theory of Natural Selection

After centuries of religious domination, the sixteenth and seventeenth centuries reopened possibilities for the accumulation of information on living things. The plagues subsided, the Church lost its stranglehold on local communities, societies became more secular, trade and science prospered, and the important question about the origin of man reappeared. Robert Browning remarked that in such a time of personal liberation, "How very hard it is to be a Christian!"

The ancient Greeks believed that fossils were layered in the earth in the order of their creation. Xenophanes of Colophone thought this as early as 540 B.C. This idea returned in the 1600's in a strong form when the French naturalist Benoiet de Maillet and the Danish scholar Niels Stensen, also known as Nicolous Steno, suggested that the more "primitive" fossils appeared in the deeper layers of the earth. Organisms died, slowly being entombed by the sediment of the ages.

Stensen knew of a peculiar fossil in the Florentine collection of the Medici family. It had a tongue-shaped form, referred to as a glossopteria. He realized that the "tongue rock" was a shark's tooth, but from a shark that was now extinct. The sediment from which it was extracted appeared much older than the earth's surface. Ever since the diluvians, who believed in the biblical Great Flood, it was thought there had been a single flood. Consequently, the evidence of prediluvial plants and animals was dismissed. Yet, there it was.

Georges Louis Leclerc de Buffon (1707–1788), the most famous of all the early paleontologists, broke cleanly with the diluvial theorists by claiming that there were many animals on earth that no longer existed—evidenced by bones of other eras. He went one step further by proclaiming that the earth was 74,832 years old, much older than asserted by the Irish Archbishop, James Usher. The exact number 74,832 years resulted from one of the first geological experiments: Buffon extrapolated to the earth's temperature using the time it took ice balls to melt, taking into account the difference between the size of the earth and the ice balls—the earth too was cooling. Yes, a ridiculous extrapolation, but in the right direction.

Estimates of the age of the earth increased with nearly every generation of scientists. By 1862 the British physicist, Lord Kelvin, concluded from his own experiments that the earth was at least twenty and no more than 400 million years old—a huge leap from the Creationists' assumption of less than 6,000 years. The geologist, Sir Charles Lyell, Charles Darwin's champion, extended this range even more, making theoretical room for Darwin's idea of slow incremental evolution. Today we know that the earth is about 4.8 billion years old, with life forms appearing within the first billion years—plenty of time for the "mischief of the genes."

Even philosophers and social commentators were thinking about evolution. Immanuel Kant (1724–1804) called evolution a "daring adventure in reasoning." He believed that the mind evolved automatically to classify sensory information and perceptions, an a priori nervous system. Voltaire (1694–1778) worried about the gaps that existed between species, gaps that should not be there if the ascent to man were progressive and continuous. In accord with today's notions, he suggested that the gaps were real, and caused by the extinction of species. His proposal echoed the thoughts of other philosophers, such as Leibnitz (1646–1716), who was close to the truth when he suggested that some species had become extinct, whereas others were *transformed*. To him, different species that share common features may have shared a common ancestor. Where he went wrong was in suggesting that species evolve toward godly perfection—as we will see, species may become better adapted over generations but they move toward specializations, not perfections.

One advance stands above the rest. In 1735 Carolus Linnaeus, a Swedish naturalist published a highly original classification of animals and plants in *Systema Naturae*. It's hard to imagine how messy things were when Linnaeus began his work. There was a bewildering diversity of animals and plants in nature which made no sense. Thomas Moufet, in his *Theatre of Insects*, published in 1590, began descriptions of grass-hoppers and locusts with this loose classification: "Some are green, some black, some blue. Some fly with one pair of wings, others with more; those that have no wings they leap, those that cannot either fly or leap, they walk; some have longer shanks, some shorter. Some there are that sing, others are silent. And as there are many kinds of them in nature, so their names were almost infinite, which through the neglect of Natural-ists are grown out of use." Moufet might as well have been lost in the jungle. What was needed, clearly, was a shorthand method for arrang-ing species in a systematic way.

And the person to do that was Linnaeus who believed that species could be logically grouped to reveal the divine plan of creation. The job seemed feasible, for Linnaeus knew of only 4,162 species, a fraction of those known today. By 1898 the known species increased to 415,000. Today about one and one-half million species of animals are known, with about 6,000 new ones, mostly insects, described each year. Amaz-ingly, the framework introduced by Linnaeus for classifying organisms works even as thousands of new species are introduced into the record. D.H. Stoever, writing a biography of Linnaeus, referred to him as "the most systematical genius of the age, the most intimate and scrutinizing minion that ever graced the bosom of Nature."

Not everyone was so pleased with Linnaeus' genius. The key attribute he used to delineate plants was male and female organs. Sex was a wise choice, as these attributes are stable and characteristic—*species-spe-cific*. Professor Dillenius a botanist from Oxford wrote to the great classifier in 1837: "I consider sexual differences altogether useless, su-perfluous, even misleading, for establishing the character of a plant. What is the point of it all? It is puerile..." Victorians were scandalized to find that, yes, love comes even to the plants—"loathsome harlotry," cried the academician Johann Siegesbeck. Yet, the ladies in particular, those whose virtue were protected from Linnaeus by Dillenius and Siegesbeck, found the system acceptable and easy to use. They, more than ever, took to the study of botany.

Linnaeus believed in creationism and the immutability of species; in his own mind he was only sharpening the Scale of Nature laid out by Aristotle. Ironically, Linnaeus established a system for viewing the ge-netic relationships among species. He never meant it that way, and knew nothing about genes in any case, but that was the eventual significance.

Linnaeus described six related classes in the animal kingdom based upon similarity: mammals, birds, amphibia, fish, insects, and worms. Starting with this general breakdown he was able to divide these classes into more specific elements.

Linnaeus believed his scheme to be a reflection of God's design—he was not out to destroy religion. But, as others would point out, the groupings clearly reflect genetic divergence—modification over time. Stephen Gould, a paleontologist and historian of biology, recently said that Darwin might not have arrived at his theory of natural selection without Linnaeus' conceptualization of animal similarities and differences. Maybe; clearly this ingenious system provided a needed practical base for describing the final outcome of natural selection. Three cheers for Carolus Linnaeus.

All of this thinking, from the Renaissance to the 1800s, a period of history between the intuitive speculations of the early Greeks and the scientific tradition leading directly to the work of Charles Darwin and Alfred Wallace, we might call Middle Thought, There were many "middle thinkers" who considered evolution as real, many who have not been recognized here. The upshot of their fervent efforts was to demonstrate the reality of evolutionary change—periodic extinction followed by the appearance of new species, or the transformation of one biological form into another.

Missing in both the Grecian and Middle Thought periods is any notion that the environment forces biological change, that the environment can destroy all ill-adapted variation, leaving the residue to reproduce itself. Every creation was believed to be unchangeable. Also missing is a clear idea of why variations occur in the first place, though some scholars, including Grecian, did think about heritable variation. Pierre Louis Moreau de Maupertuis (1698-1759) observed that both parents pass on characteristics to their offspring. He also suggested that species develop slowly as a result of changes in their heritable components, all guided by environmental conditions, or restrained by such events as geographical isolation. Buffon, for another, regarded individual differences as an expression of heritable differences.

The notion of "genetic" transmission was surprisingly strong in Malthus' classic, *An Essay on Population*, published in 1798: "size, strength, beauty, complexion, and, perhaps even longevity, are in a degree transmissible." He also said that "the children inherit the vigor of their parents." This transmissible variation could of course underlie trait differences critically important in the process of natural selection. Yet nothing came of that idea. Gregor Mendel, the Austrian monk, working on plant variations in his monastery garden had not yet demonstrated "particulate inheritance," that is, individual gene transmission. Nevertheless the seeds of intellectual growth were there.

The earth was beginning to yield its secrets in the Middle period. Slowly, as man became free of the tyrannies of disease and religious dogma, thoughts reached toward a deeper understanding of ourselves. The nature of *Homo sapiens* was taking form: it was not entirely welcome news. Yes, major discoveries and observations lent clarity to our condition, but these same advances suggested that man was a biological machine, and in this, no different from the other organisms. The knowledge was profoundly depressing for some. Omar Khayyám saw the light of knowledge transformed into the darkness of the soul.

> 'Tis all a Chequer-board of Nights
> and Days
> Where Destiny with Men for Pieces
> plays:
> Hither and thither moves, and
> mates, and slays,
> And one by one back in the Closet
> lays.

Welcome news or not, the die was cast. Charles Robert Darwin and Alfred Robert Wallace were about to fling evolutionary theory right in our faces.

References

Cited in Chapter 1

Cronin, H. (1991). *The Ant and the Peacock*. Cambridge: Cambridge University Press.
Darwin, C. (1958). *The Autobiography of Charles Darwin (1809–1882)*. New York: W. W. Norton & Company, Inc.
Degler, C.N. (1991). *In Search of Human Nature*. New York: Oxford University Press.
Durant, W. and Durant, A. (1968). *The Lessons of History*. New York: Simon and Schuster.
Eiseley, L. (1979). *Darwin and the Mysterious Mr. X*. New York: E.P. Dutton.
Moorehead, A. (1969). *Darwin and the Beagle*. New York: Harper and Row Publishers.

General References

Ackerman, D. (1990). *A Natural History of the Senses*. New York: Random House.
Barber, L. (1980). *The Heyday of Natural History*. New York: Doubleday and Company, Inc.
Boorstin, D.J. (1983). *The Discoverers*. New York: Random House.
Marks, R.L. (1991). *Three Men of the Beagle*. New York: Avon Books.

2

The Shattered Mirror

Still hundreds of miles from land, the 235-ton, two-masted vessel, *Helen*, worked its way slowly toward London. The soothing sounds of the Atlantic rocked Alfred Russel Wallace into a hypnogogic state; he was finally going home after four incredible years exploring the Amazon basin and its major tributary, Rio Negro. Stowed below deck, next to 120 tons of rubber and several tons of cocoa, was Wallace's priceless collection: crates of lepidoptera, those strange and beautiful moths and butterflies, coleoptera, the most abundant insect in Brazil, beetles, boxes of bird, reptile, and other skins. He had even brought live parrots, parakeets, a forest wild-dog, and a few monkeys, including three logothrix, New World monkeys with a human face. Near his bunk were his drawings of palm trees and fish.

Wallace lay in his bunk again experiencing an attack of malaria, thinking "I had got yellow fever after all," that dreaded tropical disease that killed his brother Herbert that very year. He had lost most of his vigor, although he still carried his entire head of dark hair, his full, almost sensuous mouth, and his cordial bearing. After all, he was only twenty-nine. He would recover his health and his contributions to science would be substantial.

At 9 a.m. Captain John Turner politely knocked on Wallace's cabin door and in an apologetic way announced, "I'm afraid the ship's on fire." Indeed it was—smoke enveloped the ship—in a short while fire whipped thought Wallace's cabin and through the skylight. Wallace grabbed his artwork and ran for the longboats. The crew threw in food and wine in preparation to abandon ship. True to the tradition of the sea, Captain Turner was the last to abandon the ship, bringing his chronometer, sextant, compass, and charts. Wallace was horrified as he watched all his work, the beautiful animals too, sink within a hellish circle of flames and black smoke. The price of this conflagration was almost too much to bear—years of loneliness, dysentery, fever, leeches, and unpredictable natives. Gone; everything gone. Later he lamented:

> With what pleasure had I looked upon every rare and curious insect I had added to my collection! How many times, when almost overcome by ague, had I crawled into the forest and been rewarded by some unknown and beautiful species! How many places, which no European foot but my own had trodden, would have been recalled to my memory by the rare birds and insects they had furnished to my collection! How many weary days and weeks had I passed, upheld only by the fond hope of bringing home many new and beautiful forms from those wild regions...! And now everything was gone, and I had not one specimen to illustrate the wild scenes I had beheld!

Wallace helped keep the lifeboat afloat by bailing water over the next three days, until the planks swelled tight. They were in the middle of the Atlantic, baked by the sun, without certainty of survival.

Wallace had not solved the problem of how species were formed; now he had lost his collection, later, perhaps, his life. Weak and sick, his mind spun ragged threads across his life. Sometime in 1844, at twenty-one years of age, Wallace had read Thomas Malthus' *Principles of Population*. He never forgot that Malthus had said that food supplies increase arithmetically, 1, 2, 3, 4, 5, whereas populations increase geometrically, 1, 2, 4, 8, 16. "Want," according to Malthus, " pinches the less fortunate members of the society; and at length the impossibility of supporting such a number together becomes too evident to be resisted." In his autobiography Wallace later said that "its main principles remained with me as a permanent possession, and twenty years later gave me the long-sought clue to the effective agent in the evolution of organic species."

Wallace had also read Charles Lyell's *Principles of Geology*, and Lamarck's, *Zoological Philosophy*, both books that had heavily influenced Darwin. And, several times he had read Darwin's book, *The Voyage of the Beagle* of 1839. Wallace, was also influenced by Robert Chambers' controversial book of 1844, *Vestiges of the Natural History of Creation.* Chambers, like Lamarck before him, viewed life as a series of small progressive steps in evolution, with the simplest and most primitive form of life giving birth to the species next above it, and that species adding to the next—deja vu all over again, as Yogi Berra once remarked. "Nor is man himself exempt from this law," wrote Chambers. This is a book that Darwin definitely did not like, probably because it was wildly speculative. But Wallace was not as conventional as Darwin and Chamber's writing was compelling.

Those books and his association with Henry Walter Bates, whom he met at a library in Leicester, Wales in 1845, finally impelled Wallace to travel to the Amazon. Bates, two years junior to Wallace, introduced him to the delights of collecting beetles. Wallace continued to work as a railroad surveyor with his brother William, but his heart was elsewhere. When William died in 1846, leaving Alfred with credits of $500 from old accounts, Alfred hatched a daring plan with Bates. Writing to Bates in 1847, he felt compelled to study beetles and butterflies with an eye toward "the theory of the origin of species." It is worth repeating: Wallace had a clear vision of his destiny, the understanding of the origin of species. In 1848, with contracts to sell specimens to collectors and museums in England, he and Bates boarded the *Mischief,* a small sailing boat of 192 tons, bound for Para on the mouth of the Amazon.

If Darwin stepped into history in Patagonia, Wallace did so too in Para. Coincidentally, that same year Charles' father, Robert Waring Darwin, died at eighty-two years of age, leaving his son the equivalent of $200,000. Secluding himself and his family at Down House in Kent, Darwin spent his time writing and corresponding with the scientific elite—including Charles Lyell and Joseph Hooker, both of whom would play historic roles in catapulting Darwin into intellectual immortality. But while Wallace and Darwin shared common visions, they were worlds apart. Darwin was wealthy; Wallace was poverty-stricken. Darwin had leisure for thought; Wallace hustled for every meal. Darwin was politically conservative; Wallace was a socialist. Darwin was connected to the scientific community; Wallace knew only Henry Bates, a scientific unknown.

Ten days after the *Helen* went down, carrying to the bottom of the Atlantic one of the world's greatest collections of animals, Wallace and the crew were picked up by the West Indian ship, *Jordeson,* bound for London. Saved from hunger, thirst, and the burning sun, the men nearly perished in three separate gales, fighting winds up to seventy-three miles per hour. The *Jordeson* rolled and plunged into the cold sea, but held. Wallace arrived in London, wiser, though the species question remained unresolved, his pockets empty.

Indonesian Nights

On the basis of his published material on palm species and fish, Wallace achieved some fame as a naturalist. Imagine his scientific impact had he arrived home with a ton of unknown specimens. While in England, he attended lectures and visited museums—his place of intellectual gestation. On one of his visits to the Insect Room of the British Museum, he met Charles Darwin, a meeting that burned into his mind but rapidly faded from Darwin's. Their next visit would be historic.

Wallace discovered that the almost totally unexplored Malayan Archipelago, halfway around the world, was a bountiful source of biological material. Maybe here was the answer to his species question. With great luck and some support by the Royal Geographical Society, our determined explorer boarded the Oriental steamer, *Bengal*, in 1854 on its way to Singapore. Singapore, thought Wallace, the gateway to Malaysia, the opening of the caldron where the origins of life might pour forth into his mind. Wallace would spend the next seven years in the jungles of the Malayan Archipelago; he would leave there with a secret of the universe.

Conditions were miserable. "I went to the celebrated Mount Ophir, and ascended to the top, sleeping under a rock. The walk there was hard work, thirty miles through jungle in a succession of mudholes, and swarming with leeches, which crawled all over us, and sucked when and where they pleased." Wallace often stayed in small thatched huts, sleeping on the floor, using a packing crate for a writing table. He even had to contend with an infant:

I must now tell you of the addition to my household of an orphan baby...which I have nursed now more than a month...But I must now tell you how I came to take charge of it. Don't be alarmed; I was out shooting in the jungle and saw something up a tree which I thought was a large monkey or orang-utan, so I fired at it, and down fell this little baby—in its mother's arms.... I presume she was a wild 'woman of the woods; so I have preserved her skin and skeleton, and am trying to bring up her only daughter, and hope some day to introduce her to a fashionable society at the Zoological Gardens. About a week ago I bought a little monkey with a long tail, and as the baby was very lonely while we were out in the daytime, I put the little monkey into the cradle to keep it warm.... I assure you, the baby likes it exceedingly, and they are excellent friends.

The infant unfortunately died, but Wallace continued his work. Work, he did, exploring Malaya, Sumatro, Borneo, Sarawak, Java, Ternate, and New Guinea, collecting a total of 125,660 specimens of beetles, butterflies, birds, small mammals, and primates. During his time in the exotic lands he undertook ninety-six separate collecting expeditions, traveling by land and boat nearly 15,000 miles, equal to a voyage half-way around the world. He would ultimately be responsible for founding the discipline of "biogeography," the study of the distribution of species. He would also be responsible for the "Wallace Line," a jagged geological line between Indonesia and Australia that distinguished species with separate affinities and origin. Observing uneven distributions of species across geographical areas, Wallace soon concluded that species changed according to environmental circumstances. Within a year he would write the profound Sarawak paper, "On the Law which has Regulated the Introduction of New Species," in which he would say, "Every species has come into existence coincident both in space and time with a pre-existing closely-allied species." He would go on to speculate that the change of life forms had been slow, resulting from a natural process of gradual extinction and creation. Evolution could now be assumed. The time of this seminal paper—1855; the journal—*Annals and Magazine of Natural History;* the origin—a small house at the mouth of the Sarawak river at the foot of the Santuborg Mountain; Charles Darwin's reaction—"Can this be true?"

Wallace continued his search for the final answer to the species question—how do species change, what is the force that propels variation into new adaptations. During this time Wallace developed a correspondence with Darwin, his only major contact with England and the scientific community. Both men were close to the species solution.

Wallace Gets a Fever; The World Gets a Theory

Unlike Darwin whose theory emerged from his mind because of what he saw, Wallace actively searched for the answer. Darwin applied induction, walking the small steps of discovery; Wallace devised hypotheses, jumping quickly to possible explanations.

Lightning struck. On Ternate Island in February, 1858, Wallace suffered a malaria attack—a fever that scrambled his brain just enough to unleash a creative surge. "At the time in question I was suffering from a sharp attack of intermittent fever, and every day during the cold and succeeding hot fits had to lie down for several hours, during which time I had nothing to do but to think over any subjects that particularly interested me. One day something brought to my recollection Malthus's "Principles of Population," which I had read about twelve years before." The answer mushroomed through his fever-inflamed mind: species evolve under pressure of life's demands; slowly, beneficial variations are synthesized into new forms until, finally, they depart from each other into new species. For every adaptive biological response many nonadaptive individuals perish. The core of the theory is captured in his Ternate paper:

> The numbers that die annually must be immense; and as the individual existence of each animal depends upon itself, those that die must be the weakest—the very young, the aged, and the diseased,—while those that prolong their existence can only be the most perfect in health and vigour—those who are best able to obtain food regularly, and avoid their numerous enemies. It is, as we commenced by remarking, "a struggle for existence," in which the weakest and least, perfectly organized must always succumb.

There it was, the final product of his agony and ecstasy, the theory of modification by descent.

Wallace Applied to Everyday Life

As Alfred Wallace understood, evolution depends on four basic conditions:

1. The production of more offspring than can survive and reproduce—the raw material of differential survival.
2. Trait variations that are heritable among individuals—characteristics of potential value for survival and reproduction.
3. Ecological pressures on individuals to change—environmental imperatives.
4. Differential survival of individuals—survival of traits that favor the continuity of individuals and populations.

The four conditions of natural selection account for trait modification over generations, the extreme of which results in *speciation*, the formation of new species. Natural selection operates under demanding environments whenever heritable variation exists. Let's translate Wallace's insights into the kinds of situations that provoke genetic adaptations.

Suppose that you live on a farm infested with field mice. They forage in two of your granaries, eating vast amounts of your wheat. Nothing you do seems to control their reproductive urge; the mice quickly learn to avoid poisons, viewing any new change with suspicion.

You study the mice, hoping to find their weaknesses. You discover that they reproduce to the limit of their space and food supplies, foraging at all times of the day and night, avoiding only you. These little beasts differ in color—some are smoky grey, others are light beige, brown, or piebald. Some are obviously faster than others, rarely stopping in open spaces. Others, spend time in open areas, showing little wariness. The populations in the two granaries appear to be equally variable in morphology (physical form) and behavior. All of this variation, no doubt genetic in origin, interests you, but you see no way in which your newfound knowledge will help eliminate your problem.

Then, one day luck comes your way. A large hungry cat strays onto your property, taking up residence in one of the granaries—let's call that granary A. About the same time, a barn owl settles into the other granary—let's call that granary B. You see hope, honoring the cat with the name, "Tabby Tiger," the owl "Winged Lightning." The two predators of mice, representing ecological selection pressures, go to work in their inimitable ways. Tabby Tiger tracks and captures mice mainly during daylight, depending almost entirely on visual information. Winged Lightning hunts only at night, relying on the rustling noises that mice make as they move about.

Within days you notice a change. Mice populations in both granaries diminish. but there are other changes as well. Over time the mice in the two granaries change, but in different ways. In granary A, where Tabby Tiger makes her home, the mice are becoming uniformly smoky grey. Moreover, while still noisy critters, they tend to forage mainly at night, rarely moving into open areas during the day. In granary B, where Winged Lightning rules, the mice are still colored and spotted in various ways, but they now forage mainly by day, becoming very quiet at night. They too, as in granary A, become more wary, avoiding open spaces. What happened to cause the two populations to differ?

You have witnessed the process of natural selection in everyday life. Mice in granary A that are light in color having "gone to join the majority," as the Roman satirist, Petronius Arbiter remarked about death, leaving only the more inconspicuous smoky-colored mice to reproduce. Those mice that are inclined to forage in daylight, in the open, are promptly snatched up by Tabby Tiger. The mice communicate mostly with vocalizations that the cat ignores. What's left is success by default—mice that are cautious by day and blend into their environment by night.

Mice in granary B, successfully avoiding the night attacks by Winged Lightning, forage by day when the owl sleeps. They are nearly silent; Winged Lightning has eaten all the genes related to noisemaking and night-foraging. Those mice that are left communicate to each other with odors and movements, but not sound. The mice retain variations in color, as color is not a relevant cue to the night-stalking predator.

The mice from granaries A and B now seem so different to you that you wonder if they would even mate if given the opportunity. You trap males and females from each granary and test them for mating preferences—they don't mate between granaries, suggesting that they have become *reproductively isolated*—they are different species. If you worked long enough at the problem you might find that the failure to mate results from different courtship signals. Remember that mice in granary A communicate mostly during the night, whereas those in granary B communicate mostly during the day. The traits, existing primarily because of predation also happen to affect sexual preferences and social interactions.

This scenario no doubt simplifies the situation—it is meant to be only exemplary—but the points are valid. The five basic conditions for natural selection were met. First, the mice in the two granaries were reproducing to the limit of their environment—a rate faster than the supplies of food. These populations offer the raw material for natural selection. Second, the mice showed extensive variation, expressed as differences in coat color, timidity, and foraging preferences. These individual differences represent genetic variations that can be of advantage to some, hazardous to others. Third, animals in both granaries had to adjust to the predatory strategies of Tabby Tiger or Winged Lightning— the environmental selection pressures. Fourth, individual mice perished or survived, depending upon how well the inherent variability prevented fatal attacks by the predators. Finally, the differential selection pressures of the cat and owl led to differences among the mice of the two granaries to such an extent that individuals from the two granaries were no longer able to reproduce. As sociobiologist E. O. Wilson put it in his book, *The Diversity of Life*, "The origin of species is therefore simply the evolution of some difference—any difference at all—that prevents the production of fertile hybrids between populations under natural conditions." It is the type of process that could explain the variations in animals forms that Alfred Wallace saw in Malaysia and Charles Darwin saw on the Galapagos Islands.

Natural selection operates very quickly, eliminating traits that are nonadaptive. The selection pressures in the environment can be multiple—predation, as in our example, or geological, meteorological, nutritional, or social. We carelessly say that natural selection creates adaptive characteristics, but what we really mean is that nonadaptive traits, those that contribute negatively to survival or reproduction, are eliminated during the process. Natural selection refers to differential death, not differential survival, as is commonly thought. Traits that help individuals to escape extinction survive, as do neutral traits that have no bearing on survival or reproduction. The British historian, Arnold Toynbee put it this way, "Death is the price paid by life for an enhancement of the complexity of a live organism's structure." Death allows life to continue.

Wallace Storms Darwin's Lair

Wallace sent the Ternate paper to Darwin at Down House by way of Singapore, Southampton, and London, asking if he thought it worth publishing. Darwin was stunned. In his hands was his own theory, the same theory that took Darwin twenty-seven years to conceive and mold. What was he to do?

Darwin entered into a controversial arrangement, advised by his friends, Joseph Hooker, the famed botanist, and Charles Lyell, the geologist. Without Wallace's knowledge a joint paper, consisting of Wallace's Ternate paper and Darwin's notes, was presented at the Linnean Society on July 1, 1858—the world would know both Wallace and Darwin as the authors of the theory of natural selection. Some claim that Darwin yanked the priority from under Wallace by this unusual move, but history will probably show that the dual presentation, in Wallace's absence, was the most satisfactory compromise in a sticky situation.

That was a close call for Darwin, in 1858, when he almost lost his parenthood over the theory of natural selection. The incident stimulated him to sit down and hurriedly write *On the Origin of Species by Means of Natural Selection or the Preservation of Favored Races in the Struggle for Life—otherwise referred to as The Origin*, or The *Origin of Species*. A single paragraph from this great book serves up the essence of the idea.

> As many more individuals of each species are born that can possible survive; and as, consequently, there is a frequently recurring struggle for existence, it follows that any being, if it vary however slightly in any manner profitable to itself, under the complex and sometimes varying conditions of life, will have a better chance of surviving, and thus be naturally selected. From the strong principle of inheritance, any selected variety will tend to propagate its new and modified form.

Compare this statement with that from Wallace's Ternate paper; they could have been written by the same person.

The day Wallace's paper was presented along with Darwin's notes at the Linnean Society—a shot continuing to echo around the world— Wallace was collecting animal specimens in New Guinea where he injured his ankle, losing one of his men to fever—not a good day for Wallace. The *Origin*, which preempted Wallace's place in history, was published November 24, 1859. That day, too, was dark for Wallace; there were "no rare birds or insects," he was sick as a dog and friendless in the jungle.

Hesitation, Convergence and the Truth of Nature

Before Alfred Wallace took his fateful trip to the Amazon, Darwin realized that species change as the result of natural selection. Wallace searched for the Holy Grail of biology, while the chalice of speciation lay quietly in a cabinet in Down House at Kent. If Darwin was concerned about the priority of his thought, why did he hesitate to unveil one of the world's greatest ideas?

Darwin was a careful man, avoiding incorrect solutions to problems, no matter what the price. He would rather be silent than wrong. He also followed the admonishments of Francis Bacon and John Sturat Mill who believed that induction was *the* method of science—Mill had exclaimed, "that great mental operation, the operation of discovering and proving general propositions." Mill, himself, was interested in applying induction to sociological problems, concluding that we might find all that is relevant to mankind by applying "Mass Observation," which apparently meant recording all raw facts about what people do and say, what games they play, what ambitions they follow. From this, a great generalization would inevitably flow.

The process of deduction, starting from a hypothesis, and searching for data to support that hypothesis, was believed to reveal only what you already knew, making explicit information already present in the axioms or premises assumed by the hypothesis. Complicated? It's the difference between counting people in populations each generation and concluding that populations expand over time—an inductive generalization—or, starting with the hypothesis that populations are large because of past reproductive efforts, a deductive hypothesis, that depends upon the assumption that births depend upon reproduction. Mill would say that the hypothesis and its assumption are simply a restatement of fact. Data, according to Bacon and Mill, were the cobblestones of the unpaved road, which when found and assembled in the only rational way, would reveal the highway. Facts speak louder than deductions; information drives hypotheses, not the reverse, so the argument goes. The great Sir Isaac Newton, next to whom Darwin would soon lie in Westminster Abbey, after all, had frowned upon hypotheses—no insignificant force in Darwin's thinking. Moreover, Darwin had little success testing specific hypotheses, leading him to conclude that "This has naturally led me to distrust greatly deductive reasoning."

It is probable that Darwin was such a fanatical collector of biological information—literally tons of information—because he believed that "Mass Observation" would eventually reveal the truth. Indeed it may have, in his case, but in all such inductive processes, it takes time, many data, luck, and unconscious perception—sort of a Kantian self-organizational brain. It also takes patience, a trait characteristic of Darwin.

Charles Darwin did arrive at the truth of natural selection, yet he refused to publish, a reluctance related to his uneasiness of challenging the Creationist view of life. Imagine what it would be like to tell your family, boss and neighbor that they and your cat, Tabby Tiger, have a common ancestor? It could hurt them and make you look silly—even today evolution has its religious and political detractors. Multiply that feeling several times in Darwin's case. For, in the era of Victorian England absolutely no one believed in evolutionary descent with modification, including the ranking members of science, such as Charles Lyell.

You can understand Darwin's dilemma. He certainly did not want to be wrong about this matter. So he waited.

But what was he waiting for? Death, it seems. He made arrangements with his wife, Emma, to have his first proper outline of his theory, written in 1842, edited and published in the event of his death. Saddled with poor health ever since his return on the *Beagle*, Charles had every expectation of dying young. Perhaps it was true in his own mind, as he insisted, that "Evolution was not in the air." He could wait, avoid the criticism and still retain priority—from the one final place of safety, the grave.

There was one miscalculation. One day Darwin looked in the mirror and saw Wallace staring back, a shattering experience. It was as if Charles Darwin believed that he was in a marathon race, far ahead of anyone else, only to find that it was a 100-yard dash with Alfred Wallace right on his heels. To save his priority he ratcheted up the pace, got his cheerleaders Hooker and Lyell to egg him on, threw caution to the wind and sprinted to the finish line with the tightly grasped baton of his *Origin*.

If there is really "truth out there," if evolution theory was as certain to appear as night follows day, who should receive the credit? Wallace, in the sense that he was the first to clearly outline the theory in writing, yet Darwin, in the sense that he held the idea in his head for years, finally painting it in detailed strokes one year later in the incomparable *Origin of Species*. We should remember, too, that Wallace and Darwin stood on the shoulders of the same giants. Thomas Carlyle was right when he said that "History is the essence of innumerable biographies." So many people, so many thoughts. For Darwin and Wallace the race was a photo finish, but many others smoothed the track.

The story of Darwin and Wallace is strange—two men so alike in their drive for understanding, both so courageous, yet worlds apart in temperament. The temporal spacing of their behaviors and thinking is perhaps the most puzzling. It is almost as if Providence stuttered and did the same story twice, spaced in origin by about seventeen years. Destiny pulled Darwin and Wallace along the same path to the same end. Consider this. As young men both collected beetles, both read Malthus, Lyell, Chambers, and Lamarck; both understood that the key problem was to decipher the formation and modification of species; both began their search in South America; both displayed extraordinary courage in the face of danger; both ventured upon long ocean trips leading to the theory—one on the *Beagle* and the other on the *Bengal*; both nearly died at sea; both developed a theory so similar that even the words describing the theory were nearly identical. In 1858 when the mirror at Down House shattered, revealing Wallace, Darwin wrote Lyell in panic: "I never saw a more striking coincidence; If Wallace had my MS. sketch written out in 1842, he could not have made a better short abstract!"

Even later, after the two men became strong friends, the independently derived similarities continued to unfold, the same sense of family responsibility, the same sense of humbleness, the same drive to write and publish, even the same kind of odd writing board that they both used. It was almost as if they were identical twins expressing their inevitable similarities. Or, as someone put it; they seemed to be connected by cellular telephone, with an initial delay circuitry of seventeen years that over time cascaded into instant communication.

Methodology and temperament were the great differences between the two men, which makes potent the imagery of Darwin and Wallace reflecting each other in the mirror. Darwin was methodical, careful, patient, inductive—he waited for the world to voice its opinion. Wallace was the antithesis—radical, bold, impatient, and deductive—he squeezed the world for its opinion. What Darwin lacked in gusto, he made up for in deliberation; what Wallace lacked in patience he made up for in passion. With Darwin and Wallace the march of science from the early Greeks to the theory of natural selection is complete, a vivid demonstration of the reality of evolution and the courage of those committed to its understanding. There is much left to know, more oceans to cross, dangerous storms ahead, but the really tough paths on the road to the complete understanding of man have been opened by those who went before. Loren Eiseley captures the poetic nature of our situation:

> (Man) is an inconceivably rare and strange beast who lives both within himself and in his outside environment. With his coming came history, the art of the mind imposing itself upon nature. There has been no previous evolutionary novelty comparable to this save the act of creation itself. Man, imperfect transitory man, carries within him some uncanny spark from the first lightning that split the void. He alone can dilate evil by drawing upon the innocent powers contained in nature: he alone can walk straight-footed to his own death and hold the world well lost for the sake of such intangible things as truth and love.

> Man, in short, has, like no other beast, tumbled into the crevasse of his own being.

The grand theory of natural selection propelled man along the new philosophical path of biological determinism. The evolutionary appearance of man appeared inevitable. But this certainty would soon evaporate—there was something strange and unsettling about man's beginnings.

References

Cited in Chapter 2

Bowler, P.J. (1989). *Evolution: The History of an Idea.* Berkeley: University of California Press.
Brackman, A.C. (1980). *A Delicate Arrangement.* New York: Times Books.
Smith, J.M. (1989) *Did Darwin Get it Right?* New York: Chapman and Hall.
Wallace, A.R. (1855). "On the law which has regulated the introduction of new species." *Annals and Magazine of Natural History,* 26, 184–96.
Wallace, A.R. (1905). *My Life: A Record of Events and Opinions.* London: reprinted Farnborough, Gregg International, 1969, two volumes.

General References

Grizimek, H.C.B. (ed). (1976). *Encyclopedia of Evolution.* New York: Van Nostrand Reinhold Company.
Strickberger, M.W. (1990). *Evolution.* Boston: Jones and Bartlett Publishers.

II

Valley of Becoming

Into this Universe, and why not knowing,
Nor whence, like Water willy-nilly flowing;
*   And out of it, as Wind along the Waste,*
I know not whether, willy-nilly blowing.

—Omar Khayyám

Chance dogs our history—miracles, seen in
retrospect.

3

Uncertain Survival

I returned, and saw under the sun, that the race is not to the swift, nor the battle to the strong, neither yet bread to the wise, nor yet riches to men of understanding, nor yet favour to men of skill; but time and chance happeneth to them all. For man also knoweth not his time: as the fishes that are taken in an evil net, and as the birds that are caught in the snare; so are the sons of men snared in an evil time, when it falleth suddenly upon them.

—Ecclesiastes 9: 11-12

Charles Darwin's and Alfred Wallace's theory of natural selection developed into a biological dynasty, where all species are viewed as interconnected through common ancestors, where all biological disciplines ascribe to the same evolutionary principles. This scientific perspective of evolution, now referred to as "Neo-Darwinism," is the keystone for the understanding of ourselves. According to this theory, nature seems predictable, progressive—even judicious—with the genetically "fit" individuals defeating the "unfit," victory going to the swift, the world running toward perfection. The theory of natural selection may have compromised our belief in God, but it replaced our agnosticism with the belief that we sit firmly as biology's perfected species, Aristotles's Scale of Nature confirmed. Or so it seemed.

Yet, the Devil is in the details. The English physician, Thomas Brown, agonized: "Thus the Devil played at chess with me, and yielding a pawn, thought to gain a queen of me, taking advantage of my honest endeavors." A detailed look at the process of natural selection presents a cold assessment, the Devil giving us an apparent advantage, only to snatch it away. We may feel that we have reached a summit of evolutionary importance, only to find that our existence is improbable and without special design.

The unexpected nature of natural selection unfolds in this chapter. First, we examine the belief that evolution has a destiny, demonstrating, instead, that evolution is mechanistic and impersonal—there is no vital force guiding evolution. Second, we show that our evolution is at best, improbable, nearly impossible at worst. The chancy business of our existence is indicated in two ways: (1) in factors that "wobble" life's processes, leading to unexpected evolutionary outcomes; and (2) in the physical pounding of the earth—asteroid impacts, earthquakes, continental shifts—that drive some species to extinction, while releasing the potential of others. The chapter ends by merging the theory of natural selection with the crazy-quilt pattern of unexpected events. Inevitably, granting the historical improbability of our life forces a new view of evolution, one that will influence the interpretation of ourselves.

Cracking the Myths of Evolution

There are three major speculations surrounding ideas of evolution: (1) evolution has a goal, and we are nearer to that goal than other animals; (2) evolution is progressive; directional change again illustrating our superior rise within the river of life; and (3) human consciousness and free will are the defining signature of our evolutionary preeminence. But, let's search for the Devil in the details.

Contrary to most beliefs, evolution has no predestination, no goal, no purpose—in technical terms, no *teleology*. Birds may *appear* to migrate *in order to find more food*. Humans *seem* to reproduce *in order to have more children*. These are teleological views, because we respond to the apparent dedication of animals to some distant end. But animals, including humans, are not animated with ambitions for themselves and their offspring *because of a sense of destiny*. True, they do behave as if they sense these goals, but they are expressing behaviors and attitudes that allowed their ancestors to survive and reproduce. We are not pulled by the future, yet unknown; we are pushed by history, long insistent— the genetic recipe of the past.

Second, evolution is not progressive. Species don't sprint toward evolutionary perfection; instead, populations adapt to local environments— the immediate stresses of life having precedence. Consider this: you live in the mountains where climbing is difficult. In the village an old man gives you his spiked climbing shoes—he's retiring to the plains of Kansas. What a change in shoes. Now you can almost fly up the mountains. Like a genetic mutation, the shoes become a permanent part of your life. Walking, as before, is out of the question. Nothing much changes for awhile, but one day, climbing up a steep valley you find some discarded pitons, spikes that are driven into rock to secure ropes. Had you not had the special shoes, you would not have reached the elevation of the pitons. Now, not only can you climb steep grades easily, but you can go up and down the face of cliffs. It all looks like progressive evolution—first walking, then climbing, and finally rappeling down cliffs.

Viewing this from afar, as would a biologist from Mars, you might conclude that the trend was "written in the wind." In fact, two accidents occurred in a row, one contingent upon the other: first, the acquisition of the climbing shoes that allowed you to explore mountain heights, and second, the finding of the pitons to climb vertical rocks. These contingent events worked well together and brought the climber to new heights of capability, one event contingent upon the other, each a reaction to specific circumstances.

Many genetic lineages show definite but not inevitable directional changes over generations, just like the story of our climber. Moreover, trends do not tell us whether things are good or bad; things simply evolve toward larger or smaller size, toward one kind of camouflage or another, toward more or less complexity. For example, hominids—humanlike species in the family Hominidae—show a striking increase in brain size during the past 3.5 million years (MY), beginning at around 400 to 500 g (grams) with the earliest form, *Australopithecus*, expanding to over 1350 g with *Homo sapiens*. The changes are certainly a trend, one of great interest to us, but the trend is not foreordained, or even of special relevance to the animal kingdom at large. It is not apparent that large brains are generally better as tools for survival or reproduction than small brains, and are therefore destined to emerge. Other species actually evolve toward smaller brains, for example the mammalian tapir (an ungulate), and several diving species of seals. Depending upon the ecology in which species live, large or small brains may be adaptive—it may, among some, pay to be bright or stupid. The important determinants of brain size and other adaptations are simply survival and reproductive competence.

Local adaptations often give us the illusion that evolution is progressive. As they adapt to variations in temperature, continental geology, sea level, food supplies, or predation, species track incremental shifts in environments with small and continuous changes. They do this over large sweeps of history, leaving only a vague record of causes. When we examine *extant* (existing) organisms, or fossil remains, we see the successive adaptations, but not the changing environments—all long gone—that dictated the adaptations.

The third major belief about evolution is that consciousness sets us apart from other species, both as a product of a unique evolution and as a cause for our superiority. Consciousness does seem to be the signature of our success—giving us free will and other qualities that are almost soul-like. The interesting, and unsettling, nature of consciousness, is that it seemingly allows us to step beyond the specific history of our evolution; even more unnerving, it looks within itself to see its own future. Consciousness gives us the power to unravel our own history, at the same time creating the superstitions that we have free will, making the unraveling more difficult. Nevertheless, as complex as it seems, consciousness does not rate a special explanation—the same old evolutionary principles will do.

Simple or not, consciousness gives us the ability to solve unique and complex problems. It also allows us to peer deep within ourselves. But those abilities alone do not separate us qualitatively from other species. Other species show the rudiments of our own capabilities. Neither is consciousness necessary for many species to implement complex and effective behaviors. Many do without it entirely. Again, it's the same old game of natural selection—chiseling out different adaptive traits, contingent upon environmental demands. Applying the strongest criteria of evolutionary success—survival and reproduction—we are neither more or less superior because of it.

The Stormy Path of Evolution

The most startling truth about evolution is its chance qualities. Many events that could have occurred in life's record did not; events that did occur, need not have. It's the old poker game on a devilish level—we draw to an inside straight and win, but the odds were heavily against us. And don't forget all of those times when the cards fell to someone else's advantage. Cards fly recklessly across the table according to probabilities, leading to exuberant success in some cases, but more often to agonizing defeat—extinction at the poker table. There are some basic rules to the game of poker, as there are to evolution, but within that framework, things sort themselves out, not according to dreamy images of aces full, but according to what cards you have, what cards are left, and their position in the deck. The best advice—bet with the house.

We have not evolved after billions of years *simply* because of a string of adaptive changes brought about by natural selection. Many chancy things occur among the cards of evolution. Catastrophes impinge on species, often driving them to extinction. Luck of the draw occurs with others, as they survive to become our ancestors. Evolution is a contingency matrix, as uncertain as any poker game—just more serious and unpredictable—"There is many a slip 'twixt the cup and the lip," as the Greek writer Palladius told us long ago. What can we discover along that slippery path?

Pictures in Life's Gallery

We are latecomers in the evolution of life, appearing in the fossil record less than 200,000 years ago. We are, therefore, less than a critical event in evolution. Picture it this way: if a seventy-foot-high live-oak tree, with its thousands of branches, represents 3.6 billion years of proliferating life, a half-inch twig at the top is the history of man—unpredictable from below and nearly invisible at the top—nothing special. Unless one believes that nearly all of the 3.6 billion years of life were in preparation for the ascent of man, our view of our own importance must be modest.

Modest, indeed, for we are a singularly lucky experiment in the vast laboratory of species diversification—just one tiny fraction of what is now out there. Edward O. Wilson, the premier biologist from Harvard, estimates that there are now about 1,413,000 *known* species of organisms, of which 1,032,000 are animals. Arthropods, which include insects, the spider and scorpion group, and crustaceans, including lobsters, shrimps, and crabs, account for about 80 percent of animal species. Mammals, including ourselves, amount for about 4,000 species, or 0.3 percent of all known animals. *Homo sapiens*, then, is only 1/4000 of the total number of mammals, numerically, at least, insignificant. The distribution of the world's fauna, that is, all animal forms, is shown here (Figure 3.1).

FIGURE 3.1
Number of Living Animal Species Currently Known
(According to Major Group)

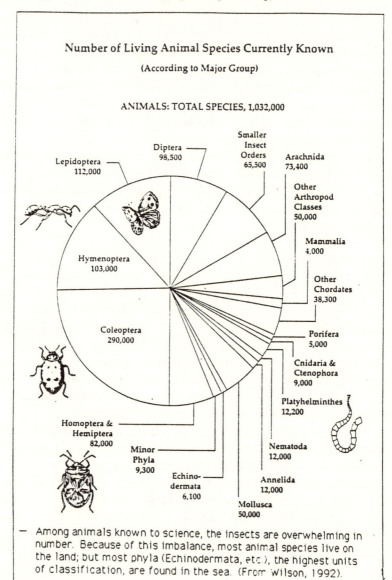

Number of Living Animal Species Currently Known

(According to Major Group)

ANIMALS: TOTAL SPECIES, 1,032,000

Smaller Insect Orders 65,500

Diptera 98,500

Lepidoptera 112,000

Arachnida 73,400

Other Arthropod Classes 50,000

Hymenoptera 103,000

Mammalia 4,000

Coleoptera 290,000

Other Chordates 38,300

Porifera 5,000

Cnidaria & Ctenophora 9,000

Platyhelminthes 12,200

Homoptera & Hemiptera 82,000

Nematoda 12,000

Minor Phyla 9,300

Echinodermata 6,100

Annelida 12,000

Mollusca 50,000

— Among animals known to science, the insects are overwhelming in number. Because of this imbalance, most animal species live on the land; but most phyla (Echinodermata, etc.), the highest units of classification, are found in the sea. (From Wilson, 1992).

Source: Wilson, 1992

Again, these are *known* species that do not include all those hidden, undetected and undescribed. The total number may be between 10 and 100 million, a number difficult to estimate. About 6,000 species come to light each year, including an occasional mammal, such as the sheep-sized, horned ungulate discovered in 1993 in the forests of Vietnam. In the final tally, insects are expected to be extremely high in number because of their critical symbiotic connectedness to flowering plants. They fertilize and decompose plants into nutrients required for the growth of innumerable other species. Insects also speciate quickly, dispersing their talents widely. Then there are microscopic organisms that rarely come to our attention. For example, pinch a gram of soil between your fingers, and you hold about 10 *billion* bacteria. Who knows, worldwide there may be several millions of bacteria species. We are a small part of this staggering diversity.

It's time to explore how contingent events drive evolution—how momentary influences determine who succeeds and who fails—why we have tremendous diversity of species.

The River of Life and the Burgess Shale

Alfred Russell Wallace laid his life on the line when he explored the great Amazon River. This gigantic river, nearly 4,000 miles in length, drains over 2.7 million square miles of land. This river of life is responsible for the world's largest rain forest, and supports the highest density of species anywhere: 2 million insects, 100,000 plants, 2,000 fish and 600 mammals—give or take a few million. The Amazon carries nearly 20 percent of the Earth's total river waters, more than the six next-largest rivers combined. The powerful flow dilutes the salinity of the Atlantic ocean 100 miles or more beyond the coastline. Oceangoing ships can travel inland to the town of Manaus, 2,300 miles from the mouth.

Dangers lurk everywhere for the unwary, providing us the perfect setting to illustrate the contingent nature of evolution. The river is analogous to the branching contours of evolution, with its many points of potential change, environmental instability, and hidden dangers. The Amazon is constantly changing, affecting climate, daily weather patterns, and species survival. It is in constant fluctuation, its banks expanding and contracting, its tributaries running strong or drying completely. Within this environment, like any other, there are both limitations to organismic survival and change. Tributaries, with strange-sounding names, like Xinga, Tapajos, Madeira, Negro, Japura, and Puricus, fan out from the river like silver spider webs. Legend has it that Francisco de Orellana, the Spanish explorer, named the river after a Greek myth, claiming that he was attacked by fierce Amazonian women. If there, they are yet to be rediscovered. No one knows the portent of this watery domain.

Now, let's build an image of contingent evolution by reference to the chancy events that occur on the Amazon. Imagine that 1000 boats of various kinds and sizes start their journey up the Amazon from the sea port of Para, Wallace's point of departure in 1848. The boats compete for supplies, waterways, and resources of the Amazon, all within a fluctuating environment. Over time many things happen to the boats, some helpful to the individual boats, some not. Some wear down, some crash, some are rebuilt, and occasionally successful crews build new boats. There are no obvious goals for the boats; they simply attempt to survive under uncertain circumstances, perhaps trading, sometimes carrying passengers. They know not where they came; they know not where they go. The Amazon remains indifferent.

The early phase of the journey brings sudden destruction to nearly 40 percent of the boats. Some are swamped by tidal waves sweeping up the Amazon from the Atlantic Ocean. Others mistakenly turn up hazardous tributaries and are wrecked. Now and then a single boat cannot be found. Other boats go aground on rocky shores during dark nights or foggy days. Later, another 20 percent of the boats fail because of rotting planks, poor construction or inept navigation. Annual rains sink another 10 percent; disease decimates an additional 20 percent. Finally, 2 percent vanish up river, perhaps rammed by other ships or captured by competing boats. Only 8 percent of the original fleet of 1000 boats remain, and half of these appear on the verge of ruin.

Looking back on the Amazonian adventure, as we might look back on the evolution of animals, we are stunned at the capriciousness of history. We can see a cause for many of the events—a boat heaved onto the shore by a great wind, one rotting from under its crew, another losing its way up a winding tributary, still another gaining control over its environment and its crew building another boat. But much of what happened could not have been predicted in advance; it neither occurred because of inherent differences in the quality of boats, nor because of specific planning by their crews. Rather, the outcomes, like evolutionary change, were contingent upon individual situations—the escape of danger, the jeopardy of unexpected forces, "A chapter of accidents," remarked the English statesman, Earl of Chesterfield. "Pure chance, absolutely free but blind, at the very root of the stupendous edifice of evolution," asserted the great biologist, Jacob Monod.

Here is an entirely different type of question. Supposing we had an opportunity to rerun the history of the boats—we again start with the same 1000 boats, the same set of founding boats. Would the outcome be the same? Would the same 8 percent of the boats survive? Certainly not. Everything would be different, as Heraclitus said: "You can't step into the same river twice; everything flows and nothing stays." The Amazon—the environment for the boats—is never the same. Storms and waves break at different times; fog obscures some tributaries and diverts boats into different streams. Some boats crash into each other; others sail into pockets of disaster and are lost forever. Rarely are the same boats exposed to the same fortunes or misfortunes. Lightning strikes twice, but not in the same place.

Evolution depends upon time and place, running down various paths and up different grades in unpredictable ways. If we knew the trajectory of every molecule in the entire universe, precise outcomes could be guaranteed. But our limitations are vast and allow no predictions beyond the most primitive; we are barely able to predict tomorrow's weather, let alone 600 MY of contingent evolution. As Winston Churchill remarked, "It is a mistake to look too far ahead. Only one link of the chain of destiny can be handled at a time." We must tighten our intellectual belts and admit that predictable determinism is a quality of theory, but not fact. Chance calls out the roll of the dice. The message is powerful and unpleasant: *Homo sapiens* is a contingent species, one that would probably never appear again if the game of life were replayed. There is nothing inevitable about our appearance and no assurance that we will make it past the next roll.

The Amazonian scenario of unpredictability is very much like our own evolutionary history. Our understanding of that history rests in part on fossil evidence gleaned from the Burgess Shale, a unique shale quarry in Yohy National Park in the Canadian Rockies, on the boarder of Alberta and British Columbia. The details of these finds are considered in Steven Gould's recent book, *Wonderful Life*. The implications of the fossil record are rich in irony, for if correct, *Homo sapiens*, with its complexity and undeniable uniqueness, is perhaps no more likely to have been an evolutionary success than any other species, including trilobites, saber-tooth tigers, or mammoths.

The fauna of this remarkable quarry were first discovered in 1909 by C.D. Walcott, a famous paleontologist. The diggings were destined to change our conception of life. The story—one of the greatest detective stories in biology—really begins with Mrs. Walcott and her horse, at least as the story is often told. At the end of the 1908 fossil hunting expedition, just before the winter snows in the Rocky Mountains, Mrs. Walcott's horse stumbled over a block of shale that had obviously fallen from a higher elevation. In it were some of the most peculiar fossil forms ever seen—500 to 600 MY old representatives of the first multicellular organisms to appear in the Cambrian Period.

The search for the origin of this block of shale had to wait until the next year when the Walcotts returned for another season of paleontological investigations. C.D. Walcott quickly found the source of the breakaway shale—peppered with thousands of soft and hard-bodied organisms, surviving as fossils only because of an anaerobic (oxygen-free) environment caused by an apparent landslide. Thus, accidents were compounded in this great mystery—the accident of nature and the accident of discovery. Were these new forms of life, never before known, or were they simply old forms in new carapaces?

By accident or not, C.D. Walcott and his wife Helena had touched the crucial joint of evolutionary transition where almost all the representative designs of multicellular organisms are found. The radiation of new species occurred, as Steven Gould said, "in one great whoosh called the Cambrian Explosion about 525 million years ago." But what happened to this great diversity? Did it suffer the same fate as our 1000 Amazonian boats? If so, then, as we have suggested, the implications for the evolution of *Homo sapiens* is rich in irony, for we were no more likely to become an evolutionary success than any other species. In fact had dinosaurs not perished, allowing mammals to diversify and radiate out into many species, humans most certainly would never have arisen—a startling conclusion that puts chance before adaptation, contingency before determinism, luck before good design.

C.D. Walcott's conservative view of the evolutionary record suggested to him that all the forms in the Burgess Shale could be pigeonholed in existing categories, even though some were so strange that they nearly defied description. For example, one form called *Opabinia* had five eyes, a flexible nozzle at the front, bending back to the mouth below—an uncommon little creature. Others were equally strange, propelling themselves on their backs, moving and clinging with sharp spikes, hooks, and peculiar appendages, even swallowing other organisms whole.

It took subsequent investigators, Harry Whittington, Simon Conway-Morris, and Derek Briggs, to understand that the diversity was well outside the range of anything known. The mystery deepened. Some species, apparently perfectly and complexly adapted for a time, nevertheless lost it all in the contingency game. In all, about twenty alternative phyla existed, only about four of which we recognize today. There are another fifteen to twenty designs so peculiar that they defy classification—none exists today. Other sites, like the Ediacara mines of Australia, northeast Siberia, and Nambia, Africa indicate that even earlier aquatic soft-bodied forms, failed to survive through the Cambrian Period and beyond. Apparently mass destruction is par for the course.

Pikaia, one chordate form in the Burgess Shale, was one of the first representative of the vertebrate group leading to man. It was sparsely distributed in the Burgess Shale, a fragile organism whose good luck is behind our ultimate success. If the Burgess Shale organisms were eliminated differently by life's events, like our 1000 boats, or our drawing to an inside straight, we simply would not be here today. Without Pikaia, on a related form, there would be no chordate; without chordates there would be no vertebrates, including us. Perhaps, then, an organism like the cockroach would be the dominant type—our worst nightmare.

The mystery of the Burgess Shale is not completely solved. We do know that the Cambrian Explosion occurred worldwide, not just as a peculiar happening in a few places. Decimation of untold numbers of species happened at the same time around the world, occurring perhaps within a period of a few thousand years, leaving only a unique sampling of species from those available. Many of the details of the species radiation and ultimate death escape our gaze. We have no idea what kinds of tragedies befell most of the Cambrian organisms, and why so few made it through the maze of evolution. But we have some ideas. One thing seems clear: the species, genera, and families seemed to be adequate poker players at the start of the competition, but some lost against a pair of aces with a pair of kings, others ran out of luck completely, and a very few drew successfully to an inside straight.

And this was only the beginning of life's gamble; powerful forces would break the continuity of evolution many times.

Sticks and Stones and Broken Bones: Dreams and Reality

The night sky cracked apart with scorching fire, the Devil, himself, straddling the blazing shaft of death. The white hot asteroid, 100 miles in diameter, plunged through the sea and deep into the earth, like a burning spear, transforming its primal roar into a cacophony of ripping destruction. Between heartbeats, earth, water, and fire exploded 50 miles into the stratosphere, blotting out the lunar light, showering the trembling world with blistering heat and jagged rocks. Night became a hellish blaze—the earth visited by damnation.

Shock waves swept behind the impact, driving sound before ruination, trailing bonfires—affirming the penultimate apocalypse. The dawn, that day, did not appear, nor did it for years, as debris born of catastrophe swirled into the tradewinds, mixed with clouds and rain, falling again to wrap the earth in a sticky umber clay. Large reptiles, like the plant eating dinosaur Brachiosaurus and its bipedal carnivorous cousin, Megalosaurus, lost their way, abandoning their families, choking on grime and phlegm. Archaeopteryx, with 36 feet wingspans, crashed crazily into mountains, or simply died of starvation. Small mammals scurried to safer havens, digging deep to avoid acid rains and plunging temperatures. Plants, dependent on intense light and mild temperatures, withered to soggy masses, allowing more adaptable varieties to persist. Insects, small and opportunistic, went on their mindless ways, hardly jarred by the structural collapse of the world. Death came in innumerable forms, but life held at the edge of chaos. The earth survived, changed forever.

Reasonable people subscribe to this historical reconstruction of an era, 65 MY ago, at the end of the Cretaceous Period, when dinosaurs were doomed, giving mammals freedom to expand. Today, remnants of the asteroid that changed everything—making man possible—is believed buried silently beneath the sea off the coast of Yucatan, near the city of Cancun. The sky above that mountain of iron is again a Caribbean azure, with dawns peacefully revolving every twenty-four hours. Saturating the senses with this beauty, it is difficult to believe that the universe is wobbling and Earth is at risk.

But they are.

The earth heaves and moans. Continents split apart and scrunch together at the rate your fingernails grow, floating on plates that send them through belts of equatorial heat and polar colds. The last supercontinent, Pangaea, was breaking apart about the time the dinosaurs evolved 250 MY, causing seas to form and altering climates inexorably. But that's only part of Earth's shifting nature. Meteors and asteroids pockmarked the earth since its beginning. There is growing evidence that around 65 MY not just one impact delivered a knockout blow to animals and plants. Instead, several meteors combined their individual devastation, causing worldwide catastrophe. One recent candidate for extended damage is a meteor about seventeen miles in diameter that struck in north-central Iowa, near the town of Manson. It's remains now lie peacefully under fields of golden corn. There were obviously others, with more impact sites identified every year. The damage from the combined extraterrestrial impacts was apparently exaggerated by volcanic action, and a deteriorating environment, beginning about 10 MY earlier.

According to Luis Alvarez and Walter Alvarez, who proposed the extraterrestrial cause for the Cretaceous extinction, two geological aberrations give us convincing markers for massive geological changes and associated extinctions. The first marker is *iridium*, a rare element found in high amounts in meteors, asteroids, and comets. The heavenly giants that crashed into the earth, known as *bolides*, fragmented, sending iridium and other debris around the world to finally settle at the surface. Today that iridium is buried in sediments dated at 65 MY. The impact of bolides also left shocked crystals—quartz melted by high heat and compression. This is the second major marker. These shocked crystals are visible at the same age as the extinction, matching the age of the impact sites and the associated iridium. The evidence, though not definitive, certainly supports the impact theory of extinction.

The Cretaceous extinction did not affect species equally. The percent dying varied from zero to 100. From 38 to 60 percent of all fish perished; around 33 percent of amphibia took the count; all the dinosaurs died, although other reptiles derived from dinosaurs were relatively unaffected (the crocodile made it). Among mammals 43 percent went extinct. In general, the massive extinction was worldwide, with large animals more severely affected. Fourteen percent of families were wiped out, 38 percent of genera (groups of species) and about 68 percent of all species. Remember that when a family is lost, so are all its genera and species. Thus, when the decimation is described in family units, the full extent of the tragedy is hidden.

The most vulnerable species were likely to share the following characteristics:

- Few in number and unevenly spaced.
- Large body size.
- Specialized feeding strategies.
- Inflexible reactions to changed ecologies.
- High dependency on other species.
- Unstable genetic, physiological and behavioral traits.
- Direct exposure to the atmosphere (e.g. terrestrial species).
- Strong adaptations to a particular range of temperatures.

Obviously, not all species are equally at risk, making it possible that differential survival in cataclysmic environments is just another response to natural selection—natural selection of gigantic proportions, with a twist of contingency.

Clearly, the Cretaceous extinction was extensive, but there are others of greater magnitude. Five major extinctions have been logged for the nearly 600 MY of vertebrate evolution, occurring with an average interval of 120 MY. The figure below pinpoints their times and the species associated with each.

The extinctions at the ends of the Ordovician, Devonian, and Permian Periods were the greatest of all—each eliminating a higher percentage of marine families than the later Cretaceous event which swept away the dinosaurs. Fully 90 percent of all marine and terrestrial species died during the Permian extinction. Unselective death came to many organisms, those forms never to reappear in the fossil record—chance running wild.

As terrible as these extinctions were, they do not stand alone as apocalyptic events. By far the most frequent extinctions are small, that in combination account for most of the deaths. Within the life span of your grandparents, the Earth has trembled from many natural catastrophes. It has many times before; it will many times again. In 1815 the volcano Tambora on the Indonesian island of Sunbawa lifted tons of rock and ash into the atmosphere, killing tens of thousands of people and eliminating

FIGURE 3.2

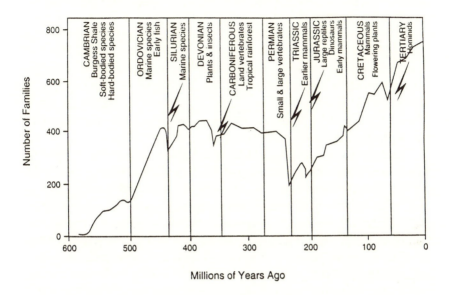

Family marine diversity has increased over time, with occasional setbacks through mass global extinctions. There have been five such extinctions indicated here by lightning strikes.
Source: Wilson, 1992

the island's plants and animals. Less than forty years after Alfred Wallace left Malyasia, Krakatau exploded. The island, the size of Manhattan, located in the Sunda Strait between Sumatra and Java, ended on August 27, 1883. The volcano's force, equivalent to 100–150 megatons of TNT, threw magma, rock, and ash four miles into the air, sent thirty-foot waves crashing into Java and Sumatra, where 40,000 people were killed. The plumes of ash and sulfuric acid spread around the world, creating magnificent sunsets, lowering temperatures by an average of two degrees centigrade. Had humans been few in number, as during their early history, either of these tragedies could have eliminated the species.

Extinction of species comes in many forms, some abrupt and devastating, as with asteroid impacts and volcanic explosions. Other extinctions slip up on species, as with slow transformation of rain forests into deserts, and glaciation that occurs when continents skirt over polar regions. Whatever the causes, the total number of extinctions is staggering. According to the paleontologist David Raup, it is sheer luck that any species is alive today. There may have been about 40,000,000,000 species formed in the past, of which only about 40,000,000 exist today, most of which are yet to be tallied. Thus the odds of going extinct is about 1000 to 1, a ratio that is close enough to 0 to be within the range of statistical error—a 99.9 percent failure. Man is not the only improbable species—all are improbable.

The Cretaceous extinction that made the movie *Jurassic Park* possible, may have occurred because of a large bolide crashing into Earth, but that as the sole reason is questioned. At the time of the extraterrestrial impacts there was great volcanic activity, probably severe earthquakes, and a lowering of the atmospheric temperature. Moreover, the timing was not razor thin, but may have happened over several millions of years, during which time the environment was deteriorating. The other four major extinction periods are not closely timed with impact craters; rather, they all appear to be associated with cooling temperatures and glaciation as the continents moved over polar regions.

Whatever the cause, there is evidence that major extinctions occur in patterns. In 1984 David Raup and Jack Sepkopski gave statistical support to the notion that extinctions are spaced about 26 million years apart. Perhaps as many as eight extinctions are patterned with this interval. These investigators speculate that the earth plunges through an asteroid belt every 26 million years, showering destructive comets to the earth's surface. Astronomers have not been able to verify this periodicity, and in any case the evidence is not good that most major extinctions involved asteroid impacts. But there may be other clock-like super events that could be the culprits, such as continental drift, volcanic eruptions, major changes in temperature, the drying of inland seas, and variations in food supplies. These potential catastrophes could have a long-term rhythm linked to internal upheavals of the earth, or even astrological events. While mainly speculative at this point, the possibility of rhythms of extinction and speciation may be of great importance in our understanding of forces of chance and necessity.

One astrological physicist estimates that there are 1,500 asteroids and comets, some the size of mountains, crossing and recrossing Earth's orbit—disaster in the making. "Sooner or later, one of them and Earth will arrive at the same place at the same time." In 1989 that intersection nearly occurred, when an asteroid a half-mile in diameter, streaking at 44,000 mph, shot by Earth only twice the distance to the Moon. Had it hit, the explosion would have been equivalent to 20,000 one-megaton hydrogen bombs.

Hundreds of meteors impact the earth each year, and hundreds of others explode like small atomic bombs as they plunge through our atmosphere seventeen to twenty miles above the earth. Most impacts are less than the equivalent of ten to a hundred tons of TNT, but about once in a millennium one hits with the force of about 15,000 tons of TNT, which is equivalent to the atomic force that leveled Hiroshima. Then, perhaps every 10 million years or so a "doomsday rock" hits with a force that causes death on a planetary scale. Clearly, we live at the capriciousness of nature, life hanging on the fringe of chaos.

The possible effects of major rock impacts on earth was recently seen when twenty-one fragments of a comet slammed into Jupiter. The largest fragment exploded with an estimated 6 million megatons of TNT, an explosive power far larger than all of the world's nuclear bombs put together. Had this comet's shard struck the earth it would have enveloped the planet with debris and darkness. Nitrogen would have been thrust into the air, producing acid rain, killing the majority of plants and animals and acidifying the water and soil. The resulting greenhouse effect would elevate temperatures up to fifty degrees Fahrenheit that might last for decades. Sobering thoughts.

Sobering too is the thought that the Earth is in constant flux, bringing with it major changes in ecosystems and temperatures, many of which can be devastating. Now we are faced with another potential disaster—man destroying himself and many other living things. Faced with dark circumstances, we might agree with the Yiddish proverb: "Better an ounce of luck than a pound of gold."

The Middle Way

The Big Three of human evolution—survival, reproduction, extinction—turned on chance or catastrophe: the lucky remains of the chordate Pikaia in the Cambrian Period, the continuous reproduction of small mammals during the reign of the dinosaurs, the cataclysmic extinction of the dinosaurs at the end of the Cretaceous, the roll of the biological dice. Herein lies the riveting drama of our lives.

Nevertheless we can go too far in dwelling on chance and catastrophe. Yes, colossal events swung the pendulum one way or another, early luck catapulted vertebrates forward, and asteroids cleared the path for mammalian diversification. But life is also measured on a thinner and more extended line. There is continuity across taxonomic groups; we show fundamental vertebrate structures and functions; we evolved adaptations to local environments. Despite the ecological upheavals, massive extinctions and sheer immensity of change, there is still the dual threads that bind one species to another, that unite every species to its environment. In these matters small changes etch their imprint into the tapestry of life—mutations and genetic recombinations are pressed into service by demanding environments—the species are molded by natural selection.

The multitudinous forces that give life and take it away—the large and small, the catastrophic and mundane, the quick and lingering—are all contingencies, nevertheless. It's the level of action at issue. An asteroid triggers a century of winter, killing large reptiles, allowing mammals to proliferate—humans evolve. Contingencies of the large kind. A rainforest dries over centuries, giving advantage to individuals who withstand desiccation—desert adaptations evolve. Contingencies of the small kind. Contingencies both, however, as luck wields both the axe and the scalpel, leaving the improbable in its wake. "There's no limit to how complicated things can get, on account of one thing always leading to another," the essayist E.B. White remarked. The life stream is like a mountain stream, abruptly cascading over rocks and falls, twisting unexpectedly, then running serenely for long distances. The contingencies are everywhere, not only in the falls and twists, but in the steady flow as well. Our thinking must adjust to both.

Paleontologists Neils Eldridge and Steven Gould gave us a theoretical model that we can adapt to large and small contingencies. Their view of the fossil record suggests that species show little or no change for millions of years, followed by sudden diversifications and/or abrupt extinctions. The evolution of North American horses, for example, shows this pattern in the fossil record, with early forms remaining unchanged for millions of years, eventually splitting into new types, with some going extinct. Eldridge and Gould describe the lengthy periods of no apparent change as *stasis*, and the rapid changes as *punctuational events*. Stasis results in consistency over long periods; punctuational events result in quick changes that alter the course of evolution. Hence, the theoretical model is referred to as *punctuational equilibrium*.

The model is controversial, resolving to the questions of "how fast is fast," and "are species not changing during periods of stasis?" Most investigators agree that some evolutionary events are faster than others, and deserve some special recognition as punctuational. Mass extinctions and rapid radiation of new species naturally fall into this category— the big punctuational events that redirect life. Other investigators quibble over the definition of stasis. "No change" is difficult to demonstrate in the fossil record where physiology and behavior cannot show themselves. The bones of saber-tooth tigers may look the same over millions of years, yet who knows what behaviors were supported by these bones. In the interval between origin and extinction—between punctuational events—species are likely to show evolutionary reactions to local environments. Regardless of their origin, species must adapt to the demands of predators, food supplies, meteorological conditions and needs to reproduce. These relatively small changes in function and structure may not be visible among the dead bones. Punctuational events are reactions to contingencies of large magnitude, stasis may not be stasis at all, but reactions to contingencies of small magnitude.

Our Shaky Past and Uncertain Future

Our evolution is obviously not as gradual or predictable as Darwin and Wallace once thought. Adaptations often do evolve according to principles of natural selection, but the truly big changes—most speciation and extinction—seem outside the boundaries of gradualistic natural selection. The commonality is that the engine of evolution is always associated with environmental change—small change, little evolution; large change, big evolution. In neither case is there evidence for goal-directed evolution. The products of evolution reflect contingencies not inevitabilities. We, along with all other species, are improbable outcomes, unpredictable from the start and unreplicable at the end. We sense it in ourselves and we see it in the bones of our history.

References

Cited in Chapter 3

Eldredge, N. and Gould, S.J. (1972). "Punctuated Equilibria: An Alternative to Phyletic Gradualism." In T.J.M. Schopf (ed.). *Models in Paleobiology*. San Francisco: Freeman, 82–115.
Gould, S.J. (1994). "Jove's Thunderbolts." *Natural History*, 10, 6–12.
Gould, S.J. (1989). *Wonderful Life*. New York: W.W. Norton and Company.
McNamara, K.J. (ed.). (1990). *Evolutionary Trends*. Tucson: University of Arizona Press.
Raup, D.M. (1991). *Extinction: Bad Genes or Bad Luck?* New York: W.W. Norton and Company.
Stanley, S.M. (1987). *Extinction*. New York: Scientific American Library.
Trfil, J. (1989). "Stop to Consider the Stones that Fall from the Sky. *Smithsonian*, 20, 81–92.
Wilson, E.O. (1992). *The Diversity of Life*. Cambridge: The Belknap Press.

General References

Eldredge, N. (1993). "History, Function, and Evolutionary Biology." In M.K. Hecht et al. (eds.). *Evolutionary Biology*, 27, 33–50.
Dunning, A.J. (1992). *Extremes*. San Diego: Harcourt Brace and Company.
Mayr, E. (1976). *Evolution and the Diversity of Life*. Cambridge, MA: Harvard University Press.

4

Bones and Stones of History

A strange animal, indeed: so very quiet when one turns over the mineral-hardened skull in a gravel bed, or peers into that little dark space which has housed so much cruelty and delight. One feels that something should be there still, some indefinable essence, some jinni to be evoked out of this little space which may contain at the same time the words of Jesus and the blasphemous megatons of modern physics. They are all in there together, inextricably intermixed, and this is how the mixture began.

—Loren Eisley

Oppressive black clouds thundered over the savannah, casting huge webs of blazing white light in every direction. Dru felt the storm grip him, its malevolent force transmigrate into sensations of doom. He had been lost, now, for about eight days, separated from his brothers when the wildebeest plowed headlong into their living noose. The rains had come early, the thunder spooking the animals. Perhaps he alone survived—somehow—with no memory of his escape.

Darkness came all at once. Light erupted irregularly—jaggedly—the Devil's heartbeat. Dru trudged on through the stinging rain, measuring his steps from one lightning burst to the next, a broken branch his only companion. His stomach cramped from fear and hunger—eight days with nothing but tubers, nuts and grasshoppers. At least, he thought, the big cats and heartless hyenas would be in their lairs. His fatigued mind wandered toward home—if only he could find the river. Mar would be waiting.

Suddenly, silhouetted against the furious sky, was a double-humped knoll. Was it familiar? He plodded upward, his strength nearly gone.

His feet were on a trail. Pushed forward by the restless wind, he was at the top. Dru wiped his eyes with his hand and looked with wonderment through the piercing light. The river flashed below him like a silver snake! He filled his lungs with air, felt the power of survival ripple through his stout frame, and flung his arms and stick to the angry sky.

The last lightning bolt of his world stabbed his head, surging through his twisting body. He spiraled down the steep slope toward the river, settling bow-shaped at its very edge. His eyes stared blankly at the water. The rain continued for days, slowly entombing him in layers of sediment from the knoll. Dru, the knoll and the river became one.

A million years later a paleoanthropologist extricated him out of the ground where he had fallen—his mineralized disarticulated bones turned a dirty brown. The scientist carefully lifted Dru's skull in one hand and peered within. The essence of man silently peered back.

Our Ancient Relatives

Agreeing with Christopher Stringer and Clive Gamble, the authors of *In Search of the Neanderthals,* "There is nothing obvious in the pre- historic record. There are no simple answers, just a cornucopia of dis- coveries, observations, ideas and theories. These are the resources with which to investigate our long-term ancestry." The conclusions, how- ever tentative, will tie us more tightly with our evolutionary past.

Looking for the Family Jewels

Searching for our ancestors' remains is like looking for a needle in a haystack. Even worse, the needle may not be there at all. The paleoanthropologists who sift through this haystack, wager a large frac- tion of their lives on finding rare evolutionary relics. In the field where they work, they tolerate the most barren and inhospitable conditions, usu- ally coming up with only dirt, grime and backaches. But the stakes of the game are high, driving them on, for on rare occasions the ghostly past unveils itself in genuine splendor. In these rare moments they touch the spark of life that most of us take for granted but few of us clearly sense. Paleoanthropologists are daring, forcing nature to reveal our beginnings.

Often the fossil remains are simple fragments that tell only part of the story; sometimes they remain utterly silent. Pieces, big and small, must be assembled, dated, and interpreted. The dating of fossil "finds" is particularly tricky, depending on (1) accurate determination of clock-like molecular transformations going on in bone matrices; (2) the dating of sediment layers in which fossils are found; or (3) knowing the age of other species or artifacts found along with the critical fossils. The details of these problems we ignore, but the problems are there. Paleoanthropology is not an exact science; new finds challenge old for a place in the timetable of man; errors are inevitable; personalities get in the way of objective science; and profound and rational disagreements occur regularity. The evolutionary record sometimes is reshaped by a single fossil find, part of a skull, perhaps, or even a single tooth. That record is only now being written, and will be rewritten many times.

It's all worth the effort, for we seek it all, the Rosetta Stone of our creation, the source of our biological river, the roots of our consciousness, our tempest in the teapot. And, with trepidation, we see a pattern emerging.

Who are Our Living and Dead Relatives?

Paradoxically, we understand the diversity of life—species and individual differences—by clumping organisms into discrete categories. Like a tax accountant who distributes numbers into columns and rows of debits and credits, we make sense out of variations by dividing them into columns and rows of similarities and differences. Tax accountants derive conclusions from the summary of numbers; we seek taxonomic truths out of our diversification. We must know something of this classificatory process before we can know where to find the answers to our questions about life.

Carolus Linnaeus provided us a simple and clever biological accounting system for classifying contemporary species; it can help us understand our place within the kingdom of animals. In it, animal or plant *species* are grouped together in *genera*, and similar genera are grouped into *families*. Occasionally *"super-"* or *"sub-"* headings are added to denote extended relationships, such as super families (many families) and sub species (populations that have not quite speciated). Linnaeus intended the classificatory system to reflect the rationality of Divine creation, but in fact it provides us the key to the understanding of our own evolution—a correlational system for ordering organisms in the environment according to genetic relationships.

The classification system applies a *"binomial nomenclature,"* meaning that two Latinized names paired together entirely describe an organism's evolutionary position. The first name specifies the genus and the second, the species. Thus, Tabby Tiger, your cat, is *Felis catus*, genus *Felis*, species *catus*, a very specific designation within the family Felidae. You are *Homo sapiens*, genus *Homo*, species *sapiens*, within the family Hominidae ("hominids"). The Latin designations are italicized. Incidentally, when multiple references are made to the same organism, it is common to spell out the genus the first time, abbreviating it with subsequent references. Thus, in the discussion of *Homo erectus*, for example, it is acceptable to refer to the species as *H. erectus* after the first reference to *Homo erectus*.

Now let's look at the application of this method of clumping species according to similarities and differences.

Capturing the Essence of the Bones

The bones of the past that require a Linnaean classification are hidden within the sediments of time. The invisibility of our bones among the stones may be the reason we have for so long believed in our uniqueness and our divine creation. The gap between us and the next most recent primate, the chimpanzee, looms large when intermediate forms are absent, so large, that, for a pessimist, it is easy to believe in man's singular loneliness, or, for an optimist, his special creation. But fill in those gaps with the bones and stones of the past and the gap diminishes, providing the most compelling evidence of our evolution and our links with the past. Pessimist or optimist, there is only one reasonable conclusion when confronting the family of man: we evolved from apes and other hominid species, and we did it within a "geological second," extending back in time only about 7.5 million years. The Pleistocene epoch, dating from 1.6 million years ago to about 9,000 years ago, was the "epoch of *H. sapiens* evolution," but arguably what went before formed the fundamental imprint of our behavior.

The gaps between us and the "Ancients" are filling. Over the past 130 years we have acquired much information about our ties to other animals, including our ancient ancestors. The species can now be arranged,

FIGURE 4.1

CLASSIFICATION

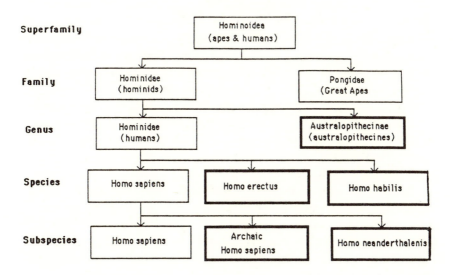

Classification of hominid species. Those in dark outlines are extinct.

as Linnaeus might have done, according to physical, physiological, and genetic similarities and differences, then plotted according to relationships as they are here.

From this plot we can see the broad links between humans and apes, and between humans and our major ancestors. At the genera level, our ancestral species include *Homo* and *Australopithecus*. At the species level, *Homo sapiens* is related to *Homo erectus*, and the well-known *Homo neanderthal* (or simply "Neanderthal"). All of our close relatives within the hominid family are extinct, but their fossils remain. Emerging from these fossils is the story of our evolutionary history.

The Branches of the Family Tree

Charles Darwin believed that "the missing link" between humans and ape would be found in the land of the Great Apes, Africa, as he saw that we share many qualities with the apes: "We must, however, acknowledge, as it seems to me, that man with all his noble qualities, still bears in his bodily frame the indelible stamp of his lowly origin." And the first traces of this identity were indeed found in Africa. But the first hominid fossils were actually dug out of the limestone quarry in the Neander Valley, near Düsseldorf, Germany, in 1856. The bones remained an enigma for some time, as they were initially thought to be a modern European, possibly a Turkish cavalryman. The cranial cap was human in size, but possessed heavy brow ridges incompatible with human skulls. Similarly, the leg and arm bones were heavier than those coming from a human skeleton. In 1864 the Irish anatomist, William King, courageously labeled the find as *Homo neanderthal,* marking its critical distinction from *Homo sapiens.*

Since then about 500 individual Neanderthal finds have been unearthed, all of them in Europe and the Middle East. They are not *monomorphic,* that is, of one form only, but vary in height and bone structure, probably reflecting their range of habitats from the western plains of Europe to the mountain regions of the Ukraine. A product of the ice ages in Europe, they adapted to the rugged life of hunting and surviving in dry and cold terrains.

Rugged it was. About three out of four skeletal remains of individuals over twenty-five years of age show evidence of damage—broken or withered bones, smashed skulls, and healed fractures. No one knows why they were at such risk, perhaps because of encounters with big prey, battles among themselves, or skirmishes with their contemporaries, *H. sapiens.* Neanderthals were tough, had a brain that on the average was larger than our own, hunted with sophisticated stone and wooden weapons, built camp sites and perhaps huts, used fire, buried their dead, and probably had a rudimentary language. They sometimes lived to be fifty-five, but forty was more likely. Only about 8 percent of adults lived past thirty-five years. They tended toward monogamy, and had an extended period of infant development. There is evidence that Neanderthals may have taken care of their old and infirm. An "old man of forty" showed degenerative joint disease in the skull, jaw, spinal column, hip and feet, as well as tooth loss and abscesses, and rib fractures. Obviously this man had suffered for a long time, and probably survived only because of help from others. In many ways they were like us—trim the hair of a Neanderthal man, name him Joe Wyoming, put him in a Dallas

Cowboy uniform, and he would pass as a successful lineman. The English playwright W. S. Gilbert saw the deeper resemblance: "Darwinian Man, though well-behaved, at best is only a monkey shaved."

H. neanderthal and *H. sapiens* overlapped in time of origin and in geography. We did not evolve from Neanderthals, as near as we can tell, but we did have common relatives among *Homo erectus*, who was the first hominid to walk out of Africa. There are new finds at Atapuerca in northern Spain that show that Neanderthal, *H. erectus* and *H. sapiens* share several skull characteristics. The dates of these finds are too old for either Neanderthal or human, but may represent transitional forms. Clearly *H. neanderthal, H. erectus* and *H. sapiens* are of the same genus and may be no more different genetically than the several species of finches that Darwin encountered on the Galapagos Islands.

H. neanderthal and *H. sapiens* have similar birthdates, around 150 to 200 thousand years ago, a coincidence that leaves us with the unsettling thought that we made it but they didn't. The fossil evidence for the evolution of *H. sapiens* indicates that the early ("archaic") human was born in Africa and its later forms spread rapidly around the world. Modern man's coming out of Africa occurred long after *H. erectus* had gone extinct in Europe and Asia. By 40,000 years Before Present (BP) *H. sapiens* were in Europe, Southeast Asia, and Australia. By 25,000 years BP humans had spread to Japan and Siberia. They entered Alaska about 15,000 BP, and the North and South American continents around 12,000 years BP. The first European discoveries of 500 years ago found their likeness everywhere, including the many islands of the Pacific Ocean, where *H. sapiens* had migrated from one to 4,000 years ago.

Everywhere *H. sapiens* went in Europe it replaced *H. neanderthal*, until, finally, about 30,000 years ago, the historical curtain came down on Neanderthals. What happened? The new humans entering the stage from the south and east brought new adaptations and capabilities—symbolism, for example, and a newer tool industry, involving spears, hand axes, blades, horn-tipped weapons, and ivory.

But, it may not have been hand-to-hand combat that brought an end to Neanderthals. There are caves in Israel where the two species may have lived side by side for thousands of years. There may have been trade between the two groups, and even some crossbreeding. More than likely, changes in ambient temperatures and flora and fauna ended their career. The glaciers from the last ice age were at their peak and the world changed. At the Eocene-Oligocene boundary, about 48 to 32 million years ago, there was a monumental transition of animal forms in Europe. The change was so great that it has been dubbed "*La Grande Coupure,*" the great break. As many as 60 percent of European mammals went extinct, replaced by Asian rhinos, primitive deer, antelope, and modern carnivores, such as cats, dogs, and weasels. Apparently what happened was that the severe glaciation of the north caused a drying of the seas and a lowering of temperatures that allowed Asiatic forms of life to swarm into Europe. Perhaps the large mammoths, the favorite prey of Neanderthals, were disappearing. In any case, *H. neanderthal* was unable to compete with the lighter and mentally agile *H. sapiens*; they slipped away with a whimper. The full lesson, however, is not that we were better than *H. neanderthal,* just different, and by happenstance adapted to those times and places. It could have been otherwise, and there would have been no historical rendering of the events. The paleobiologists Stringer and Gamble have it right: "The Neanderthals were not ape-men, nor missing links—they were as human as us, but they represented a different brand of humanity, one with a distinctive blend of primitive and advanced characteristics. There was nothing inevitable about the triumph of the Moderns, and a twist of Pleistocene fate could have left the Neanderthals occupying Europe to this day. The 30,000 years by which we have missed them represent only a few ticks of the Ice Age clock."

Into Africa

The engine of human evolution began in Eastern and Southern Africa. The relatives of both *H. sapiens* and *H. neanderthal* originated there. A great diversity of ape species existed in Africa about 10 million years ago—perhaps twenty, but only four, the chimpanzee, gorilla, orangutan, and gibbon survived to the present. Sometime around 5 to 7.5 million years ago bipedal hominids branched away from the apes and diversified into *Australopithecus* and *Homo* species.

Molecular genetic data suggest that we are related closely to the chimpanzee, sharing about 98.6 percent of our cellular DNA. That obviously means that (1) hominids, coming from the same line as chimpanzees, were all closely related; (2) very few genes are at the basis of our evolution; and (3) evolution happened rapidly.

Missing are two or three million years from the actual division of the pongid (ape line) and hominid lines and our first finds of hominids in the fossil record. Perhaps the gap is due to dating problems, or simply that we have not recovered the critical fossils. In any case, the earliest sign of hominid activity comes from a recent finding by paleoanthropologist Tim White in a region of Ethiopia known as the Middle Awash. The evidence is based primarily on tooth finds, but recently White and his colleague Yohannes Heile Selassie, and Meave Leakey in Kenya, have found several fragments, including a pelvis bone, and leg, ankle, and foot bones. No skull bones have been found. The characteristics of the teeth suggested a new form, tentatively referred to as *Australopithecus ramidus*, or "root." It appears to be midway between the great apes and the early bipedal forms of Australopithecus. *A. ramidus* has been dated at about 4.5 million years old, making it the earliest transition form leading to more advanced hominid forms. It may eventually prove to be a new genus (*Ardipithecus* has been suggested), resting between our ancestors to the great apes and the hominid species. The metaphor of the "missing link" has been misused in the past, but may be a suitable epithet for the Middle Awash species.

Prior to this find Don Johanson's discovery of *A. afarensis* was considered to be the earliest form of hominid, and yet may be, because it is uncertain if *A. ramidus* was more ape-like than hominid-like, or even if it were bipedal. As a clearcut, upright, hominid, *A. afarensis* still reigns supreme. This early hominid was common in Africa from about 3.9 to 3.0 million years ago—nearly a million years of stasis.

The earliest signs of hominid behavior comes with the finding by Mary Leakey in east Africa of fossilized footprints in volcanic ash. The footprints, date to about 3.6 million years before the present, are of three individuals, two larger and one smaller. A bonus of these footprints is that the smaller individual walked closely to the left, following the slightly wavy walk of the larger individual. The tandem walk has led to the speculation that the larger and smaller individuals were holding hands, thus perhaps supporting the idea that the earliest hominids were social and solicitous. On the other hand, perhaps the smaller individual was on a leash. Whatever the case, the prints clearly establish the individuals as Australopithecines, and as bipedal. There were no stone tools evident, although it is believed that they may have used sticks for probing and digging, just like their pongid relatives.

TABLE 4.1
Major Hominid Species*

MYA	Finding or Common Name	Technical Name	Discoverers
4.5-4.3	"Root"	Australopithecus ramidus	1994 Tim White
3.5-3.7	Laetoli Footprints	Australopithecus	1978 Mary Leakey
3.0	Lucy	A. afarensis	1974 Don Johanson
3.0	First Family	A. afarensis	1975 Don Johanson
2.6	Black Skull	A. aethiopicus	1985 Alan Walker
2.5-1.75	ER 1470	Homo habilis	1972 Richard Leakey
2.5-1.75	Handy Man	H. habilis	1964 Jon. Leakey
2.0	Taung Child	A. africanus	1924 Raymond Dart
2.0	Paranthropus	A. robustus	1936 Robert Broom
1.75	Zinj	A. Boisei	1959 Mary Leakey
2.0-1.5	Turkana	Homo erectus	1975 Richard Leakey Alan Walker
0.7	Java Skull	H. erectus	1890's Eugene Dubois
0.3	Atapuerca Skulls	H. sapiens	1993 Juan Arsuaga
230K	Neanderthal	Homo neanderthal	1856 Neander Valley

*MYA = millions of years ago. Dates are approximate for earliest finds. Individuals given credit for the finds often represent a group. Space does not permit a detailed discussion of the discoveries, and the moving experiences associated with each. Notice that the first African hominid was found in 1924 by Raymond Dart, a find that would go unrecognized for a couple of decades. Other discoveries came pouring in, with legendary investigators, such as Louis and Mary Leakey, Eugene Dubois, Phillip Tobias, Robert Broom, Richard Leakey, Donald Johanson. These individuals and their research teams are truly the pioneers of paleoanthropology and have pointed the way for a new generation of scientists who, as a result, know what to look for and where to look. The "Out of Africa" theme supported by these data has been challenged by a less-substantiated theory (e.g. Milford Wolpoff and Alan Thorne) that suggests a multiple-origin for H. sapiens in Asia.

The most important hominid finds in and out of Africa are summarized in table 4.1. They cover only a fraction of the thousand or more discoveries, but they are representative.

The historical map of man is uncertain, comparable to the map of the world about the time that Ferdinand Magellan's ship sailed around the world in the 1520's—the basic outline is there, but most of the details are missing. The rough diagram of human evolution beginning with the split between apes and A. afarensis, is depicted in figure 4.2. It is called a cladogram, a sort of map showing the relative relationships among the hominid species, without regard to the dates of origin or extinction. The skulls of major types of *Australopithecus* and *Homo* are indicated in this same figure, along with their approximate brain sizes. Most investigators would agree on the general map of human evolution, but would be uncertain about the details.

Australopithecines appeared from 3.5 to 4.0 million years ago, with *A. afarensis* and *A. africanus* making their appearance early, followed by larger Australopithecines and *H. habilis*. The smaller Australopithecines are known as gracile, referring to their slender build. The larger relatives are known as hyper-robustus, denoting their heavier build. Picturing these species as bipedal apes with promising futures would not be entirely inaccurate. Both types of Australopithecines were mostly vegetarian, as indicated by their tooth and face structure, with the male being considerably larger than the female. Their faces were flatter than the great ape, appearing more juvenile than their apish relatives. Brain size was around 500 cubic centimeters (cc), not much larger than the gorilla or chimpanzee. There is no evidence of stone tool use or manufacture.

Balanced on the Narrowest of Girders

With these early hominid forms, chance continued to exert a primary force on evolution. Chasing the evolutionary line backward from *Homo sapiens* to *Australopithecus afarensis* or *A. ramidus* gives one the sense of predestination—how could it have been different? But, just as Neanderthals might have emerged victorious over *H. sapiens*, *A. afarensis* might have failed in its quest for survival and reproduction, cutting the historical line to man. Richard Leakey and Roger Lewin, both well-known paleoanthropologists sum it up in this way: "Under appropriate conditions of natural selection, *afarensis* could have become a quadrupedal fruit eater, for instance. It didn't; that's all. What happened to this species is a contingent fact of history, not the march down a predestined evolutionary path. It is futile to speculate what might have happened had this or that circumstance been different, but we need to understand that what happened in history was only one of a range of possibilities. *Homo sapiens* was one of a range of possibilities in the evolution of the hominid group, not an inevitable product of that process."

Chance, yes, but nevertheless a major change in the evolutionary record occurred with *H. habilis*. The brain increased in size to about

FIGURE 4.2

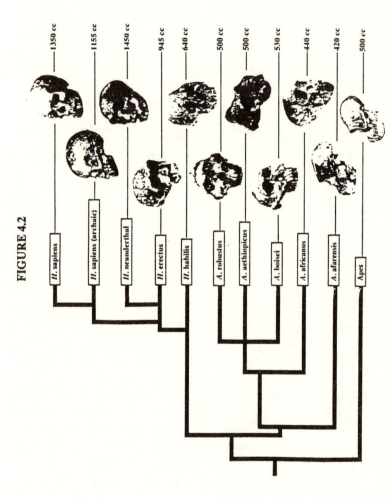

H. sapiens	1350 cc
H. sapiens (archaic)	1155 cc
H. neanderthal	1450 cc
H. erectus	945 cc
H. habilis	640 cc
A. robustus	500 cc
A. aethiopicus	500 cc
A. boisei	530 cc
A. africanus	440 cc
A. afarensis	420 cc
Apes	500 cc

A cladogram illustrating possible relationships between the Great Apes, *Australopithecus* and *Homo* species. Representative skulls are illustrated, along with approximate brain size. The cladogram does not depict exact times of differentiation of species.

750 cc, permitting new adaptations, including simple tool manufacture. Quartz rocks were deliberately shattered in crude patterns and used as choppers, hammers, and scrapers. The type of tools used by this species are known as *Oldowan*, marking the advent of a new lifestyle. Unfortunately, little is certain about *H. habilis*, and its relationship to other hominids is contentious. As new discoveries appear, the portrait of *H. habilis* will become clearer.

Australopithecus overlapped in time with *H. habilis* and to the next major form, *H. erectus*. But *Australopithecus* did not prevail, ending its evolutionary career in Africa about one million years ago. *H. erectus* was a new type of hominid entirely—much more modern in morphology and behavior. One of its key features was a brain of about 1000 cc, a size that overlaps with the distribution of brain size in *H. sapiens*. The anatomist, Arthur Keith, considers this brain size as "beyond the cerebral Rubicon," implying that for the first time a hominid stepped across the neurological river separating simple mentation from complex cognition.

No doubt *H. erectus* was something different in the heart of Africa. This hominid used fire, traveled widely, hunted meat with weapons, and perhaps even had a simple language. The evidence for language is slight but provocative, hinging on the curvature of the base of the skull which is shaped according to the position of the sound-generating larynx. The larynx in *H. erectus* was more like that of *H. sapiens* than the earlier hominids, suggesting an elementary form of language. We will return to this possibility in a later chapter.

H. erectus developed a tool industry of greater sophistication than seen with *H. habilis*, called *Acheulean*. There were more types of stone tools, and they were more specialized for certain tasks. The hallmarks of the Acheulean stone culture were large flakes up to eight inches long, struck from core boulders. The classic pieces were oval, teardrop, or pear-shaped handaxes. Among these were small choppers, picks, points, borers, and a variety of scrapers. The earliest know Acheulean "toolkit" is about 1.5 million years old. While most of the evidence indicates a gradual improvement in toolmaking, extending from *H. habilis* to *H. sapiens*, actually toolmaking was uneven in quality throughout hominid evolution.

Characterizing *H. erectus* with certainty is compounded by more accurate dating of *H. erectus* finds in Java. The discoveries include skulls that are around 1.8 million years old, or about the same age as the earliest discoveries of *H. erectus* in Africa. If *H. erectus* originated in Africa, which is likely, they traveled into Europe and Asia early, and did it apparently without stone tools. At least no Acheulean tools have been found associated with these ancient bones. Future finds may clarify this paradox.

Perhaps most surprising about the toolmaking industry of hominids is that it progressed so slowly and led to so little during the course of nearly 2.5 million years. Only with modern *H. sapiens* do we see giant strides toward the understanding and control of the environment. Like a developing child that requires a long period of maturation before creativity and symbolism flourish, hominid evolution apparently requires extraordinary time before novelty and mental advancements emerge. The question remains: why didn't *H. neanderthal*, with a brain larger than our own, or even *H. erectus*, with a sizable brain and substantial social complexity, show greater tool sophistication and symbolism? For that matter, why hasn't the dolphin, with all of its neurological sophistication, developed a comparably sophisticated behavioral system? These questions will lead us to an analysis of the evolution of cognition and consciousness.

Standing Tall

As expected, major human characteristics are represented or presaged by the qualities of our ancestors: the poker game of life that we play out today depends on the cards that were dealt millions of years ago. We share with mammals a vertebral column, hair, warm bloodedness, internal gestation, and milk production. We share one other trait with hominids, that of upright bipedal locomotion. We walk with legs linked in a straight line with our pelvis, and with our head balanced centrally on the spinal column. Bipedal locomotion is the signature of hominid evolution; it begins with the earliest Australopithecines and extends through the *Homo* lineages to *H. sapiens* of today.

It is strange that we still do not understand why the bipedal gait emerged or was retained over millions of years of evolution. This has not stopped speculation, nor will it now. Several possibilities are listed below, not necessarily in the order of possible importance.

- Results from a genetic and developmental "quirk," and continues because of associated advantages.
- Facilitates the transport of food and other items.

- Allows parents to carry infants, and the female to lactate while on the move.
- Permits the carrying of tools and weapons.
- Extends the reach from the ground to higher objects (in trees).
- Frees the hands for toolmaking.
- Increases the efficiency of traveling long distances.
- Increases body cooling during running.
- Exposes more body surface to breezes for evaporative cooling.
- Reduces the percent of body surface exposed to the sun.
- Helps to distance the body from ground micro- and macroorganisms.
- Increases height and hence visibility across the savannah.
- Enhances the visibility of hand signals over distances.
- Extends auditory signals over greater distances.
- Allows rapid standing and aggressive bluffs toward predators and competitors.
- Exposes body parts (breasts, hips, face) as sexual signals.

A couple of things are clear. First, bipedal stance and locomotion appeared early in our divergence from pongids, and was retained and refined thereafter. Second, the onset of bipedalism is not associated with any tools, hence it does not appear that the change from quadruped (four-footed) locomotion had anything to do with toolmaking. Third, bipedalism occurred two million years before a significant increase in brain size, hence bipedalism was not stimulated by neurological complexity. Fourth, the appearance of bipedalism is not associated with the use of weapons or the hunting for meat. The Australopithecines were primarily vegetarians and probably did not forage widely—early hominids were "reach, grab, and gnaw" dinners. Thus, most of the "cultural" advances of hominids *made use of* bipedal locomotion—toolmaking, weapon use, meat hunting, distant foraging, and complex communication—but none of these things *caused* it. What did, then?

The origin of bipedalism may hinge on a "quirk" in development and not on natural selection for upright locomotion. The difference between a "quirk" in development and natural selection is analogous to the difference between a bridge created by a tree falling across a crevice and a bridge structured over time to serve a particular need. The first bridge occurs because of a confluence of unforeseen events; the second bridge depends on environmental pressures for an adaptive outcome.

Surprisingly, the chimpanzee shows a critical precursor to bipedalism. The *adult* chimp walks in a bipedal hunch, using its knuckles for support. However, the *infant* chimp shows a hip and leg articulation that is bipedal in form. In other words, the infant chimp begins its life with bipedal characteristics, but *loses these traits during the process of development.* The infant bipedal traits differentiate into the adult form of knuckle walking. Hominids, diverging from the pongid line, retain some juvenile traits of pongids. One of these characteristics is bipedal locomotion. Hominids retain juvenile traits, even though they become adults and reproduce.

Evolving Toward Flat Face

More generally, the retention of juvenile traits among reproducing adults is called *neoteny,* and is known to occur among primates. Neoteny becomes more apparent as early primates evolved into later forms. New World monkeys are, on the average, more neotenized than their ancestors, the prosimians. Old World monkeys are more neotenized than their predecessors, the New World monkeys; the more recent Great Apes are more neotenized than Old World monkeys; and humans are more neotenized than Great Apes. It's as if a higher degree of neoteny emerged with every new primate group.

Thus, neoteny is associated with the sudden appearance of bipedal gate among Australopithecines—a simple retention of juvenile pongid traits. Its continuation in subsequent species may be because of the several benefits associated with bipedal locomotion—*if it works, evolution won't fix it.*

Perhaps we are approaching a general principle that will help us account for the evolution of other juvenile traits among recent hominid species. Consider this: the chronology of evolved changes from early to late forms of hominids include:

- flat face and reduced tooth size,
- upright stance and walking,
- refined bone structure,
- spherical ("vaulted") cranium,
- reduced facial and jaw muscles,
- reduced body hair,
- increased brain size (absolute and relative to body size).

These traits are all common to infant, but not adult chimpanzees, suggesting that the majority of critical traits found in hominids are simply developmental hangovers from earlier juvenile primates.

In the broad evolutionary trend for neotenous traits noted above, it seems that Australopithecines are more neotenized than the earlier evolved Great Apes; the later forms, *H. habilis* and *H. erectus*, are more neotenized than Australopithecines, and the latest form, *H. sapiens*, shows even greater neoteny. Neanderthals may be an exception to this trend, as they seem to have both neotenous characteristics, such as increased brain size, yet share differentiated traits with earlier species, as with heavy brow ridges and heavy bone structure. The full story on Neanderthals is yet to be told.

In any case, none of the several "juvenile" traits in humans, like those listed above, requires the assumption of long periods of gradualistic natural selection. Small genetic/developmental events can account for many structural and behavioral characteristics, forcing major reorganizations of morphology, physiology, and behavior— changes leading to neoteny. The proposal is not unreasonable, considering the very short history and dynamic changes that occurred in just 7.5 million years. It is improbable that natural selection, no matter how intense, could have resulted in extensive and multiple changes that we see in human history. A developmental "quirk," on the other hand, can happen "in a minute."

If neoteny offers an explanation for human evolution, we must refocus our thinking. It may not be true that each and every hominid change was in response to an environmental requirement. Nor would it be accurate to view evolutionary transitions between species as slow and cumulative. What is perhaps likely is that neotenous traits are favored in dealing with unpredictable contingencies, creating advantages under a variety of environments. Relatively large brain size, in particular, enhances survival under a wide range of environments. This generalized advantage would not, of course, preclude the evolution of other adaptations, according to the principles established by Darwin and Wallace. Natural selection could account for the refinement of many adaptive traits.

Tracing Our History Through the DNA

Fossils are the bones of genetic survival, the endpoint of differential selection, the conduits of genes to future generations, and finally extinction. Though life is quirky, studded with unpredictable punctuational events, fossils retain the imprint of genetic history—one reflects the other.

New techniques of genetic analysis promise precise measurements of evolutionary change. From these analyses two sorts of "evolutionary clocks" have been devised. The first is a "molecular clock" that depends on the rate of genetic mutations over time. The molecular clock depends on the fact that random mutations within DNA molecules occur on the average at a constant rate. The longer populations or species are separated from each other, the greater the probability that the groups will acquire distinctive mutations. Older populations will also acquire more mutations than newer populations. Theoretically, it is possible to assemble populations and species in terms of evolutionary distance by noting the divergence in the number of random mutations—the fewer mutations that differentiate groups, the closer they are in evolutionary time. Conversely, the more frequent the differences in mutations, the longer the separation between groups. When the rates of mutation are known, the time-course of evolutionary change can be estimated.

The second kind of evolutionary clock is one based on the degree to which populations are genetically similar, independent of genetic mutations. We refer to this evolutionary clock as a "gene flow clock," because it depends on the degree to which genes move from population to population. The gene flow clock is not as precise in its determination of absolute time, as the molecular clock is, but it can indicate the genetic relatedness among groups.

We can illustrate how gene flow works in human populations by noting a hypothetical example of blood type differences between three populations. Blood types are excellent markers of gene frequency differences among populations because they are directly determined by genes. Populations can thus be assembled according to their genetic relatedness. For three populations that differ in major blood types in the following manner, we can hypothesize that populations 1 and 3 are more closely related to each other than they are to population 2, because 1 and 3 share more similar frequencies of blood types. By the same reasoning, populations 2 and 3 are more similar than populations 1 and 2. From this it appears that the relative similarity among groups is 1, 3, and 2, in that order. Of course, estimates of population similarity are strengthened by analyzing large numbers of gene traits, not merely a few blood types.

Percentage of Different Blood Types

Population	AA	AB	O
1	50	25	0
2	25	13	46
3	35	26	10

The gene flow clock can give estimates of evolutionary change over time if combined with a molecular clock where the rate of mutations are known, or if gene frequency variations are correlated with fossil and arecheological evidence where points in history have already been established. It is becoming abundantly clear that there is a convergence of fossil finds, historical evidence, and genetic data that will allow more precise measurements of evolutionary time.

It is feasible that behavioral changes that correspond to genetic changes can be pinpointed in time and traced through the distribution of populations around the world. Among those traits are bipedal locomotion, toolmaking, hunting, art, language, agriculture, domestication of animals, warfare, and the building of city states. We already have rough estimates of the origin and spread of these traits, but our estimates will be refined by the convergence of techniques now at our disposal.

The Clocks are Ticking

We differ in our DNA material from our closest ape relative the chimpanzee by only 1.6 percent, less than the differences shown by closely related populations of birds. The figures below show the approximate genetic differences among several recently evolved primates.

Percent Genetic Difference Between Monkeys, Apes, and Humans

Human vs Chimp	1.6
Human vs Gorilla	1.8
Chimp vs Gorilla	1.8
Old World Monkeys vs	
Great Apes	7.2

The implications for the evolution of humans are:

1. Of all of the great apes, we are closest in genetic relatedness to the chimpanzee.

2. Evolutionary variations among the great apes are founded on few gene changes.

3. All of the morphological and functional variations from *A. ramidus* to *H. sapiens* rest on a small range of variations in DNA.

DNA changes occur because of recurring mutations in the nucleotide bases that comprise the hereditary molecules. Assuming that the base changes are random across the genotype, and occur at a constant rate, it is possible to use DNA as a digital molecular clock. For instance, in a particular form of DNA responsible for generating energy in the cell, called mitochondrial DNA, the mutation rate is close to 12 percent per million years. This molecular dating approaches the known age of the earliest known modern human fossils in Africa and the Middle East.

Other DNA dating techniques converge on a similar date of origin, and even suggest how the human species has diversified and spread around the world. Luigi Luca Cavalli-Sforza and his colleagues at Stanford University have outlined the paths and temporal history of human evolution. The genetic markers they use include genes that code for well-known blood groups A, B, O, and the rhesus (Rh) blood factor, and a variety of other protein variants known to be regulated by specific genes. The researchers now have variations of more than 100 genetic markers from over 3,000 samples taken from 1800 aboriginal populations around the world.

One must be careful about accepting the assumption that the molecular clock runs at a constant speed and is identical across species groups. Based on early work by the molecular geneticist Morris Goodman it now appears that spontaneous DNA changes have decreased from earlier mammals to *H. sapiens*. For example, the nucleotide base changes that makeup DNA have slowed from 4.8 per billion years in the rat to 2.1 changes in New World monkeys, to 1.8 changes in Old World monkeys, to only 1.2 changes in humans. What this means is uncertain, although it seems clear that the more generations per unit time, the higher the number of mutations. It may also be the case that as animals evolved larger brains that the pressures for new mutations to cope with environmental change decreased. In other words, genetic evolution may be slowing.

The details of the measurements and the statistical estimates of distances and time are complicated. Nevertheless, the principal conclusion remains: modern humans, referring to *H. erectus*, originated in Africa at least a million years ago and spread to the rest of the Old and New Worlds.

How do Populations Come to Differ in Gene Frequency

Populations and ethnic groups often differ in the frequency of genes because of random events (genetic drift). When small groups of people move into a new area they carry with them a chance number of possible genes. For example, if a population has an equal representation of A, B, O blood types, but a few individuals who happen to be mostly type O move to a new region, the developing population will become characterized as type O. It's very much like having a big bag of marbles with an equal number of green, white, and red marbles. If you drew out only three it is unlikely that all three colors would be represented, $(1/3)^3$. They could be all red, or white, or green. So it is with genes carried by people—small samples are rarely representative of larger populations. The result is that small migrating populations establish new populations with unusual genetic combinations. Biologist Ernst Mayr refers to this outcome as the *founder effect*.

Gene frequency can also vary because of differential survival of genes. Conceivably, blood type O may survive better in harsh climates; type A may correlate with disease resistance in equatorial regions; and type B may prevail because of correlations with the presence of particular predators. Whatever the selection pressure, over time populations diverge in blood types. Hypothetically, many different gene types would be affected in similar ways, thus clearly differentiating populations.

The point is that either because of small sampling events when groups migrate and establish new populations, that is, random drift, or because of long-term adaptations to different environments, populations will diverge in gene frequency. Populations that have only recently separated will share more genes in common than populations that have been apart for long periods. When numerous genes are studied in many populations one can determine how the populations differ and in what sequence the populations appeared. Coupled with other evidence on hominid evolution—fossils, archeological finds, and geographical data—the speed of genetic and functional changes can be calculated.

What Can the Gene Flow Clock Tell Us?

The genetic data of Cavali-Sforza's group identify seven major ethnic groups that share more genes within groups than they do between groups. They are African, Caucasian, Northeast Asian, Amerindian, Southeastern Asian in the Pacific Islands, in Australia, and in New Guinea. If the genetic difference between Africans is arbitrarily set at 1.0, Australians and Asians differ by 0.62, and Europeans and Asians differ by 0.42. In other words, Europeans and Asians are more closely related to Africans than are Australians. These relative differences correspond with readings from the fossil record, where it is known that Africans and Asians have been separated by 100,000 years, Asians and Australians by 50,000 years, and Asians and Europeans by 40,000 years.

In 1988 Cavalli-Sforza extended his gene frequency analyses to include the spread of languages around the world. Languages, like species, evolve over time, thus in principle making it possible to reconstruct a linguistic phylogeny that correlates with the spread of genes. Until recently about 5,000 languages existed. If modern humans evolved out of Africa, all of these languages must be descendents of a single, original language, that some call the Mother Tongue.

There are some seventeen language superfamilies or phyla that are derived from the original Mother Tongue. Examples are Indo-European, Indo-Pacific, Altacic, and Amerindian. When these language phyla are compared to the frequency of marker genes (those genes that differentiate populations), there is a very close correlation. To a high degree the language phyla correlate with ethnic variations established on the basis of gene frequency differences. The picture is one of cohesion between transitions among languages, ethnic variations, and gene frequencies. The relations are seen in figure 4.3.

The coincidence between independent sources of data are astonishing, verifying the African origin of *H. Sapiens*, and demonstrating that divergent cultural traits ebb and flow along with variations in genes. The cultural and genetic traits are not causally related—one does not cause the other—but the linkage provides evidence that the temporal course of behavioral change has a deep-rooted relation to genetic changes. One predicts the other, as both indicate rates of change across populations and ethnic groups.

FIGURE 4.3

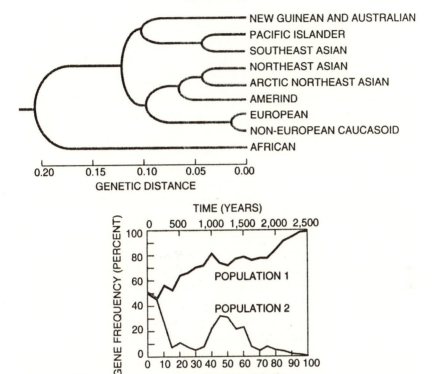

Change over time produces genetic differentiation, such as that reflected in this ethnic family tree *(left)*. Drift, the mechanism of change, can be modeled by computer *(right)*. When two halves of a population are first separated, they carry a gene at equal frequencies, but time and chance can eventually push them in opposite directions.
Source: Cavalli-Sforza, 1991

The Boundless Past

There is a bothersome truth to our fossil record—our ancestors appeared in a geological flash, lasting no longer than a million years, quickly dropping into oblivion. No hominid species has outlasted our great age ancestors; our ape ancestors were bounding through the rainforest millions of years before the hominids, and their representatives are still here. We are the last surviving hominid: the first hominid lasted perhaps a million years, with more recent forms lasting no longer, and in most cases less than several hundreds of thousands of years.

For whatever reasons hominids lacked stability, perhaps correlated with increased complexity, perhaps with increased vulnerability in capricious environments. Edgar Allen Poe had this in mind when he said: "Men have called me mad; but the question is not yet settled, whether madness is or is not the loftiest intelligence—whether much that is glorious—whether all that is profound—does not spring from disease of thought—from *moods* of mind exalted at the expense of the general intellect." The signs are distinctively ominous—we came a long way quickly and probably will vanish just as fast. High intelligence may yet be our nemesis.

Molecular geneticists have added to our philosophical concerns. Francis Crick, the co-founder of the double-helix structure of DNA, with James Watson, was at least partially correct when he said of their insight: "We have discovered the secrets of life!" We not only carry much of the morphology of the great apes, but also most of their genes. The spooky conclusion is that we share with other primates a cognitive style, a method of logic, a temperament of character, an inner-directed focus of attention. We see the world through their eyes as well as our own. We are enriched by the associations with our ape relatives, as well as constrained. No matter what kinds of culture we construct, they will always be primate cultures. The signature of our destiny is found in the bones and genes of our past, not in our technology or in our hope to populate outer space.

References

Cited in Chapter 4

Arsuaga, J-L., Martínez, I., Gracia, A., Carretero, J-M., and Carbonell, E. (1993). "Three New Human Skulls from the Sima de los Huesos Middle Pleistocene Site in Sierra de Atapuerca, Spain." *Nature*, 362, 534–37.

Cavalli-Sforza, L. (1991). "Genes, Peoples and Languages." *Scientific American*, November, 104–10.

Falk, D. (1993). "A Good Brain is Hard to Cool." *Natural History*, August, 65–67.

Gould, S.J. (1994). "Lucy on the Earth in Stasis." *Natural History*, September, 12–20.

Johanson, D. and Johanson, L. (1994). *Ancestors: In Search of Human Origins*. New York: Villard Books.

Johanson, D. and Shreeve, J. (1989). *Lucy's Child: The Discovery of a Human Ancestor*. New York: William Morrow and Company, Inc.

Lewin, R. (1993). *The Origin of Modern Humans.* New York: Scientific American Library.

Leakey, R. and Lewin, R. (1992). *Origins: Reconsidered.* New York: Doubleday.

McHenry, H.M. (1994). "Tempo and Mode in Human Evolution." *Proceedings of the National Academy of Science,* 91, 6780-6786.

Stringer, C. and Gamble, C. (1993). *In Search of the Neanderthals.* New York: Thames and Hudson, Ltd.

Wood, B. (1994). "The Oldest Hominid Yet." *Nature,* 371, 280-81.

General References

Shapiro, R. (1991). *The Human Blueprint.* New York: St. Martin's Press.

5

Bone Talk

Some examples will make it obvious that there are inescapable biological consequences of size and design. For example, swimming with the aid of cilia or flagella is possible only for very small organisms, and fishes use a different propulsive mechanism. A paramecium covered with cilia swims many times its body length in a second, but a giant shark covered with cilia would get nowhere. The laws of fluid dynamics can, in a more formal way, explain why microorganisms and fish, from this point of view, seem to live in different worlds.

—Knut Schmidt-Nielsen

Bones are so much a part of our lives that we treat them with no more respect than we do sticks and stones. Bones are everywhere—bones on our dinner plates, bones in fields, bones for Bozo, bones in movies, museums, and doctors' offices. We feel the bones in Tabby Tiger, and we sense our own skeleton. Bones seem as insignificant as metal girders, and utterly dead. We would sleep undisturbed in a warehouse full of them. But they are alive, or were, and therein lies a tale.

Can Bones Talk? The Energetic Constraints of Evolution

Do the bones of our ancestors have a story to tell? Fortunately, we can learn something about the physiology and behavior of our ancestors simply by knowing their body and brain size, measures readily available from the fossil record. The reason: we share a mammalian body plan with early hominids. Shared body plans limit the expression of physiology and behavior—know one, know the other.

We make extrapolations to earlier mammals in much the same way that we might attempt to understand the functioning of a car that we have never seen before, one, perhaps, that had been lost, but only recently discovered. It's possible because our current cars share a similar body plan with the antique version—our current cars evolved from the past, allowing us to apply our knowledge about structures and functions in present cars to the antique car. To better understand the antique car we can compare such things as engine monitoring dials, piston displacement, gear ratios, engine mounting, and carburetor efficiency, giving us insights into the nature of the antique. Knowing how those things work in today's vehicles, we can surmise how the antique car worked. We may never be absolutely certain about the performance characteristics of the antique car, but major processes are knowable—physical and functional relations do not change. In any case, making estimates based on similarities of structures and functions provides a more accurate picture of past functioning than had we assumed that every car is absolutely unique.

Energizing Our Ancestors

The present is shaped by the limitations of the past. Limitations imposed by our genetic history are referred to as *phylogenetic constraints*—"phylogenetic," referring to evolution, and "constraint," referring to the range within which functions can vary. Thus, all vertebrates share structures and functions in common, simply because the basic body plan has been used over and over. The "vertebrate plan" means that there are limited variations that can occur and still be viable—the nature of variation is constrained. The similarities among present-day and historic species are constrained, giving us the power to estimate the functions of one species by knowing another. For example, energetic functions that are common to current mammals, including *Homo sapiens*, were also common to our earlier relatives. Our behaviors, supported by energetic processes, are similar to our common ancestors. We can therefore generalize the present back to our past—history lessons taught in reverse. The beauty of this approach is that we can estimate many energetic mechanisms, and associated behaviors, by comparing what we know about existing species with skeletons of the past.

Let's look at both the energetics and behavior of existing and long-dead species, using methods of measuring energy that allow us to generalize across species. The energetic functioning of organisms is the key to figuring out the daily habits of our kind. Here, too, major processes are knowable.

Hominid species have increased in size during the past 4 million years, showing increases in brain size and changes in metabolism. *Metabolism* is shorthand for expressing the rate that energy is converted to physiological and physical activity. It is often measured indirectly by monitoring the rate of oxygen consumption, a direct reflection of cellular metabolic activities. It can also be expressed as the number of calories burned per unit time, such as calories burned per twenty-four hours. Metabolic processes change according to body size: the number of calories burned while at rest, called total resting metabolism, scales among mammals to 3/4 the power of body weight. That is, for every unit increase across species in body weight, there is a 3/4 increase in resting metabolism. Brain size scales in the same way, such that an increase of one unit of body weight is associated with a 3/4 unit increase in brain weight. Thus, it is apparent that as animals become larger, their *absolute* brain size and *total* metabolic rate increase, but their *relative* brain size and *relative* metabolic rate decrease. Knowing these relations among living species allows us to estimate the metabolic demands and capabilities of extinct hominid species— the "3/4 power law" applied to our ancestors.

Behavior scales right along with body and brain size and metabolic rates. For example, enlarging body size among mammalian species is associated with larger foraging areas, and a greater tendency to exploit new environments—large animals consume relatively less energy and are therefore capable of long-distance foraging. These behavioral features are directly related to changes in metabolic demands. Also, behaviors become less stereotyped in larger species as the brain enlarges, with social systems increasing in corresponding complexity. Parental care also becomes exaggerated, perhaps because of increased neural capabilities, but also because of the increased energy demands required to support long periods of development. Remember, the relation we see among extant mammals are no doubt similar to those of early hominids, allowing us to peer inside our ancestors' metabolic and behavioral functions. Essentially, all we have to know is body size and, as we will see, cranial capacity.

There is a revealing relation between brain size and *resting brain metabolism*, the proportion of total metabolism used by the brain at rest. It's a bit more complicated than the 3/4 rule of thumb applied to brain size and body size, but indicates that for every increase in brain size, there is a disproportionate increase in brain metabolism—*bigger brain, much higher metabolism.* Among anthropoid primates (ape-like primates) the brain constitutes about 1.5 percent of body weight and consumes about 8.9 percent of the total resting metabolism. The human brain represents about 2.5 percent of body weight and consumes an amazing 22 percent of the total resting metabolism—a 60 percent increase in relative brain size in humans, resulting in more than a doubling of energy use.

In summary, here is what we know about the relations between structures and functions of present and past species of mammals—the constraining envelope within which physiology and behavior vary. Arranging species in increasing body size, we find that the brain and total resting metabolism increase at a 3/4 power of body size. Overall metabolism decreases relative to body size. And as body size increases, so do brain size and brain metabolism, with brain metabolism increasing at a faster rate than brain size. Apparently the high resting metabolism of brain tissue is a necessary consequence of increasing body size, signaling that larger and more recent hominid species have an especially high resting brain metabolism. In other words, the brain becomes more energetically demanding than the body. With a stepped-up brain metabolism energetic demands increase, but, at the same time, the brain is capable of new and more complex functions. The critical evolutionary shift among recent hominid species was the shunting of relatively more metabolic energy to neural processes.

Walking Among the Hominids

Many structures and functions correlate among hominid species, allowing us to deduce life-history events in our ancestors. The reproductive milestones for humans, *H. erectus* and Australopithecines are estimated below.

These are rough estimates based on body size variations and *H. sapiens* longevity; nevertheless, they are informative. The earliest hominids moved through life with a swiftness not seen in later biological forms, driven on by time's short arrow. They lived only about forty years, reached sexual maturity around ten years of age, and compressed their reproduction into shorter intervals. *H. erectus* spread these events out

TABLE 5.1
Life-History Traits for Hominids
(Approximations expressed in years)

Life Variable	Homo sapiens	Homo erectus	Australopithecus
Life span	66	52	40
Length of gestation	9 (mo)	5.7 (mo)	4.4 (mo)
Puberty	14	10.4	8.0
Sexual maturity	17	13.5	10.4
Birth interval	5	3.9	3.0

over a lifetime of about fifty-two years, delaying maturation and reproduction. We are an extension of these trends.

As reproductive features stretched like a rubber band across hominid species, other things changed as well. Brain size increased nearly threefold in about 100,000 generations, and behaviors became more complex. These shifts in life processes introduced more opportunities for learning and social organization, but they also imposed severe energetic costs and psychological pressures to cope with delayed reproduction.

The following table shows the crucial relations among hominid species for body weight, brain size, total resting metabolic rate of the body (RMR), and brain resting metabolism (RM). Here we can see the basis for behavioral and mental qualities that distinguish our ancestors and anticipate ourselves.

Notice from table 5.2 that brain size takes a small jump with *H. habilis*, and then bounds upward with *H. erectus* and early *H. sapiens*. Brain metabolism increases conspicuously with *H. erectus*—a 100 percent increase within a span of 0.5 MY. Necessarily, the daily caloric intake increases, reaching about 1075 kcal/day for Australopithecines, expanding by 400 kcal/day for *H. erectus* and early *H. sapiens. Homo erectus* was definitely on the move about a million years ago. The problems were to maturate an exquisite brain, feed it, and conserve energy when possible.

Recent hominids evolved a protracted period of infant development—the high levels of energy required for complete human development were spread over a long period. The use of energy by the human brain is extremely high at birth, approaching 87 percent of the total resting metabolism. It then drops to about 44 percent of the total rest-

TABLE 5.2
Approximate Body Weight, Brain Size and Metabolic
Requirements of Common Hominid Species
(Modified from Leonard & Robertson, 1992)

Species	Time Span MY	Body Wt. (kg)	Brain Size (cm³)	Total RMR	Brain RM	RM/RMR (~%)
A. afarensis	3.0-4.0	37.1	404	1149	95	9.0
A. africanus	2.0-3.0	35.3	441	1106	103	10.1
A. robustus/boisei	1.5-2.5	44.4	516	1322	118	9.8
H. habilis	1.6-2.0	48.0	640	1404	142	11.1
H. erectus	0.5-2.0	53.0	945	1517	200	14.6
H. sapiens (early)	0.2-0.5	57.0	1155	1605	238	16.4

ing rate at year five, and eventually reaches the adult level of metabolism of 22 percent. Since the price for growth is too high to pay all at once, development is prolonged and the energetic payments are spread evenly over a number of years. The process is similar to buying an expensive house without much cash up front, using a thirty-year mortgage that can be paid in small monthly amounts. The extended development of large hominid species could be the reason for the evolution of long periods of parental care of infants. At the same time, the extended period of growth allows for the maturation of an incredible brain and a long period of socialization.

Hominid evolution illustrates almost unbelievable changes within the short span of 3 MY. Many things happened at the joints of evolutionary change, the most important of which involved changes in size, metabolism, and reproduction. Of course we know few of the particulars, but general processes followed the "vertebrate plan." Within the short time of 1.5 million years a souped-up hominid arose in East and South Africa—large, more complex, and preset for extraordinary mental feats. Shakespeare might have been referring to H. erectus when he proclaimed, "There is a tide in the affairs of men, which, taken at the flood, leads on to fortune; Omitted, all the voyage of their life is bound in shallows and in miseries." Homo erectus weighed his fortunes and prepared to move out of Africa, initiating the tide that engulfed the world. But he first needed the food to fortify his extraordinary voyage.

Calories: The Big Contingencies

Food is energy—our lives and history depend on it. Structural and functional differences among the *Australopithecus* and *Homo* species rest on the fine edge of diet. High quality food items—foods that provide many calories, such as fruits, insects, seeds, and meats—are widely spread and difficult to acquire. Consequently, species that forage over wider areas generally have better diets. Or to flip the coin over: larger species with extended and more energetically demanding brains, require higher quality foods, traveling greater distances to get them. Early Australopithecines required about 1075 kcal/day for its activities, whereas *A. robustus* and *H. habilis* averaged 1260 and 1340 kcal/day, respectively. *H. erectus* and early *H. sapiens* averaged over 1450 kcal/day, an increase of about 35 percent in less than a million years. It appears that *H. habilis*, *H. erectus*, and early *H. sapiens* were the species adapted to high energy requirements and extended foraging. The biggest jump in energy requirements occurred with *H. erectus*.

The early Australopithecines lived in wooded and forested habitats. They adapted to low quality plants for their calories and did not forage widely. Their teeth are clearly structured to deal with vegetable and leafy foods, although they may have occasionally eaten meat. Between 2.5 and 1.5 MY ago there was a drying trend in Eastern and Southern Africa, associated with a loss of wooded and forested areas. *A. afarensis* and *A. africanus* may have lost the contingency game at this point, unable to change their diets or forage more extensively. They were replaced by larger Australopithecines, such as *A. aethiopicus*, *A. robustus* and *A. boisei*, who were able to extract greater numbers of calories from plants, using the crushing strength of larger posterior teeth. They foraged more intensely in restricted areas. Eventually this too was a dead end—food supplies diminished, their feeding strategies overspecialized.

Species of the genus *Homo* made the transition to changing environments, expanding their home ranges and supplementing their diets with high caloric foods. *H. erectus* may have begun hunting meat to increase the number of calories necessary to support heightened activity and energetically expensive brains. The importance of meat for the evolution of *H. sapiens* cannot be underestimated. Meat provides about 150 kcal of metabolizable energy for each 100 g consumed, compared to approximately 75 kcal from 100 g of fruit and 15 kcal from 100 g of leaves.

meat, rather than plants, is important for evolutionary change, as meat supplies proportionally more metabolizable energy than plants. Under natural conditions not enough calories can be obtained from plants to support high levels of activity and a hungry brain.

Current-day human foragers fit the pattern begun by *H. erectus*. The !Kung and Ache populations of Africa forage widely (the males about 15 to 20 km/day; the females about 9 km/day), and derive from 33 to 56 percent of their energy from meat. More broadly, among anthropoid species there is a strong correlation between total energy intake and the range of foraging. Male *H. erectus* foraged about 12–15 km/day, less than present day human foragers, but more than the *Australopithecus* species and much more than any current anthropoid.

Contingencies Revisited

Deteriorating environments changed the evolutionary landscape, forcing species to compensate for diminishing nutrients. Aridity and falling temperatures reduced the lush plant life and rain forests of Eastern and Southern Africa, expanding the savannah, putting premiums on the abilities to extract more nutrients from existing plants and find additional sources of energy. Energy became more patchy and difficult to acquire. *A. afarensis*, and *A. africanus* failed to adjust, replaced by two distinct lines, (1) *A. aethiopicus/robustus/boisei* that for a time was able to increase the extraction of nutrients from plants, and (2) the genus *Homo* that explored wider areas and quickly evolved strategies for maximizing caloric intake. *H. erectus* was at the pivot of change, increasing its brain capacity, adjusting its metabolic requirements upward, and moving into new areas with high sources of calories.

Behaviors were locked into these same dietary requirements. The increased brain capacity experienced by *H. erectus* was both a burden and a blessing. Social interactions involving hunting and foraging ratcheted to the forefront. Cooperation was now needed more than ever before—learning of social relations and obligations took on greater salience. New areas were exploited and new sources of calories found. The down side was that everything was more expensive. Development of a large brain required increased energy; maturation was therefore extended in time to cut daily costs. This meant a longer period of infant dependency, greater parental investments, and extended cooperation between males and females. There was also a neverending search for more calories, focusing behaviors around intestinal demands. As long as this was true, brain activities centered on survival. Later, as humans learned to domesticate animals and cultivate and store foods, the brain, exquisitely fashioned to deal with life's contingencies, turned toward understanding ourselves and our relations with the environment—a burden or a blessing?

One can only register surprise at the rapid evolutionary changes. Every event was a contingency, dependent upon momentary circumstances and earlier changes—droughts that forced species to rely heavily on existing foods or new foods in patchier areas, increased brain size that triggered new quests and demanded new inflows of energy, huge energetic costs that protracted development and led to long periods of parental quid pro quo, and new management skills that facilitated complex social interactions. Each of these changes had a low probability of occurring, each a product of previous adaptations—none predictable in advance. The result: man, the improbable species, sporting dazzling capabilities, burdened with an existential headache.

The Evolution of Anti-Risk Behaviors

Risk is like a disease—dangerous, edged in fear and tinted with hidden desire. Risk is the soulmate of contingency, a path toward glory, a step into the abyss. The amazing fact about man's evolution is his success in spite of large and small catastrophes. We could have exploded with a bang—shattered with a quake, been blanketed with volcanic fire and rock, or raked by a burning comet. Luck held. More likely it was our fate to disappear in a whimper—frozen tight into a glacier, sucked dry by parasites, dismembered by a lion, starved into anorexia, broken from work, crazed by uncertainty.

> This is the way the world ends
> This is the way the world ends
> This is the way the world ends
> Not with a bang but a whimper.
> —T.S. Eliot

We did survive, though. Indeed, we prospered. We could have done that only by evolving strategies to overcome disaster—acquiring ways to minimize risks, learning tricks to outwit adversity. Here is the paradox: we were born of contingencies, and we became their enemy.

In this last section we probe the evolution of man's being—the adaptations allowing us to live in constant danger and in the certainty of our death. We blame it all on *Homo erectus.*

Reproductive Imperatives and Risk

Natural selection builds defenses against a risky environment to the degree that risks interfere with reproduction—the expense of building defenses is paid only if necessary. Traits like cryptic coloration to avoid predation, immunoreactions against parasites, and fat deposition as insulation are adaptations to minimize risks. Darwin described the opposite among animals of the Galapagos Islands: in the absence of threat, defenses do not evolve, thus, for example, birds on these islands show no fear of man, never before a danger.

Risk and reproduction shift at opposite ends of a balance beam, such that risk does not on the average overpower reproduction. Animals can adjust this equation in one of two ways, either by reproducing early and frequently, the "To hell with the risks," approach, or by minimizing risks until reproduction is accomplished. The equation is pictured below.

FIGURE 5.1

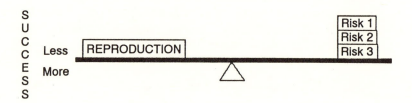

TABLE 5.3
Reproductive Strategies

r Strategies "To hell with risk—go for it"	K Strategies "Take it slow—your time will come"
Rapid maturation	Slow maturation
Early reproduction	Late reproduction
Many offspring	Few offspring
No infant care	Intense infant care
High death rate	Low death rate
Dependency on environment	Manipulation of environment

Let's name the two strategies, giving them more definition. Refer to the following table for the extremes of risk management. The "To hell with risks" strategy we will call *r*, after a biological designation that refers to opportunistic mating. Species that follow this course of action attempt to mate as quickly as possible, regardless of the risks involved—the "now-or-never" approach to reproduction. The risk management strategy we will call *K*, after a designation which refers to long-term concerns for reproduction. Species following this strategy must live longer in order to reproduce, and therefore defer reproduction in times of dangers. Species often align themselves on one or the other side of that division. Insects and small vertebrates typically follow an r strategy; large vertebrates and primates, in particular, follow a K strategy. Remember, if reproduction is accomplished early in life and opportunistically, few anti-risk behaviors would be expected to evolve, but if reproduction is delayed and expensive, anti-risk behaviors will predominate.

Among primates, and presumably our hominid ancestors, many reproductive processes correlate with body size, which in turn stipulates the degree of risk management. Arranging primates along a size continuum, from small to large, we find that increasing size is correlated with the following changes in structure and function:

- Increased longevity
- Enlarged brain
- Heightened brain metabolism
- Delayed sexual maturation
- Few offspring

- Long interval between births
- Intense offspring care
- Extended home foraging range

Large body size is associated with an intensified K strategy, requiring the need for constant risk management. An example will help our understanding.

The female chimpanzee matures sexually at about ten years of age, being more or less dependent upon her mother for that length of time. The mature female gives birth to one infant about every five years. Thus, if a female reproduces twice in her lifetime, she must live a minimum of twenty-five years, ten years devoted to maturation and fifteen years devoted to infant and juvenile care. This is a long period of time for risks to be minimized given the vicissitudes of jungle life. The long periods of infant dependency and reproductive quiescence act as strong selection pressures for risk reduction. In females it takes the form of effective disease resistance, assuring predictable food supplies, avuncular behaviors to help sustain infants, and cooperation from, and protection by, males. That is the situation with chimp communities.

Contrast this briefly with the hectic lifestyle of the house mouse. A female mouse reproduces within two months of birth in an incredibly varied and chancy environment. Each litter may consist of up to thirteen pups, and several litters can be produced in a year—an r strategy with little risk management. Her offspring survive and reproduce on a roll of the environmental dice. A meal missed, a night of cold, may be the difference between life and death. Whenever reproduction is feasible, it will occur.

Finally we come to hominid species. Based on similarities between early Australopithecines and the great apes, we hypothesize that risk management among hominids was similar to that described for chimpanzee. Considerable. Australopithecines were probably *polygynous*, with males competing for females, but not contributing heavily to infant care or mate survival. *Polygyny* is defined as males competing with each other for access to females. Competitive behaviors are suggested by the fact that Australopithecus males were about twice as large as females, a difference characteristic of polygynous species, where males hold contests with each other and females have the major responsibility for infant care.

Risk management became more telling with the appearance of *H. erectus*. Longevity increased, infant development was protracted, the birth interval was extended, the search for calories fanning out over a wider area. Apparently *H. erectus* evolved toward sexual parity, with males only about 20 percent larger than females—still a significant difference, but one which suggests that monogamy was evolving in response to needs for male/female cooperation in infant care. Parental cooperation is an obvious index of monogamy and high risk management.

Now, instead of the acquisition of separate sexual mating strategies, there appeared an amalgamation of parental roles, aimed toward the reduction of risk over the lifetime of the parents. Females reduced their risks by limiting their foraging—it would not work to have the female carrying an infant into unknown and dangerous territories. She still had to nurse the infant, and locomotion would take away energy from infant growth. She remained closer to the core community. The greater risk was left to the male, who had to (1) venture farther into dangerous areas in the search for increased levels of calories and (2) still cater to the female's needs. Nevertheless, he reduced his risks, in part through cooperative hunting, the use of weapons, and by the reduction of continuous intramale competition for females.

The gist of this argument is that increased reproductive demands, spread over long periods of life, initiated a series of evolutionary changes to minimize the risk of reproduction. Risks were still necessary, nay, unavoidable, but now they were carefully managed. *H. erectus* led the way, followed more easily by *H. sapiens.* The new weapons against the free play of dangerous contingencies were (1) a high degree of male/female cooperation in rearing offspring; (2) elaborate communication between the sexes and within each sex; (3) centralized areas of community life, offering more security and protection to the female and infant; (4) increased tool use, including weapons for acquisition of calories; (5) a shift of male risk management to group cooperation in hunting and community vigilance; and (6) a greater tendency toward monogamy that reduced the dangers of male/male competition for females.

A Philosophy of Risk

A mouse, with little tendency toward risk aversion, is likely to have a "philosophy of life" unconcerned with long-term dangers and eventual death. More likely, its philosophy has something to do with short-term goals, centering on chemical cues of aggression, sexual status, and quick reproduction—a paucity of mental concerns, no doubt, but adequate for successful reproduction.

Man, by contrast, carries a strong sense of danger in his mental lexicon, an inclination toward caution. As the American humorist Kin Hubbard advises, "If at first you do succeed, don't take any more chances." The central importance of risk assessment spans a lifetime, as do considerations of individual and kinship reproduction. One expects, then, that man's philosophy would be filled with concerns about male/ female liaison, social status, sex, reproduction, and food acquisition, and, above all, with unmitigating fears of injury, disease, and death— paranoia on small and grand scales—dreams of deluge, fire, falling rocks, fierce predators, land of the dead, quiet graves, superstitions, and personal salvation. We stand in awe of risk-takers, because they tread the line between glory, with its happy correlates to reproduction, and abject failure, with death at the ready.

We have complicated philosophies because we have complicated brains, yes, but in structure these philosophies are tuned to the vibrations of the world as they played themselves out over millennia. We did not simply walk through nature; nature walked through us. There is no separating the two. Living long enough to reproduce requires a high sensitivity to potential dangers, large and small, short-term and long-term. The willy-nilly characters of our past environments cut themselves deeply into the human mind.

Crowning risk with central importance in the evolution of human mentality, we are left with the conclusion that man did not evolve complicated moral and philosophical systems in response to specific evolutionary demands for ethics and morality. Rather, he evolved strategies to minimize danger and prolong life, some of which can be served by moral imperatives, religious beliefs, and superstitions—bread and survival disguised as philosophy.

References

Cited in Chapter 5

Leonard, W.R. and Robertson, M.L. (1992) "Nutritional Requirements and Human Evolution: A Bioenergetics Model." *American Journal of Human Biology*, 4, 179-95.
Lovejoy, C.O. (1987). "The Origin of Man." In R.L. Ciochon and J.G. Fleagle (eds.), *Primate Evolution and Human Origins*. New York: Aldine de Gruyter, 289-98.
Shreeve, J. (1994). "Erectus Rising." *Discover*, September, 80-89.

Stearns, S.C. (1992). *The Evolution of Life Histories*. Oxford: Oxford University Press.
Susman, R.L. (1994). "Fossil Evidence for Early Hominid Tool Use." *Science*, 265, 1570–73.

General References

Johanson, D.C. and O'Farrell, K. (1990). *Journey from the Dawn: Life with the World's First Family*. New York: Villard Books.
Parker, S. (1992). *The Dawn of Man*. New York: Crescent Books.

6

Invisible Imperative

*The diseases which destroy a man are no less
natural than the instincts which preserve him.*

—George Santayana

We emerged in Africa, the product of the struggle to survive and re-produce—heroes of battles with the elements, victors over others who would take our place—wars of gigantic proportion. But the greatest wars, the battles that clearly define our character, were largely invisible, laying waste to millions, yet barely evident in the fossil record. These wars were with fleas, mosquitoes, flukes, worms, bacteria, and viruses. The battlefields were our bodies.

Contingencies wrote the history of these battles. Nothing was certain. Some populations evolved defenses against microbes; others did not. New diseases threatened certain species and individuals, while leaving others alone. Microbes took advantage of hominids, but hominids responded in kind. Everything was in flux—the evolution of man resting on the fate of chance encounters.

Strangely, our abilities to reproduce and evolve may have been determined by microorganisms. If this is true, then everything we are, including our sexual differences, reflect our evolutionary fight with disease. But this is only one adaptation. Our ancestors evolved several strategies to deal with pathogens, including the immune system that recognizes and destroys foreign invaders, and cognitive and behavioral processes that permit the detection and avoidance of infestations. None of these adaptations were fail-safe, but the advantages swung toward our ancestors, enough so that reproduction was possible.

These battles, with their great costs and benefits, course through our evolutionary history, defining our individuality, specifying how we re-

111

TABLE 6.1
Major Diseases Affecting the History of Human Populations

Disease	Infecting Organism	How Transmitted	Symptoms	How Treated
Bubonic Plague	Bacterium *Yersinia pestic* (formerly *Pasteurella pestus*)	Fleas harbored on rodents	Fever, vomiting, muscle pain, mental disorganization, delirium, infected lymph nodes (buboes with pus). High death rate	Antibiotics
Pneumonic Plague	Same organism	Same, but acquired by inhaling infected droplets	Same, but highly contagious. Death within 3 days.	Same
Typhus	Different richethsia micro-organisms, especially *Richettsia prowazekii*	Human lice, whose feces penetrate mucas membranes of eye, respiratory tract or breaks in skin	Headache, fever, skin rash, high mortality	Vaccine antibiotics
Cholera	Bacterium *Vibrio cholesal*	Contaminated water	Diarrhea, loss of body water, cramps, coma, death	Vaccine, antibiotics Electrolyte replacement
Smallpox (variola)	Virus	Discharges from nose and mouth, dried scabs, contact	Chills, fever, aches, nausea, rash with pus, high death rate	Vaccine
Chicken pox	Virus *Herpes Zoster* (also causes shingles)	Respiratory, blood borne in last days of pregnancy	Rash, itching, blisters. Can be life-threatening to children	Medication to reduce itching

TABLE 6.1 (continued)
Major Diseases Affecting the History of Human Populations

Disease	Organism	Transmission	Symptoms	Treatment
Malaria	Plasmodium parasite of the subphylum Sporozoa; *Plasmodium falciparum* is an example	Female mosquito of the genus *Anopheles* introducing plasmodium into bloodstream, going to liver and reproducing, feeding on cellular hemoglobin	Fever, chills, headache, weakness and enlarged spleen	Quinine
Diphtheria	Bacillus *Coryneba terium diphtheria*	Fever, swollen lymph glands, nerve damage, heart failure, paralysis	Formation of a false membrane in the air passage	Antitoxin and antibiotics
Influenza	Virus of the genus *Orthomyxovirus*	Respiratory; animal to human	Fever, muscle aches, pneumonia	Bed rest, aspirin, fluids and antibiotics
Measles (rubeola)	Virus	Sneezing, coughing, personal contact	Fever, malaise, sore muscles, eye irritation, skin rash, encephalitis	Vaccine, antibiotics
Syphilis	Spirochete, *Treponema pallidum*	Breaks in skin, mucus membranes of genitals, mouth, rectum; with cancre initially	Stages from chancre to brain and spinal degeneration, damage to heart	Antibiotics
Rabies	Virus	Contact with wild animals: bats, skunk, coyotes, racoon, rabbit, rodent, etc.	Depression, restlessness, fever fatigue, convulsion, paralysis, suffocation	Series of shots
Leprosy	Bacillus *Mycobacterium leprae* (same family as that which causes tuberculosis)	Skin to skin; nasal discharge	Skin necrosis, damage to nerves and mucus membranes, paralysis	

produce, how we respond to invaders, and how we behave. But conflicts with microbes extend beyond our individuality, affecting the larger sweep of history. Throughout history pathogens dictated migratory routes. Entire civilizations met their fate in the struggle with parasites. Nothing remained untouched in the wars for survival and reproduction. Here are the major diseases modifying the history of human populations.

The actions between microbes and their hosts seem willful, with the microbes attempting to do one thing, and the host another. However they are not choosing their fate; that fate was decided by natural selection for survival and reproduction of traits that increase gene transmission. When our explanation seem to suggest a self-initiated behavior, it is only for ease of explanation—there is no willful process acting.

We are what we are, then, because of our struggles with microorganisms. But, have we won the wars? Is our superiority assured? Has our evolution ceased? Or, are there microbes lying in ambush, ready to alter our future, perhaps for the worse? These may be the most important questions of all.

Quirky Sex

Reproduction comes in two styles, asexual and sexual. We see both and engage in one. Asexual reproduction duplicates all of the parental genes in one rush. A cell divides, a propagule buds off, a single sex clones, and it's all over—complete genetic replication. By contrast, sexual reproduction is complicated and wasteful. Two individuals contribute genetic material to an offspring, usually by producing gametes (sex cells) which unite to form a new generation. In the latter case, each parent contributes *half* its genes to the offspring.

And there's the rub. Sexual reproduction is a loss, in that only 50 percent of one's genes reach the next generation in the first reproductive event, not 100 percent as with asexual reproduction. If natural selection maximizes gene reproduction, why would sexual reproduction ever evolve? Why take at least two reproductive efforts to duplicate one's genes when one might do? After all, asexual reproduction allows one to replicate completely—it's quicker, more efficient, and doesn't require complicated social interactions. Sexual reproduction makes no sense at all, *unless* the extra effort is worth it. At one level it is obvious that the answer has to do with the costs and benefits. If the genetic loss is 50 percent for each reproductive event, then the benefit associated with that loss must be at least twice that. But what could be so beneficial that it would make up for such an extensive genetic loss? Scientists have proposed several hypotheses (see especially *The Red Queen* by Matt Ridley); the hypothesis that helps us explain the evolution of sexuality suggests that reproductive behavior is the optimal adaptation to invading microorganisms. We refer to this hypothesis as the *microbe theory* of sexual evolution.

Microbes Move Us to the Extreme

When our thoughts turn to microbes, we think about the diseases they cause and our attempts to bring them to their microscopic knees. What we forget is that microbes, like us, are the end product of a long history of natural selection for successful reproduction.

Microorganisms have evolved ingenious strategies for avoiding destruction and for moving their genes into the future. They lie in wait and ambush their prey; they move from individual to individual through the air and water and through personal contact. Some use intermediaries, or vectors, like fleas and mosquitoes, to jump from host to host. The vectors themselves may be minimally affected, acting as a reservoir and conduit to an appropriate host. Other microorganisms take up permanent residence in hosts, replicating every time the host's cells divide.

Microbe strategies are even more complex than that, involving the manipulation of their hosts for their own purposes. For example, the rod-shaped bacillus, *Helicobacter pylori*, which is responsible for most stomach ulcers, hides from the destructive gastric juices and killer cells of the immune system by burrowing deep into the stomach lining and flushing its environment with nutritive blood. Occasionally these organisms may be burped through the mouth into the air to infect their next victim. The measles virus of the genus *Morbillivirus* passes from host to host with personal contact and sneezing and coughing. Influenza of the genus *Orthomyxovirus* is carried on the breath. Leprosy rides from skin to skin and with nasal discharges. Syphilis and gonorrhea and possibly other minor diseases are transmitted with genital contact. Historically smallpox was transmitted with scabs and mucus discharges; cholera spread in contaminated water, and bubonic plague spreads with fleas and exhaled droplets from the respiratory tract. All of these devious devices for transport may have evolved from pressures on microorganisms to reproduce, each changing its hosts' behaviors in unique ways.

More ingenious, many microbes evolved techniques for *motivating* their hosts to assist in their transport to other hosts. Viruses and bacteria, acting through the immune system, often cause sneezing, coughing, and mucus drainage, all saturating the environment with millions of their kind. Most propagules sprayed into the air, dropped in water, or smeared on objects, die quickly and never reach another host. But as we know, some do, there to be devoured by the immune cells or to carry on their devious methods of duplication and dispersal.

The malarial parasite, *Plasmodium falciparum*, carried by the *Anopheles* mosquito, manipulates both its carrier and its ultimate host. The parasite destroys the salivary glands of the mosquito, preventing it from obtaining its blood meal in one feeding. It must, instead, probe a host several times for its food, thus insuring that the malaria plasmodium gets into the host. When finally in its host, the microorganism reproduces and bursts forth at night when the host is most susceptible to mosquito attacks. The associated high fever and sweats drive the parasites to the periphery of the body where they are easily accessed by mosquitoes and transported to other victims. The plasmodium is a supreme example of how natural selection has maximized its opportunities to reproduce.

The life cycle of rabies is perhaps the most bizarre; it alters behavior as well as physiology. The virus responsible for the disease is transmitted by animal bites. It infects the spinal cord and moves to higher regions of the brain, causing an irrational rage and a compulsion to attack and bite other animals. The deadly virus, proliferating in the frothy saliva, infects the blood stream of its victim. The rage, biting, and duplication of the virus in the salivary glands are all calculated to facilitate viral transport and reproduction.

After noting these compelling examples, we may even wonder why the kiss is so sweet and why we love sexual intercourse. Is it because hedonistic pleasures advance our own reproductive cause, or could it be that microorganisms maximize their own genetic advantage by altering our own pleasures? A single kiss, with probing tongues, results in the exchange of millions of bacteria and viruses. Not surprising, if you were a bacterium with a mission to reproduce, you too would want the kiss to be sweet. Sexually transmitted diseases (STD's), including HIV, may also enhance our appetite for sex. STD's do not show themselves early, allowing time for their transmission before detection and morbidity. More to the point, gonorrhea and other venereal diseases, cause irritations that possibly increase the desire for intercourse. It's been noted that gonorrhea increases penile erection. There have been suggestions that sexual intercourse is more pleasurable during the early stages of bacterial or viral infections, even with the common cold and the flu. Perhaps these microbes can move between partners with the intimate exchange of sweat and other bodily secretions. Heightened sexual delight may be a bug's way of making more bugs. If so, we face philosophical questions that a few years ago would have been inconceivable.

Microorganisms may sweeten the kiss for their own reproductive benefits, but they can also stifle sexual reproduction. It all depends. If microbes maximize their reproduction by encouraging sex, as with gonorrhea or the common cold, they may rely on host sex behavior for transmission. However, if they reproduce better by inhibiting sexual reproduction of their host, they may do that. There are protozoa single-celled organisms that destroy the testes of male invertebrates that they infect, and that cause the host to shift its energy from sex to bodily growth. The energy devoted to bodily growth is then translated into protozoa reproduction—a nasty trick in this biological war.

At the extreme, microbes force the host to adopt an unnatural mode of reproduction. For example, infecting bacteria prevent the female wasp of the genus *Trichogramma* from reproducing sexually, forcing the host to shift to an asexual mode of reproduction, producing only females like itself. The bacteria benefit from this shift because they are transmitted to the next generation through female ova; they cannot be transmitted along with sperm. Thus by encouraging asexual reproduction, the bacteria reproduce twice as frequently as they would with sexual reproduction— every sexual propagule carries the bacteria. This mode of transmission may be quite common. Incidentally, the bacterial inhibition of sex was demonstrated when it was found that "asexual" females given antibiotics, killing the bacteria, subsequently gave birth to an equal number of females and males. The paradox is that microbes will at one time use a host's sexual reproduction for its own purpose, or, if beneficial, prevent sexual reproduction from occurring at all—unsettling news in either case.

The major conclusion from all of this is that microbes do not simply cause diseases: they organize their hosts' behaviors to facilitate their own reproduction and transmission. There seems to be no limit to their deception: altering aggression, causing explosions of microbes into the environment, stimulating personal contacts among hosts, shutting down host sexual behavior altogether, and even, perhaps, adding charm to human courtship. At this point one begins to lose perspective as to who is doing what to whom and why. Are we in a battle with microorganisms, or are we a huge colony of bugs with a big brain?

Fighting Back with Sex

What can a host organism do in the face of millions of microbes that, in hours or days—with mutations and genetic recombinations—exploit every defense? The answer in many cases, according to the biologist W.D. Hamilton and others, was to abandon asexual reproduction and develop two sexes. That may be the reason that sexual reproduction evolved independently in several groups of species, in insects, invertebrates and vertebrates, including ourselves.

Conceptually, the microbial explanation for the evolution of sex is simple. Asexual individuals not only give birth to themselves, they pass along their parasites—parasites that are equally adapted to the new clones. If the parasites are costly, as they often are, every generation is affected—perhaps resulting in slowed metabolism and impaired reproduction. A way out, at least for a time, is to outwit the parasite by combining genes with a genetically different individual, so that offspring are no longer genetic clones and therefore not susceptible to the same parasites. It's like a farmer introducing a new hybrid variety of wheat so that the existing viruses that damage the wheat are ill-prepared to exploit the new. Essentially, the farmer floods the battlefield with new individuals that are invisible to the specialized aggressors. The war is never over, however, and new viruses may appear to seek out and destroy the new variety of wheat. But the process is delayed long enough for a bountiful harvest.

The explanation, then, for the evolution of sex is an attempt to stay one genetic step ahead of parasitic attack. The biologist John Rennie has set out the costs and benefits of the war: "The guiding metaphor for most biologists looking at parasitism is the coevolutionary arms race. Parasites should be adapting relentlessly to take more resources from their hosts for the purpose of making baby parasites. Hosts should be vigilantly adapting to stop them. If both sides are evenly matched, the result should be a kind of biological détente in which neither parasites nor hosts can afford to relax but neither faces immediate extinction." In 1973 ecologist Leigh Van Valen of the University of Chicago labeled such a situation a Red Queen's race, referring to the character in Lewis Carroll's *Through the Looking Glass* who says, "Now, here, you see, it takes all the running you can do, to keep in the same place." Yes, 50 percent of a parent's reproductive potential is lost in a reproductive attempt, but 50 percent duplication, with the potential for more, is better than 100 percent duplication, with ruination by parasites.

The evidence supporting the microbial theory of sexual reproduction is accumulating. Many snails, for example, reproduce asexually in an environment low in parasite number, but switch to sexual reproduction in environments high in parasite number. Similarly, clones of asexual fish are parasitized by trematode worms less often than sexual fish, except where inbreeding is high and the fish share many genes in common. In general, as conditions facilitate the growth and proliferation of microbes, sexual reproduction is favored, as with the following.

- Long-lived host species, where many generations of microbes live on the same host.
- Close kinship in host groups, or groups with high levels of inbreeding, where generations share similar genes and environments.
- Close assortative mating among hosts, where individuals with similar genes mate, producing offspring that are genetically similar to both parents.
- Non-dispersing host populations, where inbreeding occurs and where generations share similar genes.
- High host densities, where parasites can pass readily between individuals.
- Environments that are warm, moist, low altitude and low latitude (e.g., equatorial zones), where microbes flourish.
- Populations with fewer genes coding for parasitic defense mechanisms, as with the human major histocompatibility complex (MHC), responsible for recognition and destruction of foreign invaders.

These conditions seem disparate, but they share the fact that as microbes become a greater threat, and they do in all of the preceding conditions, the hosts tend toward greater genetic diversity—wherever microbes live, sex is likely to follow. The theory can therefore be condensed to this: where microbes flourish 'tis better to sex with others than sex with self.

The Power of Genetic Diversity and the Sweet Smell of Success

The crucial diversity for disease resistance is at chromosomal locations that regulate immune reactions to infected cells. Sexual reproduction magnifies this diversity, providing resistance in offspring that does not appear in parents. The chromosomal sites for this diversity has already been mentioned, the major histocompatibility complex (MHC). In humans the MHC system is also referred to as the human lymphocyte antigen (HLA) complex. Every individual, with the exception of identical twins, is different at the MHC sites.

The importance of variation at the MHC is illustrated by the observation that there are two MHC genes that confer resistance to malaria. One of the genes is carried by 40 percent of the population of Nigeria, where malaria is endemic, but occurs in only 2 percent of South African blacks and in whites and Orientals not subject to malaria. The parasite, *Plasmodium falciprum* apparently forces humans to increase the population frequency of this gene, an evolutionary response that would be much slower without its spread through sexual reproduction.

The MHC molecules protect against invaders in part because they tag the individual's cells as being part of "self." Soldiers of the immune system can therefore recognize invaders as foreign troops. But the ramifications go well beyond this function. Variation among the MHC genes deter microbial adaptations because they offer a greater variety of genetic defenses against microbes. As a result there is mate selection for the production of cues that reflect the variability. Indeed, there are cues stimulated by MHC genes that can be sensed by others. The MHC genes are responsible for the production of unique chemical signals that are excreted at the surface of the body, and detected by others. Scent-trailing by dogs is apparently possible because of differences among individuals in the odor qualities associated with MHC genes. The chemical cues may be used by humans to denote individuality, genetic differences, *and* disease resistance.

Mice, for instance, can discriminate body odors among other mice that differ only in their MHC genes. When they are given an olfactory choice between animals of the opposite sex, they choose individuals who are different than themselves at these genetic sites. The net effect is that any offspring resulting from these differential choices are different than themselves and, presumably, can resist diseases that normally infect the parent. Once we know which MHC genes are most important for disease resistance, we will perhaps have found those genes most closely linked to the sweet smell of genetic success.

It's not just mice that make these discriminations. Humans also seem to prefer individuals with certain MHC genes, although the evidence is weak. In one case a woman disliked a male associate. Later it was found that their MHC genes were highly similar. Could her aversion be because of the inherent rejection of high degrees of similarities in potential mates (just like mice)? In a sample of fifty-one subjects with "intense" body odors, twenty-nine out of fifty-one (60 percent) were classified as having similar types of MHC genes. Can the similarities and differences in odor be discriminated, and do they evoke different emotional reactions? Certainly the ideas are interesting, and compatible with findings among other species.

Feathers, Bugs, and Sexual Preference

Females use a variety of cues for mate selection, not merely odors created by MHC genes. They select males who are superior in male/male competition, or vigorous, or large and muscular, or who have long feathers. How do these traits relate to disease resistance and how does this form of selection work?

To see how these traits relate to disease resistance and natural selection, let's pretend that you are a bicycle manufacturer, producing bicycles that you hope will out-compete other manufacturers. Over many years you learn that customers want light, fast, but rugged bikes that are easy to ride and inexpensive to maintain. They especially want bikes that can withstand major changes in terrain. You work on these goals by testing various metals for the frame, altering gear ratios and devising tough long-lasting tires. To market the bicycle you patent these developments so that customers know that they're getting consistent quality. You also offer a limited guarantee on your product, develop a unique "look" to your bike, and advertise. Everything is geared toward offering the customer high quality that can be counted on. Your cost is high, but when bicycle enthusiasts see your product they know it's good, and they covet it in their hearts. You sell all you can manufacture, while less efficient companies dwindle in number.

This is an inspiring story, one with a lesson in natural history. Mating systems rely on customer needs and product development, just as with the manufacturing of bicycles. For example, when she needs additional resources or disease-resistant genes to supplement her heavy investments in reproduction, a female chooses the best male available. Her insistence on a high quality product acts as a selection pressure on males to develop that product. Eventually, continual selection by females will produce at least some males that females prefer. The system is just as capitalistic as is the competitive business of making bicycles—the demand forces the market to move toward meeting that demand.

The system of mating that most closely follows the capitalistic strategy is *polygamy*, where either the female or the male is the customer and the other sex evolves the traits in demand. The female generally has the higher reproductive investment, as with gestation, lactation, and offspring care, thus, she is the customer who makes the selection. The male is the product competing for her favors. In this system, where females select and males compete, the mating strategy is a form of polygamy called *polygyny*. In rare instances, where the male has the greater investment in offspring, males are customers and females are the products subject to choice. This mating system is known as *polyandry*.

Polygamy often does not involve long-term sexual or social bonding. Rather, like the successful sale of a bicycle, once the deal is consummated, the two sexes may not continue to cooperate (any guarantees are ultimately limited—*caveat emptor*). The sex with the heavier investment must therefore be very careful in selecting a product. Polygynous females, for example, must choose wisely, or suffer the long-term consequences; their careful discrimination enriches their own reproduction. But females also have long-term effects on the male. Only a few males will measure up—most males will fail the customer test, perhaps not reproducing at all—the severest cost of biological capitalism.

Darwin coined the term *sexual selection*, for sexual preferences applied by one sex to the other. Although much like natural selection, sexual selection can result in the evolution of impractical traits, such as extremely long and gaudy feathers, exaggerated courtship displays, and aggressive behaviors. For example, females may prefer males with long tail feathers because only disease-resistant males can afford to grow long feathers. At the same time, long feathers may hinder movement and ability to hide from enemies. In such a case, sexual selection for long attractive feathers is working in opposition to natural selection for avoidance of predation. Clearly, individuals give up a certain degree of safety from predators in order to attract mates.

We can now understand why females are interested in males with certain extreme characteristics. Females are interested in traits that are true signals of quality—the costly genetic patents, the unique design features, the ruggedness for different terrains, that inform the female that, despite all odds, she is getting what she wants. One of her demands is for a male who is disease-resistant, a male able to provide her offspring with good genes. Obviously, her insistence for this trait will be greater among populations where pathogens occur in great numbers. To use the bicycle analogy once more, if most manufactures produce bicycles of dubious quality, the customer must increase her resolve to find those few that produce true quality.

Bright colors and elaborate feather plumes and vocalizations, true signals of disease resistance, should therefore increase in environments that harbor dangerous parasites. This was found to be true among 109 species of song birds. It was this finding that strongly suggested that females become more demanding as discriminations become more important. It also suggested that within any one particular species, the female should always go for the most disease-resistant male.

Note, there are two major predictions here. The first is that males of *species* most threatened by pathogen damage will evolve exaggerated signals, such as colorful, long feathers, that females can use to discern disease resistance. The second prediction is that *within a species* the female will use these signals to select the most disease-resistant male.

Considerable controversy surrounds these notions. Sometimes females seem to act as discerning consumers; sometimes they don't. Disease resistance, health, and vigor may be only a part of what females seek out. They may ignore disease resistance if the male can still invest heavily in offspring, as with resource acquisition, territorial defense and longevity. As always, her problem is to optimize certain concerns, not limiting her selections to one trait while ignoring others that might be of equal importance.

In other cases, females may have little choice with whom she mates, being forced to mate with socially dominant males or harem masters, regardless of their resistance to disease. The female may simply select a high-resource territory, mating with whatever male is there. Often, however, the female will be rewarded with a disease-resistant male. Finally, there is no absolute guarantee that the male who is currently free of parasites is in fact the most disease-resistant. The hills and valleys of evolution are covered with the tangled bushes of contingency.

Human and Microbial Mating Meet Head-on

At least 90 percent of all world cultures are polygynous. The defining characteristics are unequal mating opportunities among males, and sexual selection of "good" males by females. The most successful males are healthy, ambitious, and possess a disproportionate amount of community resources. They often have access to several females, as with multiple wives, high rates of divorce, and/or extramarital relations.

The male signature for "good" includes resistance to diseases. Where pathogen levels are especially high, females look for disease resistant males and discriminate against disease susceptible males. Sexual selection moves societies with high levels of disease toward polygynous mating.

There are two studies that address this issue in different ways. In the first, it is demonstrated in 186 cultures by Bobbi Low that the degree of pathogen load is related to the percent of men and women marrying polygynously. The second study of twenty-nine cultures by Steven Gangestad and David Buss shows a relationship between the degree of pathogen load and the societal value of physical attractiveness, a presumed measure of disease resistance, analogous to long, beautiful feathers in male peacock birds.

Both investigations used the same seven microorganisms or diseases to determine pathogen load. They include forms of leishmanias, trypanosomes, malaria, schistosomes, filariae, spirochetes, and leprosy. All have an acute, sometimes fatal, initial stage of infection, followed by long-term chronic debilitation or recurrence of acute episodes. Both groups of investigators scored the level of pathogen involvement as "absent or not recorded," "present, but no indication of severity," and "present and serious, widespread, or endemic."

Figure 6.1 shows Low's data for five major geographical areas encompassing the different societies.

The striking correlations between polygyny and pathogen load is an impressive demonstration that the extent of microbial disease determines

FIGURE 6.1
Male and female polygyny associated with level of pathogen stress in five populations.

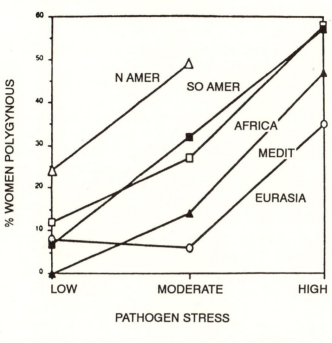

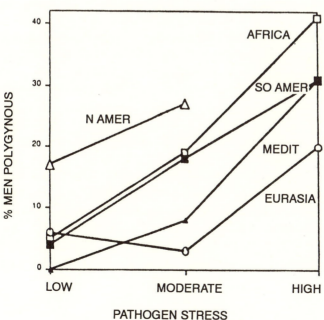

the mating system: low disease level is related to monogamy; high disease level is related to polygyny.

The second study adds the additional point that male and female attractiveness may be especially important in societies where diseases are prevalent. The hypothesis is that high attractiveness in a male is a signal to the female of disease resistance. Her own attractiveness is presumably because males are also selecting mates on the same criteria, or are using good looks as a measure of reproductive competence. The assumption is that microorganisms causing disease detract from physical attractiveness—if one cannot see the deleterious germs, at least their presence can be discerned by their effects on facial and other features of beauty.

As expected, the degree of pathogen prevalence among the twenty-nine societies correlated highly with the degree to which individuals believed attractiveness was important (the correlation, which can range from 0.00 to 1.00, is 0.72, exceptionally high as correlations go). If no other factors are causing the correlation, it appears that sexual selection is acting to increase attractiveness in pathogen-stressed societies. One wonders, then, if men and women in monogamous societies are less concerned with beauty. It may be too early to evaluate the significance of these studies; while they are few in number and perhaps harbor undetected flaws, they do appear to support the microbial theory of mate selection. In any case, one should consider the implications. If females force a polygynous style of mating through mate discrimination, the outcome is the sexual dimorphism apparent in so many societies. Any social theories about sexual differences must take this into account. The other implication is that selection for differential disease susceptibility among societies sets the stage for the march of social history. Societies emerge, collapse and spread amongst the slings and arrows of microscopic outrage.

Disease and the Birth of Modern Man

In 1344 the Mongol Tartars, related to the empire of Kublai Khan, swept down on the Italian trading post of Caffa. A fortified city on the Crimean shore of the Black Sea, Caffa was the highly prized trading link between Europe and China. By sea and land the Tartars laid siege to the city. The Italians repulsed the attacks for over two years, until fate overtook them.

In the winter of 1347 a devastating disease broke out on a Tartar ship, killing many of the sailors. As one version has it, the marauders saw this as a dark opportunity. Gathering the diseased and rotting bodies, they catapulted the corpses over the walls of Caffa. The effects were devastating, killing many who had resisted the Mongol attacks for years. From this place of death the disease spread widely, carried by tradesmen, and travelers northward into Russia, eastward into India and China, southward into the city of Genoa, and beyond to North Africa. The bubonic plague, aptly named the Black Death, had arrived—a plague that decimated Europe, ending the Middle Ages and changing the world forever.

The bubonic plague, caused by the bacillus, *Yersinia pestis*, was carried from host to host by a flea. The flea lives and feeds on the black rat, but also thrives on almost all other animals. Rats are especially dangerous because they harbor the plague bacillus without much damage to themselves, and travel with humans from country to town and across all seaways and land routes. The bacillus moves easily from rats to fleas to humans and back to rats.

From its recorded entry into Europe at Caffa in 1347 until it first ran its devastating course in 1351, the bubonic plague brought grief and horror, killing perhaps as many as 50 million people, between 30 to 50 percent of the population of Europe.

> The first symptoms of bubonic plague often appear within several days; headache and a general feeling of weakness, followed by aches and chills in the upper leg and groin, a white coating on the tongue, rapid pulse, slurred speech, confusion, fatigue, apathy and a staggering gait. A blackish pustule usually will form at the point of the flea bite. By the third day, the lymph nodes begin to swell. Because the bite is commonly in the leg, it is the lymph nodes of the groin that swell, which is how the disease got its name. The Greek word for "groin" is *boubon*—thus, bubonic plague. The swellings will be tender, perhaps as large as an egg. The heart begins to flutter rapidly as it tries to pump blood through swollen, suffocating tissues. Subcutaneous hemorrhaging occurs, causing purplish blotches on the skin. The victim's nervous system begins to collapse, causing dreadful pain and bizarre neurological disorders, from which the "Dance of Death" rituals that accompanied the plague may have taken their inspiration. By the fourth or fifth day, wild anxiety and terror overtake the suffer—and then a sense of resignation, as the skin blackens and the rictus of death settles on the body. (Mee 1990)

The chronicler Agnolo di Tura summarized the events with simple power, "And so many died that all believed it was the end of the world." The impact of the disease was incalculable, causing changes in population demography and society that affect our lives even today.

The three orders of feudalisms—clergy, peasantry, and nobility—were altered forever. The church, already under political pressures because of its excesses, suffered severe loses of its own clergy. Ultimately, the church was unable to explain why God damned to the horrors of purification the young and the innocent. As the Black Death spent it fury, the power of religion went with it. The world turned to materialism and self-indulgence—man stood in direct relation to God without the intermediate layers of church dogma. The new feeling of freedom and rationality made scientific investigations of life possible for the first time since the classic Greeks.

The high mortality among the aristocracy strained the transfer of power and property, allowing the growth of wage earners and small land owners. The plague did not honor nobility, killing perhaps three of four children before the age of ten, with a maternal mortality of around 20 percent. In England, fully 75 percent of the nobility failed to produce a male heir during two generations. The populace began to replace the old regimes.

Demographic growth was impossible for a century after the Black Death. Other infectious diseases, smallpox in particular, added to the death toll. Europe's population in 1430 was nearly 75 percent lower than it was in 1290. It was not until the middle sixteenth century that Europe regained its earlier population levels. By then the zeitgeist was spinning toward worldwide conquest and the likes of Charles Darwin and Alfred Russell Wallace.

Barriers and Colonization

Bubonic plague was one of the first major "crowd" diseases, spreading like a prairie fire through dense and nonprotected populations. The bacillus reached Tunis in North Africa in 1348, killing 1000 people each day. Yet the Berbers of the western desert escaped the disaster, primarily because they lived as nomads in small tribes.

The different killing in cities and nomadic tribes is perhaps one of the greatest lessons of historical biology. It may explain why early hominids escaped heavy infestation. In our search for our African ancestors, no permanent living sites were ever found. *Homo erectus* and early *H. sapiens* established hunting camps, but never for long periods. They were nomadic. According to the paleobiologists Stringer and Gamble, "There is scant evidence for the structured organization of living areas among any of the Ancients—Neanderthals included. The Ancient's use of living space, be it a rock shelter or an open site, is unfamiliar to us, and even something as basic as a permanent open-air, stone-lined hearth was absent in Europe until 60,000–40,000 years ago."

The usual explanation for the nomadic behavior of our ancestors is that limitations of food and water prevented the building of permanent sites. More likely early hominids were forced to move as living and butchering sites became contaminated by microbes. Other primates escape major diseases in that way. The yellow baboons at Amboseli National Park stay at a nest site for only two days and do not return to that site for nine to eleven days, a day or two longer than the longevity of parasite larvae in feces. It would seem that the baboons may have been selected for a nomadic life of hunting in order to avoid heavy infestations.

Perhaps *Homo erectus* did not so much walk out of Africa as run from the threat of tropical disease. More northern latitudes, with their cooler and dryer climates, harbor fewer microorganisms, presenting increased opportunities for expansion and reproduction. It is not surprising, then, that the routes of colonization followed northerly paths before they again converged on equatorial regions. According to the historian McNeill:

> Parasites that could spread from host to host by direct bodily contact, like lice, or the spirochete of yews, could survive in temperate climates within small and migratory hunting communities. As long as the infection acted slowly and did not incapacitate the human host too severely or too suddenly, such parasitisms could and probably did travel with hunting communities from humanity's tropical cradlelands throughout the earth. But the array of such infections and infestations was vastly diminished from what had thriven in the tropical luxuriance of humanity's oldest habitat.

Many human behaviors may have been shaped by the evolutionary pressures of endogenous and exogenous parasites, including those listed in the table 6.2. They range from simple hygienic habits to complex avoidance responses and medicinal habits.

The balance between life and death shifted dramatically about 12,000 years ago in the Jordan River Valley with the advent of agriculture. For the first time, large permanent settlements were founded, fields were irrigated and plowed, populations increased in size, and crowd diseases appeared as if by magic. The major killers were plague, smallpox, measles, influenza, typhus, pertussis, tuberculosis, diphtheria, mumps,

TABLE 6.2
Pathogen-Induced Behavioral Evolution

Disease Avoidance Strategies	Evolutionary Consequences
Avoidance of Contaminated Areas	Nomadic life style
Use only temporary campsites	Preference for fresh foods
Avoid spoiled foods	Dislike of insects
Avoid disease vectors (insects)	
Acquire Taste Avoidances	Food selectivity
Avoid tastes and smells related	Food-induced nauseousness
to sickness	Sensitivity to parental eating
Monitor parental food habits	likes and dislikes
Self-Medicate	Obsessional hygienic behaviors
Clean wounds	Botanical knowledge
Find medicinal plants	
Reduce stress and malnutrition	
Destroy disease vectors	
Control Social Interactions	Fear of strangers and strange
Avoid contact with strange groups	behaviors
Reduce population density	Sensitivity to disease-related traits
Quarantine or exclude the diseased	Outbreeding to reduce
Choose disease-resistant mates	inbreeding depression
Avoid "genetic weakening" (incest taboos)	

malaria, and yellow fever. The sudden appearance of these diseases does not suggest that the responsible pathogens were not carried in the population, but only that they remained "silent," only multiplying and spreading as population density increased.

Not only were populations susceptible to new diseases, they were generally less healthy than hunters and gathers. High starch diets were common with a lack of vitamins and minerals. True, more people could be fed, and good harvests could be stored for lean years but at the price of overpopulation, malnutrition, and pestilence. The biologist Jared Diamond believes that women became "beasts of burden," with the advent of agriculture, supposedly as a result of work demanded of her in the fields, plus the additional burden of caring for offspring. We might add that men at the same time increased their work load, lost their freedom as hunters, and diminished their sense of male camaraderie. We entered into the modern world with the biological baggage acquired in Africa, often turning that baggage to advantage.

Disease has always been a major determinant of human survival and the barrier to the spread of nations. Because of tropical diseases, nearly 1,000 years elapsed between the birth of China and the taming of the Yellow River flood plain. The climate shift from north to south was from dry and cool to wet and warm—from a place of minor infestation to a place of severe parasitism. The Yellow River was an invincible barrier as real as the Great Wall. It is this same barrier that prevented the early colonization of Africa, and, to some degree, still prevents the complete devastation of the equatorial rain forests.

Nations did spread into disease-infested areas, but they paid a price for adaptation. The battle between man and disease resulted in a coevolution of man's immunity and the parasite's virulence—a resolution that costs each but spares both. Sometimes humans take an active part in the conquering of disease, opening up new vistas for exploitation. For example, it was the French who first attempted to build a canal across the Isthmus of Panama, but were beaten back by malaria and yellow fever. In 1901 an American medical team, led by Dr. Walter Reed in Havana, found that yellow fever and malaria could be eliminated by attacking mosquito-breeding sites. This medical advance allowed the United States quickly to rid the Panama area of these parasites, completing the canal in what had previously been one of the worst fever regions of the world. Thus, the United States, not France, became the dominant power in Central America.

The greatest conquest in history by the Spanish in the Western Hemisphere turned on the transmission of smallpox from the Spanish armies to the populations of Mexico, South America, and eventually North America. In 1519 Cortez with 600 Spanish soldiers landed on the coast of Mexico with a military mission to conquer the Aztec Empire. He was initially defeated, losing two thirds of his army. But, when Cortez returned in 1521, the outcome was much different. The advantage went to Cortez because of the arrival into Mexico of one slave infected with smallpox in 1520, the start of a major epidemic. The Spanish were spared because of their acquired immunity to this European disease, but the Aztecs lost at least half of their population to the ensuing smallpox epidemic. By 1618 the initial Mexican population of 20 million had plummeted to around 1.6 million. The Aztec nation crumbled and Mexico fell because of a lack of resistance to an invisible army of microbes.

In 1524 the Spaniard Pizarro was successful against the Incas of Peru for the same reason—the Inca population was severely depleted by a smallpox epidemic that killed the Emperor Huayna Capac and his son, the designated successor. Pizarro exploited the political vacuum that followed and conquered the Inca nation.

The conquistadores of Spain rode into North America carrying their advanced weapons and millions of microparasites to which the American Indians had no defense. It is difficult to say how many died, but one estimate is that within two centuries of Columbus's arrival in the New World, 95 percent of the indigenous population perished—not just from smallpox, but from measles, influenza, and typhus, and a half-dozen other alien diseases strange to this continent.

Today we feel smugly safe from epidemics as florid as bubonic plague, smallpox, malaria, yellow fever, and the like. With vaccinations, antibiotics, and sterilized food and water, we thumb our nose at epidemics. Yet as recently as 1918, 20 million people died from influenza, at the end of World War I. Some of the diseases we thought defeated and buried are raising their ugly countenance in even stranger forms. And then there is AIDS, with all the signs of a pandemic, and some strange and new deadly bacteria and viruses coming, ironically, from our original home, the heart of Africa. What new deaths stalk our evolutionary trail? Do we still have some genetic tricks up our sleeves? Will the arrow of history again turn on a germ that can be measured only by the smallest of rulers?

Our Moment of Truth

When first described on the European continent in 1495, syphilis was one of the most deadly diseases on record. It struck quickly, leading to pustules over the entire body—the skin literally falling from the face, and death occurring within months. Today the same disease is less virulent, causing only genital sores initially and developing slowly over years, eventually resulting in death. The disease evolved toward relative benignancy in about a century.

Many diseases progress in this fashion, reaching an equilibrium with hosts, thereby conferring immunity to infested individuals—both pathogen and host surviving to reproduce. If this be the general rule, given enough time for mutual adaptation between microbes and hosts, all diseases must run toward a favorable conclusion. Perhaps, pathogens eventually integrate themselves into the working machinery of the body, benefiting themselves and their hosts. Such was the case with mitochrondrial DNA, responsible for energetic activities of the vertebrate cell. This DNA may have its origins with invading parasitic bacteria.

Unfortunately, that is not the usual path of evolutionary history. The general rule for pathogens *and* hosts is "reproduce at any cost." If reduced virulence among pathogens facilitates reproduction, the direction of change is for reduced virulence. But, if increased virulence is compatible with high rates of reproduction, the opposite will occur. The problem for the host is how much energy can and should be allocated to the problem of deactivating the pathogen. The two sides of the equation don't always match.

Pathogens should be less virulent if their reproduction depends upon their host's viability, than if they can easily move from host to host. Infecting bacteria become more benign when their fate is tied to a "mother-daughter" (vertical) mode of inheritance, that is, when the bacteria transmission is within an isolated line of hosts. Under this condition the virus quickly begins to produce fewer harmful toxins. When the virus can spread laterally to new linages of bacterial hosts—the "multiple stranger" mode of inheritance—virulence remains high. In the first instance, pathogen survival is correlated with host survival; in the second it is not. The facts strongly suggest that the fate of the host results in a genetic adjustment of the pathogen's virulence.

When ticks and insects transport pathogens from individual to individual, virulence can remain high, especially if the pathogens reproduce rapidly and there are many potential hosts around. Yellow fever, sleeping sickness, and malaria are examples of this mode of transmission. Likewise, when pathogens are transported easily in air or water, toxicity remains high. In the most deadly form of bubonic plague the bacillus is acquired by inhaling infected droplets. Influenza and tuberculosis follow the same pattern of dispersal. Cholera, caused by the bacterium *Vibrio cholesal*, results in diarrhea, allowing the pathogen to contaminate waterways where it is transported to other unfortunate hosts. Cholera results in a severe loss of body water, cramps, coma, and death. The finish comes within days of infection. Even hospital attendants and doctors can be inadvertent vectors of disease transmission, spreading highly toxic bacteria, viruses, and protozoa among their many patients.

The folklore is that doctors can deal with the sick without themselves becoming infected. The truth may be that they are infected, but as with other vectors, they may be minimally harmed.

Our ancient ancestors lived in small groups that moved ahead of contamination in their environment. They were too few in number to support lateral transmission of pathogens, so that their worst microbial enemies lived in balance with them. As long as our early relatives remained hunter-gathers, a fairly high degree of good health was assured. It was when populations increased in size and began building farming communities and cities that new crowd diseases appeared and spread widely. Where did these new diseases come from?

What New is in Store for Us?

In September of 1976 in northern Zaire a new virus appeared in human populations. It was named Ebola, after the river which runs through that area. The virus erupted simultaneously in more than forty villages, killing approximately 88 percent of the people it infected. Apart from HIV, which causes AIDS, and rabies, Ebola has the highest rate of mortality of any contemporary human virus. The symptoms are headache, fever, blood clots, and hemorrhages. The clots lodge everywhere, including the liver, spleen, and brain. The immune system is severely depressed, leading to death within a week. Ebola is spread through contact with bodily fluids and blood.

A form of this virus, strange, new, and deadly, was inadvertently transported to the United States with a shipment of Philippine monkeys in 1989. Fortunately this particular type of Ebola virus was not infectious to humans. However, it did kill the monkeys and had the potential of mutating to a deadly form in humans. Thanks to some fast thinking by the laboratory personnel and the Army, we may have missed a pandemic by a hair.

Altogether the Ebola virus has struck Africa five times in sixteen years. At the time this is written a new outbreak has killed nearly 200 men and women in four towns in Zaire. It appears to have been contained, but it could reappear at any time. Obviously there is a high risk that the virus could spread widely. There is no cure, and it is not even clearn how it spreads.

Ebola is not the only virus of concern. New pathogens leap from animal species to humans, especially where humans disrupt the ecology where they live. The problems are multiplying and their solutions could quickly be out of reach. The Oropouche virus, appearing for the first time in Brazil in 1960, caused a flu-like epidemic in 11,000 individuals. They suffered from headaches, fevers, and muscle aches. The virus was spread by forest-dwelling midges that underwent a population explosion after the clearing of a forest. It took nineteen years to discover this.

Then there is the hantavirus, otherwise known as "Rodent Pox," which killed an estimated fifty or more people, mostly native Americans living in New Mexico, Arizona, and Colorado. Often mistaken for the flu, the virus causes chills, muscle aches, and fatigue. Unfortunately, it doesn't stop there; it goes on to turn the lungs into soup. The virus is apparently carried by deer mice and is inhaled with dust contaminated by urine or saliva from the infected mouse. Biologist Robert Cocke has suggested that this or a related virus may have been responsible for the devastation of the Anasazi culture of the Southwest in the 1100s. Although the disease was first detected in the 1980s, it did not show an infectious distribution until 1993. It could be our next pandemic.

Other viruses, including, Rift Valley Fever and a new form of yellow fever, originate in animals and threaten humans. Then, of course, there is HIV. We understand none of these viruses completely, and there are no cures. No doubt many more will appear as rain forests are stripped and pathogens leap to man. The problem is compounded by the fact that a virus can be picked up in the Amazon or Zaire on Tuesday and walk through airport customs in Los Angeles on Wednesday. There is absolutely no way to check their lateral spread, and there is no reason to think that they won't be virulent.

But, if the new items on our plate weren't bad enough, the old is coming back to haunt us. Tuberculosis strains have recently appeared that are resistant to more than one drug—some are resistant to all known tuberculosis drugs. About 5 percent of the 27,000 people known to have active tuberculosis have drug resistant forms of the disease.

The demise of communist regimes has left post-Stalinist countries vulnerable to disease. In Albania, for example, migrant workers from other countries have brought syphilis, hepatitis-B, and AIDS—all diseases that can be transmitted with hypodermic injections and unprotected sex. Infant mortality in Albania is the highest in Europe. Old diseases in new populations can be especially virulent.

Now a new strain of cholera-causing bacteria is blowing through India and Bangladesh. *Vibrio cholerae*, known as 139 (there have been 138 others), is the microbial culprit. Current vaccines are ineffective. In its severe form it causes diarrhea, vomiting, muscle cramps, and eventually the collapse of the vascular system. The bacteria did in fact walk through customs with a woman at an international airport this year. It is yet to be pandemic, but the potential is there.

The United States is not exempt from the rapid spread of old and new pathogens. In the spring of 1993 the most extensive waterborne disease outbreak ever reported in the U.S. occurred in Milwaukee, Wisconsin. More than 400,000 persons became ill with the pathogen crytosporidiosis, showing profuse watery diarrhea. The source of the outbreak was traced to municipal water contamination. Unfortunately there is no national surveillance for human infections such as this. It often takes thousands of cases within an urban area before public health officials become aware of the dangers.

A survey conducted by the World Health Organization (WHO) in 1993 underlined the urgent need for improving global surveillance capabilities. Only 56 percent of the thirty-four laboratories surveyed had the ability to diagnose yellow fever, a condition that may have contributed to the yellow fever outbreak in East Africa from 1992 to 1993. Fewer than half of the laboratories in this survey had the ability to diagnose Japanese encephalitis, hantavirusus, Rift Valley fever virus, or California encephalitis.

Many of the diseases now spreading worldwide are evolving resistances to common antibiotics. It's the old evolutionary game, where resistant microbes have a selective advantage, eventually replacing all nonresistant forms. Bacteria have evolved two powerful defenses: sturdier membranes to prevent antibiotics from entering the cell, and "eflux pumps" that expell any substance that does penetrate the cell. Other specific devices for sabotaging antibiotics have also appeared. Hiroshi Nikaido, a microbiologist at the University of California at Berkeley, believes that most of the antibiotics developed during the past fifty years will soon be obsolete.

A table reproducing recent infectious diseases is shown below. As microorganisms adapt to multiple changes in our societies, we remain vulnerable to drug-resistant infections and new forms of bacteria and viruses.

TABLE 6.3
Emerging Infectious Disease

Pathogen and year of emergence	Disease manifestations	Epidemiologic characteristics	Current surveillance	Comment
Drug-resistant pneumococci 1970s	Middle ear infections; pneumonia; meningitis	Person-to-person, especially large child care centers	Magnitude of problem unknown	In 1993, outbreaks of drug-resistant strains in communities in Tennessee and Kentucky
Cryptosporidium 1976	Prolonged watery diarrhea; life-threatening in immunosuppressed persons	Waterborne: person-to-person in child care centers	Reportable disease in two states	Since 1984, multiple outbreaks have been recognized involving municipal water supplies; in each outbreak, water met state or federal standards for quality
E. Coli O157:H7 1982	Bloody diarrhea; acute kidney failure	Foodborne, especially ground beef; person-to-person spread in child care centers	National surveillance being initiated	Multiple outbreaks recognized since 1982; estimated 20,000 cases annually
Vancomycin-resistant enterococci 1988	Life-threatening blood-stream infections; surgical wound and urinary tract infections	Person-to-person spread in hospitals	Trends monitored by voluntary system of reporting to CDC by 166 hospitals	Since 1988, increasing number of outbreaks recognized in hospitals on east coast of U.S.
Hantavirus 1993	Hantavirus pulmonary syndrome; 60% mortality	Rodent reservoir; spread by inhalation of an aerosol of rodent urine, feces, or saliva	Case reports investigated by health departments and CDC; trapping and lab exam of rodents part of investigations	Confirmed to have caused deaths in previously healthy adults in the United States for more than a decade

The Next Step

As dangerous as the world has become, two things remain clear. The first is that our species is resilient, showing capabilities of responding genetically to the most severe environmental and biological shocks. There is plenty of genetic variation inherent in our population, and a range of possible adaptations to any microbial threat. Moreover, we are already equiped with exquisite defense mechanisms, ranging from the immune system to our cognitive capacities to grasp new opportunities. The second thing in our favor is our scientific methodology, now being mobilized to meet the demands on the biological battlefield. The genetic code is "cracked" and we are beginning to understand the cellular biology that underlies our defense mechanisms. We can expect new drug and other therapeutic assaults on virulent pathogens, and a more determined effort to restrain and understand disease processes. In the end, we may find that there are only a few general principles by which microbes interact with their hosts. If so, we may be able to construct generic preventative measures that allow us to control all diseases.

On the other hand, we should not be overly optimistic. Population growth has accelerated lateral transmission of diseases, and hence virulence of microorganisms. More diseases are in the making, more plagues in our future. To the extent that we fail to control population growth, we face a growing uncertainty in our attempts to control diseases.

References

Cited in Chapter 6

Beauchamp, G.K., Yamazaki, K., and Boyse, E.A. (1985). "The Chemosensory Recognition of Genetic Individuality." *Scientific American*, 253, 86–92.
Bull, J.J., Molineux, I.J., and Rice, W.R. (1991). "Selection of Benevolence in a Host-Parasite System." *Evolution*, 45, 875–82.
Cartwright, F.F. (1972). *Disease and History*. New York: Dorset Press.
Diamond, J. (1992). "The Arrow of Disease." *Discover*, October, 64–73.
Ewald, P.W. (1994). *Evolution of Infectious Disease*. Oxford: Oxford University Press.
Ferstl, R., Eggert, F., Pause, B., Schuler, M., Dagmar, L., Westphal, E., Zavazava, N., and Müller-Ruchholtz, W. (1989). "Immune System Signaling to the Other's Brain: MHC-Specific Body Scents in Humans." *Sixth International Symposium on Neuronal Control of Bodily Function: Basic and Clinical Aspects*. Irvine, CA, October 23–27.
Gangestad, S.W. and Buss, D.M. (1993). "Pathogen Prevalence and Human Mate Preferences." *Ethology and Sociobiology*, 14, 89–96.

Garrett, L. (19YEAR). *The Coming Plague*. New York: Farrar, Straus and Giroux.

Gottfried, R.S. (1983). *The Black Death*. New York: The Free Press.

Hamilton, W.D. and Zuk, M. (1982). "Heritable True Fitness and Bright Birds: A Role for Parasites?" *Science*, 218, 384–87.

Low, B.S. (1990). "Marriage Systems and Pathogen Stress in Human Societies." *American Zoologist*, 30, 325–39.

McNeill, W.H. (1976). *Plagues and Peoples*. Garden City, NY: Anchor Books.

Mee, C.L., Jr. (1990). "How a Mysterious Disease Laid Low Europe's Masses." *Smithsonian*, 20, 67–79.

Preston, R. (1992). "Crisis in the Hot Zone." *The New Yorker,* October, 38–81.

Tooby, J. (1982). "Pathogens, Polymorphism, and the Evolution of Sex." *Journal of Theoretical Biology*, 97, 557–76.

General References

Earnest, M. and Sbarbaro, J.A. (1993). "A Plague Returns." *The Sciences*, September/October.

Ghiselin, M.G. (1988). "The Evolution of Sex: A History of Competing Points of View." In R.E. Michod and B.R. Levin (eds.), *Evolution of Sex*. Sunderland: Sinauer Associates, Inc., 7–23.

Read, A.F. (1990). "Parasites and the Evolution of Host Sexual Behaviour." In C.J. Barnard and J.M. Behnke (eds.), *Parasitism and Host Behavior*. London: Taylor and Francis Publishers, 117–57.

Rennie, J. (1992). "Living Together." *Scientific American*, January, 124–33.

Ridley, M. (1993). *The Red Queen*. New York: Macmillan Publishing Company.

Williams, G.C. and Nesse, R.M. (1991). "The Dawn of Darwinian Medicine." *The Quarterly Review of Biology*, 66, 1–22.

7

Undaunted Reality Submerged in Beauty

*The progress of science is strewn, like an ancient
desert trail, with the bleached skeleton of discarded
theories which once seemed to possess eternal life.*
—Arthur Koestler

Every college freshman knows truths of evolution for which Darwin
and Wallace would have sacrificed their lives. In retrospect it seems that
knowledge came as an inevitable flood. But it wasn't that simple. In the
words of Robert Pirsig, who wrote *Zen and the Art of Motorcycle Maintenance*, "Traditional scientific method has always been at the very best,
20-20 hindsight. It's good for seeing where you've been." To the person
looking toward the future, knowledge is the golden nugget lying deep
in a forbidding mountain. The fact of the matter is that nature reveals
her colors reluctantly.

If the principles of nature escape our casual view, how, then, are they
found? How do scientists actually deal with uncertainties and arrive at
generalities? What are the methods, and from where do they come? What
are the hazards? If truth is really out there, what does it look like? Sifting
through these questions will help us arrive at the knowledge about evolution, and how we can gain entrance into the mind and body of humans.

The Measure of Tomorrow

The longing for truth is part of our genetic makeup, born of practical
concerns for survival and reproduction. Natural selection stamped us
with abilities to perceive dangers and opportunities, and to reconstruct
our environment to better serve our needs. The upshot was brain power
enough to begin to understand ourselves, coming to full fruition about

200,000 years ago with the appearance of *Homo sapiens*. So here we are today, a genetic reflection of our history, not only measuring our chance to succeed in a contingent environment, but looking for our cosmological purpose.

Using the brain power acquired as part of our survival mechanisms, we have slowly built philosophies to explain our existence and methods to verify their reality. The philosophies dictate the kinds of methods we use to reveal our nature; the methods, in turn, give rise to new philosophies. The two, philosophies and methods, are inextricably intertwined. In that sense, what we pursue and how we conduct the chase is relative.

But the process is neither random nor arbitrary. The goal is a greater understanding of ourselves and our environment. There are facts out there; there are invariant principles in the universe, and there are causal relations between structures and functions. As long as we continually strive to match our thinking with the hard reality beyond our senses, truth will eventually emerge. The proof is seen in what we have accomplished in the last three hundred years, and in the exponential rush toward new knowledge. Like it or not, we have tasted the fruit from the tree of knowledge—there is no turning back.

Our discussion of philosophy and scientific methods comes deep within this book. We saw the struggles of Darwin and Wallace in their search for truth; we traced our evolutionary history through the fossil record, and we became acquainted with the environmental contingencies that shaped our destiny. Now we are in position to pick at the lock blocking our way to the inner qualities of human behavior. We do it by applying theories and experimental strategies. Throughout the rest of the book you will see the engrossing pattern of philosophy that guides our search for new knowledge, and the strategies of observation and experimentation that shed light upon the cold realities of our deepest visions and our harshest nature. Where we are wrong, the self-corrective actions of science will expose our theoretical weaknesses. The service we can provide is not to be cautious and hesitant, but to be explicit in our contentions, so that our propositions can be subject to rigorous test.

Creativity and the Science of Knowing

The overarching goal of science is to understand the universe—no small task. In its reach for knowledge, science describes the universe in relations, which if they clearly reflect reality, seem like beautiful paintings. The scientist, in that sense, *is* an artist, discovering, creating, and composing. The discernable difference between the scientific painter, such as Albert Einstein, and the artistic painter, such as Salvador Dali, is that the scientific painter must construct works of art that have verifiable relations to the external world. The pictures of the universe, whether mathematical or metaphorical, must be reducible to time and place. No such restrictions guide the artist working on canvas. Other than that, the scientist and artist stand together in their attempts to perceive and describe the nature of the universe.

But, ask a scientist how discoveries are made and relations formed, the conversation becomes murky. Some processes of discovery are the result of what we perceive and learn, whereas others are not observable, residing beyond the range of communication. The latter come from within, seemingly the workings of our instinctual nature. The idea of built-in knowledge has a long history. The great German philosopher Immanuel Kant believed that the mind is equiped to categorize sensations—an *a priori* intuition about the nature of the world—evolved knowledge, etched into the protoplasm of the brain. Kant believed that everything sensed and understood has quality, quantity, relation, and modality—axioms of intuition. The extreme of this notion goes back to Plato who propounded a doctrine of recollection, positing that we possess universal truths, but, which unfortunately, are driven from consciousness by the shock of birth. Accordingly, in a vague sort of way we know everything, with experience enabling us to recall this knowledge with some precision.

Today we might call Kant's intuition *genetic knowledge*, referring to a set of mental rules built through natural selection for dealing with the vagaries of sensory experience. This goes beyond Kant's original axioms by suggesting that most of our behaviors and thoughts have been programmed into the brain as adaptations to solve environmental puzzles. For example, we have rules to deal with the physics of the universe, rules on how to learn and comprehend language, and rules to evaluate cause and effect relationships. These and other similar rules are absolutely essential for solving critical problems. Many of these rules, as we will later see, are apparent in infants, who develop extraordinary abilities without any specific training at all. Of course knowledge cannot flow from instinct alone. We learn from our environment; even genetic rules of the mind are drawn forth and modified by the environment. It must be granted, then, that knowledge is some mysterious combination of gene expression and environmental canalization—two sides of a coin that blend together to form new alloys of the mind.

To the degree we have evolved rules of the mind, the principles of the world are locked within our brain. The nature of the world, including the principles of evolution, may be packed into our nervous system as a result of natural selection for practical knowledge of our surroundings. Our task, then, as Plato suggested, is to unleash that knowledge and allow those principles to emerge into consciousness.

Probing the Universal Mind

Stories of sudden insights—discontinuous and radically new thoughts—fill our books on the history of science. They tell of the abrupt and often uncanny emergence of new concepts, as if fundamental templates of the brain had gained their voice in an instant of revelation. The stories are also compatible with the observation that the "great insights" in science and art fight their way to expression in minds *prepared* to hear the message. It is as if thoughts meander across the desert of the mind, constantly probing, until at last the "Artesian" well of illumination gushes forth—genetic knowledge released from its neural restraints. We may never know this process exactly—there will always be a fundamental mystery—but we can see examples.

One can never forget the incomparable revelation of Isaac Newton that the force causing a stone to fall is the same that holds the planets in their orbits. It is said that this startling vision of heavenly mechanics came as suddenly as an apple falling from a tree. The apple was apocryphal, perhaps, but the insight was sudden and in sharp contrast to other explanations. The forthcoming laws of gravity were reserved for Newton, not because others lacked abilities along these lines, but because the vigilance of concentration was there, moving constantly across his mind until the vision erupted.

The visions of the mind can appear in unexpected ways, not entirely a function of concentration. It was the chemist Friedrich August Kekulé who in a dream united the two loose bonds at the ends of the compound benzene, forming the famous "benzene ring," thus opening up the area of synthetic organic chemistry. According to the historian Charles Singer,

"Of the hundreds of thousands of 'organic' compounds now known, the majority have been made artificially, and the stimulus for this great advance came from the clearly visualizable model provided by the structural formulae that Kekulé described." The mind sometimes dreams its own destiny.

René Descartes, one of the world's greatest philosophers, was a mercenary in his younger days. On the night of November 10, 1619, while quartered on the banks of the Danube, he had a dream that put into his mind the principles of analytic geometry. He kept that monumental insight to himself for sixteen years and through several battles before he finally published his principles for posterity. Descartes went on to formulate the distinction between mind and body, becoming the father of the mind-body theory of interactionism, the so-called Cartesian dualism, a distinction that is still controversial.

There are many other examples of the creativity of the inner mind. The cognitive psychologist Roger Shepard in a state midway between sleep and wakefulness suddenly experienced a three-dimensional structure majestically rotating in space, ushering in a life-time of creative work on how the mind transforms mental images from one form to another. Perhaps one of the most spectacular revelations occurred with the writer Samuel Taylor Coleridge when visual images and words appeared before him in a dreamlike state (perhaps opium-induced), allowing him to write the first forty lines of the poem "Kubla Khan." His spontaneous genius is left to us in such unforgettable lines about the mythical Xanadu: "A savage place! as holy and enchanted as e'er beneath a waning moon was haunted by woman wailing for her demon-lover!" The delicacy of the images that he translated into words was shattered for all times by a knock on the door. "At this moment he was unfortunately called out by a person on business from Porlock," so said a friend.

Alfred Russell Wallace exhibited what appears to have been genetic knowledge when, in a fit of malarial fever, the principles of natural selection came to him in a flash. Deathly sick, he pulled himself to the table, writing the principles of evolution on paper before they could slip back into unconsciousness. Clearly he was prepared to understand those principles, having searched for the mechanisms of species formation for many years. Still, it took a fire in the brain to free the answer.

These are just a few examples, the emergence of preexisting knowledge into consciousness, stimulated by particular environments, drawn from deep within the mind—complete, novel, archetypical. Darwin and Wallace seemingly harbored the knowledge of evolution within their brains, knowledge which was elicited by the environments in which they worked and thought—the axioms of evolution in the hominid brain, waiting for the rational deductions to cascade into consciousness.

No one knows what principles lie within the unconscious mind. They are probably encoded in neural networks that process information according to the dictates of past evolutionary pressures, not exactly keys to the universe, but more like mental predispositions to view the world in certain ways. Sensory information probably combines with these predispositions, offering new ways of looking at the world—insights that transcend sensory information. Metaphorically, the release of genetic knowledge is like playing a concert harp—each string vibrating at a specific frequency with a touch. The frequency of each tone and the quality of the chords are brought into play by the fingers, but the fingers can only call upon the inherent structure and functions of the harp. The environment guides the mind but does not create it.

Constructing the World through the Senses

Not all science flows from the turbulence of the mind, coming to us fully formed, but is, instead, built piecemeal from the shards of the universe. Perhaps this is the most believable view of science, because it makes no claim about the hidden knowledge of the brain and is an enterprise open to everyone. The method can be traced to the English philosopher Francis Bacon, who more than any single person, led Europe out of the Middle Ages into the age of scientific enlightenment. Beginning with his *Essays*, first published in 1597, he supported the empirical method of scientific discovery. He certainly was not a proponent of the notion of built-in genetic knowledge.

The empirical method depends upon observation and measurement—a reliance on the sensory input to the mind. Bacon argued against excess generalization, mental biases, and grand deductions, supporting instead an inductive approach to knowledge based upon specifiable operations. Indeed, he believed that mental biases would have to be purged before pure scientific method could be successfully applied. The impediments to clear reasoning, he said, are the "Idols of the Mind," those mental biases that force an individual imprint on the world. For example the idols of the tribe and of the cave were the biases that stem from our human nature—in current terms the dogmatism of biology. Notice that these "idols" represent what we described earlier as genetic knowledge. Bacon argued that general conclusions only come after the elimination of "self" from the scientific equation and the systematic application of induction. The philosophy is Zen-like, in that the idea is to clear the mind of self-expression, inculcating instead the nature of the universe. In that fashion we become enlightened. Peter Urbach, a student of Francis Bacon, summarized the strategy this way: "The understanding is endowed by nature with an evil impulse to jump from particulars to the highest axioms (which is called First Principles). This impulse must be held in check; but generalizations lying close to the facts may first be made, then generalizations of a middle sort, and progress thus achieved up the successive rungs of a genuine ladder of the intellect." In short, we clear the mind, allow the information of the universe to flow in, finally bind the facts together in a comprehensible way. The method is induction.

Induction involves the stringing together of related events until a conclusion is reached. The operation of measurement literally defines the procedure and the type of outcome possible. For example, if the question is how fast does a microorganism spread within a population, the investigator focuses on a particular microorganism and samples a population over time. The operation is very specific to the conditions of the observations, and the outcome cannot be immediately generalized to a different population. Only later can the question be adapted to a different population. Generalizations come slowly, and only after the fact.

John Sturart Mill, extending Bacon's notion within a sociological context, asserted that deduction was powerless as a method of scientific discovery. Deduction begins with a premise—an assumption of fact—followed by detailing the specifics of that premise. The premise might be genetic knowledge, although it can also be knowledge derived from what has been learned. In any case, the problem with deduction is that it makes explicit only that which is already present in the premise. A rough example is this: a scientist posits that sexual reproduction creates the genetic variability in offspring to which microorganisms are not adapted. It follows from this premise that sexual reproduction should be found in species subject to high levels of invasion by microorganisms. This seems to be the case.

Mill argued that the conclusion is inherent in the original premise; one has merely collected evidence to support the assumption, hence nothing was gained by noting this correlation. In fact, he insisted, the premise biased the nature of our observations. The biggest crime of deduction is that one can *always* find something to support any premise, much like picking out passages from a book of aphorisms to support almost any assertion. As we shall see, however, deductions are important if the hypotheses that they generate can be challenged by an experimental or observational test. Deduction and induction must act together. Nevertheless, in the 1800's when thoughts of evolution were stirring, the inductive method was seen as the golden road toward truth.

Charles Darwin followed an inductive strategy, as we saw in chapter 2. Like Bacon and Mill he eschewed deductions and the testing of hypotheses, favoring the stockpiling of relevant information; he believed that the general principle of evolution would emerge from the many facts—the laying of brick upon brick until the church emerges. The inductive process actually may have slowed Darwin's progress toward the final solution of the speciation process. He might have deduced the principles of natural selection from intuition rather than data, as did Wallace. Reading his notes and autobiography, it seems that he had the notion of natural selection long before he was willing to commit to it. Always a cautious man, Darwin moved carefully with many facts toward the grand generalization of natural selection as the force for evolution. He approached the construction of theory slowly and gradually, in much the same way that he felt evolution occurred.

The philosophical impact of the inductive method was and is still substantial. It was embraced by entire philosophical movements, such as the *logical positivists*, who attempted to purge science of all deduction, mysticism, and subjectivity, substituting induction and the logic of reasoning. In one form or another, induction is still the path leading to new knowledge. All scientists and others striving for answers use inductive techniques. The powerful implication of the inductive method is that the true nature of the universe can be constructed in the mind from information flowing in through the senses. The late Frank Beach, perhaps the world's greatest endocrinological psychologist, once said that he was uncertain about the value of many deductive hypotheses, but he sure recognized a damn good brick when he saw it.

For the true inductionist *association of events*, rather than genetic knowledge, is the source of all knowledge. The mind becomes a blank slate, a *tabula rasa*, on which experience writes, so said the philosopher John Locke in his *Essay Concerning Human Understanding*, published in 1690. With its heavy emphasis on learning and the modification of the mind through experience, this view became the central theme of psychology, William James, the founder of American experimental psychology at the turn of this century, believed that infants come into the world with "a bloomin', buzzin', confusion," that is only harnessed through a lifetime of experience. The possibility for innate knowledge of our universe was discarded.

A Middle Ground

Thus, there are essentially two ways in which insights into the evolutionary process can occur. The first is by extracting knowledge built into the brain through eons of natural selection—the brain probing itself. Accordingly, when we face a problem we access the most appropriate genetic adaptation and apply it. There is no specific learning involved, although, like Newton, the brain may be prepared by experience to tap into relevant knowledge. The inborn premises we have about the world allow us to deduce consequences, permitting the construction of hypotheses that we can test through observation or experimentation. This is the type of knowledge that hits us fully formed, coming sometimes as if in a dream.

The second way in which insights are acquired is through sensory experience and learning. The method is strictly inductive, in that information is accessed from experience. The implications of the new data are then sought by looking for additional correlations with sensory events. In this way we string together related facts to arrive at a generalization. Whereas the first strategy is like an airplane flying into a new unexplored region, sometimes finding new fields, the second is like a passenger train moving systematically from station to station, the switches being thrown depending upon what went before.

Both strategies, deduction from natural knowledge, and induction from sensory experience, probably work together in bringing us closer to the truth, but neither is foolproof, completely understood, or free from controversy. As our story of humans unfolds, we will see that the primary method by which we understand ourselves and the environment is deductive, or at least our search begins that way. We seem to have intuitive knowledge about our own functions and our surroundings—internal visions of the DNA carried out of Africa. We use this knowledge to map out solutions to problems, some correct, some incorrect; we use it to categorize and evaluate the information gained from the environment.

In no way is the intuitive knowledge of our genes guaranteed to be correct; it is approximate knowledge that more or less reflects our evolved adaptations. This genetic knowledge was acquired under specific environmental demands, thus was more appropriate for solving problems hundreds of thousands of years ago than it is today. Nevertheless, it is the only fundamental knowledge we have, and the basis for viewing new information in our environment. Fortunately, deductive insights can be modified as we test them against current events.

It is in the testing of our intuitive knowledge that we apply the inductive method. We look at the world, in first measure, through the adaptations of the past. In second measure, we form hypotheses that can be tested empirically using induction: "If this is true, *then* that will also be true." It's a non-ending process of application of genetic knowledge, modified by facts.

The Resolution of Belief and Disbelief

Einstein saw no logical path leading to general laws. Theory, he said, cannot be fabricated from observation alone; it can only be invented. Thus, induction follows intuition, not the reverse. Like the molding of an amorphous piece of clay into a distinctive face, science proceeds from the ideas of the mind to observations of the environment—ideas first, logical deductions second, inductive hypothesis-testing third. Our question is how does this method allow us to verify evolutionary processes and move to new ideas?

The study of the evolution of behavior involves two levels of analysis, both of which can be subjected to the scientific method of induction. One level focuses on the understanding of *proximate causes* of behavior, those mechanisms that regulate the behavior of everyday life. They include neurophysiological processes, hormonal systems, learning strategies and abilities to react to ecological changes. Proximate causes of behavior are those that evolve to facilitate survival and reproduction.

At a deeper level are the evolutionary causes of behavior, the deep-structure events that shape the evolution of proximate mechanisms. These are the *distal causes* of behavior, the situations that determine who survives and reproduces. They include the ecological pressures that drive genetic and behavioral change—the great geological disruptions that initiate extinction and speciation, and the contingent factors that interrupt and guide the flow of evolution.

The great biologist Ernst Mayr made the clear distinction between proximate and distal mechanisms of behavior in reference to the migratory behavior of the North American warbler. This bird spends the reproductive season in the northern latitudes of North America, mating, nesting, and providing for young. It survives by eating insects. In the fall, when daylight begins to fade and the weather cools, the bird ceases reproduction, stores body fat, and begins to orient toward the south, using star patterns in the sky. Then one day a cold snap occurs and the bird migrates to lower latitudes.

The sense of this resides in knowing that the bird's behavior is regulated by insect density; it has evolved mechanisms and strategies to track insect density. When the insects of the north disappear, "thoughts" turn southward. The distal cause of its behaviors is the selection pressure of changing food supplies. The proximate cause of its behaviors are all of those hormonal, sensory, and motor mechanisms that insure that the bird tracks the seasonal variability of insects.

Distal and proximate causes are the bookends of reproductive success, bracing the history of life on one end and the contemporary strategies at the other. The distal causes of the evolution of complex brains among hominid species apparently involved under intense selection pressures to deal with variable environments. Increasing brain complexity, at the same time, offered the proximate strategies to cope with immediate uncertainties. One depends upon the other, encompassing the essential features of life.

The two levels of evolutionary analysis seem so different—distal causes referring to *why* things evolve, and proximate causes referring to *how* behaviors are regulated—that it is difficult to conceive of a scientific method common to them both. Yet there is one that not only transcends the levels of evolutionary study, but applies broadly to the investigation of everything from the elementary particles of the atom to the social behavior of humans. That strategy is called *strong inference,* a deductive/inductive strategy that had its origins with Francis Bacon. The first step is deductive, whereas subsequent steps are inductive. Here is how it works.

1.   A hypothesis is derived from an existing paradigm (theoretical deduction).
2.   Alternative hypotheses are devised that can be tested so that one or more can be excluded—a narrowing of possible answers.
3.   An experiment is carried out to get a clear result, one that has a qualitative result—a yes or no answer.
4.   The procedure is recycled as new answers are acquired and new hypotheses specified. It's like climbing a tree and choosing directions at each fork—the answer from each test suggests the direction of the next step

The power of strong inference rests on two primary criteria. The first is that the questions are framed so that the answers are clearly "yes" or "no"— "if yes, ask this question; if no, ask that question." The process deliberately pits alternative hypotheses against each other so that a qualitative answer will emerge—a yes or no. Quantification of relations normally follows the application of strong inference; it is not the essential first step. The second criterion is that the hypotheses are framed so that they can be disproved. Without possible disproof, one can never know what is true.

John Platt, the biophysicist who outlined and named the method of strong inference, was adamant on the above two criteria. With regard to "yes" and "no" answers he said: "Many—perhaps most—of the great issues of science are qualitative, not quantitative, even in physics and chemistry. Equations and measurements are useful when and only when they are related to proof; but proof or disproof comes first and is in fact strongest when it is absolutely convincing without any measurement." Stipulating our questions so that qualitative results follow, focuses our attention on what's important and how best critical hypotheses can be tested. It also poises us clearly for the next step in the investigation.

The second criterion of strong inference is that all questions asked have a possibility of being falsified. This seems strange, but is essential if a hypothesis is to gain any strength. The more critical challenges a hypothesis meets without defeat, the more likely that the hypothesis is true. In any case, if it is easily defeated, one shouldn't hold on to it. Clearly the criterion of falsifiability means that we must be able to abandon ideas and techniques when they are demonstrated to be insufficient. This strategy certainly tests the strength of the scientific soul, as it is never easy to give up on cherished ideas.

If a hypothesis cannot be falsified by any conceivable circumstances, it is of limited value. It is either too sweeping, accounting for everything in its path, or it fails to suggest alternative hypotheses that might offer even better proofs of its validity. The scientific philosopher Karl Popper who first detailed the importance of falsifiability likened this approach to the process of natural selection: "According to my proposal, what characterizes the empirical method is its manner of exposing to falsification, in every conceivable way, the system to be tested. Its aim is not to save the lives of untenable systems but, on the contrary, to select the one which is by comparison the fittest, by exposing them all to the fiercest struggle for survival." The entire scientific enterprise is much like natural selection, with differential survival of ideas from the vastness of variable thoughts.

Let's briefly follow a problem from the deductive phase through the steps leading to hypothesis testing and falsification. For example, it is generally believed that neurological activity of the central nervous system accounts for consciousness. We start with that premise—a notion of science dealing with brain function—and move toward testing the notion. Our major deduction is that brain structures that evolved recently, being associated with homind evolution, would contribute to the psychological impression of consciousness. In particular, the frontal areas of the brain could be involved, as they are known to be related to complex problem solving; they are not directly involved in sensory processing. So, we have a testable hypothesis, where the answer could be "yes" or "no." The next step is to test the hypothesis. We go about it in two ways. In the first, we look for changes in consciousness associated with naturally occurring brain damage. In the second, we record brain activity in subjects under various conditions of consciousness—sleeping, waking, attending to the environment, and so on.

Assuming that both approaches give us evidence to support the hypothesis, we can now advance our questions one more step by hypothesizing that other brain areas would not contribute as strongly to consciousness. Again, we have a testable notion that will lead to a "yes" or "no" conclusion. Each time we acquire evidence to support or disconfirm one conclusion we automatically set the stage for the next step. In this scheme, for example, we may find that other areas of the brain also contribute to consciousness, in which case our first narrow hypothesis must be rejected and replaced by another that takes into account the interaction between brain regions. And so it goes, until we reach a level of specification that gives us a satisfying level of explanation.

The system outlined above is a common method by which evolutionary hypotheses are tested. It begins with deductions—guesses, really—about how the world operates, derived usually from a common paradigm. A paradigm is simply a theory that guides the business of science. From there it proceeds to a phase of testing where alternative hypotheses are played against each other, and where qualitative answers can be obtained by observation or experiment. Whatever the answer, new hypotheses are formed and the procedure is reiterated. Hypothesis testing and the inductive strategies are those that have supported science from the time of Bacon. They are what John Platt called strong inference and what the philosopher Thomas Kuhn called *normal science*—the puzzle solving in all scientific endeavors.

Faithfully following strong inference can lead to findings that can't be accounted for by the paradigm giving them life. Theories not only generate supporting data; they often lead to data that contradict the theories. According to Kuhn, when anomalous findings pop up in a number of different laboratories, and when they can no longer be ignored or swept under the theoretical rug, they put a strain on the original notions and cause a shift in the paradigm. This is the historical process that led to the substitution of the idea of natural selection for supernatural creationism. When a new paradigm is accepted it reigns supreme and is used to generate the hypotheses that are again tested using strong inference. Paradigms bend, shift, and change. Slowly they become more informative as their hypotheses generate more and more answers. Eventually nature turns over its secrets.

Bet on the Come

Historically the human struggle with life was philosophical—the conflict that stirred the Greeks to create art and government, the Romans to build aqueducts and great empires, Shakespeare to probe the heart. As then, we wrestle with the world to find the character of our lives, and deduce our heading.

The nature of our struggle changed as the theory of evolution unfolded. For many, as science grew in strength, existential problems about God and creation lost their compulsion. With that paradigm shift came a certain hardness of attitude—not arrogance of certainty, but a determination to reduce the complex to the simple and accept the mechanistic nature of man. The Nobel winner Steven Weinberg skips the beauty of modern science altogether, saying simply that, "The reductionist worldview *is* chilling and impersonal. It has to be accepted as it is, not because we like it, but because that is the way the world works."

The only possible reason science is the warp and weft of our culture is that it works; it brings us nearer to our origin, illuminating many of the bumps and swirls of our universe. In an incidental way it accounts for our demands for comforts and our ambivalent tastes for destruction. Science feeds our desires for comfort and command. But the technological offspring of science are of little consequence next to our enriched understanding of ourselves—the elementary particles that make up all things, the double helical strands of DNA that shape our minds and bodies, the evolutionary principles that spun our lives from a primitive cell to self-reflection. These are the true accomplishments of science—the diggings of life that separate us from the pits of ignorance.

Paradoxically, the ice core of science is a center of great beauty. We sense it in the cobweby relations between structures and functions, and in the simplicity of explanations. Beauty is even a part of the process of discovery, beginning with an idea and the testing of hypotheses, leading to a new way of thinking.

Godlike Beauty

The certainty of scientific laws depends on its complete abstract generality. When we assert that the sexual differentiation of male mammals occurs because of the secretion of steroids from the gonads, we are not referring to a particular mechanism in a specified species at a designated time. We are asserting a generalization that extends beyond the individual mammal, place or time, and is always true. The assertion is abstract and general because of its independence from the particular case.

Scientific law that comes from generalization is the rocky beach on which all idealism founders: the relations between mammalian gonads, steroids, and sexual differentiation are fixed in one way or another, not because of idiosyncratic belief systems, but *because it is so*—because physiological reality is built that way. It's a hard, cold reality, yes, but still one with beauty.

There are patterns of life, as with the hormonal system, that when understood, fit together harmoniously—a biological fashioning of beauty, David bursting forth from the marble—the harmony of the universe expressed exquisitely. Inevitably, beauty becomes the hallmark of truth, a relation that the poet Keats knew well: "Beauty is truth, truth is beauty—that is all ye know on earth, and all ye need to know." Beauty becomes the first criterion of truth. If the pattern of discovery is ugly, chances are that it's wrong. Beauty need not be simple, but often is, especially in the basic sciences. The famous physicist Werner Heisenberg expressed this idea in a conversation with Albert Einstein: "If nature leads us to mathematical forms of great simplicity and beauty—by forms I am referring to coherent systems of hypothesis, axioms, etc.—to forms that no one has previously encountered, we cannot help thinking that they are "true," that they reveal a genuine feature of nature...You must have felt this too: The almost frightening simplicity and wholeness of the relationships which nature suddenly spreads out before us and for which none of us was in the least prepared." *Putchritudo splendor veritatis*—Beauty is the splendor of truth. *Simplex sigillum veri*—The simple is the seal of truth.

Beauty and simplicity are certainly properties of fundamental building blocks of life, such as elementary particles, the nucleotide bases of DNA, or the neurons—properties that are discovered by reducing the complex to its individual parts. But beauty and simplicity also flow from unity, coherence, and harmony. Some of the most beautiful scientific laws refer to emergent features—composed systems, not decomposed parts. The cell, in its intricate complexity, emerged from independent constituents, and acquired a new level of beauty and simplicity. In many of these matters, more is different, and the whole is greater and more beautiful than its parts.

The emergent qualities acquire the beauty and simplicity of self-organizing systems, those systems that flow together because of inevitable relationships between molecules. Like undulating and symmetrical traces of movement cut from water by a speedboat, structures and functions of organisms combine to upstage their individuality and propel the individual to new heights of organization. In hindsight the new organization flows naturally from its parts, though it can rarely be anticipated. Intelligence is an example of self-organized qualities of neural elements, manifested during development, evolved during the last four million years. Its properties could never have been anticipated.

The implications for the biology of humans are profound. Undoubtedly, the form of the final theory of man will depend on the simple beauty of emergent principles. Individual genes shape behavior, but they have no direct representation in behavior; there are no invariant relations between individual genes and the behaviors that they influence. Rather, genes participate in self-organized functions that are simple in conformation, beautiful in expression, functional in design, and adaptive in character.

Reproduction, in particular, expresses itself through the beauty and simplicity of organized behaviors. Mating dances, songs and sensory-motor displays comprise the aesthetics of reproduction—complex in their organization and compelling and simple in their expression. Individual genetic units do contribute to the whole, but the true beauty lies in the unified mechanization of processes whose roots go deep into our evolutionary history and project ourselves into future generations.

Human behaviors, even the most uncomplimentary, express that same beauty and organization of emergent qualities. Reducing the behaviors to their simplest parts will tell us a great deal about their physiological mechanisms, the damn good bricks of nature, but much of the beauty and functional significance can be seen only in the unity of their being.

We have barely touched on the importance of emergent qualities of human behavior, but ultimately they may prove to be the keystones of novel characteristics. Genes often influence characteristics of behavior, but the grand designs of human qualities—astonishing abilities, extreme personalities, raw courage, and new behaviors—often come unannounced, unclearly tied to specific genes or environments, rare and nonheritable. We may grant natural selection the final *arbiter* of survival and reproduction, but the *creation* of novelty may be more punctuational in nature and less predictable from ancestral DNA. Genes often come together in unusual combinations, forming new traits and new potentials, often unfolding during early development or expressed under unusual environmental conditions. From this comes the Einsteins of the world, the grand insights that overturn paradigms, the extraordinary flowering of novel traits, the exaggerated levels of leadership, and the incomprehensible depths of criminal behavior. The unpredictability of emergent traits is what limits our understanding of human behavior and which suggests that the constraints of evolution are looser than classical scientific investigations lead us to believe. These mysteries remain, but suggest that we have yet to explore the limits of biological creation.

References

Cited in Chapter 7

Boring, E.G. (1950). *A History of Experimental Psychology*. New York: Appleton-Century-Crofts, Inc.

Chandrasekhar, S. (1987). *Truth and Beauty*. Chicago: The University of Chicago Press.

Hovis, R.C. and Kragh, H. (1993). "P.A.M. Dirac and the Beauty of Physics." *Scientific American*, May, 104-9.

Kuhn, T.S. (1962). *The Structure of Scientific Revolutions*. Chicago: The University of Chicago Press.

Mayr, E. (1988). *Toward a New Philosophy of Biology*. Cambridge, MA: Harvard University Press.

Medawar, P. (1984). *The Limits of Science*. Oxford: Oxford University Press.

Platt, J. (1964). "Strong Inference." *Science*, 146, 347-53.

Popper, K.R. (1959). *The Logic of Scientific Discovery*. New York: Harper and Row, Publishers.

Singer, C. (1959). *A History of Scientific Ideas*. New York: Dorset Press.

Weinberg, S. (1992). *Dreams of a Final Theory*. New York: Pantheon Books.

General References

Ayala, F.J. and Dobzhansky, T. (1974). *Studies in the Philosophy of Biology*. Berkeley: University of California Press.

Lakoff, G. and Johnson, M. (1980). *Metaphors We Live By*. Chicago: University of Chicago Press.

Medawar, P.B. (1990). *The Threat and the Glory*. New York: HarperCollins.

Reese, W.L. (1980). *Dictionary of Philosophy and Religion*. Atlantic Highlands, NJ: Humanities Press.

Young, R.M. (1993). "Darwin's Metaphor and the Philosophy of Science." *Science as Culture*, 3, 375-403.

8

Rules of the Mind

The remarkable thing about the human mind is its
range of limitations.

—Celia Green

In mind and body we are what we were, carrying the genetic knowledge of past struggles, applying the rules of yesterday to problems of today. It is nothing less than strange that we listen to our inner self and hear the person who roamed over the African savannah.

Adaptations for survival and reproduction were selected into our genotype during the past three to four million years. It was then that our destiny unfolded, that the imperatives of survival laid waste to the unsuccessful and set the range of possibilities for the survivors. Clearly, the present and the future are made of the stuff of the past, inspiring Confucius, long before Darwin and Wallace, to write: "Study the past if you would divine the future."

It could not be otherwise, for we were long ago selected to do certain things—to be certain things. As a result, our brain is filled with rules—genetic software or operations—for dealing with contingencies of the past. Our psyche is not built for the present. It resonates to the vibrations of 200,000 generations ago.

Constraints and Brain Power

Every physical and biological machine has its functional limits. Take your car, for instance. It can move you from zero to sixty miles per hour in seconds, carry you in rain or shine from Fairbanks, Alaska to Mexico City. It keeps you comfortable, and even entertained. Versatile, indeed.

But, your car does have many limitations. It requires gasoline and oil, general maintenance, and occasional repairs. It was built to do only certain things. It won't move at 150 miles per hour; nor will it climb mountains or swim seas. And, of course, it can't grind your corn or baby-sit your child. Sure, it wasn't built specifically to travel from Fairbanks to Mexico City—it can go other places—but it was built to move over roads—period. It does what it was built to do, and little more.

The human brain is much the same. It processes sensory information, stores memories, and does such things as choose mates. It allows you to move about, communicate with others, and search within yourself for a higher purpose. But even your brain is limited. It cannot process ultra-violet light, live without oxygen or glucose, remember the details of your youth, speak three languages simultaneously, or exempt you from stress, emotional reactions, or superstitions. It does well what it was constructed to do, using rules built into the brain through trial and tribulation. But, just like your car, it does only certain things.

Looked at from this perspective, our problem is to figure out what the rules of the mind are, how they once facilitated survival and reproduction, and how they operate in today's frenetic world. What was the brain built to do; what are its limitations? We will explore our mental capabilities in this chapter and the next three. There is an urgency in this endeavor, for it may be true, as H.G. Wells prophesied, "One thousand years more. That's all *Homo sapiens* has before him." We seem to be racing ahead of the wind, twisting toward an evolutionary disaster. Perhaps by finding our biological center we can avert humankind's greatest catastrophe—extinction.

The Basic Rules of the Mind

We appear to approach the solution of problems by applying mental rules: "If this occurs, then do that; if that occurs then do this." We have hundreds of these rules, ready for application whatever the problem we face. Rules are varied, part of our mental system of logic, and often very simple in nature. No one has yet figured out what each of these rules is for; the closest is probably in our understanding of language. Whatever they are, the messages they give allow us to "mind the store," and build new libraries of knowledge. We may learn about these rules, but we don't seem to learn the rules themselves. Where did these rules originate and how do they work? As a rough measure, rules of the mind have the following features:

1. Rules are mental adaptations to previous contingencies. They are "wired" into the central nervous system through natural selection. These operative mechanisms are parts of what we have referred to as genetic knowledge.
2. Rules are evolutionary representations of environmental events. They are cognitive (mental) impressions and emotional predispositions for action, mirroring the contingencies of history that made a difference for survival and reproduction.
3. Rules are triggered into action by specific environmental conditions. The rules are the genetic harp strings upon which the environment plays.
4. Rules are typical of our species, reflecting selection pressures for adaptations to the environment. They may show individual variations in expression, but the variations are always variations around a species-typical theme. In effect, they are instincts of the mind, showing low variability in their expression.
5. Rules develop early in life, providing exact control over the environment without the need for specific learning. Learning does not ordinarily build new rules; it instead selects out appropriate ones.
6. Rules determine how we respond emotionally to our environment, causing us to seek out or construct environments that match the rules.

Rules come about because of environmental contingencies that force mental adaptations, such as needs to define space and time, categorize objects, recognize cause and effect relations, and respond adequately to danger. Rules are built into the brain that defeat predators, cope with weather and climate, find shelter and food, communicate with group members, facilitate mate selection, and rear offspring. The contingencies are demanding; the rules are the organism's responses.

The Children of Evolution

How can we be sure that our cognitive attributes—our mental guidelines—are caused by genetic influences? They could be learned, after all, giving us the latitude to respond to any environment regardless of our genotype. Learning plays a role, but apparently does not build new and complex rules—learning is mainly a device for accessing and modifying those rules of the brain that already exist. This is why we said in the last chapter that genetic knowledge is plucked from the mind by environmental stimulation, mental concentration and general preparedness to express that knowledge. The fundamental knowledge is built through processes of natural selection, to be called forth by appropriate stimuli. We may be able to learn how to elicit rules of the mind, and we may even be able to modify some, but we cannot learn new rules. Rules are primitive structures of the brain.

From the earliest time infants can be tested, they demonstrate that the mind is differentiated in function, long before imitation and specific instruction can play a significant role. Infants prefer mid-level visual complexity, preferring pictures of human faces and some checkerboards as soon as they are able to orient visually. Surprisingly, two-month-old infants show a preference for the faces of women whom adults have rated as attractive over the faces of women considered to be less attractive. Six-week-old infants can detect a simple change in geometric angle (| to \), but do not respond to a more complicated change in orientation (< to >). By fourteen weeks infants are aware of the change in orientation as well as angle. Apparently their cognitive abilities change from processing simple stimuli at a younger age to more global stimuli at an older age. Infants seem prepared to respond to features in their environment most closely related to survival. Older infants form hierarchies of mental processing, organizing whole patterns, and secondarily noting details. These are maturational changes that do not require specific environments, as long as the surrounding environment is not inhibiting.

Complex categories of stimulus objects are spontaneously forged between seven and ten months of age. For instance, infants of about this age successfully group trucks, stuffed animals, pictures of faces, or line drawings. Even as early as one or two months, they can distinguish among triangles, squares, crosses, and circles, and can categorize simple features, such as color or size. And again as they mature, their conceptual abilities become more complex. The point is that infants move through the developmental process *without specific training*. Development is a natural unfolding of instinctual qualities, expressing variations as the environment interacts with maturational events. Infants and children use the variation within their environment to call on innate rules, or to build these rules according to features of their environment. They seem prepared to express rules or to learn them readily and spontaneously.

Similarly, infants come equipped with notions that objects are solid and that one thing causes another. If a vertical screen, hinged at the table top, stops its movement when it encounters a ball that the infant knows is behind the screen but cannot see, the infant shows no particular reaction—all is as it should be. But if the ball is secretly removed and the screen folds flat against the table, that is, appears to move *through* the ball, the infant registers surprise—all is not as it should be. Or, take another example. If an infant is presented with a box that seems to block the view of the middle section of a tube, but when removed reveals two small sections of tube, with the middle section gone, the infant is surprised. In other words, the first visual impression of two solid objects—a box blocking the view of a single tube—is violated by the demonstration that the tube is really in two parts.

Infants also show surprise when cause and effect relations are violated, or when visual and auditory signals are not in natural harmony. If a moving toy car hits another car, sending it rolling, the infant does not react. But, if the situation is rigged so that the first car stops short of the second car, yet the second car moves, the infant is surprised. Laws of physical motion and inertia have been violated. Similarly, if infants are shown a movie of a car driving toward and then away from them, the infants prefer an associated sound that first becomes louder and then softer, rather than the reverse (the Doppler effect). Shown two pictures, one which has two objects and another which has three objects, they prefer the picture with two objects when they hear two drum beats, and prefer the picture with three objects when they hear three drum beats. Amazingly, infants just old enough to attend to stimuli spend more time looking at an object they had previously mouthed but not seen. The infant is able to analogize objects perceived with one sensory modality with objects perceived with another sensory modality, a kind of early metaphorical skill. Things are obviously supposed to happen only in certain ways, with fundamental syndetic relations between classes of stimuli. Cause and effect relations are difficult concepts, yet they occur naturally in infants as young as three months of age.

Many experiments verify the inherent complexity of cognitive processes. The rules of the mind—genetic knowledge—develop early, all in predictable ways, uniform for the species, and without exposure to specific environments. Infants discriminate patterns, show early preferences for certain levels of stimulus complexity, categorize objects according to multiple attributes, understand concepts of solidarity, and know about cause and effect relations. Infants come equipped with premises, assumptions, and hypotheses. They test deductions, and are puzzled if their mental concepts do not conform to the real world. The knowledge is primarily inborn, strongly suggesting its importance in providing individuals with early control over the environment.

The study of infant development gives an uncluttered view of cognitive attributes shaped by natural selection. Developmental changes, moving from simple to complex, from singular to hierarchical, may even provide us with a glimpse of the evolutionary steps leading to complex rules of the mind—the simple probably evolved first, followed by the complex. Finally, the study of infant development shows us what little power specific training has in the construction of mental rules. General environmental stimuli are needed for any behavior to be displayed, and rules can be applied in different ways and in different combinations, but specific training is unnecessary for the maturation of much of the human potential. Parents would be astounded if they realized how much their infants know and how little they teach them.

Language and Mental Rules

Language is the premier example of the evolution of specific mental tools. For all people, speaking any language, the mode of language acquisition and its formal structure are the same. The neurobiologist Michael Gazzaniga points out, "no population has ever lacked a language. There are no reports of a newly discovered band of hunter-gathers who lacked language, only to suddenly learn it from their more technically advanced neighbors." Language is a species-specific form of communication that comes forth inevitably, given a half-way decent environment. The linguist Steven Pinker notes that "Language is not a cultural artifact that we learn the way we learn to tell time or how the federal government works. Instead, it is a distinct piece of the biological makeup of our brains. Language is a complex specialized skill, which develops in the child spontaneously, without conscious effort or formal instruction, is deployed without awareness of its underlying logic, is qualitatively the same in every individual, and is distinct from more general abilities to process information or behave intelligently."

Newborn infants prefer to hear speech in the right ear. These sounds are channeled to the left hemisphere of the brain where language comprehension and language production are most often located, suggesting that the rudimentary aspects of speech are already specified at birth.

These same infants prefer to hear the sounds of heartbeats in their left ear, hence in their right brain hemisphere. This part of the brain deals more often with emotional stimuli, and could, therefore, be important in infant-mother bonding.

Language is learned early in life, typically beginning around 18 months of age. Already by seventy-two hours after birth the vocal interactions between mothers and infants are "conversational," that is, the duration and kind of infant vocalization depend on the presence or absence of the mother's voice. Babbling appears sometime between four and ten months of age. Around ten to fourteen months infants begin to reduce the range of sounds to those that are typical of their particular language. At birth they can perceive every sound used in any language, even though they don't understand any of it. The first words generally occur between ten and seventeen months. By three years children are speaking their native language, whatever that happens to be. New words are added to the vocabulary at the rate of about ten per day. Moreover, the sequence of acquisition, the maturation and use of grammatical rules, is all the same—everywhere—all without formal instruction.

The most important function of language is to communicate "predicate-referent" relations that denote who did what to whom. In the sentence, "Bill ate the red apple that I bought," the verb "ate" is the predicate and it has two "referents"—the eater, Bill, and the object, the apple. The referents must be kept separate and aligned so that the order of action is evident. All languages make the necessary distinctions so that a sensible meaning is conveyed. To this end, questions are never posed by reversing the order of words. In no language is a middle word removed and placed at the end of a sentence, and so forth.

Language grows naturally, demonstrating a critical period for learning, a universal grammatical structuring, a common rhythm of articulation, and a natural use of sounds that can be heard. Moreover, there is specificity of brain function underlying language. The function is lateralized in the brain, with the left hemisphere usually controlling both the motor and conceptual functions of language. Brain dysfunctions that affect language, called *aphasias*, show us the specificity with which language is programed into the brain. One can lose the ability to speak without losing comprehension, or the reverse. One can speak and comprehend, but the messages fail to remain in memory. Or, verbal comprehension may be lost, leaving written language intact. The nature of this communication system is very exact and specified early in infant development. We may learn a particular language, and add vocabulary at incredible rates, but how we learn and package the language is always the same. Language, in short, appears to be an instinct.

The brain categorizes language in different ways: a major way is according to parts of speech. Plural words and verbs seem to be categorized separately from other words. In one family the members fail to make plurals of words. The grandfather, father and sons all suffer from the deficit, yet the rest of the language process is unaffected. Perhaps a single gene mutation is at fault. The brain even seems to sort words according to the type of language used. For example, George Ojemann of the University of Washington stimulated areas of the cortex of a patient who was bilingual in English and Greek. Stimulation at certain places temporarily prevented the patient from using English words but not Greek ones. At other sites of the cortex the reverse was true.

In another case a stroke resulted in a woman's inability to write verbs, even though she can speak and understand verbs. In another stroke victim with damage in the area of the brain controlling speech there was the opposite problem: the affected woman can write verbs but has difficulties understanding them. Language abilities obviously have specific representation in the central nervous system—modules of form and function.

The lexical knowledge of the brain is not categorized by sounds. As a demonstration, the woman who had difficulty speaking verbs had no trouble when the same words were spoken as nouns. When asked to read, "Don't crack the nuts in here," in which "crack" is used as a verb, she had difficulty saying "crack." But when the same word with the same sound was used as a noun, as in the sentence, "There's a crack in the mirror," she had no difficulty saying "crack." Apparently words are categorized as parts of speech and not according to sound. Words stored for speaking are categorized separately from those stored for writing. Identical words are stored differently, depending on how they are used in sentences.

Studies of other aphasics indicate that the brain also sorts words according to meaning. One stroke victim correctly identified a picture of a lion as a "four-legged animal with a monstrous head which growls," but could not correctly label inanimate objects. When shown a picture of a desk drawer, he called it a "serving device" and wrote "vase."

Another patient had a similar problem, having no difficulty naming animals and vegetables, but incorrectly identifying inanimate objects. Other patients have problems naming large outdoor objects, such as bridges and airplanes, while still others have trouble naming indoor objects, such as lamps and chairs. The brain is very precise and specific in how language is categorized, building a complicated dictionary based on parts of speech, word meaning, object size, and animate and inanimate objects. Undoubtedly other categories will be discovered showing how the brain stores other features of language.

Ordinarily it is the left hemisphere of the brain that carries the details of language, whereas the right hemisphere is dominant for holistic and spatial perceptions and emotions. This distinction is known as laterality of function. The nature of brain laterality is more complex that we can discuss here; the point here is that the two hemispheres are differentiated in their communication functions apparently from birth. The kind of language built into the brain, as with English or German, is obviously learned, but the rules for acquisition and readout of information, and where in the brain they are stored, are as natural as having two arms, two legs, and one big brain.

Taken as a whole, the evidence strikingly verifies the linguist Noam Chomsky's ideas that the major qualities of language are innate. "Language is a uniquely human characteristic. Each person has programmed into his genes a faculty called Universal Grammar." Language is not the *sine qua non* of learning capabilities, as we once thought. Instead, it taps into a critical network of mental rules that evolved for purposes of survival and reproduction. Just how such a complex system evolved, and why in only humans, are open questions, although linguists have their ideas. Psychologists are mapping out an evolutionary continuum of communication in primates. They would probably agree that language is uniquely human, yet they would argue that the precursors of language are evident in earlier primate species. They note that right- or left-handedness as well as language are lateralized in the brain. In their view brain laterality of handedness associated with clinging and reaching in other primates facilitates the evolution of laterality in human language. Once an organism has brain laterality for one complex trait, it may be easier to capitalize on that laterality for the development of another. We will encounter more of these ideas in later chapters. The trend for complex functions is oftentimes toward specificity and brain laterality.

Just how this evolutionary process occurred is uncertain, but the idea offers an initial paradigm for the understanding of the evolution of man's most complex mental functions.

Cognitive Rules

Cognition is not the same as language, if by cognition we mean mental representation and understanding of the outer world. An infant may have understanding but no language; some aphasics may have language but no understanding. Cognition is a brain process—a set of mental rules used for comprehending the self and the outer world. If you show a person two pictures in rapid sequence, the first showing a person standing naturally with feet together, the second showing that same person standing with feet crossed, the perception of movement is induced, just as in a short movie. If the pictures are shown back and forth at a speed corresponding to natural limb movement, the illusion is that one foot moves *around* the other. But if the speed of picture presentation is sped up, the illusion is that one foot moves *through* the other. In other words, the brain infers normal body movement if the speed of apparent movement is similar to natural movement. If the timing is different than normal for that movement, then a quite different perception emerges. The brain has "preferred" representations of movement patterns, specified in part by the speed of their execution.

Moreover, the brain fills in missing details of the environment and makes rapid judgments as to meaning. The foot does not have to show the intermediate points of traversal if the starting and ending positions are natural and the timing is correct. Apparently evolution has provided perceptual solutions to problems where incomplete data are available— certainly an adaptation of great importance when decisions must be made in the absence of complete information.

The rules of cognition develop in children in a predictable sequence, again largely independent of specific training. Sensory and motor activities appear around two to four months of age; symbolism of objects, events, and people appears at about eighteen to twenty-four months; simple relations among objects and events are formed around four to five years; abstract thinking begins about ten to twelve years; and abstract generalizations about the world occur around fourteen to sixteen years. The important questions are how does the brain accomplish the cognitive demands placed on it, and what are the adaptive purposes of these rules?

The Nature of Cognitive Rules

The start of the scientific study of natural rules of the mind began several decades ago with the so-called Gestalt psychologists, investigators who were interested in the inherent qualities of perception. At the time of their prominence in the 1930s they were not interested in genetic influences on perception, nor did they link their discoveries to evolutionary theory. Nevertheless, they laid the groundwork for studying natural units of behavior that we now recognize as rules of the mind. Kurt Koffka, a leading proponent of the Gestalt movement, said that events run toward minimum complexity, meaning that individuals automatically organize perceptions so that they show regularity, symmetry, and simplicity. Data arranged in a crude circle are seen as a circle; incomplete triangles are seen as completed triangles; two lights flashing milliseconds apart are seen to move in a specific direction. The brain makes up for missing data and, in effect, reaches reasonable decisions as to what reality is like. The major perceptual qualities of the world automatically "pop out" of the environment. The brain does not "show its work" in arriving at decisions; it gives us the functional endproduct in a flash of insight, much like a computer hides its work but gives us the final product on the monitor.

Brain organizing devices used to integrate complex stimuli need not involve great neurological complexity, as might be expected. Individual cells in the visual cortex of the brain are programmed to respond to vertical or horizontal lines, movement, and other complex configurations. In fact, neurophysiological investigations of monkeys indicate that single neurons located in the lower regions of the temporal lobes of the brain, just above the ears on the sides of the head, respond to visual stimuli from body parts, such as hands or faces. Because some of these cells respond to whole faces they have been called "grandmother cells." These same cells fail to respond to other stimuli in the environment. That is, gestalt perceptions are mediated by individual cells in the central nervous system, something that would be expected in frogs, but not in primates, especially humans.

The procedure for studying selective attention of single cells in primates is worth noting. Tiny electrical recording electrodes are implanted into single cells in the lateral areas of the temporal lobes of the brain. The animals are then shown complex visual stimuli on a television screen. The natural electrical activity of these cells is recorded simultaneously. Thus, one can see a correlation between the presentation of an object on the television screen and the responsiveness of particular cells. A cell that is responsive to an object will show an increase in electrical activity.

Some of the neurons in the temporal area of the primate brain are highly reactive to pictures of monkey hands or human faces. Depending on the particular cell, when a hand or a face is presented, the electrical output of the cell increases dramatically. The responsiveness of these cells is highly specific, in that if the orientation of the hand changes, or if the hand is distorted, or if parts of the face are interchanged, such as eyes for mouth, the cells cease to respond. The brain takes longer to respond neurophysiologically when presented with inverted pictures of faces. It appears that the brain is prepared to react quickly to stimuli associated with important features of the body occurring in natural ways.

Facial recognition among humans may operate similarly. Recognition of faces is quite specific. If, for example, pictures of familiar faces are presented up-side-down the latency to recognize those faces is increased. This does not seem to be true for nonbiologically relevant pictures of houses, scenes, and airplanes. Moreover, individuals with specific brain damage lose the ability to recognize faces, a condition referred to as *prosopagnosia*. The posterior right side of the brain is typically involved. People with lesions in this area perceive variations between faces, as with color of eyes and size of the nose, but do not recognize the individuals, even when they are relatives or close friends. They can literally pass by a relative or a spouse without recognition. Much like the monkeys who have "grandmother" cells for recognizing others, people have brain mechanisms for identifying faces. Remember, too, how young infants prefer images of faces, a complex Gestalt perception independent of specific learning. As with language, the brain apparently has a large dictionary of perceptual templates, each of which can be matched with an actual feature in the outer environment. The organizing principles are highly specific, reflecting perceptual adaptations buried deep in the evolutionary history of primates.

The Salvation of "Just-About" Knowing

The brain runs to holistic pictures of the world, reflecting a high correspondence of brain processes to the individual's surroundings. The Gestalt psychologists referred to an organizing principle, the Law of Pragnanz, to explain how the brain operates on perceptual material. The neurophysiologist of today is still trying to decipher the brain's organizational principles, and is, in fact, making progress. The hope, of course, is that the Law of Pragnanz will be translated eventually into neurological activity and the distal influences of natural selection.

One can imagine the value of perceptual organizing principles in hunter-gatherer societies. Suppose a person gets only a glimpse of an antelope, but the form is vague and indistinct. The brain takes the information it has, organizes the data according to mental rules, and makes its best guess—antelope. Certainly the process is subject to errors, but the errors may be of less consequence than if the brain saw only a sketchy number of visual points and remained silent as to its possible form—a good guess is better than no guess at all. There is often salvation in "just-about knowing."

The brain not only organizes perceptual stimuli, it can manipulate those stimuli to see how they would look at different angles or at a different times. For example, one can visualize a common object such as a cat and then mentally rotate that object to a new position. Try it. Potentially, this ability is of tremendous significance in understanding different arrangements of stimuli and anticipating future events. The brain accomplishes these rotations in specific ways, the rotations often being nonintuitive. Thus an object may not be mentally rotated along a path of the shortest distance, but will move complexly to its new position, perhaps with an unexpected twist or arc. Apparently the brain is constrained in terms of its spatial abilities—it does it according to the way the brain evolved and developed.

The constraints of the mental processes are noted in other ways. Females and males show differences in the ability to mentally rotate objects, with males showing greater capacity. Some object rotations are difficult or impossible for either sex, especially if the visualized object in an arbitrary stimulus that has no natural ecological validity—that is, if the object is not typically represented in the environment. Ink-drawing outlines of countries are difficult to visualize in new orientations.

We take this to mean that the types of things that we can successfully rotate are those that in fact hominids constantly encountered and had to deal with in practical ways.

Like objects, time can be manipulated in similar ways. One can categorize time into different lengths, speed it up or slow it down, or anticipate how things will be after differing lengths of time. One can, for example, estimate with considerable accuracy the time needed to intercept a moving animal across the savannah. The trick is to estimate speed over distance for two objects moving at different speeds along converging tracts, a geometric problem of some significance for modern-day computers, yet one we have been able to do intuitively for millions of years. Our time sense places us in a dynamic stream of mental activity, with a past, a present, and a future.

A new technique is being developed that promises to change our way of thinking about mental space and time. It will also tell us much more about how language is organized in the brain. The technique is called fast magnetic resonance imaging, or fast MRI. Fast MRI is a brain imaging technique that measures neurological activity in specific areas of the brain. It's success depends upon the fact that activated brain cells use more oxygen than nonactivated cells. The change in oxygen utilization is detected electronically, giving a visual image of an active brain.

A person asked to imagine a face and move imaginary objects through space shows a kaleidoscopic cascade of neurological activity in different areas of the brain, depending on what is imagined. When asked to generate spoken verbs, a small area in the left frontal cortex, in back of the left eyeball, becomes active. When individuals listen passively to the presentation of names of animals, a name of a potentially dangerous animal activates more of the brain than one that is not dangerous, as if the entire brain is alerted to possible danger. Fast MRI promises to revolutionize our understanding of where rules of the mind are located in the brain and how they operate.

The Emotional Rules of the Mind

The innate qualities of emotional reactions become evident when genetic defects eliminate certain rule-making capacities. In some forms of infantile and adult autism the individual cannot understand how to interact socially with others. Emotional affect is lacking, as well as the ability to put oneself in another's place. Certain rules are simply missing. So it is with psychopathic individuals who lack traits of empathy or self-understanding.

The emotional rules of the mind develop in infants. Emotional expression matures in conjunction with the infant's need to interact with its mother and the environment. At birth the infant reacts with diffuse, general excitement, showing increased heart rate, quickened breathing, and random movements. At about three weeks this general arousal becomes more specified, with general arousal becoming distress. At three months the individual shows aggression. Around six to seven months the infant shows fear of strangers, and by fifteen to eighteen months the psychological demons of jealousy and envy unfold. Crying occurs earlier than smiling, probably because it better serves early survival.

Emotions wash over the entire world of cognition. Pure reasoning may be a fiction, as all acts are colored by emotions—indeed, reason may be driven by emotion. They remain clutched together in death-defying acts of survival and reproduction. In a general sense, emotions are organized physiological and behavioral reactions that evolved to facilitate survival and reproduction. The neurobiologist Robert Ornstein said it well: "Mental processes, I have come to believe, are not organized around thought or reason but around emotional ideas: how we feel we want something to be. These may center on getting rich, getting married, getting angry, getting even, getting ahead. These inner goals drive us. They suggest to the person where he's going, what she should do, what should happen."

As with language, emotion is located in discrete areas of the brain. Anger and sadness involve the right hemisphere of the brain more than the left hemisphere, appearing as early as a few weeks of age. Adults seem to express emotions more on the left side of the face, probably because that side of the face is controlled by the right hemisphere. We are also better at interpreting another's emotions by observing the left side of the face.

The right hemisphere not only controls our deep and darker emotions, but it also controls large motor movements, such as running. This relation allows us to move quickly at the first sign of danger. The left hemisphere controls both the more positive emotions and the smaller muscles of the body, allowing us to approach and manipulate things that please us. Apparently our motor movements and our emotional reactions are synchronized and regulated by the two halves of the brain. The linkage is clearly rational even if the outcome is not.

Emotional reactions have their antecedents in vertebrate evolution, which is easily seen with laboratory primate studies, where stimulation or lesioning of subcortical brain structures either intensify or repress emotional reactivity. Limbic structures of the brain, in particular, appear to organize and regulate emotional tone, areas that still contribute to human emotionality. Sometimes unusual electrical activity can be detected from these brain sites during emotional outbursts, as was noted in one woman who was institutionalized because she had suddenly stabbed a stranger with a pair of scissors. In this woman increased electrical activity in the limbic region was associated with attacks on medical attendants and was often associated with destruction of property. Other brain sites have been implicated as well. The basic design of the vertebrate nervous system is still evident in the human brain, as are many of its behaviors, suggesting that the human rules of the mind, unique as they seem, have their beginnings elsewhere in evolutionary history.

Bold New World

Evolutionists are following the path of the neurophysiologists who are demonstrating that the brain is a collection of specific structures and functions. What once looked like general processes of the brain is rapidly being decomposed into specific attributes. General intelligence as an inclusive mechanism is probably disappearing, for example, replaced by evidence for regional specificity of sensory input, information storage of different kinds, activation of specific rules of the mind, and chemical modulation of neural activity. Likewise, perceptual and emotional qualities are divisible into specifiable tissue areas and neural pathways. Descriptions of the brain are beginning to look like detailed topographical maps.

Evolution of behavior is also becoming more refined. Rules of the mind are seen as more and more specific, reflecting the laser quality of natural selection. In fact, it is difficult to envisage a general environment that would select for a general trait. What would be a general environment? The environment is always specific, and so, therefore, are the rules of the mind. Moreover, it is becoming clear that that the evolutionary history of humans is linked tightly to the characteristics of the brain.

For every behavioral rule that evolved there was a specific representation of that rule in the brain—one is a reflection of the other. It therefore makes sense that both the proximate and ultimate levels of explanation be spelled out in fine detail.

It is in the development of the brain and behavior that we are likely to find the principles that were selected over millions of years to regulate our behavior. We won't find them in the brain as little compartments of facts and guidelines—there are no objects or pictures in the mind—but they will be represented by specificity of brain function, neural networks, and variations in neurological patterns of activity. As we dissect behavior and brain functions into smaller and smaller units, and begin to understand their interactions, we will see the expression of our evolutionary past.

In none of this are we bound to feel comfortable, for details steal the spontaneity of life and tear at the fabric of our dogma. In John 8:32 we are promised that the truth shall make us free, but Omar Khayyám might agree that it is a strange kind of freedom when the truth discloses our limitations, for as Aeschylus long ago lamented in his *Agamemnon*, "Things are where things are, and as fate has willed. So shall they be fulfilled." Bittersweet.

References

Cited in Chapter 8

Chomsky, N. (1988). *Language and Problems of Knowledge: The Managua Lectures.* Cambridge, MA: MIT Press.

Cohen, L.B. (1991). "Infant Attention: An information Processing Approach." In M.J. Salomon Weiss and P.R. Zelazo (eds.), *Newborn Attention: Biological Constraints and the Influence of Experience.* Norwood, NJ: Ablex Publishing Corporation, 1-21.

Gazzaniga, M.S. (1992). *Nature's Mind.* New York: Basic Books.

Jackendoff, R. (1994). *Patterns in the Mind.* New York: Basic Books.

Koffka, K. (1935). *Principles of Gestalt Psychology.* New York: Harcourt, Brace and Company.

Lieberman, P. (1991). *Uniquely Human.* Cambridge, MA: Harvard University Press.

Ornstein, R. (1991). *Evolution of Consciousness.* New York: Touchstone.

Perrett, D.I. and Rolls, E.T. (1981). "Neural Mechanisms Underlying the Visual Analysis of Faces." In J-P. Ewert, Capranica, R.R., and Ingle, D.J. (eds.), *Advances in Vertebrate Neuroethology.* New York: Plenum Press, 543-66.

Phelps, M.T. and Roberts, W.A. (1994). "Memory for Pictures of Upright and Inverted Primate Faces in Humans (*Homo Sapiens*), Squirrel Monkeys (*Saimiri Sciureus*), and Pigeon (*Columba Livia*)." *Journal of Comparative Psychology*, 1994, 108, 114-25.

Pinker, S. (1994). *The Language Instinct.* New York: William Morrow and Company.
Raichle, M.E. (1994). "Visualizing the Mind." *Scientific American,* 270, 58–64.
Pringer, S.P. and Deutsch, G. (1989). *Left Brain, Right Brain* (3rd Ed.). New York: W.H. Freeman and Company.

General References

Lefrancois, G.R. (1995). *Of Children* (8th Ed.) Belmont, CA: Wadsworth Publishing Company.
Lieberman, D.A.(YEAR?). *Learning: Behavior and Cognition.* Belmont, CA: Wadsworth Publishing Company.
Povinelli, D.J. (1993). "Reconstructing the Evolution of Mind." *American Psychologist,* 48, 493–509.

III

Winds of Being

The Moving Finger writes; and, having writ,
Moves on: nor all thy Piety nor Wit
  Shall lure it back to cancel half a Line,
Nor all thy Tears wash out a Word of it.

                              —Omar Khayyám

Genes stir in the winds of time, spinning
imperatives into the fabric of life.

9

The Taming of the Irrational Mind

*The pendulum of the mind oscillates between sense
and nonsense, not between right and wrong.*

—Carl Gustav Jung

Thus far we have portrayed the mind as rational, attempting to match mental images to reality. And it is rational, to a degree. But there is another side to the mental world—a world that is by nature irrational. Consider how common irrationality is. Many people believe in astrology, demons, gods, and magic. They are superstitious, carry good luck charms, wear amulets, believe in special numbers, gaze into crystals, and profess out-of-body experiences, near-death illusions, and reincarnation. Some people compulsively count objects, do things only at special times, employ incantations, and read minds. Irrationality is part of their everyday lives. It is our life as well. Appealing to the irrational mind is also a multibillion dollar industry.

But are these irrational beliefs and behaviors actually without cause and adaptive function?

Strangely, evolutionary scientists have relatively little to say about irrationality, almost denying that it exists, as they strive to be rational about their own activities. There is something inherently irrational about any activity, an irrationality that we all try to tame. Scientists, in particular, have made significant advances in the understanding of behavior by deliberately focusing on those behaviors and mechanisms that are rational. The study of animal and human learning, so prominent within psychology, is an example. Learning depends on the logic of the mind—the identification of the relationships between stimuli and responses. In general experimental methods have been devised so that they exclude irrational hypotheses and outcomes. Maybe this is why we know so little of our irrational self. But irrationality is a property of all thought processes, deserving more of our attention. We may find that irrational rules of the mind are important adaptations, on par in significance with the rational rules.

The Foundations of Fictitious Beliefs

The Russian investigator Stubbotsky believes that "We are captured within the limits of subjectivity, and cannot leave its bounds." Magical thoughts pervade our thinking. According to Stubbotsky there are two physical regularities that are constantly violated by magical thought: (1) one object cannot be transformed into another, and (2) it is impossible to exert a force upon an object directly through thought. Most people in one way or another believe that both magical possibilities can happen.

A child shown a "magic box" that transforms stamps into rings may first look for a rational solution by examining the box, but failing that, will agree that the transformation is magic. If the investigator gives the child an incantation meant to make the transformation possible, and then leaves the room, the child will soon invoke the incantation. Having accepted the magical possibility, the child is surprised and upset when the incantation doesn't work.

The irrational behavior is not limited to children. Adults invoke magical incantations under similar conditions, showing frustration when the magic words fail. Watch people at a magic show and you will witness both the delight in the unexpected and the borderline experience of magical belief. Our inner world is a mixture of reality testing and irrational hyperbole. In ourselves we engage in magical thinking all the time, and rarely give it a second thought. It was recently pointed out that 25 percent of the population of the United States believes that their presence at a sporting event affects the outcome of the contest. Magical thinking is our mental crutch when we can find no rational explanation for our surroundings or when we have no control over the outcome.

Another strange thing about human behavior is that we tend to believe the first thing we see or hear. How could this be an adaptation? The judgment of information as true is especially strong if the new material is never analyzed or contradicted. According to the psychologist

Dan Gilbert, "People are credulous creatures who find it very easy to believe and very difficult to doubt. In fact, believing is so easy, and perhaps inevitable, that it may be more like involuntary comprehension than it is like rational assessment."

Why would natural selection build an uncritical brain, where the first thing we see or hear is accepted unreservedly? That can be hazardous in today's world of low-grade information. But during the evolution of hominids it might have made sense. For example, facing a charging tiger required an instant acceptance of the danger—an uncritical reaction of running. There was no time to evaluate the validity of the data or consider alternatives: "Is it really a tiger, or is it merely a shadow from a cloud flashing across the savannah? Do the colors validate a tiger? If your mate yells 'run,' should you first try to analyze the problem?" Zap, too late—excessive philosophical debate.

Of course, one may react uncritically, only to find that the reaction is inappropriate, making the behavior seem irrational, but during hominid evolution the consequence of disbelief and inaction could have been fatal. It's a matter of costs and benefits. Right or wrong, the first impression must drive the behavior. Only later does it make sense to reconsider. "Wow, it wasn't a tiger at all, but simply a gazelle breaking through the brush. Well, anyway, I'm still here." Survival goes before reason.

Our brain is constructed to react to the most recent information, picking the most intense, louder, bigger, riper, more delicious, more frightening alternative. We select out a few signals and then overemphasize their importance. We ignore other information and concentrate on the immediate. It is the "immediate" that demands and gets our attention. We are prepared to react quickly to novel stimuli, and eat our mistakes if necessary. Better to jump first and avoid greater risks later.

Even when we think about it, there is something peculiar about our assessment of environmental risks. Risks that are imposed by others or by the environment loom larger than those that are accepted voluntarily. For example, we react negatively to the low risk of consuming milk stimulated by growth hormone given to cows, yet happily accept the risks of skiing and driving cars which are thousands of times more dangerous. Risks that we seemingly have control over are less objectionable. Dangers associated with natural events are more acceptable for similar reasons—nothing much can be done about them. But similar dangers from technology are rejected as too high. Thus, living in the California quake zones is tolerated more than less likely radiation leaks from nuclear plants. Health officials are often perplexed by inconsistencies. For example, 84 percent of the hikers at parks in New Jersey knew about the precautions necessary to avoid ticks carrying Lyme disease, yet only 43 percent took the precautions. The same is true with the use of condoms for protection against the HIV virus: we know the risks, but often choose to ignore them.

Just how we see the environment may depend upon immediate demands as well as actual risks encountered during our evolutionary history. The irrational in the eyes of some could have facilitated survival on the savannah. In any case, it is probably not the result of a crazed central nervous system or an overstressed brain.

Even sexual fetishes that seem to have zero adaptive significance may not be entirely irrational. Sexual fetishes are defined as those things that evoke excessive reverence or obsessive devotion. They are generally symbols that seem only remotely connected to normal sex and reproduction. Objects that are soft, furry, lacy, pastel-colored (e.g., panties, stockings and garters) are often fetishes. In addition, hard objects such as high-heeled women's shoes, leather goods, gloves, and other items are fetishes, especially related to sadomasochistic fantasies.

Fetishes are used to arouse sexual feelings as part of lovemaking and as substitutes for sexual intercourse. They are often used in masturbation. Learning theorist Michael Domjan suggests that the symbolism associated with fetishes is not distinct from our evolutionary past. He may be correct. First, males display fetishes more commonly than females, in keeping with males' broader interest in sexual cues. Second, fetishes are limited to clothing and objects naturally associated with the touching or stroking of body parts. Gloves, for instance, are associated with hand-holding, touching, stroking, and fondling. Spiked heels elevate the buttock in a provocative way. Furry and soft objects may simulate touching and stroking of hair and skin. Of course, objects like lace panties, garter belts, and silk hose have clear relations to sexually provocative body parts and sexual stimulation. The sexual grip of these objects on imagination may denote a natural interest in objects that lead to sexual arousal and reproduction. Shakespeare had it right again when he described fetishes as, "The oldest sins the newest kind of ways."

Death, Irrationality, and Cognitive Psychology

Existentially, irrational beliefs seem to be attempts to understand the incomprehensible, and are used primarily when rational beliefs are assailable. Suppose you are awakened in the middle of the night by a noise in the kitchen. Several explanations jump into your mind—all of them bad. You move cautiously to the kitchen to investigate, only to find a spoon on the floor and your cat on the counter. Fine, you have a fair interpretation of the incident, your fear subsides and you go back to bed. Now, it is possible that the noise that woke you *wasn't* the spoon falling to the floor, but as this explanation is probable, you look no further—that is that. The point is that we grasp at rational explanations, and are willing to go with these unless they are challenged. If we find nothing that makes sense, then we are likely to mystify the events. Similarly, when the child investigates the "magic box" he or she is looking for a rational explanation of the material transformation. It is only because the rational explanations fail that the magical incantations take on significance.

As science provides mechanistic answers to life's puzzles, rational explanations supersede irrational appeals. Death, for example, has long been explained by irrational chance, devilish influences, and supernatural interventions. More recently death has been explained by specific diseases and accidents: these matters are expressed in probabilities that we can all understand. Death, in effect, has been reinterpreted and built into mortality tables of probabilities. Your chances of dying of a heart attack are one in three, not a comforting thought, but the odds on your making it to next year is about 118 to 1, a thought that inspires confidence.

It was the demographer William Farr in 1843 who first applied the concepts of probability to patterns of death, thus forever changing our perception of causal features of death. A modern version of a mortality table is seen here. Somehow, distributing death across conditions and assigning probabilities to each, makes death less capricious and less terrifying.

The more specific and mechanistic the explanations for death, the less need there is for the application of irrational rules of the mind. The language of probability, tied to a rationalization of events and diseases, functions to quell our irrational thoughts about our own mortality.

Perhaps other strange functions of the mind will become understandable as we consider the biological bases for the traits. Irrational cogni-

TABLE 9.1
Age-Adjusted Death Rates by Selected Causes: 1970–1989
(Rates per 100,000 population)

CAUSE OF DEATH	1970	1980	1989	CAUSE OF DEATH	1970	1980	1989
All causes	714.3	595.8	523.0	Pneumonia and influenza	22.1	12.9	13.7
				Pneumonia	20.8	12.4	13.4
Major cardiovascular diseases	340.1	256.0	194.2	Influenza	1.3	0.5	0.3
Diseases of heart	253.6	202.0	155.9				
Rheumatic fever and rheumatic heart disease [1]	6.3	2.6	1.5	Diabetes mellitus	14.1	10.1	11.5
Hypertensive heart disease [1]	4.9	6.8	5.3	Suicide	11.8	11.4	11.3
Ischemic heart disease	228.1	149.8	105.1	Chronic liver disease and cirrhosis	14.7	12.2	8.9
Other diseases of endocardium	2.3	2.0	2.4	Nephritis, nephrotic syndrome, and nephrosis	3.5	4.5	4.4
All other forms of heart disease	12.0	40.8	41.5	Homicide and legal intervention	9.1	10.8	9.4
Hypertension	2.9	2.0	1.8				
Cerebrovascular diseases	66.3	40.8	28.0	Septicemia	1.4	2.6	4.1
Atherosclerosis	8.4	5.7	2.9	Other infective and parasitic diseases	2.8	1.8	10.8
Other	8.8	5.5	5.4	Benign neoplasms [5]	2.0	2.0	1.7
				Ulcer of stomach and duodenum	3.2	1.7	1.3
Malignancies [2]	129.9	132.8	133.0				
Of respiratory and intrathoracic organs	28.4	36.4	40.3	Hernia of abdominal cavity and intestinal obstruction [6]	2.6	1.4	1.1
Of digestive organs and peritoneum	35.2	33.0	30.0	Anemias	1.3	0.9	0.9
Of genital organs	15.6	13.6	13.1	Cholelithiasis and other disorders of gallbladder	1.3	0.8	0.6
Of breast	12.6	12.5	12.5	Nutritional deficiencies	0.8	0.5	0.5
Of urinary organs	5.7	5.2	5.0	Infections of kidney	2.8	0.7	0.3
Leukemia	5.8	5.4	4.9	Tuberculosis	2.2	0.6	0.6
				Meningitis	0.8	0.6	0.4
Accidents and adverse effects	53.7	42.3	33.8	Viral hepatitis	0.5	0.3	0.5
Motor vehicle	27.4	22.9	18.9	Acute bronchitis and bronchiolitis	0.5	0.2	0.1
All other	26.3	19.5	14.9	Hyperplasia of prostate	0.6	0.2	0.1
Chronic obstructive pulmonary diseases and allied conditions [3]	11.6	15.9	19.4	Symptoms, signs, and ill-defined conditions	10.4	9.8	8.1
Bronchitis, chronic and unspecified	2.1	1.0	0.8				
Emphysema	8.4	4.0	3.7	All other causes	44.0	36.8	38.6
Asthma	1.0	1.0	1.4				
Other	(4)	9.9	13.5				

[1] With or without renal disease. [2] Includes other types of malignancies not shown separately. [3] Prior to 1980, data are shown for bronchitis, emphysema, and asthma. [4] Included in "all other causes." Comparable data not available separately. [5] Includes neoplasms of unspecified nature; beginning 1980 also includes carcinoma in situ. [6] Without mention of hernia.

Source: U.S. National Center for Health Statistics

tion must be as adaptive as rational cognition, otherwise it would have been selected out of our species. Perhaps false beliefs and strange associations are better than no beliefs or associations at all, giving peace of mind and hope for the extraordinary, and driving us to concentrate on issues most closely related to gene replication.

We have touched only the surface of cognitive processes. Research is revealing how perceptions are transformed into images and how images guide our behavior. Moreover, as with language, we are beginning to understand where in the brain these events occur. The mental rules of the brain—rational or irrational, reasoned or emotional—are universal and occur without special training. Learning may sharpen or redirect these rules, but learning doesn't create them. They occur in accord with needs to understand the external world and our inner being. They evolve and develop, springing forth in great complexity. Whatever form the "final theory" of cognition takes, it will have to account for man's irrationality as well as his rationality. Magical and emotional thinking lurks in the background of all that we do.

Gamblers and the Laws of Ignorance

The hypothesis running throughout this chapter is that people believe strange things to the degree that they lack information—irrationality melts before the heat of knowledge. But what does one say when it is discovered that many individuals shun knowledge, preferring ignorance as a steady diet?

What people don't know is truly astonishing. Two surveys on scientific knowledge are revealing, one conducted with 1,255 adults by the New York American Museum of Natural History, and another with over 3,000 adults carried out by the Chicago Academy of Science. Here are just some of the findings.

When people were asked if they were interested in botany, 39 percent of the respondents said yes, but 77 percent were interested in plants and trees. Similarly, only 30 percent expressed an interest in paleontology, but 48 percent were interested in fossils. Fifty-three percent of those surveyed were interested in geology, but only 42 percent were interested in rocks and minerals. Fully 65 percent didn't know how many planets were in our solar system, and 46 percent did not believe that humans evolved from earlier species. Only 20 percent knew that DNA was involved in genetic inheritance; about 10 percent knew that bacteria were tiny organisms; and barely 2 percent understood that science involved the testing of hypotheses.

More depressing, perhaps, are the growing indications that people know fewer basic facts than they did decades ago. When data are corrected for age differences, it is clear that the level of knowledge for vocabulary has been slipping since the turn of the century. Individuals born around 1900 could define on the average 6.47 of the following ten words: space, broaden, emanate, edible, animosity, pact, cloistered, caprice, accustom, and allusion. Contrast that to the average score of 5.24 for individuals born between 1961 and 1965. The drop may not seem great, but it does represent about a 19 percent change. Moreover, the depression of vocabulary knowledge is probably a reflection of a growing disregard for all kinds of knowledge.

It's not flattering to think that our grandparents were expected to know more than we. In Jersey City High School in 1885 students were expected to be able to answer the following questions: (1) Write a homogeneous quadrinomial of the third degree. Express the cube root of that 10ax in two ways; (2) Divide the difference between 37 hundredths and 95 thousandths by 25 hundred thousands and express the result in words; (3) Name four principal ranges of mountains in Asia, three in Europe and three in Africa; (4) Write a sentence containing a noun used as an attribute, a verb in the perfect tense potential mood, and a proper adjective; and (5) Name four Spanish explorers and state what induced them to come to America. Most of us would fail miserably on such a test.

Table 9.2 indicates the dates and discoverers of some events about which few people have any knowledge. Genetic knowledge may run deep, but certainly not historical knowledge.

Not surprisingly, most people admit that their primary source of knowledge is television, with newspapers, doctors, and magazines trailing in that order. While television viewers may not watch educational programs, it is still amazing that so many commonly accepted facts are either unknown or totally rejected. Most people are operating in a highly complex society with a level of knowledge that was current decades and even centuries ago. They choose ignorance and irrational explanations about themselves and their environment. Why?

For one thing, it takes time and energy to acquire knowledge, so why bother? Moreover, information digested may never be of value, so again

TABLE 9.2
Scientific Facts and Level of Knowledge

Who Discovered What	Majority of People's Level of Knowledge
The last and ninth planet of our solar system, Pluto, was discovered by C.W. Tombaugh	Pre 1930
Louis Pasteur isolated and later described bacteria	Pre 1857
Severo Ochoa and Arthur Kornberg synthesized DNA and RNA	Pre 1959
John Watson, Francis Crick and Maurice Wilkin received the Nobel Prize for describing the structure of DNA	Pre 1962
Charles Darwin and Alfred Russel Wallace published the theory of natural selection	Pre 1858
Sir Francis Bacon described the testing of hypotheses in the book *Historia Naturalis et Experimentalis*	Pre 1622

why bother? At a deeper level of explanation, there is rarely any punishment for irrational beliefs—survival and reproduction ride the rails of instinct, depending little on the validity of external knowledge. For instance, what are the negative consequences for believing in astrology, extrasensory perception, reincarnation, psychic pronouncements, or rabbit feet? None. Indeed, the beliefs hardly ever interfere with the biological stream of life, and can be comforting. In the words of the English poet W.H. Auden, "Happy the hare at morning, for she cannot read the hunter's waking thoughts." Forego knowledge and inherit ignorance; embrace ignorance and don happiness.

Even when knowledge could be valuable, some desist. The gambler is a prime example. The worst game in the gambling casino is the slot machines, returning only about 85 percent of the player's investment. People generally know that, yet the "slots" are the most popular game in the casino. For roulette the house advantage is about 5.26 percent; the pass line ("7" or "11") in craps gives the house a 1.4 percent advantage; baccarat favors the house between 1.06 percent and 1.24 percent; and blackjack provides the house at least a 1 percent advantage over the very best players and from 6 percent to 16 percent advantage against the average player. For a particular game individuals can tell you the approximate level of risk, as in advising others about the probability of success, but for themselves they are overconfident about their chances at the same game. Despite the common knowledge that the house with its near-infinite bankroll will always win over a player with a small bankroll, the games go on.

There is no evidence that the gambler is any less rational than the average person. Thus, the persistence of the gambler, in spite of bad odds and heavy losses, is well worth studying. The gambler in his endeavor to win (or lose) is fairly representative of many others who persist at all sorts of things when the odds are against them. As we consider the gambler, keep in mind that the strategies employed are common to everyday life.

People who lose money at gambling have generally lost money in the past. They see others win; therefore, they believe that they can too, if only they keep at it. This does not mean that they are compulsive gamblers, but only that they are willing to rationalize their losses and try again. There is some kind of positive inertia for persevering. Many gamblers have acquired the belief that they will succeed despite seemingly convincing evidence to the contrary. They continue to bet, confident that success is just around the corner.

According to psychological investigations, successful outcomes tend to be readily accepted as reflecting one's gaming skills, or the workability of some system. The result is that successes reinforce one's expectations more than losses decrease them. It is not the case that the gambler ignores his failures. Rather, the gambler rehearses the losses of the past, concluding that external factors account for the failures, as with fluke events someone sitting down and getting the good cards that he should have had, "fixed" races, and so on. The gambler is doubly reinforced by believing in his own abilities and discounting evidence for failures.

In one experiment of one season's betting behavior on NFL football games by thirty individuals, it was found that gamblers spent nearly twice as much time rehashing and rationalizing losses than they did wins. Losses were essentially "undone" with comments such as, "If Dickerson had not been taken out of the game during the last five minutes, they would have won." Wins, of course, were not "undone," as the outcome was entirely favorable. Instead, the reasons for wins were sometimes exaggerated: "Farley played his best game, as I knew he would." This study leaves little doubt as to how gamblers discount and sustain strings of losses while magnifying wins as inevitable.

The gambler's asymmetric explanation of losses and wins accounts for persistence. After all, the losses are "near wins" and the wins are the result of sound analyses. This trait is coupled with another, in which the gambler often cites some point in time when walking away would have resulted in a win: "I just knew I should have quit when I was ahead." Since there is often such a time during a string of losses and wins, the gambler can point to that moment of winning, ignoring the fact that the ultimate outcome was unfavorable.

Another odd characteristic of the gambler is his willingness to occasionally break a habit of betting to try a novel strategy, even during a string of wins. At the roulette table, for example, gamblers doing well by playing simply red or black, with nearly a one to one chance of winning, will occasionally reach out with their chips and play a number that has a one to thirty-five possibility of winning. This "breaking of risk symmetry" is not well understood, although it does suggest that gamblers carry "floating probabilities" in their minds, acknowledging that persistence is not always the way to a big payoff.

The above account of the gambler's psychology has been placed within a theory called *prospect theory*. Psychologists D. Kahneman and A. Tversky indicate in effect that the gambler decides what to do in a risk situation by mentally calculating a probability of outcome and a "value" for that outcome. In other words, the gambler assesses the probability of success and places a bet according to the probability of winning, discounted by the value of a winning outcome. Since the probability of an outcome is generally fixed and knowable, as with the toss of a coin, it is the *value* of the outcome that most often determines the betting strategy. Take the case where a gambler has "sunk" a lot of money into a series of bets, each consisting of an equal probability of winning. With each loss the importance of winning and recouping losses increase, biasing the gambler toward bigger bets and higher risks. There are few gamblers who can cut their losses and walk out of the valley of defeat if there is the possibility of regaining the advantage. Values ride the wave of emotions; probabilities fix the outcome.

According to the late B.F. Skinner, an expert on probabilities of reinforcement, the gambler is faced with an even greater threat, responding irrationally to a lopsided schedule of reinforcement. Consider the usual payoff matrix of a slot machine. There is a series of zero returns for coins deposited, interspersed with a few low payoff results and a rare high payoff. This reinforcement structure is known as a variable-ratio (VR) schedule of reinforcement—a series of losses all culminating in a positive reinforcement. It is the occasional and unpredictable payoff that keeps the gambler feeding the slot machines. Surprisingly, the VR schedule of reinforcement results in more persistence than a fixed-interval (FI) schedule that delivers the same amount of reinforcement, but distributed at predictably regular intervals. A schedule of loss, loss, *win*, loss, loss, loss, loss, *win, win,* is more alluring than one of loss, loss, *win*, loss, loss, *win*, loss, loss, *win*.

Speculatively, the VR schedule of reinforcement, with its unpredictable but delightful surprises, contributes to the compulsive optimism of gamblers. The VR schedule plays on the general optimism that success is always possible. In another context Winston Churchill spoke of the power of optimism in driving behavior: "Like the Mississippi, it just keeps rolling along. Let it roll. Let it roll on full flood, inexorable, irresistible, benignant, to broader lands and better days." Yes, but we still must remember that in a game of poker the odds of drawing to a full house with the first five cards is 693 to 1.

What does the behavior of the gambler teach us about the evolution of behavior? Perhaps a great deal, showing us that the apparent irrational strategies observed in the casino and elsewhere are the same that possessed adaptive qualities on the African savannah. There the environment was filled with uncertainties and VR schedules of reinforcement. Food was unpredictably distributed over large areas; infant mortality was high; ectoparasites and endoparasites were annoying and potentially dangerous; and love and reproduction were problematical. Given the uncertainty of critical events, *H. sapiens* had to gamble. Food gathers had to take chances on the possible toxicity of plants; individuals tried to anticipate changes in weather; hunters pursued wary game; and men and women took chances in romance and investing in offspring.

The question is, what are the best strategies for meeting and mastering a quirky environment? Well, the answer seems to fall into seven categories: (1) do what has worked before; (2) do what seems successful with others; (3) persist at things that occasionally pay off, even though the schedule of reinforcement is generally VR; (4) analyze failures to better understand what went wrong; (5) hold to a high level of optimism by exaggerating successes and discounting losses; (6) bet more on an outcome if losses are heavy but successes possible; and (7) occasionally switch strategies in an attempt to maximize reinforcement. These are exactly the things that casino gamblers do; these are exactly the things that most of us do at home, at work or on the highway. The difference is that during evolution hominids probably had better betting odds than the gambler currently does, accounting for the misapplication of perfectly good survival strategies.

Speculation aside, it is clear that gambling behavior in *H. sapiens* is just as much a part of the organism as perception, cognition, and language. To jump to the conclusion that gambling is irrational is to ignore its species-specificity and its potential use under conditions of uncertainty. Gambling could only be irrational if our evolutionary history were seamless and invariant, without requirements for risk taking. It wasn't then; it isn't now.

The Natural Rhythm of the Universe

Sociobiologist Edward O. Wilson and his colleague Stephen Kellert, have argued that we derive comfort or discomfort from certain environments that were important to us in our evolutionary history. Feelings may seem irrational, but they may express something deep within our being. We feel comfortable in an environment that contains a few trees, short grasses, and a flowing stream. This is an environment that once provided a place to live, free of spying predators. Oppositely, we shrink from images of snakes, spiders, many insects, and large predatory animals—organisms that once were of great danger to us. The general principle operating here is that we seek out and enjoy environments that reflect safety and security, what Wilson calls a *biophilic* reaction, while avoiding and disliking environments that were previously harmful, a *biophobic* response:

> Biophilia, if it exists, and I believe it exists, is the innately emotional affiliation of human beings to other living organisms. Innate means hereditary and hence part of ultimate human nature. Biophilia, like other patterns of complex behavior, is likely to be mediated by rules of prepared and counterprepared learning—the tendency to learn or to resist learning certain responses as opposed to others. From the scant evidence concerning its nature, biophilia is not a single instinct but a complex of learning rules that can be teased apart and analyzed individually. The feelings molded by the learning rules fall along several emotional spectra: from attraction to aversion, from awe to indifference, from peacefulness to fear-driven anxiety. (Wilson 1993)

The drives toward or away from some environments may not be overwhelming, but simply represents a lingering preparedness to learn certain relations and feel certain emotions about things that were part of our early history.

These behavioral and emotional propensities apply to many dimensions of our environment, yet are surprisingly specific. They help explain why we collect plants, yearn for open spaces, find flowers beautiful, and feel secure with pets. Plants and flowers are correlated with food and protection, open spaces afford views of potential opportunities and dangers, and pets offer personal protection and friendship. Our positive feeling about these things may be a reflection of a deeper and older affinity to our environment. Links to the past also help explain our fear of darkness, our dread of certain animals, and our distress in confining areas or of high places.

These are broad rules of the mind that bias our behaviors and emotions. They are as much instinctive as the kneejerk reflex, having a long history of natural selection for adaptation. They operate universally at the species level and also apply to variations among individuals. Historically it was Carl Gustav Jung, the psychoanalyst and student of Sigmund Freud, who first gave meaning to our universal motivations. According to his thinking humans possess a hereditary fabric, cut from the cloth of evolution, driving our behavior and symbolism. It is part of our common humanness, the "collective unconscious" of our history. Wilson and Kellert refer to the same universal motivational system, but now frame it in terms of natural selection.

Our affinity for the past suggests a genetic link between the results of natural selection and our common interests and concerns. But the link may also involve genetic variation across individuals. People who differ genetically may also show mental rules that correlate with their particular genotypes. For example, there is growing evidence that individuals seek out specific environments compatible with their genetic makeup. Bright people gravitate toward universities and occupations that challenge the intellect. Similarly, individuals with mechanical abilities often find themselves as engineers, auto mechanics or watchmakers. Then there is an entire range of artistic and athletic abilities that sort individuals into separate groups and occupations—painters, musicians, dancers, basketball players. Self-sorting is probably important for maximizing feelings of contentment and for increasing efficiency of performance.

Ultimately self-sorting, with it's winning profile, is critical for successful reproduction.

Psychologist Thomas Bouchard has the strongest evidence for the power of genes in the self-sorting process. Over a number of years he and his colleagues have tracked down genetically identical twin pairs who had been separated from birth, or near birth, and who had no idea that they were twins. If genetic sorting is occurring, both of the twins should show similar preferences for things and people in their environment. When Bouchard united the twins, sometimes as late as fifty years of age, they showed an amazing degree of similarity in psychological as well as physical features. This, despite the fact that they were reared in much different environments, and had many years to acquire unique experiences.

The twins often sought out similar environments, occupations and hobbies, even though they differed in childhood and adult experiences. Bouchard has found twins that have the same occupations, such as fire chiefs, smoke the same Turkish cigarettes, prefer the same kind of music, wear the same kind of jewelry, prefer the same sports, and acquire the same degree of education. Rosen, reviewing these astounding findings, refers to one striking case: "There were the Jim twins of Ohio. That they had the same name was obviously a fluke. But the Jims also smoked the same brand of cigarettes, drove the same kind of car, held the same jobs, and engaged in the same hobby: woodworking. In fact, they had built identical white wood benches around trees in their yards. The Jims were both nervous nail-biters and both developed migraines at the same age."

There is the obvious problem of how to interpret the range of similarities within twin pairs, as some of the similarities could be expected by chance. In favor of the genetic hypothesis is that the frequency of similarities is greater among twins than people chosen at random, or any siblings reared together. Moreover, quantitative measures of personality attributes, IQ, personal values, and a host of related traits, also show the same high degree of similarity between members of identical twin pairs separated since birth.

The genetic influence on these traits appears to be much stronger than the unique environmental experiences. It is not that twins share genes for Turkish cigarettes, or for building white wood benches, but they do have genetic inclinations that move them in similar directions so that it is more likely than by chance that they will hit upon the same behaviors. If each twin finally discovers something that makes him or her feel more comfortable, the chances are higher than average that the outcome will be similar in the other twin. The inclinations to do certain things and prefer certain environments are fine-grained examples of biophilia and biophobia. These astounding results with identical twins suggest that we have underestimated the power of the gene and overestimated the power of the environment in shaping individual behavior.

Individuals match their genetic programs to their environment in still another way. Instead of moving to a compatible environment, many individuals create their environments. Essentially that is what people do when they design their own home, flee to the country, surround themselves with plants and animals, and start their own business selling stamps or repairing television sets. People often do whatever it takes to establish a match between their gene-driven images and the surrounding environment.

If gene-environment matching is important for self-actualization and feelings of self-satisfaction, then today's world can present some real problems. As the environment becomes more artificial and mechanized, many individuals may be unable to establish those critical matches. People can feel boxed into a concrete and plastic environment and unattached to their "soul-stuff." Their relation with the past becomes less distinct and weaker, provoking, perhaps, psychosomatic deviations, depression, dissatisfaction with their jobs, and violent reactions to stress. If Wilson and Kellert are correct that we attempt to maximize compatibility with past selecting environments, then we can expect sharp and severe reactions to technological distortions, high population densities and common overindulgences. The paradox is that humans tend to embrace the glitter of the present, yet yearn for the greenery of the past.

What Do We Learn?

Our sights have been on the innate rules of the mind; to a great extent we have downplayed the importance of learning on the modification of behavior. In large measure, however, the ability to learn seems to define our nature. Learning apparently separates us from instinct and allows us to escape our irrationality. Now is the time to examine this important point in greater detail.

The evolutionary biologist Ernst Mayr has the comforting view that species are either *closed* or *open* to environmental experiences. The honeybee operates within a closed system, in that its behavior is tightly regulated by genes. It is locked into instinctive acts. But we, with our oversized brain, are open to environmental information that modifies our behavior in major ways. The notion that we are open to the environment pulls us away from believing that we are *nothing but* a biological machine and are *something more* than irrational. After all, isn't our uniquely human moral sense born of personal beliefs and nurtured by cultural imperatives? Don't we learn what's right? Can't we step beyond our crass animal nature?

The facts, however, do not favor the view that we have great capacity to acquire new rules of the mind. Rather, it is more like the philosopher Thoreau knew: "It is only when we forget all our learning that we begin to know." Learning, at best sharpens our inner knowledge—it replaces nothing and creates little. According to John Tooby and Leda Cosmides, all we can do is apply old knowledge to new events. According to them, what appears to be learning is simply the sorting out of evolved strategies that apply to the situation. Our cognitive strategies are rigid adaptations acquired during our evolutionary history. They may or may not be adequate for solving new problems. Tooby and Cosmides do not believe in *general* learning strategies. How is it, they ask, could we have ever acquired a general strategy to maximize genetic fitness if in fact we were selected to adapt to specific circumstances? There was no environment general enough to result in general adaptations, a point made earlier. Environments are always specific, therefore, so too, adaptations. Thus, what appears to be an "open" cognitive system is simply one with many specific adaptations that we call upon depending upon the environment at hand. To say it another way, general strategies, as with general intellectual capacities, may not be general at all, but reflect a high number of specific strategies integrated in their functioning such that they appear as a group to be general capabilities.

This appealing notion can be used to understand the specificity of language, cognition, environmental preferences, and irrational acts. As neuropsychologist Gazzaniga says, "The strong form of the argument is that an organism comes delivered to this world with all the world's complexity already built in. In the face of an environmental challenge, the matching process starts, and what the outsider sees as learning is actually the organism searching through its library of circuits and accompanying strategies for ones that will best allow it to respond to the challenge." A metaphorical selection and matching scheme is pictured below (Figure 9.1). It suggests that we react to environmental novelty or threat by applying multiple strategies, finally settling on the one strategy that is the most appropriate. The environment, according to this view, does not structure new strategies, it guides our search for the appropriate strategy that is already there. The environment both presents the problems that must be solved and helps evoke the range of strategies that might be successful to solve those problems.

We must be careful here, for obviously humans and other animals learn new things—even old dogs learn new tricks. We acquire the ability to play billiards; we remember phone numbers; and we increase our vocabulary. What we don't seem to do, however, is learn new ways of going about learning billiards, remembering phone numbers, or learning vocabulary. There may be individual differences in these capacities, but the core strategies are instinctive. If we are to learn anything new, there are a finite number of rules of the mind that must be followed.

The psychologists K. Holyoak and B. Spellman emphasize the importance of two different forms of cognition, *explicit* and *implicit*. Explicit cognition is knowledge acquired voluntarily and which can be verbalized—the usual view of learning. Implicit cognition is more primitive, involving the use of genetic strategies and the acquisition of knowledge without awareness. Implicit cognition is similar to what we previously called genetic knowledge. Holyoak and Spellman spell out that implicit knowledge is more robust than explicit knowledge, operating despite injuries, diseases and other disorders. It is also age-independent and IQ-independent, showing cross-cultural invariance and even across-species commonalties. An obvious example of implicit knowledge is mating strategy differences between males and females, being more opportunistic with the male, and more cautious and limited with the female. These strategies are indeed robust, operate under adverse conditions, are evident from puberty on, have little relationship to IQ, are common to all cultures and common to many species. Obviously explicit knowledge can modify the expression of the implicit knowledge, but the cognitive predispositions remain the same.

The distinction between explicit and implicit cognition is important. We can absorb new information according to old rules of the mind, but we cannot reformat those rules. Males and females can learn more things about each other and their surroundings, but they organize this informa-

FIGURE 9.1
Learning: Environmental Selection and Error Elimination

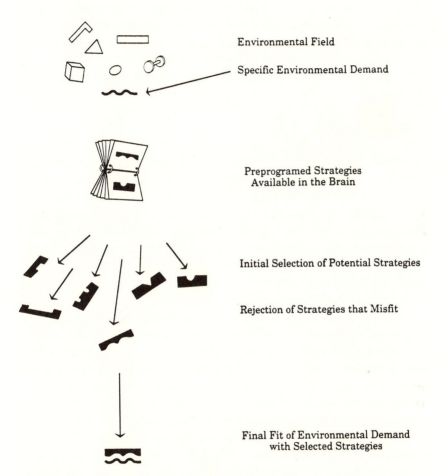

Environmental Field

Specific Environmental Demand

Preprogramed Strategies
Available in the Brain

Initial Selection of Potential Strategies

Rejection of Strategies that Misfit

Final Fit of Environmental Demand
with Selected Strategies

It is assumed that the organism has to adapt to a particular environmental demand (〰). The individual sifts through available innate strategies looking for a match. Several possibilities may be tried until the best match is found. The match may not be perfect -- novel demands must make use of available strategies.

tion along lines specific to each sex. The sex differences persist. We are no more able to shift from being a male or a female than a dog can become a cat.

Thus, what we learn are how to categorize information as to existing rules, and how to use those rules in dealing with new information. Rules are accessed when we need to deal with novel events, implying that our abilities to adjust to changing circumstances are constrained. Old dogs may learn new tricks, but only certain tricks and in certain ways—dog strategies are the only things the dog has to rely on. It's not any different for us.

The Constraints on Learning

There are obvious reasons that learning capabilities are limited. For one thing, the brain is only so large and so complex. In fact, any additional increase in complexity might cause too many mechanical failures, just like in a finely tuned racing car. Likewise, an IQ of 400 might threaten the entire system. For another thing, too much learning might contradict critical survival and reproductive drives—there is too much of importance going on for happenstantial learning to be a primary regulator of behavior. Genetic naiveté is a straighter road to reproduction than cosmopolitan sophistication.

Learning theorists have told us for nearly one hundred years that some things are more easily learned than others. Edward Thorndike found that certain responses *belong* to certain reinforcers. Cats learn to push and pull things in order to escape from confinement, but find it difficult to learn to yawn or scratch in order to escape. Presumably pushing and pulling are behaviors naturally associated with escape behaviors and therefore more easily learned than unrelated responses of yawning and scratching.

The notion that certain associations belong together suggests that there is a *preparedness* to learn specific things. This appears to be the case. Rats easily learn to avoid electrical shocks when shocks are associated with auditory or visual cues. Thus, a sound followed by shock is easily associated, so that when the sound occurs the animals quickly learns to avoid the shock. On the other hand, taste is a natural cue in learning to avoid gastrointestinal upset, but auditory or visual cues are relatively ineffective. A novel taste is easily associated with gastrointestinal distress. External cues like light and sound are associated with motor behaviors; internal cues like tastes and smells are associated with physiological reactions. Clearly there has been a genetic link honed between environmental cues and relevant behaviors.

Humans are no exception. In one study cancer patients were given uniquely flavored ice cream before chemotherapy treatment, treatment that induces gastric distress. Following this association, the patients developed an aversion to the ice cream. This natural association between foods and sickness apparently explains why patients develop aversions to whatever foods that are eaten before chemotherapy, causing them to reject those foods and thus lose substantial body weight.

Preparedness to react runs to other stimuli as well. Children readily learn to avoid snakes and spiders, but find it nearly impossible to learn to avoid neutral stimuli, such as innocuous foods or flowers. Natural selection for adaptive reactions to signals of danger is no doubt responsible for differential preparedness to learn. There is a parsimony expressed in these strategies, as we should never learn insignificant things, and we should always learn anything that might be important.

Some responses can't be learned at all, making behavior appear illogical at times. Pigs cannot be taught reliably to pick up coins in their mouth and place the coins in a piggy bank. Instead, they may do it for a few trials and then engage in typical pig behavior by rooting the coins along the ground. Raccoons find a similar behavior difficult because of their inherent tendency to dip the coins into a container, as if in water, and then rub them together—an expression of raccoon cleaning behavior. They refuse to let go of the coins. Even if the initial training is successful, the species eventually revert to species-typical behaviors, a "genetic drift" that looks very much like genetically driven environmental preferences shown by humans. As the Roman poet Horace wrote, "You can drive out nature with a pitchfork, and she will always return." The fact that we can react successfully in our present environment with old adaptations is testimony to the resemblance of today's surroundings to those that originally shaped our behavior. The truth is that we do everything in accord with what we were built to do.

The Final Interpretation of Learning

Learning apparently acts as a device for accessing the appropriate mental strategy that matches the environmental demand. No new associations are necessarily required; old strategies are accessed. The process is one of screening out inappropriate responses, finally leaving the one innate response that best matches the environment.

Another way to look at this, is to suggest that individuals exposed to a new and demanding environment first integrate *all* sensory stimuli, but only hold those stimuli in storage that contribute to dealing successfully with that environment. Consider this. There is a type of learning called latent learning, in which individuals appear to learn a lot about their environment but use none of the information until it becomes important. For instance, a rat allowed to explore a maze will later quickly learn the pattern of maze choices when reinforced with food for specific responses. The information was there all the time, but was only used when it became necessary—the rest was simply inhibited or mentally thrown away.

Language acquisition apparently occurs in a similar way. Infants show a wide range of sound production appropriate to a variety of languages, but as they mature and are exposed to their language, inappropriate sounds are inhibited or simply discarded from storage, leaving only those sounds appropriate for expressing their language. In a sense, infants do not learn a particular language, instead they discard all other language possibilities, leaving only one. That is no doubt an exaggeration, but it does seem that infants have evolved to organize incoming information in limited ways, throwing the rest away. Again it's the case of having many strategies to draw upon, but using only those that fit the environmental demands.

The substractive nature of learning, that is, the dropping of inappropriate responses, reminds one of the substractive nature of evolution and brain development. During evolution natural selection acts on genetic variation to carve out only that variation that matches the selection pressures—the rest is discarded, or at least never reproduces. Analogously, during development the brain grows thousands of neurons that regress and disappear as the brain becomes more differentiated along certain lines. What isn't used disappears. The immunologist Gerald Edelman speculated in 1989 that learning is a natural selection process among available neurons, with external stimuli selecting the most appropriate. Indeed, the theory, called *Neural Darwinism*, shares many of the aspects of the immune system, especially that quality where an antigen invading the body selects out a specific antibody response. Applied to learning, the notion is that the neurons that remain because of environmental selection are those that are necessary to regulate particular responses. Evolution, development and learning share the sequential qualities of overproduction of elements, differential selection of appropriate structures and functions, reduction of ineffective variation, and final specialization of function.

Frankly, this is not a popular view of learning, but it is compatible with evolutionary theory, and has been around for a long time. The psychologist who first recognized this filtering aspect of learning was the late Harry Harlow. He found that animals try a number of solutions during training, most of which are wrong. But with the proper incentive, such as a preferred food, they begin to inhibit or drop out responses that are ineffective. Eventually all that's left is the most efficient behavior for reaching the incentive. This "correct response" was there from the beginning, perhaps never changing in intensity, but wallowing within a sea of inappropriate behaviors. The animal facing a complicated problem continues to test hypotheses until only one response will do. It is a fact that we learn from mistakes.

After hundreds of experiments with rats and primates Harlow gave us this lasting insight:

> The learning of primitive organisms appears to be nothing more than the gradual suppression or inhibition of extraneous response tendencies. In view of modern genetic theory, which holds that evolution takes place by the selection of multiple small mutations, it is not unreasonable to hypothesize that the fundamental process of of learning has probably remained essentially unchanged for near-countless millions of years. Furthermore, there is nothing relating to the slow, but progressive, evolution of the nervous system to suggest any great master mutation giving rise to a new learning mechanism. For countless generations, development has gone along the line of slowly increasing the number and complexity of neural structures without evidence for development of essentially new anatomical units which might give basis for a sudden change in the nature of learning. Unless the assumption is made that there have been one or more large mutations which could have resulted in new learning processes, inhibition learning theory is not inconsistent with evolutionary theory. Data such as these, of course, can never be definitive but must always be judged on a "best-guess" basis. (Harlow 1959)

A new version of this theory has been proposed by the psychologist Irvin Biederman who believes that animals learn to recognize complex forms by parsing them into elementary building blocks called "geons." Superficially it looks like associative learning, in that object recognition improves with experience, but is more like shuffling through a deck of cards to find those few geons that fit the demands of the game—a matching process that takes time and is limited to the frequency and types of geons built into the central nervous system through natural selection. The individual is relying on implicit knowledge. In Harlow's terms, the organism is eliminating superfluous responses until the most appropriate one remains. The implication of it all is that we are now stuck with the mental repertory of our evolutionary past—we cannot "learn ourselves out of it."

Freedom Forsaken?

We have taken an incredible journey, for what we have discussed seems contrary to everyday life. Can it be that natural selection was so picky and insistent that it allowed us no personal freedom? Are we stuck with a mechanistic model of man—is biology all there is? Is our irrationality as species-specific as any other human trait, that no learning can ever eradicate? Do the ideas of free will and self-determination allow us hope merely by deluding us into thinking we have stepped beyond our evolutionary bounds? Is there no room for gods and devils except in our irrational compulsions? Well, we may be getting closer to the truth, forcing us to side with Robert Browning when he said, "So free we seem, so fettered fast we are!"

References

Cited in Chapter 9

Biederman, I. (1987)."Recognition-by-Components: A Theory of Human Understanding." *Psychological Review*, 94, 115–47.

Bouchard, T.J., Jr., Lykken, D.T., McGue, M., Segal, N.L. and Tellegen, A. (1990). "Sources of Human Psychological Differences: The Minnesota Study of Twins Reared Apart. *Science*, 250, 223–50.

Domjan, M. (1993). *The Principles of Learning and Behavior* (3rd. ed.). Pacific Grove, CA: Brooks/Cole Publishing Company.

Edelman, G.M. (1992). *Bright Air, Brilliant Fire*. New York: Basic Books.

Eigen, M. and Winkler, R. (1993). *Laws of the Game: How the Principles of Nature Govern Chance*. Princeton, NJ: Princeton University Press.

Farr. W. (1839). "Statistical Nosology." In *First Annual Report of the Registar General in England*. London: Clowes and Sons.

Gilbert, D.T. (1991). "How Mental Systems Believe." *American Psychologist*, 46, 107–19.

Harlow, H.F. (1959). "Learning Set and Error Factor Theory." In S. Koch (ed.), *Psychology: A Study of Science*. Vol. II, New York: McGraw-Hill, 492–537.

Holyoak, K.J. and Spellman, B.A. (1993). "Thinking." *Annual Review of Psychology*, 44, 265–315.

Kahneman, D. and Tversky, A. (1979). "Prospect Theory: An Analysis of Decisions Under Risk." *Econometrica*, 47, 263–91.

Kellert, S.R. and Wilson, E.O. (eds.). (1993). *The Biophilia Hypothesis*. Washington, DC, Island Press.

Rachlin, H. (YEAR?)."Why do People Gamble and Keep Gambling Despite Heavy Losses?" *Psychological Science*, 1, 294–97.

Rosen, C.M. (1987). "The Eerie World of Reunited Twins." *Discover*, 8, 36–46.

Stubbotsky, E.V. (1993). *Foundations of the Mind*. Cambridge, MA: Harvard University Press.

Tooby, J. and Cosmides, L. (1990). "The Past Explains the Present: Emotional Adaptations and the Structure of Ancestral Environments." *Ethology and Sociobiology*, 11, 375–424.

General References

Frankel, C. (1973). "The Nature and Sources of Irrationalism." *Science*, 180, 927–31.

Hall, C.S. and Lindzey, G. (1978). *Theories of Personality*. New York: John Wiley and Sons.

Morris, R. (YEAR?). *Time's Arrows: Scientific Attitudes Toward Time*. New York: Simon and Schuster.

Wagenaar, W.A. (ed.). (1988). *Paradoxes of Gambling Behaviour*. London: Lawrence Erlbaum Associates.

Wilson, E.O. (1984). *Biophilia*. Cambridge, MA: Harvard University Press.

10

The Strange Evolution of the Human Brain

...for several million years after the split with proto-chimpanzees, our hominid ancestors got along with ape-sized brains, in spite of becoming bipedal at least three and a half million years ago. Then, when the ice ages began, about two and a half million years ago, the Great Encephalization commenced, and was essentially completed 150,000 years ago—before the development of language, of cooking, of agriculture.

—Daniel Dennett

The Brain Game

Humans appear overbrained, oversexed, overaggressive, overself-reflective—evolution run amok. What is it that we possess that is uniquely superior for survival and reproduction? Why do we have the most complex brain on this planet? Why are we the only hominid who evolved language? For what possible reasons did we decorate the caves of Lascaux, France 35,000 years ago with mystical paintings, later elevating our skills to that of Michelangelo's Sistine Chapel and the latest graphic computer programs? Why do we need philosophy, systems of justice, and a scientific cosmology?

There is something very strange about it all, for the obvious answer is that we really did not need our quiver of complexity in order to survive. Or, so it seems. A chimpanzee does as well, without the backaches of bipedal locomotion or the disturbing abundance of self-consciousness. Its brain and behaviors seem optimally correlated for survival and reproduction. On the other hand, the gorilla, with a brain the size of the first bipedal hominid, shows no great expression of creativity. It of course demonstrates complex primate traits, but doesn't appear to match the sophistication of chimpanzees. It has some ability to symbolize, cleverly learning some American sign language, but this capacity is not exploited in the animal's mountain retreats. Day after day it pursues its vegetarian ways, reaching out little beyond its next meal. The gorilla's brain seems overbuilt for what it does.

Perhaps we do have advantages over the chimpanzee and gorilla, but why did only one hominid species survive? There is nothing obvious in the fossil record or in our geophysical nature to suggest that *Homo erectus* might not have been the apogee of human evolution—the final human form. *Homo erectus* traveled early and far, meeting and conquering environments from Eastern Africa to Northern Europe and Java. He sometimes made stone tools, apparently hunted larger game, made fire, displayed complex communication, and invested heavily in sexual bonding and infant care. What is remarkable is not that *H. erectus* survived for nearly two million years, but that this complex form was replaced by Neanderthal and, in turn, by *Homo sapiens*. As we remember from an earlier chapter, anatomist Arthur Keith once remarked that the "cerebral Rubicon" was crossed when the brain reached 700 to 800 cubic centimeters, as it did with *H. erectus*. No more cerebral power seemed necessary, yet it came.

Did hominids evolve steadily toward superior forms, or were some just luckier than others? Consider this: bipedalism was not a consequence of brain enlargement; the first came two million years before the second. The need for stone tools was not a prerequisite for the evolution of large brains, nor did tool making lead to significant changes in enculturalization—that was another million years in coming. Language and art did not flow naturally from an expanded brain. Neanderthal and Archaic *H. sapiens* had huge brains yet made no striking developments in language or art. The fact is that successful living was common before every major transition in morphology, brain growth, hunting skills, communication, and artistic abilities. The complexity of form and function, so evident in our own being, seemed unessential for survival and reproduction: it simply was, the kind of excess pointed to by Shakespeare "that was laid on with a trowel."

House Rules: The One Percent Difference

Perhaps brainy *H. sapiens* became more of a force with which to be reckoned because of the direct competition with Neanderthals across Europe.

Here's a compelling argument:

Joos Neanderthal and his comrades are stalking a mammoth. Their weapons? Throwing stones and rock hammers. They gesture and yell out their encirclement strategy, moving in for the kill. Suddenly Boish H. sapiens, lighter and quicker, darts out of the forest, yelling explicit commands to his family members. They abruptly cut off the Neanderthals and swiftly bring down the mammoth with spears and horned axes. That year only two male Neanderthals have sufficient food to reproduce. Boish and all his brothers live to have offspring, passing on their competitive advantages. The difference in speed and capabilities between the two species may have been small, but one percent multiplied over 7,500 generations is easily enough to result in differential extinction.

Or, it could have gone like this:

Juana Neanderthal is near death from mistakenly eating the leaves of the foxglove plant. She tries to tell her sisters and brothers about the dangerous plant, but the concept swirls like cirrus clouds in her befuddled brain—the mind and vocal tract inadequate to express the exact details. Several of her tribe die of poison that year until the association is finally made between the foxglove and illness. Over the next mountain Boona H. sapiens is also facing death from the same poison but during her bout with eternity she speaks of the plant and her family hears the warning. No one else dies that year. Moreover, her daughter Dia discovers that they can use the poison from the seeds, now known as digitalis, to tip their spears and more quickly bring down large animals.

Again, a one percent difference in ability to communicate is enough.

Indeed, the complex brain and competitive skills of *H. sapiens* may have been the deciding factors. Starting about 50,000 years ago early modern *H. sapiens* moved west from the plains of Poland into Neanderthal's home grounds. Everywhere *H. sapiens* went the Neanderthal disappeared; its last appearance on the evolutionary stage was about 33,000 years ago. There was no protracted war, no death by bloody tooth and claw, only competition for resources, environmental hardship, starvation, and decreased reproduction.

This story has a ring of truth, comforting our egoistic view of our inherent value, yet there are problems with the argument. First of all, Neanderthal actually had a bigger brain than *H. sapiens* if uncorrected for body weight, 1500 cc verses 1350 cc. The advantage is obviously not simply with brain size. Second, brain evolution of *H. sapiens* was essentially complete long before *H. sapiens* migrated out of Africa to encounter Neanderthal. Competition with Neanderthal was therefore not the natural selection pressure causing the brain of *H. sapiens* to balloon. Third, hominid brain evolution did not progress steadily in size over millions of years of natural selection to ensure a competitive edge. Rather, it showed quantal jumps in brain size—nothing like the steady rate one would expect if hominids were slowly honing their skills of competition and communication.

On the average the human brain increased in size during the last 2.5 million years by one-millionth of a percent per generation, but most of that change occurred (1) about 2.5 million years ago during the transition from *Australopithecus africanus* to *Homo habilis*; (2) about 1.8 million years ago during the transition of *H. habilis* to early *H. erectus*; and (3) about 0.8 to 0.6 million years ago during the transition of early *H. erectus* to early *H. sapiens*. These three major brain increases were approximately equal in size, about 33 percent each. The changes were abrupt, geologically speaking, and difficult to associate with gradual and continuous environmental pressures—they were, instead, punctuational, long-lasting, and without intermediate stages.

The conclusion is unexpected: we did not acquire a complex brain because of competition with other hominids or because of manifold long-term demands of the environment. For whatever reason, we first acquired the brain stuff, subsequently using it to dominate other hominids and our surroundings. The striking capacities of *H. sapiens* were born long before their application. Contingencies prevailed. Had *H. erectus* survived it might have characterized humans, and you wouldn't be reading this book. Had Neanderthal developed language or tracked the mammoth farther north, it might not have lost out to *H. sapiens*. Just because we know the end of the story doesn't mean that the conclusion was inevitable. Every form that entered or exited from the scene closed or opened a door for someone else.

The Storms of Brain Evolution

Hominids appeared one by one during near catastrophic changes in climate. According to Elisabeth Vrba of Yale, each major climate shift in Africa was associated with the appearance of a new experimental design. Somewhere between 5 and 6 million years ago global cooling eliminated the subtropical rain forests, and with that sixteen of twenty existing species of apes. A savannah grassland remained in its wake. For the first time a tree-dwelling quadruped gave birth to a biped savannah forager. Following shorter cycles of alternating warming and cooling, Australopithecines emerged. Then around 2.8 million years ago the forests of Eastern Africa disappeared for the last time during a severe pulse of cold. *H. habilis* and *H. erectus* appeared. About 2 million years ago *H. erectus* left Africa. It's more recent descendents, Neanderthal and *H. sapiens*, adapted to the climate cycles of Europe and Asia. The correlations are rough, and are challenged by other data, but do suggest that severe climate changes, or associated events, are at the basis of hominid evolution, driving brain complexity to the max. The paleontologists Richard Leakey and Roger Lewin explain it this way:

> Principal changes in Africa were the circumstances surrounding the opening of the Great Rift Valley, beginning about twenty million years ago. As the result of the separation of tectonic plates running roughly north-south underneath the eastern part of the continent, upwelling lava gradually caused the crust to bulge unevenly, building the Kenyan dome and the Ethiopian dome, each reaching about nine thousand feet above sea level. Like huge blisters on the continental skin, these two domes brought large-scale topography to East Africa. At the time, a swath of dense rain forest stretched across the continent, from the Atlantic coast to the Indian Ocean, home to an increasing diversity of ape species. As the two domes grew, the patterns of rainfall to the east were disrupted, the result of a growing rain shadow. The eastern forests began to fragment, and patches of open country developed, producing a mosaic of environments, from forest to woodland to shrub and grassland.... It acted as an engine of evolution.

Ecological changes have always been critical for change, and not merely in Eastern Africa. Environmental instability drives change, forging new species, creating new talents. No pain, no gain. The earth wobbles on its axis, cracks, and spews forth lava, sends its continents drifting across wide latitudes, creates and destroys glaciers, responds to moon tides, sun spots and twice-per-decade El Niños, repeatedly turning night into day, cold into hot. The earth is continually bombarded by meteorites, comets, and high and low levels of radiation. Lightning strikes repeatedly. The world shakes, rattles, and rolls. Without these shocks to the biological systems, there would be no reason for new adaptations to appear or prevail. Without them, about the most complicated species around today might be the sea slug.

FIGURE 10.1
Events During Human Evolution

EVENTS DURING HUMAN EVOLUTION

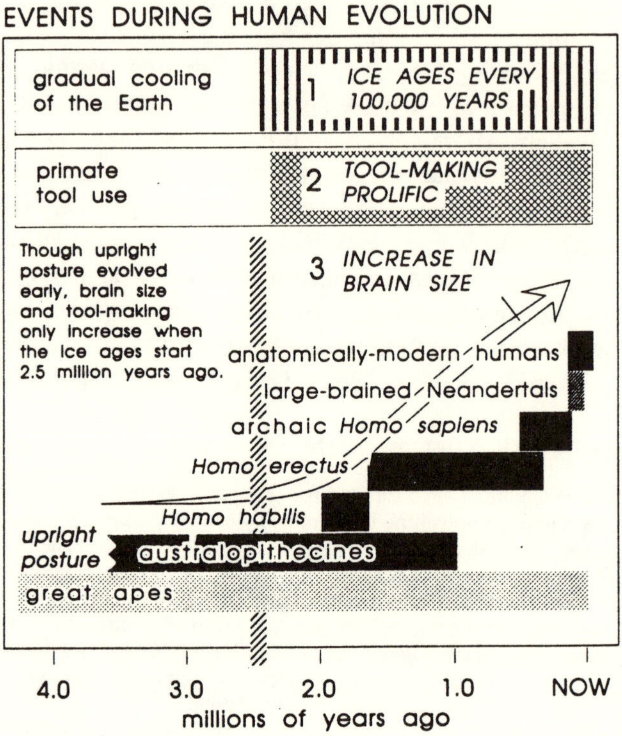

Source: Calvin, 1990

The big shocks that drove brain development were glaciations that cooled and dried east Africa. Beginning around 2.5 million years ago ice ages occurred on the average of every 100,000 years. Africa became cool, dry and savannah, generating five successive speciation events, each apparently tied to a period of cooling and each generating a larger brain. The rough correlation between periods of glaciation and the emergence of new bipedal species is seen here?

A great deal of the change in brain size may be associated with increases in body size, as more recent hominid species are heavier than older species. A general scaling rule that applies to comparisons across mammalian species is that brain size increases by .75 unit for every unit increase in body size. Measuring the body in kilograms and the brain in grams, then for every kilogram of increase in body weight there is a .75 gram increase in brain weight. Thus, there is an inevitable association between body and brain size. If cooling climates favored larger bodies that could store more energy and use it at a slower rate, then the evolution of "large brain" simply tagged along.

Investigators have shown that various structures of the brain are related in size. For example, the ratio of total cortical volume to brain volume follows a predictable mathematical formula, as does the ratio of lower centers of the brain to the rest of the brain. In rough measure, the body specifies the brain, and the brain specifies its parts. Thus, body size can be used as an initial predictor of brain size and its component parts.

The evolutionary story is complicated by the observation that brain size is not changing in size proportionally to increasing body size—yes, there is a relation, but during hominid evolution the brain was increasing faster than expected. This disproportionate growth in brain size is indexed by what is known as the Encephalization Quotient (EQ), a measure of brain size (weight) relative to body size (weight) that indicates the degree to which the brain is larger than expected based on body size. An EQ of 1.0 indicates that the brain is exactly that which is expected based on the usual mammalian relation between body and brain size— a dog is an example. An EQ of less than 1.0, say 0.5 as with an anteater, indicates a brain development that is one-half as large as one would expect with an animal of that particular body weight. Finally, an EQ of 2.0, as with the average primate, indicates that the animal has a brain two times larger than expected based on the average body weight. So, the larger the EQ, the larger the brain relative to body size.

The EQ levels of the major primates are shown in the next figure. EQ levels increased substantially from *Australopithecus afarensis* through modern *H. sapiens*. In environmental terms every increase in EQ resulted from a sharp drop in environmental temperature.

EQ is considered by many investigators to be a rough measure of relative species intelligence. An animal can take care of its general neurophysiological needs with an EQ of 1.0 or less. Anything above 1.0 suggests a "surplus" of neural tissue. Since EQ predicts neuron number, it is also associated with the ability of the brain to process information. We will see later that the "extra" neural tissue associated with high EQ is often in areas of the brain that regulate cognitive and linguistic pro-

FIGURE 10.2
Brain/Body Ratio in Hominids

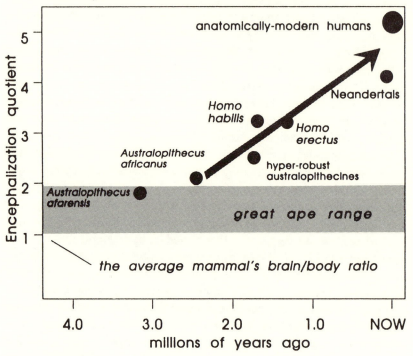

Source: Calvin, 1990

cesses—complex rules of the mind, such as with the frontal, parietal, and temporal regions of the brain. For now what we need to understand is that *H. sapiens* ended up with an EQ of 5.0 or greater, much more than any other Homo species and greater than that of Neanderthal. Perhaps we can begin to understand why *H. sapiens* beat out Neanderthal—it was probably smarter—but we are still left with the troubling question that if an EQ of 1.0 or even less is adequate for most species, why did we win the EQ lottery?

Brain size is also a predictor of human intelligence. Human intelligence is measured by standardized IQ tests. This is not the same as EQ, as IQ measures performance variations among individuals, whereas EQ measures variations among species. Nevertheless, both concern themselves with brain processes associated with information acquisition and use. Using magnetic resonance imaging (MRI), which gives a picture of the internal structures of the brain, psychologist Lee Willerman and his colleagues have found statistically significant correlations between brain size and standard Wechsler IQ scores of university students. With correlations running from 0.00 to 1.00, males and females show correlations of from 0.35 to 0.65. The findings are especially interesting because previous low-resolution techniques of brain measurement have not shown these relations. Usually significant correlations between brain function and brain size are found only when comparisons are assessed across species.

Subsequently the neuroscience team led by Nancy Andreasen has found that several specific areas of the normal brain correlate significantly with the Wechsler IQ scale. Among those brain parts showing substantial correlations between volume and IQ are the cerebrum, the cerebellum, temporal lobes, and the deeper residing hippocampus. The correlations are not especially robust, but they do consistently range between about 0.20 and 0.50. These studies are initial forays into identifying structures that might have been targets of natural selection. The fact that several brain areas, all of which correlate highly with total brain size, show relations to IQ strongly support the notion that brain size is a primary determinent of intelligence.

History Ain't Bunk; History is Everything

Understanding ourselves is like peeling an onion. We are what we are because we are a hominid. Peel that away, and our primateness shows through. More peeling and we see our mammalness. Lower yet, we find our vertebrateness—a peel that takes us back to a common ancestor about 525 million years old. The famous neurobiologist Karl Lashley put it this way: "The rudiments of every human behavioral mechanism will be found far down in the evolutionary scale and also represented even in primitive activities of the nervous system."

We retain some of the basic features at each evolutionary step: we are a fish, an amphibian, a reptile, a bird, a mammal. Like a junked car passed around the neighborhood where everyone adds and takes off parts, we are a working model of evolutionary tinkering. We call ourselves human, as if that defines our uniqueness, but in fact, we are everything that went before—at least with those traits that we didn't lose—including our thin veneer of specializations. An extended Linnaean classification of *H. sapiens* might be *Homo-prima-mammo-avian-reptil-amphibia-fisho sapiens*.

One gets a strong hint of this amalgamation of biological forms by viewing vertebrate embryological development. The early stages look the same, be it a fish, frog, turtle or mammal—gill-like, tail-like, embryo-like. Charles Darwin realized, "Man is developed from an ovule, about 125th of an inch in diameter, which differs in no respect from the ovules of other animals." Later stages of development bring differences, so that a reptile begins to look more like a reptile than a fish, and a mammal begins to look more like a mammal than a reptile. Yet, each stage is built on an existing blueprint, each donating elements to the next, each casting out improbable arrangements or unusable parts, each working its way to a new form.

Evolution preserved the most critical vertebrate and invertebrate genetic strategies, including genes for the segmentation of body parts, and for regulating basic metabolic needs. New adaptations were added through time. We are, as a result, a sophisticated Rube Goldberg device, embracing all of evolutionary history as our parents—body forms, physiology, cellular structure, DNA, behavior.

The human brain exemplifies its striped evolutionary heritage. It is part human, part primate, part mammalian, and so on, deep into the onion. One can even safely say that humans are part bird-brained. Attempting to specify the brain from this evolutionary perspective, Paul MacLean, a neurophysiologist, spoke of the "triune" evolution of the mammalian brain, suggesting that the mammalian brain retains the anatomical and chemical features of our reptilian and early mammalian ancestors. His version of the evolved brain is pictured here, along with some general functional characteristics of each evolutionary stages. The reptilian part of the brain includes the basal ganglia and midbrain structures—structures that regulate body temperature and motor functions. The older mammalian part includes the cingulate cortex and limbic systems that regulate emotion, sex behavior, learning, and some thought processes. Finally, the new mammalian part, the neomammalian component, includes the neocortex (often referred to as simply "cortex") that is responsible for abstract thought, consciousness, language, and

FIGURE 10.3
The Triune Brain (after MacLean)

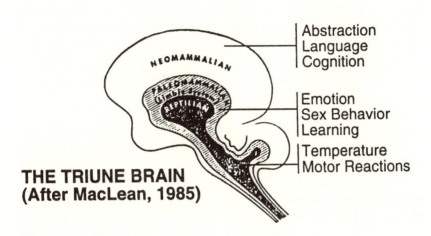

NEOMAMMALIAN

PALEOMAMMALIAN
(limbic)

REPTILIAN

Abstraction
Language
Cognition

Emotion
Sex Behavior
Learning

Temperature
Motor Reactions

THE TRIUNE BRAIN
(After MacLean, 1985)

perceptual representation of the world. The most recent elaboration of cortical tissue in *H. sapiens* provides for self-reflection and complex consciousness.

The "triune" view of the brain, simple as it is, illuminates our historical ties to earlier species. We think human-like but emote lizard-like. But evolution did more than stack species traits like bricks; evolution mortared the parts together, creating new bonds and functions. The whole of our brain is measurably more than the sum of its historical past. We are not simply a hierarchy of past evolutionary steps, for at each step adaptation was novel and species-specific.

The emergent qualities of our brain are most evident with language. Broca's area in the left frontal cortex, concerned in part with syntax and verbal motor performance, and Wernicke's area in the left temporal cortex, related to recognition and comprehension of speech, are new additions to the primate cortex. Lesions in these regions, or in their connections, are responsible for several forms of aphasia. However, destruction of identical cortical areas in monkeys does not disrupt vocalization or signaling comprehension. "Monkey talk" and "monkey understanding" are products of the underlying older anterior cingulate cortex in the paleomammalian circuitry. Lesions here will disrupt vocalization patterns. In the evolution of the neocortex among recent hominids, communication processes apparently shifted from cingulate cortex to neocortex, where they were elaborated into "universal rules of grammar."

Many functional shifts seem upward toward newer anatomical areas. But the shift in functions is downward and lateral as well. Speech and language comprehension came with Broca's and Wernicke's areas, but new connections from these sites linked up with older brain parts and with each other. Similarly, the new, large and complex frontal cortex, that is arguably the central brain region related to consciousness and self-awareness, sends numerous neurons deep into the limbic system and other subcortical regions. The ties between newer and older regions are evident when damage to the basal ganglia, the "reptilian" structures, produce speech, language, and cognitive deficits. Somehow complex and recent neocortical inventions turn backward to link again with their past.

The juxtaposition of the old and new, the relatively fast evolution of neocortex, and new lines of communication between areas are what allowed for the rapid evolution of the brain. Each new species was a related event—bringing with it adaptations from ancestors—adding here or there, breaking some neural connections, and forming others. The brain was not reinvented each time a new species came about, nor was it reorganized in major ways. Structures and functions were reiterated. At each stage of hominid evolution, the adapted structures and functions were spared, setting a foundation on which new processes were formed and, in successful designs, integrated into the whole. With that, rules of the mind acquired by *H. erectus* passed with relatively little change to Neanderthal and *H. sapiens*; other rules were added, and old ones modified. The Cadillac of the brain quickly followed once the mechanical principles of the Model-T Ford proved successful.

Brain as Growth

There are major links between periods of glacial cooling, hunting skills, changes in infant development, and ultimate brain complexity. Within this matrix lie the answers to the most perplexing questions about ourselves.

Of those links, glacial cooling seems to be the key. It's effects in Africa were to diminish the number of calories available from food gathering and to distribute resources more widely. The haven of the rain forest was destroyed to be replaced by a drier and less predictable savannah. At the same time climatic change opened opportunities for the evolution of large-bodied antelopes and other grassland species. Humans began to search out meat for sustenance, first probably through scavenging, later through active hunting. Stone tools became important for both, the breaking of bones to extract marrow, their use as projectiles.

According to the neurobiolgist William Calvin, the functional bottleneck in the ability to hunt was accuracy of throwing. No doubt more was involved than simply accuracy of throwing, such as general neuromuscular capabilities and cognitive processes, but the hypothesis is worth considering. Here it is: big game could not be wrestled to the savannah floor; it had to be brought down by stone projectiles. Precision of throwing depends on finely tuned sensory and motor capacities, which in turn depend upon large numbers of neurons. Launching a projectile at just the right millisecond to hit a small target at a distance requires the coordination of many stimulating and inhibiting neurons. Calvin estimates that accurate throwing depended on one-millisecond-in-a-thousand launch period, a precision impossible with a few jittery neurons whose individual timing was no better than ten-milliseconds-per hundred. For the required accuracy, "We are talking of *hundred-* and *thousandfold* increases in the number of brain sequencing circuits that need to be temporarily synchronized." To say it otherwise, the more neurons devoted to a task, the more stable and precise the behavior becomes.

H. habilis and *H. erectus* may not have possessed the neurological complexity to fell single prey species accurately, but they may have been able to throw stones into a herd of prey species, thus bringing down individual animals. It's impossible to know for sure, but it is in-

teresting that the Acheulean stone tools of *H. erectus* included an artifact that had the head of an arrow and the body of a discus. These stones
could have been hurled fairly long distances into a group of animals
with a substantial probability of dropping an animal to the ground, there
to be run over by other animals or clubbed to death by the hunters.

The importance of recruiting additional neurons to stabilize behavior
is easily seen in our own lives. For instance, we obtain more accuracy in
firing a pistol by holding the gun hand with the other hand, thus engaging twice as many neurons and eliminating tremors. One can also see
the effects of losing neural connections during aging on accuracy of
limb movement.

The evolutionary trick, then, was somehow to increase the production of neurons, reducing the jitters of throwing. It did happen, and faster
than can be accounted for by gradual evolution—sharp spikes of cooling followed closely by increases in brain complexity. There is, however, a reasonable developmental explanation.

The developing mammalian brain is peculiar, in that many more neurons are produced than eventually survive. As neurons grow and connect to each other, or connect to target cells, such as muscle end organs,
many more fail to make connections and die. Perhaps up to 50 percent
of all neurons produced during embryological and infant development
are lost, certainly substantial cell death. Which neurons survive and why
are mysteries of great theoretical concern. The control may lie with the
type and amount of sensory input from the environment and with the
chemical gradients of the central and peripheral nervous systems. Regardless, the fact that there is an early surplus of neurons offers a route
to the understanding of rapid brain growth. All that we need to imagine
is that early development is stopped before these excess neurons are
lost. But how could this happen?

The developmental quirk that can bring this about is *neoteny*, the
retention of juvenile characteristics in the adult individual. As we saw
earlier, neoteny is a developmental change that retards differentiation
and leads to an organism that can reproduce in a juvenile condition.
One can often identify a species that is neotenized by the similarity
between its early and later phases of development.

Clearly humans are neotenized. As adults we retain or exaggerate
many juvenile traits that are lost in most adult primates. On the list are a
highly vaulted cranium, a large brain relative to body size, large eyes,

scant body hair, small tooth size, opposable thumb and fingers, bones articulated for bipedalism, and fine facial musculature. We also continue to be playful, like infant primates, showing childlike creativity.

The argument is complex, but comes down to this: human differentiation was periodically arrested during evolution, perhaps with increased neoteny at every major node of speciation. Neurons that otherwise would have perished lived on, increasing brain size and complexity. Animals grew in size as juvenile creatures, carrying on their shoulders incomparable brains. The jitters of throwing stones was thereby reduced, giving later hominids a distinct advantage in surviving on the savannah. It also left *H. sapiens* with surplus neurological capabilities (high EQ) that were then used to effectively manipulate the environment and bring Neanderthal to its knees.

Body size interacted with neoteny, eventually to specify the most fundamental human traits. Sequential Homo species increased in size, forcing brain dimensions to increase as well. This was coupled with neoteny and the saving of neurons, thus increasing EQ well beyond expected levels.

Increases in body size are important for other reasons, as a host of variables change in correlated ways. Many of these changes occur because of reductions in metabolic rate associated with enlarged size—they are inevitable partners in the developmental process. For example, reduced metabolic rate decreases energy expenditure and allows individuals to travel more widely in the search for food and shelter. But it also has effects on almost all traits expressed during a lifetime, the so-called life-history traits. Some of these interrelations are seen here.

Life history traits spell out the lifestyle of a species—how it reproduces, how it learns, how it copes with environments. The traits are surprisingly tied together, the integration arising because of their relations to size and metabolism. What makes us human is not so much the idiosyncratic traits that define our species, but the exaggeration of traits that are common to vertebrates. Nothing much is absolutely new, but we have managed to push the developmental envelope to the extreme. The implications are far-reaching, for our analysis suggests that limited changes in one or two parameters fan out during the course of development to touch every aspect of our lives. As Shakespeare mused, "How far that little candle throws its beams!"

FIGURE 10.4
Body Size and Life History Traits

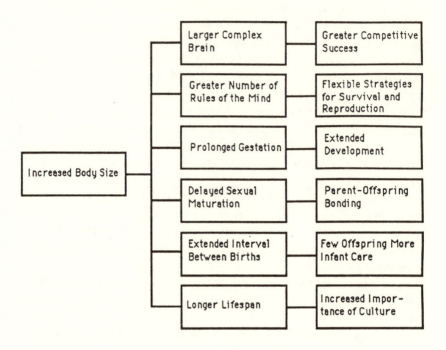

Can Big Brains be Stupid?

The question lingers, why did it take so long for bigger, better brains to realize their potentials? *H. erectus*, Neanderthal, and Archaic *H. sapiens* carried around a great deal of silent neural tissue, long before major advances occurred in tool-making, art, language, culture, or technology. Only within the past 150,000 years did incomparable traits emerge in *H. sapiens*.

Perhaps hominid species were too busy staying alive to dwell on self-origin, death, and the cosmos. The anatomist Jared Diamond argues, however, that some hominid species were actually better off before major cultural advances occurred. Early *H. sapiens* bones show little evidence of dwarfing, osteoporosis, rickets, and other disease or malnutrition. It was only after agriculture flourished, around 10,000 years ago, that humans were subjected to widespread disease and selective malnutrition. In general, early humans seemed healthy and vigorous—apparently strategically positioned to excel. But they did not.

Certainly cultural advances are cumulative, starting slowly, moving more rapidly, finally generating incredible progress. The more advanced Acheulian stone tools were necessary before spears and cooperative hunting could occur, but once these steps were taken it became possible to differentiate groups according to specific functions and social roles. One thing follows another, generating more alternatives and opportunities. It takes considerable time to generate self-sustained cultural momentum, just as it does when moving a flywheel. Perhaps, then, no special explanation is necessary to account for the lagtime between brain expansion and major innovations. The lag could have been as inevitable as the later onrush.

Another possible explanation for this cultural lag is that a sudden enlargement of the brain provided general scaffolding for adaptive change, but did not result in sophisticated interior design. Brain changes probably occurred without internal reorganization of neural networks or adaptive connections. Acquiring more neurons because of neoteny and reduced cell death is only the preface to restructuring the central nervous system. It takes time for ecological selection pressures to build in new rules of conduct and concepts. Expanded brains, according to this view, were initial reactions to climate stresses, occurring because of little-known shifts in embryological and infant development. Brain enlargement by itself did not increase survivability, but it did build the platform on which advances were made. Neoteny and the sparing of neurons may have provided a new brain field of accessible neurons for the neural selection of additional rules of the mind, in the same way that new genetic variation within populations of animals provides additional opportunities for ecological selection of new traits. Agreeing with Gerald Edelman, natural selection acts on neurons much as it does on genes.

Ecological Selection on Available Neurons

It is probably true that the major changes in the evolution of hominid brain were dramatic. Possibly cold waves and major reductions or changes in foods acted as strong pressures for updating the brain. Somehow these factors preserved genetic and developmental processes that quickly got the job done. The exact mechanisms are only vaguely known. There is little evidence showing *how* cold or diet could trigger increased body size, neoteny, and the preservation of surplus neurons. Nature was no doubt balancing costs and benefits. Perhaps climate changes were so chaotic that the rare mutation with significant advantages was the only one that survived.

Our knowledge is incomplete, to say the least. Climate shifts related to ice ages may have been of paramount importance, but even they don't reveal the environmental chaos that swirled around man. We now know . that substantial climate changes happen on the time scale of decades, not centuries. Short-term oscillations are superimposed on the longer waves of climate, interacting in complex ways. Geophysicists believe that sharp changes in temperature occurred about 115,000 to 135,000 years ago during the last interval between glacial epochs, just about the time *H. sapiens* acquired language. In one catastrophic flux the average temperature of Greeland plunged 25 degrees Fahrenheit, remaining at that level for about seventy years—and that was between major glacial periods.

If recent history is any guide to the distant past, then developing man was always subjected to an unstable and fluctuating environment. Measures of tree rings, ice crystals, and fossil pollen give a picture of radical climate instability. The record for the Northern Hemisphere for the past 600 years shows a sharp temperature drop in the sixteenth century, followed by an erratic rise over the next two centuries. A more modest drop occurred in the nineteenth century, followed by a surge above average in the twentieth century.

Moving backward in time, annual growth rings in South American alerce trees that live up to 3,600 years indicate a warming from 1400 B.C. to 750 B.C., followed by a cooling. The longest period of above average temperature was from 80 B.C. to 160 A.D. Similar changes over a 50,000 year period have been found in Florida, using oscillations of pine pollen in sediments of Lake Tulane. Fluctuations in climate occurred worldwide, some related to glaciation, some to radiation, some to continental drift, and some to meteor impacts and volcanic action.

The genetic pools around the world, including those in areas of hominid evolution, were buffeted drastically over and over, as individuals strove for self-preservation and genetic immortality. Stepping back from the details, it appears that our failure as a species was just as likely as our success—a roll of the biological dice in a stormy universe. As improbable as it was, a few big-brained souls pushed through the eye of the needle.

We are faced with a fossil record that literally boggles the mind. Remember, we are different from chimpanzees, currently our nearest primate relative, by only about 1.6 percent of our DNA. Some subspecies of birds are more distantly related. Yet, out of this small difference and in less than 4 million years came at least three forms of Australopithecines, *H. habilis*, *H. erectus*, Neanderthal, and perhaps two distinct forms of *H. sapiens*. No one can guess what is still buried in Africa, Asia, and elsewhere. Whatever happened, it was stunning in consequence, breaking on the scene with pyrotechnic speed.

Darwin and Wallace offer little in the way of explanations for the grand changes of evolution, for our understanding of these depends more on the knowledge of how punctuational events occur than on how small mutations assemble into major adaptive traits. We ultimately became human because of interrelated changes that self-organize during development. The crack of the environment that sends evolution spinning acts quickly, razor-cutting the maladaptive and sending ancestral traits careening in unpredictable directions.

But smaller changes are involved as well, and Darwin and Wallace have not been replaced by punctuational messages. Short-term fluctuations in climate or food can modify directional changes in human development and evolution. One way to put evolution into perspective is to consider that any geological or atmospheric change can initiate biological change—the greater the one the greater the other. Ecological pressures impose their effects on larger evolutionary restructuring, altering the expression of thematic characteristics.

Mace, Clutton-Brock, Paul Harvey, and other biologists are using an animal comparative approach to assess ecological impacts on brain evolution. Their basic point is that the daily demands of the environment exert their effects on brain size and complexity. For example, fruit-eating bats have larger brains for their body weights than do insectivorous bats, presumably because of the greater foraging demands faced by frugivorous species. Fruit-eaters must forage more widely, compete more intensely and learn to recognize appropriate fruits and times for hunting, more so than do insect-eating bats.

Similar dietary effects on the brain have been found in several families of rodents and primates. In every case, leaf-eating rodents and primates have relatively smaller brain weights than their related but non-leaf-eating counterparts. It's apparently tougher to make a living hunting for foods than simply reaching out and grabbing them. Incidentally, brain size differences do not seem to correspond to any other life-history trait. As usual in this world of limited resources, energy availability is a fundamental driving force of evolution, modifying brain size to a considerable degree.

Some of the variations found in brain size are apparently related to what tasks must be performed. Fossorial (burrowing) rodents, like moles, that mostly dig tunnels until they run into eatable roots and tubers, have smaller brains than closely related rodents, including moles, that prey on less predictably distributed insects.

Recent studies indicate that specific brain regions may respond to ecological selection pressures, even though whole brain does not. American passerine birds that store foods in multiple hidden areas, only to retrieve them later, show a selective increase in hippocampal size. This area of the limbic system is essential for spatial learning, the type of learning that is critical for this complex foraging strategy.

Along similar lines, it is known that nocturnal birds that depend on olfaction have enlarged olfactory bulbs, relative to diurnal birds. Comparably, male birds that sing have larger brain regions devoted to this skill than those that don't. And so on within the animal kingdom: structure relates to function.

Such observations are significant for two reasons. First, it is clear that the environment and life-history traits determine the rate of brain growth. These changes are probably superimposed on climate influences of a greater magnitude. Second, species exhibit what the evolutionary biologist Harry Jerison calls, "The Principle of Proper Mass," which says that parts of the brain that mediate special functions acquire tissue mass comparable to the need for those functions—the mosaic character of the brain reflects the mosaic character of its environment.

The Bottom Line

The interim picture of human brain evolution suggests that the major changes were extensive, happening fast, and correlating generally with deep ecological changes. Major changes were possible in part because of scaling relations between body size and brain size—the first increase magnifying the second. But the changes were also possible because the fundamental vertebrate brain with many of its ancestral traits was transmitted to new species as a whole, there to acquire new dimensions of sophistication. Brains were not built anew at each taxonomic junction; they moved in quantity and quality more like an inflating balloon—ever so new, but ever so redundant.

Changes in developmental trajectory are probably responsible for major brain change, as neoteny and reduced cell death probably underlie the magnitude of change from species to species. Whatever climate demanded, it vented its wrath against those unable to remain young. Juvenilization is the face of evolutionary success. The more general message is that most evolutionary changes, not just brain changes, are generated in the uterus and in the nest. Evolution is really a process of developmental change. Obviously that is where we should look for answers.

Last, there are the day to day details of making a living—the constant press to adapt to the ecology at hand. Ecologically driven changes in brain size and specializations bridge the periods of punctuational change. If individuals can't adapt to the routine of environmental insults that they experience daily, they will certainly not withstand the lightning strikes of greater proportions. Punctuational changes may account for the large changes among hominids, but interim changes occur as the result of adaptations to local environments.

References

Cited in Chapter 10

Andreasen, N.C., Flaum, M., Swayze, V., O'Leary, D.S., Alliger, R., Cohen, G., Ehrhardt, J. and Yuh, W.T.C. (1993). "Intelligence and Brain Structure in Normal Individuals." *American Journal of Psychiatry*, 150, 130-34.

Calvin, W.H. (1990). *The Ascent of Mind*. New York: Bantam Books.

Crick, F. (1994). *The Astonishing Hypothesis: The Scientific Search for the Soul*. New York: Charles Scribner's Sons.

Dubrovsky, B. (1993). "Evolution of Nervous Systems and Psychiatry: Consequences of the Vertical and Horizontal Duality of the Evolutionary Process." *Journal of Psychiatric Neurosicience*, 18, 245-59.

Eccles, J.C. (1989). *Evolution of the Brain: Creation of the Self*. London: Routledge.

Foley, R.A. and Lee, P.C. (1991). "Ecology and Energetics of Encephalization in Hominid Evolution." *Philosophical Transactions of the Royal Society of London B.*, 334, 223-32.

Hodos, W. (1988). "Comparative Neuroanatomy and the Evolution of Intelligence." In H.J. Jerison and I. Jerison (eds.), *Intelligence and Evolutionary Biology*, 93-107.

Hofman, M.A. (1983). "Encephalization in Hominids: Evidence for the Model of Punctuationalism." *Brain, Behavior and Evolution*, 22, 102-17.

Jerison, H.J. (1985). "Animal Intelligence as encephalization." *Philosophical Transactions of the Royal Society of London B.*, 308, 21-35.

MacLean, P.D. (1970). "The Triune Brain, Emotion, and Scientific Bias." In F.O. Schmitt (ed.), *The Neurosciences, Second Study Program*. New York: The Rockefeller University Press, 336-49.

Mace, G.M., Harvey, P.H. and Clutton-Brock, T.H. (1980). Is Brain Size an Ecological Variable? *Trends in NeuroSciences*, August, 193-96.

Willerman, L., Schultz, R., Rutledge, J.N., and Bigler, E.D. (1992). "Hemisphere Size Asymmetry Predicts Relative Verbal and Nonverbal Intelligence Differently in the Sexes: An MRI Study of Structure-Function Relations. *Intelligence*, 16, 315-28.

General References

Arbas, E.A., Meinertzhagen, I.A., and Shaw, S.R. (1991). "Evolution in Nervous Systems." *Annual Review of Neuroscience*, 14, 9-38.

Bullock, T.H. (1993). "How are More Complex Brains Different?" *Brain, Behavior, and Evolution*, 41, 88-96.

Jastrow, R. (1981). *The Enchanted Loom: Mind in the Universe*. New York: Simon and Schuster.

Edelman, G.M. (1992). *Bright Air, Brilliant Fire: On the Matter of the Mind*. New York: Basic Books.

Prochiantz, A. (1989). *How the Brain Evolved*. New York: McGraw-Hill, Inc.

11

The Motor Basis of Mind

The separation of psychology from the premises
of biology is purely artificial, because the human
psyche lives in indissoluble union with the body.

—Carl Jung

Compared with our attempts to understand the mind, all other biological problems pale. We hardly know where to begin our inquiries, nor what to expect. The Noble Laureate Francis Crick is quick to conclude that "your joys and your sorrows, your memories and your ambitions, your sense of personal identity and free will, are in fact no more than the behavior of a vast assembly of nerve cells and their associated molecules." True, no doubt, that neural activity drives our consciousness, but "molecules in motion" hardly catches the essence of our experiences. The mind seems irreducibly subjective. Metaphors somehow strike closer to the truth: the mind is like a rippling breeze, invisibly shifting in force and direction, leaving small eddies in our character. We are a long way from understanding how neural activity can do that.

Our history may tell us something. We acquired an exceptional brain, a brain that evaluated the opportunities and threats of its surroundings, a brain that anticipated future happenings, and a brain that reflected on itself. Built into the brain were mental rules, concepts, thoughts, language, and a shimmering sensation of selfawareness.

Where did it all come from? Certainly a demanding environment left adaptive traits in its wake—traits that were used to neutralize threats, traits regulating individual mating strategies and social interactions. But cognitive capacity also evolved as part of a body moving through space and time. The mind and body were minted together, never apart, never in isolation of their bonding. Mind and consciousness are not perched on a body; they are the body.

Roots of the Mind

World-famous child psychologist Jean Piaget (1896-1980) believed that an infant's thoughts are based on its physical action. An infant reaching for its mother is showing a sensorimotor understanding of its environment. The infant extends its hand toward an object, thus identifying that object as distinct from self, yet obtainable through action. A self-action concept is forming, a basic unit of cognition that Piaget called a scheme.

Initially, the infant only reacts to its environment, demonstrating no thoughts, no concepts. Concept formation takes time, unfolding in increasing complexity as the child matures. Piaget likened the journey as one of self-discovery, akin to what we earlier referred to as the revelation of genetic knowledge. The infant does not learn so much as it blooms like a rose in the richness of its soil. Over the months and years the infant assimilates new information from its perceptions and motor acts and accommodates to changes in its environment. The rules of cognition develop through several stages until the child can solve hypothetical problems, make complex deductions and test elaborate hypotheses. An outline of Piaget's cognitive development is given below.

We should understand that the development of concepts, or rules of the mind, is not simply a time-release of pre-stored operations. There may be genetic biases for the formation of neural regulatory networks with particular functions, but these networks assume their final form within a complex neural ecology, continually modified by shifting environmental input. Infants construct adaptive processes from past outcomes of natural selection and contemporary influences.

It is important to emphasize three aspects of Piaget's theory. The first is that the origin of schemes is sensory-motor: all mental architecture comes from finding meaning in muscle movement and the perceptual qualities of its environment. Second, like the formal logic of universal grammar, cognitive development is innate, reified through exposure to complex environments, and logical in its sequence. Third, concepts detach themselves progressively from muscle action and perception, becoming more subjective and independent of objects—the formation of

TABLE 11.1
Stages of Cognitive Development

Sensorimotor Period (0–2 Years)	
Stage 1 (0–1 mo):	reflex activity without thought
Stage 2 (1–4 mo):	self-investigation
Stage 3 (4–8 mo):	coordination and reaching out
Stage 4 (8–12 mo):	goal-directed behavior
Stage 5 (12–18 mo):	experimentation with the environment
Stage 6 (18–24 mo):	mental combinations and problem solving

Preoperational Period (2–7 Years)
Logical operations applied to concrete problems
Conservation and reversibility obtained: knowledge that distortions do not change
  the amount of substance, and the reversals of operations can be imagined

Period of Formal Operations (11+ Years)
Can solve hypothetical problems, make complex deductions, and test advanced
  hypotheses
Can analyze the validity of different ways of reasoning (the foundations of science)

the Ghost in the Machine, as the philosopher Gilbert Ryle put it. Still, the concepts themselves—concepts of proximity, separation, order, enclosure, and continuity—stray little from the Euclidean nature of the environment. The imprint of muscle movement within space and time remains a part of us, no matter how subjective the mentation.

Piaget's theory is brilliant because of its wide scope, its specificity, and the postulation of causal mechanisms of cognition centered on motor movements and the interaction of the child with its environment. Recent hypotheses have gone beyond these notions, but there is no argument that Piaget formed the cornerstone for a new way of thinking about the development of cognition.

He did more than that. He placed human development squarely within an evolutionary framework. Consistent with evolutionary theory, Piaget considered development as an outcome of adaptive selection. Every state that the child goes through reflects the complexity of development needed at that time. As expected, psychologists who are inclined to believe that most concepts result from cumulative learning take issue with the genetic implications of Piaget's thinking. These critics disagree that cognitive development is staged in progressive and discrete ways, and quarrel with his near disregard for learning.

One of the most critical challenges to Piaget's notion that sensorimotor interaction is necessary for developing concepts are the occasional cases of congenital paralysis where the child cannot interact with its environment, and yet appears to have full concept formation. However, according to the developmental psychologist S.J. Segalowitz the evidence for complete paralysis is not strong. Even in severe cases the person still may have feedback from swallowing, tactile interaction with other people, and kinesthetic input from sheets and other objects. Where motor paralysis does seem complete, as in the Guillian-Barre syndrome, the paralysis usually appears after the person has acquired mature concepts.

It is also the case that the infant's perceptual and conceptual development is closely tied to its early motor movements. The onset of crawling at about eight months of age seems to induce a cluster of spatial abilities, such as searching for hidden objects and appreciating the danger of heights. Just dragging oneself along the floor will not induce these skills. Moreover, handicaps that prevent crawling, including spina bifida and orthopedic problems, delay the normal range of cognitive development. A group of leading investigators of child development headed by psychologist Bennett Bertenthal recently concluded that "some of the most significant early experiences are those produced by the infant's own actions. This finding represents a radical departure from the traditional perspective of viewing these actions as merely products and not processes of development." It is doubtful that cognition and adaptive reactions can form in ways other than sensorimotor.

No doubt there are uncertainties in Piaget's encompassing theory. Current methodologies are better and more revealing. Nevertheless, it appears that Piaget was correct in broad outline if not always in specific detail. Development is arranged and expressed according to level of maturation, concepts do apparently form from early interactions with the environment, and identical sequences of change are found in all societies and races. It was our good fortune that as a Swiss, relatively unknown to American psychologists until about 1959, Piaget was uninfluenced by the American eagerness to interpret all behavior as externally derived. Our notions of biological development were enhanced accordingly.

From Piaget's ideas of cognitive development came radically new ideas about the importance of sensorimotor and kinesthetic (muscle feeling) control over the genesis of concepts. According to these new views, thought, language, and consciousness are not simply epiphenomena of neural activity; they are the consequences of motor movements, associated with maturation, driven by natural selection. In much the same way that we acquire morphological and physiological traits, we assume the mental reflections of our sensori-motor existence. Can in those circumstances the mind be anything but its motoric creation?

The Birth of the Modern Mind

Rene Descarte split the mind from the body in 1650 with his publication of *Passions de l'ame*. He accepted that the body was mechanical and animistic, but retained the mind as an unextended soul which is "all that is in us and which we can not conceive in any manner possible to pertain to a body." The soulful mind perceives and wills, interacting with the body through the pineal gland of the brain. Ah, the mind is not animal, not mechanistic; it is different from body.

This great philosopher and scientist described the dualism of the mind and body with such force and clarity that the distinction remains even today. His loyalty to the Catholic Church reinforced his position on the dualistic qualities of body and mind, a position not distinct from the Church's belief even today. However, for those who wanted to entangle the mind and body inexorably, that dualism retarded scientific progress for about 300 years. We inherited the philosophical dualism, and also a not-so-innocent vocabulary that keeps this dualism alive—a host of opposing terms that structure our view of mental activities—"physical" versus "mental," "body" versus "mind," "matter" versus "spirit," "brain" verses "consciousness."

Moreover, within the well of our emotional beliefs, many of us want to believe the Cartesian dualism—it provides us a mental sanctuary against material determinism, for what are we if not free, soulful, and self-determined? Ask a man who is dying and he'll tell you his body is failing him. Marcel Proust expressed our tenacity in this duality when he said, "It is in moments of illness that we are compelled to recognize that we live not alone but chained to a creature of a different kingdom, whole worlds apart who has no knowledge of us and by whom it is impossible to make ourselves understood: our body." The mind remains our haven from the ravages around us, giving us the hope of survival—that last refuge from the pains and suffering of the body. The messages of the mind that contradict objective evidence are compelling, engulfing, deceptive, telling us that all will be well. Madame de Maintenon, the wife of Louis XIV of France, put it bluntly: "Hope says to us constantly, 'Go, go on,' and leads us to the grave."

In spite of history and personal beliefs, psychologists have long believed that the mind is not distinct from the body. The trouble was that no one could find an adequate way to study the mind. Ironically, it was the fear of an unfounded dualism that kept many scientists from investigating mental processes. If one couldn't get at the mind, perhaps it was not worth getting at. Psychologists therefore turned to "behaviorism," attempting to interpret all processes of signiflcance in terms of behavioral responses. John B. Watson the "father" of behaviorism said it authoritatively: "The time seems to have come when psychology must discard all references to consciousness."

For what it was conceived to do, behaviorism was very successful, especially for understanding stimulus-response relations. It showed us the degree to which behavior could be modified with conditioning, giving psychology a level of objectivity never before obtained. The problem was that the subjective qualities of the mind, those which psychology first intended to study, were shoved into the theoretical closet for fear that they might contaminate an objective explanation of human functioning. As a result, mental experiences continued to live a closet life, never eradicated by the behaviorists, half-forgotten by the psychologists.

Mental processes, once regarded by scientists as mirror images of neural activity, have recently jumped out of the theoretical closet wearing new clothes. The "mind" is again the focus of investigations, this time by the cognitive psychologists and linguists who are concerned with "attention," "object representation," "thinking," "concept formation," and "language." The subjective and private aspects of mentation are being transformed into "rules of the mind," sometimes using computer metaphors, at other times by looking for physical and psychological correlates to our experiences. No one knows where all of this effort is going, but it's an exciting time in science, for finally the mind seems to be giving up its secrets.

One of the most exciting developments is the growing understanding of the links between motor movement (muscular activity), muscle sense (kinesthesiology), and the evolution of mental concepts. Here the gaps between Descartes' willful mind, the mechanistic body, and Piaget's motor-perceptual theory of development are closing. The message is not as Descartes asserted, "I think, therefore I am," but quite the opposite, "I do therefore I think."

Muscle Concepts

Helen Adams Keller (1880-1968), the world-renowned author, lecturer, and humanitarian, epitomized her life with this comment: "Security is mostly a superstition. It does not exist in nature.... Life is either a daring adventure or nothing." She spoke from deep wisdom, for as a young girl she was considered mentally retarded and emotionally disturbed. At the age of nineteen months, as a result of a damaging brain fever, she became blind and deaf. She could communicate only through hysterical laughter or violent tantrums. She had no conscious concepts of how the world was or how she fit into it. Her inherent brightness was shrouded in the darkness of her inner walls. Her companion Anne Mansfield Sullivan tried to get her to associate her movements with things around her, but there was no entry into her inner self.

Her epiphany was said to have come in a single day when suddenly she made the mental connection between the feel of water coming from a pump and the general notion of "water." It was a revelation of the deepest kind, for she instantly understood that the world around her could be represented by mental concepts. From that moment on she was a sponge for knowledge. With the help of Anne Sullivan she learned to read Braille and to write on a special typewriter. The world had opened for her, so much so that in her autobiography, *The Story of My Life*, she wrote, "Literature is my utopia."

The story of Helen Keller is not only an inspiration for those handicapped by sensory-motor deficits or circumstances, it is a lesson in how we form concepts. Concept formation is the intrinsic business of the brain, but for the brain to build a concept it must be in contact with the environment—there must be a sensory-motor corridor.

There are other instructive cases like that of Helen Keller, but the outcomes are not always as happy. In one case, an infant of six months of age, referred to as "X," was permanently paralyzed with encephalitis. He was thereafter mute and could only communicate by moving his upper lip for a "yes," and smiling for a "no." As an adolescent his tested IQ was only 8, even though he had three brothers with normal intelligence. In any case, his facial gestures, with the binary code of "yes" and "no" allowed him to name the day of the week for any date from 1915 to the present—a savant with a specialized yes versus no form of counting—but little more. One can perhaps attribute his general deficits to his low IQ, but it is remarkable that his only talent was keyed to the yes-no muscle movement of his face. It seems more evident that the focus of conceptual development was restricted by the individual's inability to move and react widely with his environment.

The third remarkable case is that of Harriet, the sixth of seven children. She was largely ignored and isolated from other children. Her mother habitually placed Harriet's crib directly against the grand piano of the studio when she taught piano and singing. One evening when Harriet was seven months old her father heard a familiar tune coming from her room. Exploring the sound, he found Harriet lying on her back in her crib humming in perfect pitch, tempo, and phrasing the "Cara Nome" from *Rigoletto*.

Harriet developed head banging and rocking, a common feature of infantile autism. Because of this disruptive behavior she was kept in relative isolation. But the obsession with music grew. By the age of four she played the piano, violin, trumpet, clarinet, and French horn—all of the instruments that her siblings played. She, too, was a mnemonic savant, memorizing weather reports, pages of the Boston phone book, and calculating calendar dates over a fifty-year period. At nine years of age she developed some speech. Her IQ was measured at 73. Music became her connection with the world.

The psychiatrist Harold Treffert who studies exceptional people like "X" and Harriet, believes that many savant individuals with limited mental concepts are closed to much of the world, developing only a narrow bridge with the world. Autistic, and very much isolated from motor experiences and sensory input, they view the world through a small iris. Normal individuals vary their width and intensity of focus. In contrast these exceptional individuals concentrate on a few details without awareness of the background.

As with Piaget's notion of scheme, we capture two important points from Helen Keller's experiences and from the exceptional lives of savants. The first is that the brain is prepared to take in and categorize sensory experiences. The second is that motor and kinesthetic experiences are crucial in the formation of mental concepts. Natural selection establishes the preparedness for concept formation; development resurrects these concepts for everyday living.

Apparently, concepts of the mind, mental rules, and even language evolve from muscular movement and the relation of that movement with perception. Tactile-kinesthetic experiences are incorporated into the mind as phylogenetic memory—genetic knowledge, the preparedness to form concepts. Those who did it best had a leg up on others, passing these refinements on to their children.

From the beginning the body knew the mind only through touch and movement, the movement of the limbs, the sense of balance, and one's place within spatial surroundings. Gradually the brain evolved concepts about these tactile-kinesthetic experiences and generalized them to the surrounding environment. For example, bipedal hominids, moving their heads up and down, standing and sitting, drew that feeling of muscle movement together with their spatial perceptions, forming the concept of verticality. Helen Keller made a similar association when she joined together the kinesthetic feeling of flowing water with the concept of water. The idea of water could then be generalized to many other situations in the environment.

The anthropologist Maxine Sheets-Johnstone even believes that our experiences of chewing and masticating food were conceptually translated into stone tools that performed analogous functions. "Thus, in chewing, the creature catches itself in the act of grinding something to pieces. An 'I move' clearly precedes an 'I can.' In this sense, corporeal powers are the spawning ground of corporeal concepts. As the creature that is already chewing finds itself grinding something to pieces, so the creature that is grinding something to pieces is at the brink of conceptual awareness, namely the corporeal concepts of transforming a material object." She goes on to point out that the older Oldowan stone flakes used as hammers, grinders, and scrapers look much like teeth.

Many concepts are presumably built on corporeal experiences— experiences that are common to all hominids. For example, spatial ordering is evolved from the body's experiences—ideas like "up-down," "forward-backward," "in-out," back-front," "here-there," all set against the compass points of the body. It is similar with temporal ordering— concepts such as "now-later," "close-far." These concepts are evident from body movement, and position in space. All represent prepared concepts, cut from the drama of natural selection, reexpressed during individual development.

Below is a list of some of the many mental concepts seemingly based on tactile-kinesthetic experiences.

Concepts of Action

General Concept	Specific Concepts of Tactile-Kinesthetic Experience
Spatial Ordering:	up-down, forward-backward, in-out
Temporal Ordering:	now-later, close-far, closed-open
Texture:	solidarity, softness, rough, smooth, flowing
Transformation:	hitting, cutting, twisting, squeezing
Irreversibility of Action:	unidirectionally of change
Repetitiveness:	cycles, rhythms, back-forth
Equivalence-nonequivalence:	same-different, comparisons
Numbers:	fewer-more, there-not there
Sexual displays:	bipedal displays

In the formation of these concepts the muscle sense was analogized to the environment. For instance, closing and opening of the fist is a systematic change of movement felt by the body and applied to anything that closes and opens. Similarly, smashing, cutting, and twisting objects in the environment stimulates the evolution of transformation. Those concepts that increased genetic fitness eventually became species-typical adaptations of the mind.

Even sexual displays and courtship differences between males and females are extensions of the "body in movement." Bipedal locomotion changed our social and sexual lives. When the woman stood upright for the first time her vagina was hidden from the male's view. This allowed her effectively to hide her receptivity, perhaps gaining her greater solicitation and cooperation from the male. At the same time her waist, hips, and breasts were exposed, allowing these physical characteristics to become sexual signals.

When the male stood up his penis was exposed for all to see. The female could then judge his sexual interest in her and his potency. Anthropologist Donald Symons has suggested that women are much more interested in males with erect penises than in those with flaccid penises. Bipedal movement of the male automatically guaranteed the female a continuous gauge of his sexuality.

The details of concept formation are obviously speculative, but the overall importance of the body in knowing the environment is undeniable. A swimming fish, a flying bird, a digging mole, and a walking human obviously have different conceptions of their environment, each concept is species-specific, each is based upon specialized muscle movements and brain processes.

At the neurological level there is a telling relation between the area of the brain related to motor dexterity and the frontal region of the brain associated with "mental dexterity." In mammals the cerebellum, resting just above the brain stem, controls movement and balance. Recently this same area has been implicated in learning and the retention of memories. In higher primates, especially in humans, the dentate nucleus of the cerebellum has expanded, evolving ties with the frontal cortex. What this connection accomplished was to link motor movements, including those for speech, with areas of the brain involved in concept formation, planning, and anticipation.

In children with autism who have normal intelligence but depressed language abilities, the dentate region of the cerebellum is shrunken. Apparently the motor functions of language are not connecting with cortical areas that interpret language. On the other hand, in children with a bizarre form of mental retardation called Williams Syndrome, in which language is not impaired, or is even exaggerated, the same areas of the cerebellum are longer than average. The motor-language functions are expanded, despite the lack of comprehension.

It has been known for years that the normal development of vision in animals depends upon unrestrained body movements. Restrict movements and visual processing of information is retarded. Dru and her colleagues in discussing these findings additionally show that when cortical lesions destroy vision in rats, visual functioning eventually recovers, but only if the rat is allowed to physically locomote in its visual environment. Visual cognition depends heavily on normal movement through space.

Finally, Lawrence Parsons and his colleagues demonstrated that human discrimination of hand movements in space activate motor regions of the brain normally involved in hand movement. In other words, cognition of movement depends upon implicit motor activity even when actual movement does not occur.

These new observations are shedding light on the essential relations between sensory-motor processes and complex cognitive abilities. One always seems to involve the other. The evidence is compelling that motor functions form the evolutionary and developmental bases for the acquisition and use of complex mental concepts. The origin of cognition is motor—tactile-kinesthetic—forever linked to evolutionary history.

The Physical Properties of Language

The general consensus among linguists with interests in evolution is that true language appeared in recent *Homo sapiens*, perhaps 125,000 to 150,000 years ago—long after thought evolved but sometime before art and agriculture. The antecedents are unclear. Noam Chomsky, the father of the concept of universal grammar, believes that human language is so unique and species-specific that "...it is quite senseless to raise the problem of the evolution of human language from more primitive systems of communication that appear at lower levels of intellectual capacity."

But language did evolve, and from structures and functions already in place, a "genetic tinkering," The use of one trait as the basis for the evolution of another is referred to as *exaptation*. Almost always, a complex system has its evolutionary precursor in simpler form—"descent by modiflcation," as Darwin put it. The classic example is seen with the evolution of the malleus and the incus, bones of the middle ear of vertebrates. The gill arch of fish was first modified into jaws and then into two of the three bones of the middle ear. The end result was a more effective auditory system. Similarly, flight in insects may have evolved from body extensions that originally acted as heat exchangers with the environment. And so it is with every other intricate biological system; one thing becomes another.

Chomsky is correct that universal grammar is species-specific, and it can be viewed as instinctive, as the linguist R. Jackendoff defines it. The problems with these ideas are that language is not clearly recognized as an emergent system of earlier systems or as a set of operations that has to refine itself through development. It has the appearance of the touch of God. But, as we know now, language does have its "animal-istic" origins, and it can only develop in interactions with the environment. Exaptation is evident at every step.

Indeed, there is an entire melody of language that is tuned to its early origin. In the simplest terms language is timed respiration. The rhythm of the lungs drives the vocal cords, giving them power and trajectory. Amazingly, while talking we inspire just enough air to complete a sentence with expired air, regardless of the sentence's length. Unconsciously we regulate the amount of air going in and out of the lungs to suit the segmentation of our thoughts. It's as if we know the complexity of an utterance before we construct it.

Language was born of earlier adaptations in even a more startling way. The linguist M. Donald believes that human language derived from the more generalized mimetic capacity of *Homo erectus*. *H. erectus* did communicate with each other and probably had a sophisticated culture. The hominid no doubt had significant cognitive capacity, but probably no language. But if not language, then what sort of communication was it? It may have involved tones of voice, facial expressions, eye movements, hand gestures, whole body movements, differential speed of movement, and postural attitudes. Similarities between chimpanzee and hominids make these forms of communication quite likely. In addition, *Homo erectus* may have had tribal rituals, music, dance, games, and singing, all of which depend upon enriched cognition, all of which communicate ideas, symbols, and emotions. Donald's argument is that muscle movement and postural attitudes were the precursors of elaborate social communication, and perhaps language. Certainly it is easier to think that language flowed from mimesis rather than the reverse. Again, the tie is evident between physical movements and the evolution of language.

The origin of our voice box, the larynx, is prototypic of evolutionary tinkering. The larynx, situated above the lungs as part of the trachea, is responsible for generating the acoustic source that enters the upper vocal tract. Its original function, however, was to protect the lungs from intruding foreign objects. Coughing reflexively closes the larynx, protecting the lungs from the intrusion of liquids or solid objects. The larynges of most primitive air-breathing animals served the same purpose. Thus, the starting point for the evolution of our vocalization apparatus was a minor change of some lungfish's larynx.

Psycholinguist Peter MacNeilage argues that asymmetrical function-ing of the left and right hemispheres of the brain is a prerequisite for lan-guage. The left hemisphere normally is responsible for language production and interpretation. This brain imbalance did not evolve simultaneously with language; it occurred much earlier in primate evolution. Even the earliest living primates show asymmetrical handedness, and in rhesus monkeys the left hemisphere is more sensitive to vocalizations than is the right. According to neurobiolgists Doreen Kimura and Y. Archibald, the asymmetry of symbolic functions is the consequence of left hemispheric adaptations for expressive motor activities: gestures, signals, and panto-mime. The left hemispheric control of the right hand became the founda-tion of a communication system that began with right hand movements but eventually involved left hemispheric control of language.

MacNeilage makes the point that motor imbalance was important for primates in arboreal environments where animals had to steady them-selves with one hand, while reaching for objects or gesturing with the other hand. Perhaps these functions were mediated by the dentate nucleus of the cerebellum. It makes sense that this asymmetry of movement would be conserved because of its greater efficiency—laterality of func-tion reduces behavioral ambiguity and increases the speed with which movements occur. Movements were always either left or right, with no hesitation of decision. When later primates dropped to the ground and became bipedal, they carried with them a brain asymmetry so complete that any new function like language could only appear in an asymmetri-cal form.

At the level of word production one clearly sees the import of motor movement. The frequency of opening and closing of the vocal folds of the larynx, resulted in changes in perceived pitch. In virtually all speech production, the mouth oscillates between open and closed. The open phase is designated as vowels (a, e, i, o, u); the closed phase corre-sponds to consonants (b, t, d, f, r, etc.). Thus the complete motor cycle of open and close results in a syllable with a vowel and a consonant, as with of, the key sound element in the construction of words.

In all of the communication processes discussed, including respira-tion, larynx variations, gestures, dance, and music, there is oscillation of structure and function—a rhythm of motoric response inherent in the nature of the machine—co-opted as symbols of sound communication and eventually as language.

Press inward into the brain and similar motoric rhythmicity is evident. MacNeilage points out that the same mandibular oscillation that is responsible for vowel and consonant production is part of ingestive motor reactions associated with sound generation—rhythmic lipsmacks, tonguesmacks, sucking, and teeth chattering. Stimulate Broca's area of the monkey cortex, that is what you get. Do the same with the human cortex and the effects are rhythmic movements of the lips, tongue, mandible, pharynx, and larynx. The rhythms in combination with the air moving through the larynx produce what we identify as language sounds.

Apparently the motor oscillations based on ingestive behavior became a rhythmic frame within which syllables and words are formed. You can see this in the repetitive babbling that goes on in seven month old infants—ba, ba, da, da, da, ma, ma—but you also see it in the invariant form of syllable production among adults. There is something very rigid about the pattern of sound production. Consonants and vowels have exact relations to each other, and if language errors occur, they occur in definite and predictable places. For example, "Well made" is sometimes transformed into "Mel wade," a transposition of consonants in the initial position of each word. In the case of transformation of "ad hoc" to odd hack," the vowels *a* and *o* are exchanged, again at the same position of each word. The general case is stated by MacNeilage: "two consonants beginning a syllable, exchange with each other, or vowels exchange, or consonants terminating a syllable exchange. Occasionally consonants occupying different positions in syllables interact with each other (e.g. 'top' 'pot'). But what appears totally inviolate is the independence between consonants and vowels (errors such as 'abstract' 'bastract'). Errors such as this never occur in speech even though in another linguistic output medium, typing, such exchange between adjacent items, are the most common kind."

According to this motor-llinguistic theory, words and meanings, stored elsewhere in the brain—the "content" of language—are shuttled through the oscillating "frame" that structures and releases them into the world. It is all motor-driven, rhythmic, and derivative of earlier primate adaptations. Think about the generation of language and you think about frame and content; think about the abstractions formed with words and sentences and you think about universal grammar. The distinctions, not withstanding, word production and language structure flow from motor movements, and language results from descent with modification.

What Did Neanderthal Know and When Did He Know It?

Why do linguists believe that hominids, except for recent *H. sapiens*, were without formal language. Several species hunted, made stone tools, used fire, and all had complex social systems. Their concepts and thoughts were obviously complex; Neanderthal even had religious burial practices. So why not language?

It all comes down to the hyoid, a small bone at the base of the skull, a bone connected to the larynx by muscles and ligaments. In chimpanzees, in human infants, and in *H. erectus* and Neanderthal, that bone is positioned so that the larynx is elevated relative to the upper supralaryngeal airway. Speech sounds are limited and nasal in quality. As human infants mature and begin to form syllables the larynx sinks and the position of the bone changes accordingly. Thus, when a fossil skull is found with the hyoid bone in place, one can make an estimate of speech capabilities—high larynx, as in chimps, infant humans and early hominids, no language—low larynx as in adult humans and earlier *H. sapiens*, language. There are other physical characteristics of fossilized skulls that are suggestive of speech characteristics. Some of these variations, along with the hyoid bone and larynx as seen here.

Language speeds up communication, hence its value. Non-speech animals transmit up to seven to nine sound units per second, but humans can transmit as many as fifteen consonants and vowels per second. Considering that the output of Neanderthal was quite similar to nonhuman primates and human newborns, it is obvious that Neanderthal was not producing sounds at the same rate as adult humans. Moreover, due of the configuration of the vocal tract, Neanderthal could not form the vowels *i*, *u*, and *a*. Its speech was possibly like that of a babbling human infant. Because it was also nasalized it was subject to a high rate of errors, perhaps as much as 30 percent higher than ours. Obviously Neanderthal had a limited capacity for speech, although it could have had a rich repertoire of nonarticulated sounds, as well as gestures, pantomime, dance, and music. Jean M. Auel the author of the famous novel about Neanderthal, *The Clan of the Cave Bear*, probably is near the truth with this description: "With a need for silence so as not to warn the game they were stalking, they developed hunting signals that evolved into the more elaborate hand signals and gestures used to communicate other needs and desires. Warning cries changed in pitch

FIGURE 11.1

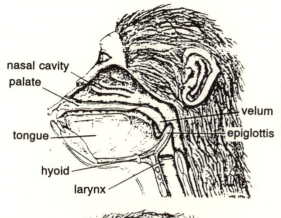

nasal cavity
palate
velum
tongue
epiglottis
hyoid
larynx

Chimpanzee
The chimpanzee is positioned high.
The hyoid bone is connected to the
larynx, jawbone and skull by
means of muscles and ligaments.

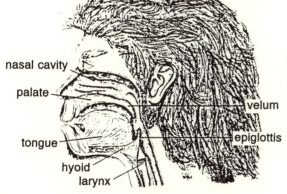

nasal cavity
palate
velum
tongue
epiglottis
hyoid
larynx

Neanderthal
A reconstructed airway of the
Neanderthal fossil. The larynx is
positioned high, close to the
entrance to the nasal cavity. The
hyoid bone is positioned much like
that of the chimpanzee.

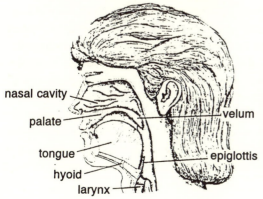

nasal cavity
palate
velum
tongue
epiglottis
hyoid
larynx

Human
The larynx and hyoid bone are low,
making it impossible for the larynx
to lock into the nose. The position
of the larynx relative to the supralaryngeal airway is what makes
complex speech possible.

TABLE 11.2
Structural and Behavioral Adaptation for Speech

Australopithecus
Pipelike vocal tract
No speech

Homo Erectus
Slight lowering of larynx
Speech limited to range of sounds of nonhuman primates
Brain mechanisms for automotized speech control?

Neanderthal
La Chapelle-aux-Saints (France)
Long palate, shallow basicranial angle, slight lowering of larynx Nasal speech, no quantal vowels *(a, i, u)*
Brain mechanisms for automatized speech control?

Anatomically Modern Homo Sapiens
Broken Hill (Africa, 150,000 years ago) Vocal tract generating all sounds of human speech, but with less stability
Brain mechanisms for automatized speech control
Jebel Qafzeh and Skhul V (Israel, 125,000 years ago)
Modern vocal tract, all sounds of human speech
Brain mechanisms for automatized speech control

and tone to include greater informational content. Though the branch of the tree of man that led to the people of the Clan did not include sufficiently developed vocal mechanisms to evolve a full verbal language, it did not impair their ability to hunt."

As we acquire more information about the fossil record and the development of language we will better understand the differences among evolving hominids. For now, the generalized view is sketched here.

Australopithecine species were ape-like in communication, with a brain to match. *H. erectus* showed a lowering of the larynx and a brain capability that together suggest primitive speech. Neanderthal perhaps had greater speech capacities, and certainly its brain was bigger. With *H. sapiens*, especially the more recent form, everything was in place for sophisticated articulation and the translation of thoughts into sound.

Human development shows aspects of our evolutionary history—we develop through earlier to later evolutionary steps. In the parlance of the evolutionist, ontogeny recapitulates phylogeny, or, more clearly, development duplicates genetic history. This is the notion we explored earlier when it was suggested that in our embryological development we seem to display a sequence of traits from fish, through amphibia, reptiles, and higher vertebrates. Our human structure, while obviously unique, still shows those earlier traits that were parts of our early evolutionary history. Assuming that recapitulation does occur and applies to language, MacNeilage estimates that the first *H. sapiens* had about 100 words. He bases this estimate on the universality of seven consonants and three vowels found among two year olds using 317 different languages. The consonants are p, t, m, n, w, y, and g, and the vowels are a, i, and u. The three vowels are those that Neanderthal couldn't construct, suggesting that these made a world of linguistic difference. In any case, seven consonants and three vowels can be combined to form about 100 simple consonant-vowel arrangements—the babbling of babes, the talk of early *H. sapiens*. It wasn't *Hamlet*—more like *The Call of the Wild*.

Language develops in characteristic ways, and it is driven by motor patterns and brain differentials. It is so remarkable in form and function that it might never have happened, and probably never will evolve again. Thought doesn't depend upon language, but once language appears, thoughts can be expressed and shared with others. Language may be the key to the evolution of cooperative societies, where technology can develop, kinship rules are defined, and reciprocal interactions are implemented. Language is that quintessential step that humans took that set us far apart from our closest nonlingual relatives—the telling adaptation, providing us with competitive and reproductive advantages. A teacher of Helen Keller, and therefore one able to appreciate the power of language, Anne Sullivan gave language this deserved endorsement: "Language grows out of life, out of its needs and experiences.... Language and knowledge are indissolubly connected; they are interdependent. Good work in language presupposes and depends on a real knowledge of things." We can add that language gives us the labels, the symbols, and the metaphors to understand our own wispy consciousness.

The Rock Bottom Seat of the Soul

Our oldest marine ancestors were probably sessile filter-feeders, hardly moving, living the passive life, ingesting what came their way. More like a plant than an animal, these organisms charted no seas and reflected not.

But as resources dwindled and competitors arrived, the advantage went to those organisms that could extend their appendages, sense the currents swirling around their bodies, and move to a more strategic location. So it went, evolution toward feeling and manipulating the environment—motor movements resulting in new sensations and perceptions, allowing organisms new command over their environments.

Movement led to interpretations of new qualities of the environment—sharpened sensitivity, enlarged perceptions, induced knowledge of location, opened discrimination between beneficial and harmful stimuli, and created the anticipation of change. Motor movements shifted their force inward, building neurological analogues of the encircling world, composing relations among movement, position in space, sensations, perception, and causality. Knowledge, action patterns, and self-reflection were the new tools for survival and reproduction.

Born out of the turmoil of survival were many evolutionary successes, some maturing into mammals, and some of these becoming primates, including hominids. The process moved through exaptation—the periodic evolution of new specializations built on older structures and habits. As our neurological system became more complex, and our relations with the environment more extensive, the exaptations enhanced our cognitive understanding of the world until, finally, about 125,000 years ago language was first heard and understood.

It seems farfetched to argue that all of our mental finery emerged from the transformation of motor movements into cognition, but that's what it looks like. The mind was never separate from the body, contradicting Rene Descartes; it was always a part of that body—the body in movement, the movement transformed into concepts and rules of the mind. Our nature is earthbound in a very literal sense, emerging from the interaction of the body with the earth, shaping our concepts, rules of action, and our human philosophy.

References

Cited in Chapter 11

Baillageon, R. (1994). "How Do Infants Learn about the Physical World?" *Current Directions*, 3, 133–45.

Chomsky, N. (1973). *Language and Mind*. New York: Harcourt Brace Jovanovich.

Corballis, M.C. (1989). "Laterality and Human Evolution." *Psychological Review*, 96, 492–505.

Donald, M. (1991). *Origins of the Modern Mind: Three Stages in the Evolution of Culture and Cognition.* Cambridge, MA: Harvard University Press.

Dru, D., Walker, J.P., and Walker, J.B. (1975). "Self-produced Locomotion Restores Visual Capacity after Striate Lesions." *Science,* 187, 265–66.

Gazzaniga, M.S. (1992). *Nature's Mind.* New York: Basic Books.

Jackendoff, R. (1994). *Patterns in the Mind: Language and Human Nature.* New York: Basic Books.

Kimura, D. and Archibald, Y. (1974). "Motor Functions of the Left Hemisphere." *Brain,* 97, 337–50.

MacNeilage, P.F. (1994). "Prolegomena to a Theory of the Sound Pattern of the First Spoken Language." *Phonetica,* in press.

MacNeilage, P.F., Studdert-Kennedy, M.G., and Lindblom, B. (1993). "Hand Signals: Right Side, Left Brain and the Origin of Language." *The Sciences,* January/February, 32–37.

Parsons, L.M., Fox, P.T., Downs, J.H., Glass, T., Hirsch, T.B., Martin, C.C., Jerabek, P.A., and Lancaster, J.L. (1995). "Neural Basis of Implicit Motor Behavior: Evidence from PET Studies of Visual Shape Discrimination." *Nature,* in press.

Piaget, J. (1970). "Piaget's Theory." In P.H. Mussen (ed.), *Carmichael's Manual of Child Psychology.* (Vol. 1, 3rd ed.). New York: John Wiley.

Segalowitz, S.J. (1980). "Piaget's Achilles' Heel: A Safe Soft Spot?" *Human Development,* 23, 137–40.

Sheets-Johnstone, M. (1990). *The Roots of Thinking.* Philadelphia: Temple University Press.

Treffert, D.A. (1989). *Extraordinary People.* New York: Harper and Row.

General References

Crick, F. (1994). *The Astonishing Hypothesis: The Scientific Search for the Soul.* New York: Charles Scribner's Sons.

Lieberman, P. (1991). *Uniquely Human.* Cambridge, MA: Harvard University Press.

McCrone, J. (1991). *The Ape that Spoke: Language and the Evolution of the Human Mind.* New York: William Morrow and Company, Inc.

12

The Light and Dark Sides of Consciousness

*Man is only a reed, the weakest in nature; but he is
a thinking reed. There is no need for the whole
universe to take up arms to crush him: a vapor, a
drop of water is enough to kill him. But even if the
universe were to crush him, man would still be
nobler than his slayer, because he knows that he is
dying and the advantage of the universe has over
him. The universe knows nothing of this.*

—Blaise Pascal

*Consciousness is much more than the thorn, it is
the dagger in the flesh.*

—E.M. Cioran

Our reflections on ourselves and the cosmos are the junk dividends
of evolution past. Self-reflection is not necessarily adaptive, appearing
as a consequence of our responses to the environment. We are in first
measure a creature of action, with our mental adaptations mirroring our
motoric nature. We evolved to understand our world through actions—
the need to detect and avoid predators, the foraging strategies necessary
to find food, the imperatives of building habitats and acquiring mates.
We were not specifically designed to understand ourselves, contemplate
the universe, or philosophize about our origin. These matters were never
direct responses to natural selection, as they ultimately have little to do
with survival or reproduction. To believe this, one need only consider
the absence of a concrete relation between cognitive capacity and reproductive rate.

Often, higher mental functions interfere with reproduction. As scary
as it sounds, the evolution of brain complexity appears negatively associated with species survival. Early *Australopithecus afarensis*, with a

249

brain hardly bigger than the chimpanzee, about 500 cc, survived about a million years. *Homo erectus*, sporting a brain of about 1,000 cc lived perhaps 750,000 years. Neanderthal, with a huge brain of about 1450 cc, lived only about 300,000 years. And *Homo sapiens*, with a brain size of about 1350 cc—larger than that of Neanderthal relative to body size—has a recent origin and an uncertain future. Newer hominids were always more complex, but perished more quickly. Several small-brained great apes are still around, but only one hominid. Perhaps it was neural complexity that ultimately interfered with reproduction, cutting hominid lives short.

In any case, brain complexity is not always a blessing. Some individuals may profit reproductively by being smart and clever, but in the long run it may pay to be bright about the immediate environment and stupid about metaphysics. The problem may be, however, that when one is bright about the surrounding environment, one has to contend with thoughts about the cosmos.

The Emergence of Consciousness

Consciousness is the apparent miracle of all time, our sense of life, an irreducible nugget of self-reflection, the door through which we move outside ourselves. Memory, language, and even thoughts seem to have substance and brain location, but consciousness floats like a ghost throughout our head. If there is anything that apparently supports the mind-body dualism it is consciousness. Consciousness seems worlds apart from body.

The separateness is there, alright, but only conceptually. There is a tight relation between the activity of neural networks and the conscious state—mess with neural activity and watch consciousness change. The curious thing is that the neurological state is measurable in microvolts, while the other flies like the wind: isomorphism is there, but the measurements differ.

The word "conscious" comes from the Latin word *con*, which means "together with," and from the word *scire*, which means "to know." Originally the word consciousness referred to what was shared with others, but eventually it was restricted to sharing knowledge with oneself, therefore taking on the subjective qualities as we now understand them. But are we alone in what we experience and from where does it come?

There has been a continuing argument about the phylogeny of consciousness, just where it appeared in the evolution of organisms, and how it varies across species. For the philosopher John Searle consciousness has an on/off switch: the system is either conscious or not. But once conscious, the system is regulated by a rheostat—there are different degrees of consciousness. Most of us might agree that the great apes have consciousness, even though ape-like in character. But what about your dog or cat, or the rat you saw running under your shrubbery this morning? Would you go that far in ascribing consciousness to these animals?

The major reason that we believe other persons to be conscious is that we are similar; we share similar bodies and environments, and probably, therefore, mental states. It is unlikely that you would be much different from someone who shares your history and your general evolutionary composition. We apparently possess the same conscious state, even though we are unable to describe it properly or understand its origin. Extending this reasoning, it would seem that we share consciousness with other animals to the degree that we share their genes.

Where Did it all Begin?

There was a time in evolutionary history when there was no consciousness anywhere. The fact that it did evolve, finally, is evidence of its adaptive character. The evolutionary scenario that the neurobiologist Nicholas Humphrey favors is an "outside-inside" hypothesis. According to this notion there was *first* a localized peripheral stimulus-response reaction that was reflexive and had no lasting impact. The example would be a single-cell protozoan that reacts to an irritation of the outer membrane with an avoidance reaction. No neural activity is involved, little is remembered, and the cell anticipates nothing.

The *second* evolutionary step was to send the information about a local irritation along a neuron to a central ganglion (group of neural cells) and back again to cause an avoidance reaction. Again, the system is reflexive, but the difference is that the information coming in can be stored as a neural change in the ganglion. The "memory" of the local event can alter subsequent responses to similar local events. Consciousness is not assumed here either.

In the *third* and critical evolutionary step the incoming information reverberates in the ganglionic neural network—it circulates over and over, even in the absence of continuous peripheral excitation. Moreover, the central circuit can be reactivated by minimal external excitation and perhaps by adjacent neural activity not directly related to the peripheral event. The reverberation in the ganglion is a representation of external events— an isomorphic "anticipatory" activity that reflects a possible peripheral state. We might now call this "elementary consciousness."

Humphrey's model, accounting for the origin of consciousness, is compatible with the hypothesis that concept formation, language, and consciousness are tactile-kinesthetic in origin. From tactile-kinesthetic origins, strategies, concepts, and rules of the mind evolve—dependent and causally determined by their origin—taking on forms and independence hardly recognizable in their new attire. Much like gaseous bubbles breaking free from their seething caldron, mental traits strip their bonds from their substrate and float free. But the freedom is illusory, for, like the bubbles from the steaming caldron, the mental traits depend entirely on the substrate, and merely represent its content. Mental freedom is like that gaseous state—it seems real—but when the bubble bursts we are reminded of its primitive beginnings. In the case of consciousness the organism builds a neurological system to reflect sensory-motor events, then, like concepts and language, the central representation appears more or less autonomous.

The implication of the "motor origin" hypothesis of consciousness is that natural selection magnifies those mental structures and functions that reflect motor activities which enhance reproductive performance. Individuals who best represent their interaction with the environment with consciousness have competitive advantages in being able to assess the qualities of their environment and in anticipating future events. Thus, natural selection is tending to maximize mental representation of motor actions that increase reproductive performance.

The Strange Case of the Bicameral Mind

Psychologist Julian Jaynes believes that human consciousness appeared only within the past 3,000 years. Prior to that *Homo sapiens* was a virtual automaton, lacking the concept of self-fulfillment and a sense of independence. There was no "I." Everywhere, people heard voices in their heads, calling them gods. The mind was divided into two centers: there was an executive center, called "god," and a follower center called "man." When writing and other complex behaviors appeared this "bi-cameral" mind began to break down—the gods became silent and consciousness was born.

According to Jaynes the "speech of the gods" occurred in the right hemisphere of the brain and was heard by the auditory and speech centers of the left hemisphere, the information moving across the connecting fiber tracts of the cerebral commissures. Thus the "silent" right hemisphere containing the gods ranged freely, influencing the actions of man through speech and perceptual processes of the left hemisphere. While Jaynes might not agree with this, it appears that his theorizing is another version of the mind-body distinction stressed by the philosopher René Descartes. It is also reminiscent of Descartes' idea that the spirits (Jaynes' "gods") interact with the body (Jaynes' "man') by way of a single unifying organ of the brain. Descartes chose the pineal gland of the brain as the point of spiritual entry into the body; Jaynes, more than three hundred years later, chose the connecting fiber tract uniting the two brain hemisphers.

Where did Jaynes get the idea that consciousness is only 3,000 years old? He supports his contentions by reference to ancient history and literature, where heros never act without reference to the gods. To him, the people depicted by Homer in the *Iliad* were not conscious. The Greek warrior Achilles, for instance, like all bicameral people of that period, had a split brain: the executive god-part stored up experiences and told the follower person what to do through auditory hallucinations.

Jaynes believes that the bicameral mind began to break down as language and writing became more important. To him consciousness is largely constructed from culture and what we learn.

The theory of Jaynes is a bold attempt to localize the origin of consciousness, but, alas, is at variance with what we know about chimpanzee cognition and inferences about our ancestor hominids. Chimps have a sense of self, hardly compatible with the idea that the self was commanded by the hallucinations of gods. Handed a mirror, chimps will look at their reflection, attending to paint spots placed on the head by the experimenter. Clearly they see the image in the mirror as a reflection of self, and can act accordingly. Moreover, hunter-gather hominids from *Homo habilis* on displayed many complex mental processes that are consistent with the concept of "I"—tool making, hunting, differentiation of labor, fire making, art, dance, and probably music and story telling. There was no deficiency of self-awareness. God-like commands may have existed, but they involved natural attributes of power to unknown and unpredictable surroundings. Certainly by the time of Homer there is no question that consciousness was as complex as *H. sapiens* will ever experience. Here, Homer speaks through the *Iliad*: "As is the generations of leaves, so is that of humanity. The wind scatters the leaves on the ground, but the live timber Burgeons with leaves again in the season of spring returning. So one generation of men will grow while another dies." Shakespeare couldn't have consciously done better.

Jaynes may have been wrong in ascribing man control to the left hemisphere of the brain and god control to the right, but he was still correct about the bicameral nature of the brain. The left and right hemispheres process information differently. To simplify, the left hemisphere is generally the language hemisphere, forming abstractions and dealing directly with the environment. The right hemisphere, by contrast, tends to be more emotional, viewing the world holistically, and involving itself in visual-spatial matters. Each hemisphere has a different form of awareness, as it were, a different form of consciousness.

According to the neuropsychologists Sully Springer and Georg Deutsch the left hemisphere may govern our conscious life, while the right hemisphere controls our unconscious life. The right hemisphere seems less accessible to observation, yet is a reservoir of cognitive and emotional force. Included here are an extensive use of images, involvement in the perception of time and sequence, and a limited language of the kind that appears in dreams and slips of the tongue. Yet it gives emotional tone to the qualities of our lives, is perhaps responsible for dreaming, and quietly processes information independent of language. The bicameral manifestation of consciousness offers an explanation for the duality of our mental processes, the conflicts of the mind, and the hidden influences of our unconscious mind from which incredible insights and thoughts of despair emerge.

Neural Structures and Functional Design of Consciousness

Consciousness reflects the activity of specific brain processes. While this is true, it is the case that it is difficult to define consciousness and we have only begun to detail the nature of its neurological substrate. Investigators often end up describing mechanisms that are thought to be associated with consciousness, but not consciousness itself. *Attention* is an attribute of consciousness that is assuming experimental importance. Attention is that characteristic of mental life that focuses awareness on ourselves as well as those things around us. It is the conscious awareness that allows the necessary separation between "us" and "them;" it is the "I" of consciousness. Cognitive psychologist Michael Posner believes "that an understanding of consciousness must rest on an appreciation of the brain networks that subserve attention, in much the same way as a scientific analysis of life without consideration of the structure of DNA would seem vacuous." Posner doesn't believe that attention *is* consciousness, but only that the understanding of attention is essential for figuring out the substance of consciousness.

According to Posner there are three major attentional functions: orienting to sensory stimuli, detecting significant events, including ideas stored in memory, and maintaining an alert state. These functions can be described to some degree in terms of neural processes. For example, when subjects in experiments switch attention from location to location the lateral posterior outer cortex of the brain becomes more active. The left hemisphere seems to be more involved when the individual is attending to local information that is used in recognizing objects, whereas the right hemisphere appears to be more involved when more global features of the environment are attended to.

An individual's attention provokes neural activity. For example, when a person attends to a color, form, or motion, regions of the brain that normally process that information are increased in activity. Similarly, attention to motor movements activates regions of the brain used to generate the movement. Even creating a visual image of an object produces activation in areas of the cortex that are used to process visual input of the same type. In other words, areas of the brain that normally process stimuli in the environment are the same ones that are activated when a person pays attention to these stimuli. To some extent, then, attention, arousal, and information processing are the same.

When attention is focused on colors, forms, and motion, the frontal areas of the cortex are activated, but no lateral or posterior regions. It thus appears that there are two activational systems, one involving target location in space (lateral-posterior brain areas) and another involving attention to color, form, and movement (frontal areas of the brain).

There are of course more details to the neural representation of attention, and there is much more to learn. The same areas involved in attention seem to be involved in memory. Also, it appears that brain activity is amplified in the right posterior cortex when features of the environment are attended to, and in the left frontal area when language is being used.

One of the most important functions of attention is to increase the speed with which information is processed. It does not increase the accuracy with which information is processed, but it does facilitate the speed of action taken toward a target. The speed of processing information is related to the chemical neurotransmitter norepinephrine. Neurons controlling norepinephrine originate deep within the brain and distribute themselves in the areas of the brain used in attentional functions. Norephinephrine arouses those areas, increasing the speed with which decisions are made.

At the moment there are major limitations to our understanding of consciousness. It is increasingly apparent that consciousness is not a global characteristic of the mind, even though our metaphors make it appear so. Consciousness is a distributed function that depends on whether decisions are made about locations, forms, colors, or words. It interacts with the memory system and is carried along by physiological mechanisms of arousal. There is not only a bicameral mind based on left and right hemispheres, there is a hierarchy of functions depending on the specificity of the environment and the differential activity of the brain. It seems that there is a plethora of "I's," a variety of consciousnesses, degrees of attention, and several uncertain visions of ourselves.

A recent theory of consciousness expounded by the neuroscientist Rodolfo Llinás suggests that the attention mechanism is related to a neural scanning of the sensory areas of the cortex by waves of electrical activity originating in a lower brain structure called the thalamus. This neural center generates a 40-cycle-per-second wave that sweeps the cortex from front to back every 12.5-thousandth of a second. The sweep continuously samples sensory information, synchronizing cortical activity and sending back sensory patterns to the thalamus.

When the sensory picture of the world changes, as when a dog suddenly appears in the visual field, the pattern of activity between the thalamus and cortex changes. It is this specific and ever changing pattern that represent our conscious view of the world. Although the activity of the brain is periodic, the 40-cycle-per-second electrical waves from the thalamus and their return happen so fast that, like a movie film, we appear to have a continuous monitoring of the outside world. How the changes of activity are interpreted as consciousness, attention, or self-reflection is not known, but at least we have an emerging theory that can be subjected to experimental test.

The Use of Consciousness

Whatever is in the brain—electrical rhythms, genetic knowledge, rules of the mind, thoughts, emotions, concepts, consciousness—is coded neurologically to allow the organism to track and anticipate the environment. At no evolutionary stage did the individual respond dispassionately; there were always causes that initiated change; there were always consequences that brought organisms before the governing board of natural selection. The organism's more basic needs were to respond to the immediate future, without memory or representation, just the plunge straight ahead. Later, as Humphrey believes, short-term anticipation was built in, allowing the organism to "dodge bullets." The more that genetic fitness depends on environmental circumstances, the more clearly that the conscious mind perceives those relations, the less variable the behavior. Thus, economic behaviors, such as job acquisition or the investment of discretionary money, are typically flexible, whereas universal grammar, incest avoidance, predatory avoidance, and aggression are more tightly programed, allowing for fewer conscious reactions.

Neurophilosopher Daniel Dennett believes that one of the more important pressures leading to an anticipatory brain was another individual staring. Eyes are potent signals, sometimes specifying predator, at other times signaling a mate, still at other times warning of aggression. Being informed in advance was a great advantage. Eyes, as well as other potentially "evil" or "good" stimuli triggered a vigilance that served the animal's needs.

When an organism is alarmed by eyes or other startling events consciousness jumps into action. It's as if the attention system says "All hands on deck." The organism is prepared to respond to any danger or potential danger. It scans; it anticipates; it reflects on its own capabilities; it digs into its bag of evolutionary tricks. The brain remains vigilant until the potential danger passes. It's as if every second of consciouness is a discomfort looking for a solution. Once the situation is resolved, it's "Hands stand down," and consciousness fades into a choppy dream-like state. Sigmund Freud described it beautifully: "The conscious mind may be compared to a fountain playing in the sun and falling back into the great subterranean pool of subconscious from which it rises."

The specificity to the system is that we must be conscious of something. As with the specificity of attention, we are not just "conscious," we are conscious of the blister on our heel, the blaring television in the background, the letters moving across the computer monitor. Our consciousness refers to figure-background variations, colors, forms, movements, novelty, other individuals, space and time events, eyes and other social signals, and muscular movements. This is the environmental representation in the mind that took millennia to forge. Pretty primitive stuff, all of which we share with each other.

Consciousness also carries the stamp of individuality. It is colored by our emotions of joy, fear, surprise, anxiety, hate, and love; it is shaped by "background" features, consisting of dispositions, know-how, intelligence, ways of behaving, extrinsic and intrinsic cognition, memories, and savoir faire. The intermingling of moods and background with consciousness creates an enriched mind that sees the world both with the primitive perspective of evolutionary history and the parochial view of the individual. The fundamental nature of consciousness remains, but is colored by our personal dispositions and history.

Dennett disagrees by asserting that to a great degree human consciousness is a product of cultural evolution. By that he means more than the shading of significance through individual experience. For him, ideas surge through generations not only on our strands of DNA but along with our cultural brains. Dennett draws the biological line where culture and learning carry our most complex ideas, ideas of philosophy, religion, science, and business.

There was, perhaps, an emergence of "soft-wiring" (read: *learning*) to our nature that went beyond food-seeking, shelter-searching, mate-selection, and predator-avoidance. As Dennett sees it, "The design improvements one receives from one's culture—one seldom has to 'reinvent the wheel'—probably swamp most individual genetic difference in brain design, removing this advantage from those who are slightly better off at birth." In other words, culture takes us beyond biology and irons out any genetic differences that might be there at birth.

But culture is a creation of evolution, not simply of learning, and even what we learn is constrained by our biology. No doubt there are things we cannot know, and we are restricted to forms of culture that allow us to pursue old goals—feeding, mating, dealing with dangers, and feeling good—old genetic wine in new cultural bottles. Dennett, and others who would divorce us from our millions of years of evolution, fail to make a distinction between rules of the mind and content of the mind. The former are the strategies by which we deal with the basic requirements of the organism—the evolved plans of survival, and yes, the consciousness of these plans. These mechanisms don't change. Content, as with the content of consciousness, is variable; it does not alter strategies, although it does give the mind new tools to work with. The analogy is the frame and content of language, where the frame determines how we select words and produce grammar, and the content, which can include any number of arbitrary words. We can surround ourselves with technological innovations and read Shakespeare until the cows come home, but we will never change the nature of consciousness, our basic needs, or the strategies that satisfy them. Culture, in the sense of learned content, is overrated as the mother of behavior—mere shadows cast on the torrents of evolution.

The Validity of the Unconscious Mind

Sigmund Freud believed that "The unconscious is the true psychic reality: in its inner nature it is just as much unknown to us as the reality of the external world, and it is just as imperfectly communicated to us by the data of consciousness as is the external world by the reports of our sense-organs." To understand consciousness, we must delve into the processes that lie beyond.

What we are and what we think we are, are two different things. Consider memory. We do not store memories like letters in mailboxes; we construct them out of fragments of our sensory world and our past experiences. Memories are shaped by the context in which events occur, the emotional color that surrounds them, and the circumstances of the learning. For example, if a person sees a reddish-orange sphere and is told it is a tomato, that person will remember the disc as red. On the other hand, if a person sees the same sphere but is told that the sphere is an orange, that person will remember the sphere as orange. Distortions are the rule not the exception. Most of the time our memories represent reality enough so that we get by, but there is no doubt that we build memories from fragments of the truth.

One thing is clear: people believe that memories drop from consciousness to unconsciousness, there to remain as hidden influences on our lives, until called back through special circumstances. Little wonder we believe that, for it is a fact that we are aware of only a tiny fraction of what we know at any one time. As you read this, your consciousness is cluttered with thoughts about mental processes, but little else. However, you could be reminded of what you had for breakfast, what your last sexual experience was like, or who your favorite teacher was in grade school. A great deal is stored in your brain, but very little of it "flashes before your eyes" for review. Self-awareness is specific and ephemeral—it comes and goes in fragments, many of which are incomplete sparks of reconstructed events.

The writer Arthur Koestler told a story about the chemist Otto Loewi who came up with the idea that neural activity involved chemical transmission. For seventeen years he neglected the idea for a lack of a technique to test the idea. Then in two nights his unconscious brain gave him the answer:

> I awoke, turned on the light, jotted down a few notes on a tiny slip of thin paper. Then I fell asleep again. It occurred to me at six o'clock in the morning that during the night I had written down something most important, but I was unable to decipher the scrawl. The next night, at three o'clock, the idea returned. It was the design of an experiment to determine whether or not the hypothesis of chemical transmission that I had uttered seventeen years ago was correct. I got up immediately, went to the laboratory, and performed a simple experiment on a frog heart according to the nocturnal design.

The insight won him the Nobel Prize in 1936.

Loewi had prepared his mind to work on the problem of chemical transmission many years before the solution came. When it did come, it was swift, simple, and complete, a bit of genetic knowledge expressed through the unconscious filter of the brain—fragments of the mind quietly built into an edifice.

Deep-Seated Problems of Explanation

It is difficult to understand how the brain ties incoming information to existing memories, concepts, and new experiences. We don't even know whether we think in images or in propositions. A brain is a mass of interconnected neurons; it is not scaled from high consciousness to low unconsciousness; it is not compartmentalized into storage areas for memories, emotions, and instincts, with mixing bowls here and there. There are no pictures, words, predators, or sex objects in the brain. Nor is there an omniscient brain official who applies rules and directs traffic. There is just the brain, magnificently complex, laced with millions of overlapping neural networks, responding to inner metabolites and electrical events, and outer sensory stimuli.

Somehow, though, the brain takes care of our needs. It builds consciousness into neural maps that can be referred to later. It labels information and tucks it away for later recall. The brain scans the environment for potential danger and things of interest. It works through hierarchies, grouping processes into general categories, and activating rules of the mind, concepts, and systems of grammar. It also represses.

However it does all these things—no matter how roughly it works— it gives us a general logic of survival and an inclination toward reproduction. Everything else more or less fits in—partial memories, variable emotions, specific concepts, and a whole bunch of individual differences in physiology and behavior.

Most of the time the machinery works silently and efficiently—there is no need for consciousness—a quality that only disrupts the flow of life. Consciousness is there to update the brain and allow it to hum on without distractions. The neuropsychologist Robert Ornstein says it better than most:

> Consciousness is involved when deliberate, rather than automatic, control of intervention is needed. The main operations of the brain do not really include thought and reason, but blood flow, blood chemistry, and the maintenance of the *milieu interieur*. Pain interrupts philosophical dialogue; the longing for food eventually disrupts concentration; disruptions in the weather, which disrupt brain functions, also disrupt thought. Very few of our decisions get shunted up to consciousness; only those that need a top-level decision about alternatives. We thus live our lives without knowing how we are doing it and what is happening to us. The simpletons just go about their work.

The brain has one other astonishing feature. It allows unrecognized information to shape its destiny. Our genetic past and current sensory-motor processes are not just held quietly below the surface of consciousness; they work constantly and silently to guide our behaviors, just as it did with Otto Loewi. One major hypothesis to explain the function of our unconsciousness is that it acts as a storage mechanism of evolved and personalized information—information that works its way to consciousness when the brain is stimulated to solve a problem. The English novelist Aldous Huxley might have been writing about the brain when he said, "Silence is full of potential wisdom and wit as the unhewn marble of great sculpture." Most of what we do seems unhewn. Consider common events.

Facial recognition occurs outside of consciousness and is delegated to the right hemisphere of the brain. We don't mull over the characteristics of a face in order to decide whether we recognize it or not. We do or we don't. Consciousness is around only if the face is significant and requires some action. Similarly, we awaken when our name is called, but not someone else's. During sleep the sound of our name will profoundly excite the brain, but other names provoke no change.

Subliminal perception acts in the same way. There are experiments showing that individuals can guess at better-than-chance levels the nature or color of a picture that is shown so rapidly that a person can't see it. When geometric figures are flashed at rates faster than we can recognize them, people will still pick out ones they were exposed to when later asked to select favorites from a set of figures. In one final example, people who are asked to write stories, write shorter stories when the phrase "Don't write" is displayed subliminally, and write longer stories when the phrase is "Write more." Stimuli and commands slip into our brain unannounced, there to bias our behaviors in specific ways.

Not all experiments aimed at demonstrating subliminal perception have been successful, but certainly enough have to make us wonder just how much of our behavior is mediated by things that we do not recognize or deal with consciously. The brain is a powerful system for getting things done. There is no more reason for it to announce its intents, than it would be for your automobile to announce its shock absorber responses as it moves along. The brain was selected to solve problems along the road of survival and reproduction, not explain to us what it's doing.

The Final Structure of Man

About 125,000 years ago evolution closed its books on *H. sapiens*—its structure complete, little more destined to change. Thereafter, humans applied their hard-won capabilities to introduce agriculture and horticulture, build city-states, and spread around the world. It's a different ball game today, yet we still use the same bat and ball.

Before we go on to describe the social dimensions of our species, let's pause to summarize what we know or think we know about the structure of *H. sapiens*. Above all, our history was quirky, with hominids rising or falling in the turmoil of catastrophe, riding the cusp of survival, only sometimes meeting the challenges of the environment— luck spread thin upon the water. Climates shifted, rain forests came and went, resources were distributed in new ways, and competition with microorganisms and other species fluctuated. In response, hominids speciated, acquired larger brains, evolving new techniques for survival. Chance, body/brain scaling and neoteny were our benefactors, but in addition—*always*—the environment pressuring populations to evolve adaptations—natural selection lurking everywhere.

The prime movers of survival are *strategies*, essentially the drives toward self-protection and reproduction. They take many forms, as in phobias to avoid danger, heroism to overcome odds, aggression to defend against destruction, and mating to serve the future. The strategies are the most general attributes of life, but are only managed through more specific mechanisms, including *knowledge* of self and the environment and *operations* that move the strategies to fruition. The entire system and the interaction of its parts are constantly being trimmed by natural selection and influenced by information from the environment.

The evolutionary knowledge are *concepts*—inferences about the world brought about through sensorimotor interaction with the environment. Concepts are essentially genetically hardened beliefs about the world, its characteristics, and its influences. Operations are *rules of the mind* that mobilize concepts in specific ways to activate programs of survival and reproduction. Both concepts and rules of the mind are driven by *implicit information*, such as genes and their interaction with the environment, and *explicit information*, as in what we experience during our lifetime.

What we have described are the essential ingredients of survival and adaptation for most complex species. But primates, especially, and hominids, in particular, acquired an even more complex and potentially useful adaptation, and that was *consciousness*. Consciousness allowed the organism to monitor important changes in its environment and glimpse within itself the knowledge and operations that might be used to solve particular problems. The system was no longer simply reflexive and limited in responsiveness—it acquired a self-imaging capacity that afforded more alternative actions and allowed deferment of impulsive behaviors. It also provoked deferment of reproduction—the complex brain allowed extended parental care, the judicious spacing of offspring, and the shunting of activities into nonreproductive behaviors.

Consciousness, in effect, loosened the organism's connections to knowledge and operations, and expanded the boundaries of interaction with the environment. The individual could now *evaluate* its environment, *reflect* on itself within a changing world, and *anticipate* the consequences of external change and the application of concepts and rules of the mind. Some individuals who were better at these things were more likely to survive and reproduce, passing these same characteristics to their offspring. Others, caught in the glittering distractions of hedonisms or the metaphysical cusp of life and death, spurned reproduction, rushing headlong toward individual extinction.

The final adaptation that ended the evolutionary history of *H. sapiens* was *language*. Language evolved on the back of consciousness; it could not have evolved among organisms in the preconscious state. Language is useful only when consciousness affords access to knowledge and operations. Then, and only then, can access to the self and the world be transformed into symbolic representation through vocalizations.

Language is neither fish nor fowl. It is not the knowledge of the brain, or the operations that underlie our adaptive responses. Nor is language thought or consciousness, although it can influence both. Thought and consciousness are separate from language, evolving much earlier. Language is the translator of survival traits into more or less understandable forms, and the orator of thoughts, emotions, and conscious activities. Language literally gives voice to the primitive drives of individuals and transforms tidbits of consciousness and unconsciousness into messages.

Below is a hypothetical time-line for the evolution of the major components of the mind and their general functions. Its value is in trying to sort out the specific features of mentalism and show how they interrelate.

The assumptions of this model are that (1) evolution was stepwise, moving from general to specific adaptations; (2) genetic imprints on the mind are modified by the environment, either through development or individual experience; and (3) consciousness and language provide access to more primitive mechanisms, including the unconscious memory

FIGURE 12.1
Structure of the Mind

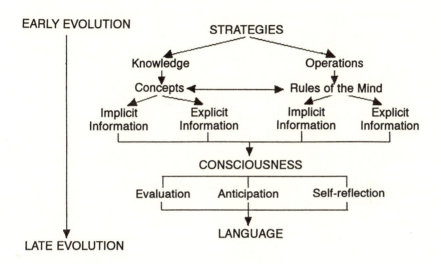

of the past, allowing them to be more carefully evaluated, affording the know-how and the flexibility that ultimately sent humans along a path of cultural development.

References

Cited in Chapter 12

Dennett, D.C. (1991). *Consciousness Explained*. Boston: Little, Brown and Company.
Freud, S. (1915). "The Unconscious in Psychoanalysis." In J. Riviere (tr.), *Collected Papers*, 4, 98-136.
Gallup, G.G. and Beckstead, J.W. (1988). "Attitudes toward Animal Research." *American Psychologist*, 43, 474-76.
Humphrey, N. (1992). *A History of the Mind*. New York: Simon and Schuster.
Jaynes, J. (1976). *The Origins of Consciousness in the Breakdown of the Bicameral Mind*. Boston: Houghton Mifflin.

Ornstein, R. (1991). *Evolution of Consciousness*. New York: Touchstone.

Posner, M.I. (1994). "Attention: The Mechanisms of Consciousness." *Procedures of the National Academy of Science*, 91, 7398-7403.

Posner, M.I. and Rothbart, M.K. (1994). "Constructing Neuronal Theories of Mind." In C. Koch and Davis, J.L. (eds.), *Large-Scale Neuronal Theories of the Brain*. Cambridge, MA: The MIT Press.

Searle, J.R. (1992). *The Rediscovery of the Mind*. Cambridge, MA: The MIT Press.

Springer, S.P. and Deutsch, G. (1989). *Left Brain, Right Brain*. (3rd ed.). New York: W.H. Freeman and Company.

General References

Dawkins, M.S. (1993). *Through Our Eyes Only? The Search for Animal Consciousness*. Oxford: W.H. Freeman.

Griffin, D.R. (1992). *Animal Minds*. Chicago: University of Chicago Press.

Koestler, A. (1967). *The Ghost in the Machine*. New York: Macmillan.

IV

Rush Toward Tomorrow

Ah, Love! could thou and I with Fate conspire
To grasp this sorry Scheme of Things entire,
Would not we shatter it to bits—and then
Re-mould it nearer to the Heart's Desire!

—Omar Khayyám

Culture salutes the grandeur of our evolution,
guiding us inexorably toward reproduction.

13

Years Without Solitude

Ah love, let us be true to one another! For the world,
which seems to lie before us like a land of dreams—
so various, so beautiful, so new—hath really neither
joy, nor love, nor light, nor certitude, nor peace, nor
help for pain; and we are here as on a darkling
plain; swept with confused alarms of struggle and
flight, where ignorant armies clash by night.

— Matthew Arnold

We have only recently begun to think of culture as an evolutionary adaptation. Indeed, our history shows that we normally think of culture as a unique adaptation that depends almost entirely on our complex brain. In other words, culture appears to be learned—an arbitrary product of our ideation. The general public, as well as the disciplines of sociology, anthropology, and psychology generally adhere to this belief. Today, however, orthodoxy is crumbling under the weight of arguments based on natural selection.

The study of human cultural behavior turned the philosophical corner when the biologists William D. Hamilton and Robert Trivers gave us the theoretical models to show that the individual goals of reproduction are served through social interactions. These scientists established two very important points, that genes propagated through relatives were just as significant for genetic fitness as genes propagated through individuals, and that genetic benefits flow from social "give" and "take" among nonrelatives. The effects of these advances were that Darwin and Wallace's theory of natural selection was easily extended to social organizations. Social behaviors were seen as spawned from the "selfish gene."

269

The grand synthesis of biological theorizing and principles of natural selection was heralded by Edward O. Wilson, who wrote the benchmark book in the area entitled, *Sociobiology: A New Synthesis*. Wilson defined the area as the study of the evolution and organization of social systems. The fundamental assertions of this discipline are surprisingly few in number, but are perhaps the most powerful statements in all of biology. Here they are in brief form.

1. Natural selection acts on individual traits and genes, not on groups or species.
2. Natural selection preserves genes and traits that correlate with reproduction, favoring some individuals in a population over others.
3. Evolutionary adaptations are specific to particular selection pressures ("domain-specific"), reflecting the specificity of selection pressures. There are, apparently, few if any general adaptations ("domain-general").
4. Cooperative acts follow lines of gene similarity (nepotism) or the social exchange value of interacting with nonrelatives (reciprocal social exchange).
5. The two sexes differ in their investment in offspring, as with male-male competition and female gestation and lactation; as a result the sexes differ in morphology, attitudes, aggression, sexual behaviors, and reproductive strategies.
6. Crime, war, and revolution turn on individual adaptations for economic gain, social dominance, and exploitive behaviors.
7. Proximate adaptations are those mechanisms that evolved to serve ultimate selection pressures, such as the hormone system serving sex behavior and reproduction.

The tenets of sociobiology are controversial because they emphasize the "selfish gene" as the foundation of all social behavior. The basic argument is this: natural selection acts to increase individual genetic fitness, and it does this in large measure by selecting attributes that allow individuals to take advantage of social interactions for purposes of reproduction. Sociobiology is also controversial because, when pressed to the extreme, culture is viewed as an inexorable product of gene activity— roughly explainable, starkly mechanistic. The "magic nature of man"— his culture—becomes just one more adaptation of evolutionary history.

Our story begins with a brief history of thought about human culture and why it is commonly believed to be a creation of man's ability to rationalize. The exploration is revealing. Two things become clear, the first is that our general belief in culture as arbitrary and learned is in part a belief about what we "ought to be" and "ought to do." The belief does not necessarily reflect "what is." The second observation is that most people, including scientists, really don't want to believe that we are tightly linked to our biology. The conclusion that we are *nothing but* biology is simply too austere and troublesome. But, the die is cast.

Our System of Belief

Some of us never step on ordinary dirt for days at a time. We move from our apartment to our car and into our place of business, always on concrete, wood, or carpet, completely insulated from the ground that spawned us, riveted to a man-made culture that is increasingly elegant and beguiling. In many societies we are caught between some vague dream of godly salvation and the attitude that we are unique and independent from other animals. Either way, we find ourselves drumming out our own rhythms of life, uneasy about our biophilic and biophobic inclinations. Little wonder we feel unaccountable to our early evolution, and unrelated to the plants and animals around us. We have been separated from our roots as much as a tooth pulled from our jaw.

In a typical upper division undergraduate class at a major university, approximately 20 percent of the students indicate that they do not believe in evolution—evolution of any species, not just themselves. This belief prevails even after studying the subject of evolution for the entire semester. A survey of 225 undergraduates revealed that most students believe that nearly all human traits and behaviors are environmentally determined, including personality attributes, rape, child care, feelings of bereavement, and moral values. Students are slightly more inclined to assign a genetic influence to intelligence, aggression, athletic ability, and sexual orientation. But even with these traits it is felt that the external influences on behavior are nearly as strong as any internal biases. The environmental explanation for human behaviors is uniformly strong in our society—a cultural attribute, as it were. That's what we're taught; that's what we believe.

The most cited sociologist of all time, Emile Durkheim, fanned the environmental storm that swept across intellectual disciplines, when he said in the early part of this century that only "social facts can explain other social facts." In other words, one could not reduce social questions to other levels, certainly not to the biological level. Durkheim asserted that the alleged innate tendencies of religion, sexual jealousy, filial piety, and paternal love lacked empirical support. By the middle of this century anthropologists had crystalized the belief that culture moved across generations without the benefit of evolutionary constraints. L.A. White, one of the most recognized anthropologists at that time, believed that culture "embraces the members of each generation at birth and molds them into human beings, equiping them with their beliefs, patterns of behavior, sentiments, and attitudes. Human behavior is but the response of a primate who can symbol to this extrasomatic continuum called culture."

The view that culture is free of biology remains dominant in sociology and anthropology to the present, supported by two related theoretical developments of this century. The first was the behavioristic movement, headed up by John B. Watson, which emphasized the critical importance of learning in human affairs, reinforcing the cultural stereotype that the mind is a blank slate upon which experience writes. The second development was Marxist thought that underlined the notion that human nature is determined by specific historical-material conditions—that there are no "universals" of behavior that might suggest innate qualities. Marxism meshes perfectly with other environmental explanations of behavior, in that it suggests that humans and culture are changeable, and that we can strive for their betterment. Economist Joseph Schumpeter in 1942 declared Marxism a religion for change: "which implies a plan of salvation and the indication of the evil from which mankind, or a chosen section of mankind, is to be saved."

The environmental movement in our colleges and universities was not merely intended to understand social behavior. It had an agenda for righting social wrongs, destroying racism and sexism wherever they appeared. In fact, the concerns for remedies to social inequalities may have been responsible for the widespread public acceptance of the environmental explanations of human culture. The assertions were these: If all individual, group, and gender differences were a matter of environmental circumstances, then everyone could reach social and economic equality; social problems could be engineered away. Durkheim, White, Marx, and Watson provided both the theoretical structure for social change and the methodology for implementing these goals. The agenda of equality seemed "right," allowing academic leaders to climb the moral high ground, proudly remaining ignorant of genetic differences, taking on an evangelical and monotheistic character.

TABLE 13.1

		Aspect of Social Behavior		
	Academic Performance	*Lifetime Earnings*	*Race Differences in Academic Performance*	*Sex Difference in Occupational Interests*
Genetic	16.7	6.8	4.6	3.0
Prenatal	5.4	2.3	3.4	0.5
Nonsocial Postnatal	6.1	3.1	5.3	1.2
Total Nonsocial	28.2	12.2	13.3	4.7
Family	36.1	34.6	27.2	35.2
Community	17.4	20.1	23.0	22.2
Society	18.0	33.0	36.5	37.7
Total Social	71.5	87.7	86.7	95.1

Source: Ellis, 1993

This is not an exaggeration of scholarly beliefs today. Recently, a biologically sophisticated sociologist, Lee Ellis, did a survey of 168 fellow members of the prestigious American Sociological Association. Ellis asked his colleagues to indicate the degree to which various human traits were influenced by nonsocial (genetic, developmental) or social (cultural) causes. Here is the tabulation of the results of that survey.

Depending on the social behavior, professional sociologists believe that from 70 to 95 percent of the differences among individuals and groups is socially determined. Ironically, their numbers are the opposite to those often obtained by behavior geneticists who have demonstrated that about 50 to 70 percent of the variability of behaviors is genetic.

Environmental arguments extend to our views on human violence and war. Twenty social scientists at the 6th International Colloquium on Brain and Aggression held at the University of Seville, Spain, in 1986 issued a statement of beliefs that was meant to dispel any notions that humans are inevitability disposed to war as a result of innate, biologically aggressive traits. The statement has been endorsed by several scholarly groups, including the well-known American Psychological Association. The series of propositions have become known as the Seville Declaration.

1. *"It is scientifically incorrect* to say that we have inherited a tendency to make war from our animal ancestors."

2. *"It is scientifically incorrect* to say that war or any other violent behavior is genetically programmed into our human nature."

3. *"It is scientifically incorrect* to say that in the course of human evolution there has been a selection for aggressive behavior more than for any other kinds of behavior."

4. *"It is scientifically incorrect* to say that humans have a 'violent brain.'"

5. *"It is scientifically incorrect* to say that war is caused by 'instinct' or any single motivation."

The conclusion of this group is that biology does not condemn humanity to war, and that humans can be freed from the "bondage of biological pessimism," becoming empowered with confidence to undertake the steps needed in the "International Year of Peace."

While well-intended, the Seville Declaration misses the mark. The propositions seem written by political activists who are fearful of the dark side of human behavior, wishing it weren't so, hoping that violence and war can be expunged from human nature. At best they are naive about the dimensions of behavior, making an appeal to divide genes ("nature") from environment ("nurture"). The formulations obviously promulgate "what ought to be," not "what is." Psychologist Gerald Beroldi says that "The signatories were trapped in the dualistic ideation that separates biology from culture, as if culture could exist without human beings, who are quite biological."

Politics continue to influence scientific investigations of genes and violence. At a 1995 conference sponsored by the National Institute of Health's Center for Human Genome Research, the mood was clearly to reject any connection between genes, evolution, and crime. Instead there was much discussion of historical precedents for misuse of science and eugenics in particular. Like many others of the conference, Dr. Diana

Fishbein, a criminologist of the Department of Justice, refused to "look through the telescope," as Galileo urged his critics, and pleaded for more "bleeeding heart programs." To that Galileo would have said *"Eppur si muove"* (Yet it moves), as he did after his recantation of belief in the Copernican system.

What the propositions don't point out is that adaptive strategies always express themselves within environments. True, there are no genes or instincts specific to violence or war, but there are evolved strategies for optimizing reproductive potential, sometimes in devious and harmful ways. Distinctions between "self" and "nonself," and between "us" and "them" invariably lead to self-serving behaviors, sometimes involving violence. It all depends, as adaptive responses are contingent on available alternatives for survival and reproduction. We may not like it, but the ebb and flow of life-sustaining processes were entombed into our neural networks by eons of natural selection. The appearance of their ghosts depends on the demons at hand.

Anthropologists John Tooby and Leda Cosmides pull no punches in summarizing their opinion about "pseudoscientific" statements like the Seville Declaration and the lack of progress in the social sciences. They insist that the social sciences have a weak cultural tree because they have no biological roots. "After more than a century, the social sciences are still adrift, with an enormous mass of half-digested observations, a not inconsiderable body of empirical generalizations, and a contradictory stew of ungrounded, middle-level theories expressed in a babel of incommensurate technical lexicons. This is accompanied by a growing malaise, so that the single largest trend is toward rejecting the scientific enterprise as it applies to humans." The Seville statement is an illustration where social scientists have pursued a belief system in preference to an open-minded avenue of investigation.

The analysis of belief systems is a strong indictment of traditional disciplines with long historical shadows, but it is not the first, nor the last. The social sciences and the political activists have painted themselves into an untenable corner by ignoring the cornerstones of all behavior—genes and natural selection. They cannot continue to exist as they are today—the evidence for the evolution of culture and the genetic influences on behavior are simply too great—they must either embrace evolutionary theory or self-destruct on the political shoals of "genelessness."

TABLE 13.2
Some Costs and Benefits of Sociality

Benefits	Costs

1. Gathering food
  a. More searchers to help find food
  b. Use of information obtained by others
  c. Ability to take on larger or more difficult prey
	1. Gathering food
	  a. Chance of warning prey
	  b. Need to divide any food obtained
	  c. Reduced input with subordination

2. Social facilitation and conditioning the environment
  a. Synchronization of activities
  b. Conditioning of the environment (e.g., increasing plant growth)
	2. Social facilitation and conditioning the environment
	  a. Environmental pollution
	  b. Limitations on times of activity

3. Avoiding predation
  a. Greater alertness to predators
  b. Ability to defend against predators.
  c. "Selfish herd" effects (hiding in a group)
  d. Glutting of predator appetites
  e. Confusion effects
	3. Avoiding predation
	  a. Greater conspicuousness to predators
	  b. Becoming more efficient target for predators
	  c. Energy expenditure in avoiding predators
	  d. Metabolic energy used to produce anti-predatory devices (e.g., poison, cryptic coloration)

4. Avoidance of parasites
  a. Material grooming of ectoparasites
  b. Avoidance of areas that cause sickness
	4. Avoidance of parasites
	  a. Rapid spread of disease among animals

TABLE 13.2 (continued)
Some Costs and Benefits of Sociality

5. Intraspecies competition
   a. Dominance of individuals in groups over solitaries or those in smaller groups

6. Division of Labor
   a. Greater efficiency of the social unit—and hence of each member

7. Social transmission of information
   a. Gain in information from the experience of others, without comparable risks

8. Reproduction
   a. Aid in finding a mate
   b. Aid in rearing young
   c. Mutual stimulation of sex behavior

5. Intraspecies competition
   a. Greater competition within each group
   b. Physiological stress effects

6. Division of labor
   a. Possible reduced fitness of those less specialized for reproduction or particular roles

7. Social transmission of information
   a. Opportunity of being deceived or manipulated

8. Reproduction
   a. Competition with others
   b. Competition with others and also misdirected parental care toward a nonrelative

The Initial Appearance of Social Systems

Perhaps as few as one-tenth of one percent of all species are truly social. The count is even fewer if we include single cells. Individual cells occasionally exchange DNA, but one would be hard-pressed to call that behavior social. Similarly, most insects get together for the purposes of reproduction, but little more. The exceptions are the *eusocial* species—those with nonreproductive casts—such as Isoptera (termites) and Hymenoptera (bees, wasps, and ants). While these insects have evolved complex social systems, they represent only two of the thirty or more orders of insects. Finally, there are several vertebrate social species, including some mammals. The total picture of social evolution is that of a simple nonsocial origin, followed by various forms of eusociality and more complex social systems.

Another way to look at the evolution of social organizations is to note that they won't evolve unless the benefits outweigh the costs. Individuals, not groups, respond to natural selection pressures, thus any elaboration of social organization must have benefits for the individual. The former prime minister of Great Britain, Margaret Thatcher, was alluding to the importance of individuals in the formation of societies when she insisted, "There is no such thing as society; there are individual men and women, and there are families." Intricacies of social organizations in their last analysis say more about individuals than they do cultures; individuals create societies, not the reverse.

Below are illustrations of the potential benefits and costs of most forms of social organization. Given that benefits are often balanced by costs, we can understand why sociality is a relatively rare event.

There are problems with defining social systems because their characteristics vary so much. The next table illustrates the range of social systems and presents several examples.

The most striking generalization is that the environmental contingencies determine the nature of the social system. In some cases individuals aggregate simply to conserve body heat, whereas in other cases individuals gather together to ward off predators, find food, or in other ways facilitate reproduction.

One of the best examples of an environmental impact on the evolution of social behavior is sociobiologist David Barash's work with species of marmots. These ground-dwelling rodents have adapted to a wide

TABLE 13.3
Classification of Animal Grouping Patterns

Type of grouping	Definition	Examples
1. Aggregations	Groups formed by simultaneous attraction to a common source, rather than to each other, and/or the result of physical factors acting on individuals.	Earthworms under a rock Bears at a garbage dump Gulls following a plow Hawks migrating along a ridge Human spectators at a sporting event
2. Survival groups	Groups formed largely by nonbreeding individuals based on mutual attraction; the members are only randomly related.	Herring schools Wildebeest and zebra herds Night roosts of starlings Winter foraging flocks of blackbirds
3. Mating groups	Groups within which breeding occurs; this may involve a monogamous pair, a harem, or a troop (several males and several females), and often includes extended families, formed by offspring remaining with the parents rather than dispersing.	Gibbon and bald eagle pairs Elk harems Baboon troops Mexican jay extended families Human families
4. Colonial groups	Groups formed by distinct breeding pairs or harems, often unrelated to each other, that seek the close company of other, similar breeding units.	Gull and other seabird colonies African weaverbirds Some bats and seals Most human residential systems

TABLE 13.3 (continued)
Classification of Animal Grouping Patterns

5. Unisexual groups	Groups of one sex, usually male, formed because of the breeding system, either as a means of attracting mates (lekking groups) or because of failure to do so (bachelor groups).	Prairie chicken or sage grouse lekking groups Uganda kob lekking groups (a species of antelope) Bachelor groups in elk, deer, and seals Human fraternities and sororities?
6. Clonal groups	Clones; groups formed by asexual reproduction and therefore composed of individuals each of whom are genetically identical to each other and are typically in permanent physical contact.	Certain marine invertebrates, such as jellyfish polyps Multicellullar organisms?

Source: Barash, 1982

TABLE 13.4
Correlations between the Sociobiology of Marmots
and the Environments in which They Live

| ENVIRONMENT | | | | SOCIOBIOLOGY | | |
SPECIES	ELEVATION	GROWING SEASON	AGE AT DISPERSAL	AGE AT SEXUAL MATURATION	REPRODUCTION	SOCIAL SYSTEM
Woodchucks	Low	Long	First year	Second year	Annual	Solitary, aggressive
Yellow-bellied marmots	Medium	Intermediate	Second year	Third year	Occasionally skip a year	Colonial, moderately aggressive
Olympic marmots	High	Short	Third year	Fourth year	Biennial	Colonial, highly social, tolerant

Source: Barash, 1977

range of ecologies, showing consistent correlations between the environment and social behavior. The three major species investigated are the woodchuck, yellow-bellied marmot, and olympic marmot. They range in elevations from the low-altitude woodchuck of the eastern United States to the high-altitude olympic marmot of the Olympic National Park.

The characteristic differences between the three species are summarized below. The most important environmental factor driving evolutionary differences among the species is not altitude of the habitat, but the availability of food supplies. In lowlands where food is available year round, and social cooperation is unnecessary for infant survival, the animals are aggressive toward each other, rarely associating except for copulation. In the highlands where food is scarce and available only seasonally, the marmots are highly social, cooperating for the welfare of the offspring. Marmots living at intermediate elevations with intermediate food availability are midway in behavior between the lowland woodchuck and the highland olympic marmot. In harsh climates where the growing season for food is short, maturation must be delayed, social dispersion is retarded until the young can make it on their own, the animals can only breed infrequently, and social cooperation is imperative. Other species, such as the hoary marmot that lives at high elevations with short growing seasons, are predictably similar to the olympic marmot.

The conclusion from this work is that even among species that share many genes in common, and tend to resemble each other because of common origins, there is considerable variation in social behavior, its form depending upon the need for coping with particular environments. No doubt social behavior is costly, occurring only where necessary. Certainly, there is no evidence for the progressive evolution of social systems, except that larger and more complex species show a higher probability of social interaction. Rather, the appearance of social organizations seems constrained by the phylogenetic history of species, and by the nature of the ecology in which behavior evolves. Consequently, hominids show sociality because of their common primate background, as well as because of the need for cooperation in managing reproduction and environmental contingencies.

The Shaky Step Beyond the Gene

Cultural attributes are in some ways discrete units of social creativity that have analogies with gene activity. They include attitudes, beliefs, myths, ideas, and symbols—all which, like genes, pass to the next generation, sometimes unchanged, sometimes modified in expression. In an attempt to specify how cultural units are reproduced British biologist Richard Dawkins proposed a cultural "replicator," called the *meme*, which is transmitted across generations in much the same way as a gene. In Dawkins' words, "Memes are ideas, bits of consciousness, beliefs capable of evolving, combining and flowing down the generations. Our ability to choose between replicating genes or memes is what distinguishes humans from other animals." The image is that of a cultural product duplicating, mutating, and recombining with other products in unique ways, exactly the way that genes do. The differences are that the memes change faster and command more of our attention—a shift from gene to meme; a step beyond the gene.

If memes act like genes, but are not genes, we have a situation that appears Lamarckian. Jean-Baptiste Lamarck (1744–1829) posited that traits influenced by the environment are transmitted to new generations, as with the long neck of the giraffe which exists because of generations of stretching upward to forage in tall trees. Learned cultural traits share Larmarckian characteristics, showing modification and transmission due to environmental pressures. It's odd to conceive of one aspect of cultural as gene controlled, and another aspect as Lamarckian. Of course Lamarckian notions have been disproved, replaced by genetic transmission, yet they still linger on in the form of memes. This is not necessarily an unhappy comparison.

The value of the meme is that we can begin to conceive of genetic and cultural transmission using the same biological images of gene reproduction. Memes and genes may behave similarly, leading to theoretical generalizations that include both the artifacts of culture and the genetic mechanisms that underlie the formation of culture. If the units of measurement can be made similar, then comparisons are possible in rates of change, degree of variability, and combinational abilities. The correlation between the sweep of languages around the world and variations in gene frequencies is an example of what can be achieved. Dawkin's meme may not reveal much about the *origin* of culture, or its genetic structure, but it may be able to define the units of society that display regularity of transmission across generations.

A more extensive form of this idea was later developed by physicist Charles Lumsden and sociobiologist Edward Wilson. Their cultural unit of transmission, called a *culturgen,* is very much like the meme of Dawkins, except that the unit of cultural transmission evolves together with the genotype, often expressing itself during early development. Culturgens include such things as universal grammar, particular mating strategies, sensory organization, facial recognition, and concept formation. A culturgen is thus a replicating unit of social behavior that coevolves with genes under the influence of past and present environments. The units of cultural transmission are not independent of natural selection; there is always a gene-environment covariation.

Culturgens do not specify all of the rules of the mind that are needed, but *create a preparedness to learn any number of things.* They have "domain general" capabilities. The argument is persuasive that culturgens must be flexibly related to the environment. Lumsden and Wilson point out that the brain is not complicated enough to build in pure genetic rules to cope with every contingency. Genes must act in concert with the learning of culture. For example, to have an inborn vocabulary of only 10,000 words, and a sentence dictionary of ten words each, one

would have to have an astonishing number of DNA variants, an estimated 10^{16} kilograms of DNA, far more than the weight of the entire
human species. This is a powerful argument for the necessity of a flexible brain, with culturgens and memes *prepared* to interact in any environment. The conclusion from this is that behavioral strategies are not
rigidly built into the brain but bias behaviors in various ways depending
upon the environmental contingencies. In any case, Lumsden and Wilson are emphasizing the importance of cultural learning, independent
of strict genetic codes of behavior.

The difficulty with the culturgen model is that each cultural unit
evolves as part of a complicated developmental program, that itself
has been selected for. Lumsden and Wilson estimate that for one
culturgen to evolve into another, such as monogamy evolving into
polygamy, requires about 50 human generations, or about a 1,000
years of natural selection. But they are really modeling simple gene
changes that are uncharacteristic of complicated behaviors that we
wish to understand. Reproductive strategies, for example, are composed of multiple genes, requiring many gene changes to completely
overhaul a complex strategy. More than a 1,000 years would be
needed, perhaps ten times that number. Moreover, for gene substitution to be successful in a large population, and in such a short time,
environmental selection forces would have to be unusually consistent and intense. As they admit, "the overall gene-culture fitness depends on the length of the period that the population tracks the
environment." But culture varies too radically to provide the continuous directional pressure necessary for culturgen substitution. The
unique and changeable nature of culture, the large size of the breeding population, and the diversity of civilizations are not the kinds of
atmospheres that drive evolution.

The value of the meme and culturgen is in dealing with cultural
changes that are not obviously genetic in kind, an admission that culture is not simply genetic activity. The meme is conceptually more independent of the genotype than is the culturgen, yet both accept a dualism
of cultural origin, and emphasize the human's abilities to learn new things
and create novelty. What is puzzling is that cultural artifacts seem to be
confused with the evolution of cultural capacity. Cultural artifacts are
things that we produce—symbols, tools, laws, history, and all the rest—
but they do not represent changes in our being.

The disappointing fact is that humans have changed hardly at all, even though culture has taken wing. Memes and culturgens can be used to describe and measure the attributes of culture—they can be analogized to gene transmission—but they have little to say about the evolution of human social behavior. What does it matter that the Mercedes Benz replaces the wooden wagon, that we live in high-rise apartments, rather than natural caves or thatched roofed houses, that we watch television sports, while forsaking storytelling, that we exchange academic degrees for knowledge of plants and the prediction of weather? We may enjoy our technology, and even feel better and live longer as a consequence, but the real questions are: Do these things change our basic character? Are our culturgens any different today than 200,000 years ago? Is our psychology today different from that of yesterday? Are we better for all of it? Are we somehow more human because of it?

The fact is, we carry the mountain of Pleistocene evolution within us, tipped only lightly with the snows of recent culture, eroded little by our learning. The character of our love, desires, and yearnings exalt us now as they have for thousands of generations. Jealousy, hate, and paranoia stalk us like the tigers of old; hunger, thirst, and tiredness consume us no less than ever; and dread of death still fills our moments of contemplation. Nothing fundamental has changed by our experiences, languages, science, or technology—not one biological thread, not one genetic breath, not one trivial emotion. We are no less *H. sapiens* because of our cultural knowledge than a dog on a skateboard is other than a dog. Our psychological designs are those of our parents, their parents, and their parents, and so on to our "African Eve." It is our destiny to be what we were, what we are, and what we ever will be. Memes and culturgens will help us describe cultural units, and will allow us to propose modes of cultural transmission, but they won't reveal our fundamental nature.

What Do We Tell Our Children?

We share a dilemma. We move through life as if detached from biological history, constructing moral, ethical, and religious systems based on a belief in learned culture, an attitude that is particularly strong in the United States. Then, along come Darwin, Wallace, and the sociobiologists, and our institutions are threatened by the concept of the selfish gene. If we decide that "the new genetic religion" is correct, do we revamp civilization to more accurately fit the biological model; do we live a dual life, giving lip service to the past, but believing in the malleable future? Or, do we repress the information as we might the knowledge of a galactic bomb?

In a recent interview sociobiologist Sarah Hrdy expressed her dualistic approach in teaching our children.

> I question whether sociobiology should be taught at the high school level, or even the undergraduate level, because it's very threatening to students still in the process of shaping their own priorities. The whole message of sociobiology is oriented toward the success of the individual. It's Machiavillian, and unless a student has a moral framework already in place, we could be producing social monsters by teaching this. It really fits in very nicely with the yuppie "me first" ethos, which I prefer not to encourage. So, I think it's important to have a certain level of maturity, with values already settled, before this kind of stuff is taught. I would hate to see sociobiology become a substitute for morality. It's a nasty way to live.

While one can sympathize with this view, ultimately it must be rejected. Sociobiology is a tough road, as reality often is. When we understand something to be true it must never be hidden because it is unfriendly toward a view of life. Not knowing the truth is an obvious excuse for not teaching it to our children, but knowing what it is and *then* not teaching it, can be hypocritical, dualistic, elitist, and unethical. The fact that it's done all the time, does not make it meritorious; those actions can lead to great social mischief.

The strong message of sociobiology is that society is comprised of selfish individuals striving for advantages at the expense of others. Rather than hiding these notions from our children until they learn to believe something else that is perhaps less damaging but untrue, we need to explore the details of sociobiological theories, help people to understand them as early as possible, and demonstrate how selfishness is regulated by nepotism, reciprocal social exchange, and law and order.

A full understanding of the biology of *H. sapiens* will not automatically make us more ruthless or insensitive to social justice. We are what we are in any case, and it's best that we find out just what that is. Power to change one's self and adjust in cultures comes from knowledge, not from rationing information that has an unhappy message for some. The nuclear physicist Enrico Fermi shrugged his shoulders when he said, "Whatever Nature has in store for mankind, unpleasant as it may be, men must accept, for ignorance is never better than knowledge." The mirror on the wall is there to catch our biological image. It's better that we look, even if we prove not to be "the fairest of them all."

So, what do we tell the children? The biologist Richard Alexander believes that there is something "incompatible about telling young children all about natural selection and rearing them to be properly social in the ways that we always have." Alexander believes that we should teach our children about genetic selfishness so that their genetic fitness is enhanced. In other words, children should be taught about the selfish gene and when and when not to extend cooperation. Since genetic fitness is enhanced by helping relatives, parents should reinforce children more for helping close relatives than for helping distant relatives or strangers. The concepts of "right" and "wrong" would be instilled into children in a fashion that would increase their reproductive potential and that of their relatives with whom they share genes.

Realistically, children would also learn that the two sexes differ in reproductive functions, attitudes, and behaviors, not because of any social attempt to honor one sex over the other, but because the two sexes have genetically diverged in child investment responsibilities. This realization would clear the ambiguous waters of sexual interactions, making it evident that inequality of opportunity is a different concept from inequality of biology.

It also might be helpful for children to realize that to obtain what they want, they should understand that everyone else is in the same business. The great Scottish economist Adam Smith may as well have been a sociobiologist when he wrote, "It is not from the benevolence of the butcher, the brewer, or the baker, that we expect our dinner, but from their regard to their own interest. We address ourselves, not to their humanity but to their self-love, and never talk to them of our necessities but of their advantages." According to Alexander, it is better ultimately to teach children the true implications of sociobiology and not impose a system of justice and personal conduct that are disadvantageous to the individual and highly unrealistic in everyday affairs.

Pragmatic training would not preclude social cooperation, because it is often to an individual's advantage to engage in nepotistic or reciprocal interactions with others. For instance, humans subscribe to laws against murder, rape, and robbery because they realize that by enforcing social order the probability is lessened that they and their relatives will become victims. For similar gains we learn to cooperate in matters of love relations, friendships civil contracts, and work relations. Like the Yin and Yang of Oriental philosophy, if individuals interact so that each is helped, then differences will mesh harmoniously, serving the next generation. The selfish gene has its delicate sides.

It's surprising that Alexander's ideas are not discussed more frequently; they focus on what is and not what we would like. If children actually inculcated moral values of absolute truth-telling and sacrificial behaviors, "they would be the rubes of society, of whom advantage would be taken at every turn." Indiscriminate altruism is the fast track to genetic extinction. What children seem to inherently know, and what they eventually learn, regardless of what we might like, or the guilt we instill, is that total sacrifice is not profitable in the long run. Fortunately, children seem to follow the Selfish Gene more than they do the Golden Rule.

Many people reject this philosophy because they simply do not want to accept our manipulative tendencies; they would rather believe that if somehow everyone would simply learn to "love" each other all would be well. The French writer Jean de la Bruyere shows the irony of this attitude. "That man is good who does good to others; if he suffers on account of the good he does, he is very good; if he suffers at the hands of those to whom he has done good, then his goodness is so great that it could be enhanced only by greater suffering; and if he should die at their hands, his virtue can go no further; it is heroic, it is perfect" Self-deception runs deep. Rarely will true altruism work because natural selection has built in strong competitive drives that for generations have allowed us to continue to reproduce. We do what's necessary and give in to others reluctantly. That's the evolutionary game that got us where we are; that's the game that continues to be played.

At the same time, scientists who are not as philosophically strong as Richard Alexander, find it difficult to push sociobiological notions to their ultimate conclusions. The serpent of doubt insinuates into the sharpest minds, there to frighten off the drafting of the last human equation that completely separates us from personal salvation. We want something more, yet the cold facts suggest that the final explanation of human social behavior will be no more satisfying than what we know today. Unnerved that we may finally unveil the Rosetta Stone of behavior, we lose our courage, telling others more what they want to hear, than what we actually believe in our solitary moments. Few, it seems, can stare our nature in the eye without blinking. Even the greatest scientists recoil at the last moment, speaking hopefully of the incomparably flexible brain, the emergence of novel behaviors, the probabilistic character of mental processes, the ability to overcome the dictates of evolution with intelligence and technology. Most biologists, in some measure, reach for the thinnest thread of humanity, the smallest illustration of altruism, the rarified sense of equality, the tiniest glimmer of God—the memes and the culturgens.

Inviolable Human Nature

Culture has always been with us as an inseparable part of our evolution. *Homo erectus* had culture, so did Neanderthal, and early *H. sapiens*. With vocalization, ritual, fire, stone tools, food gathering, and hunting, mating rites, child care, and possibly music, dance, pantomime, and worship, hominids expressed a rich mixture of individual and group adaptations. Reproductive success probably always depended on mate choice and bonding, infant care, regard for relatives, cooperation with others in foraging and hunting, sharing of knowledge, political alliances, and ability to distinguish between "we" and "they." The complexity was there in the antecedents of *H. sapiens*.

Culture does change, even progressively sometimes, but its development cannot be measured simply in terms of artifacts, art, language, science, business, and politics. Any definition must focus on the most consistent and fundamental aspects of behavior, personal needs, rules of kinship, forms of economic exchange, and moral imperatives. Largely invisible, these basic processes—all responses to natural selection— shaped everything to come. Know these; know culture.

The extension of biological theory to the evolution of social behaviors does not mean that we inherit the details of our culture, but only that we inherit a preparedness to respond in ways that will facilitate using culture as a stepping stone toward reproduction. The possible variations on a strategy are endless. For example, a male Yanomamo Indian may be able to secure copulations with a woman by the demonstration of warlike violence. In the !Kung society of Africa the same result may be associated with demonstrations of successful hunting and the sharing of meat. Then, as a member of a Western society, currency as a mate may depend upon the individual's occupation or prospects in the free-market arena. The point is that competitive skills hammered out during our Pleistocene evolution millions of years ago, play themselves out in various ways depending upon the characteristics of a culture. What is common to all cultural inventions is their ability to provide demonstrations of individual fitness and differential reproduction. Culture essentially produces the goods and services than can be hoarded, dominated, sought, prized—in short, the commodities of reproduction. Beads, bread, money, leisure time, healthful aids, medical care, automobiles, prestigious jobs can all be used to our advantage. It doesn't matter what these things are, as long as they are scarce and valued. We live for barter, sale and display, and through tenacity, strength of will, intelligence, and just plain luck, transform the obvious into reproductive success. Behind it all are the deep-seated drives of survival and reproduction, maximizing personal advantage, provoking the great Italian sociologist Vilfredo Pareto to remark: "The centuries roll by, human nature remains the same."

References

Cited in Chapter 13

Alexander, R.D. (1979). *Darwinism and Human Affairs*. Seattle: University of Washington Press.

Barash, D.P. (1977). *Sociobiology and Behavior*. New York: Elsevier.

Barash, D.P. (1982). *Sociobiology and Behavior* (2nd ed.). New York: Elsevier.

Beroldi, G. (1994). "Critique of the Seville Statement on Violence." *American Psychologist*, 49, 847–48.

Dawkins, R. (1994). In T.A. Bass (ed.), *Reinventing the Future: Coversations with the World's Leading scientists*. Reading, MA: Addison-Wesley Publishing Company, 109–29.

Ellis, L. (1993). Preface to volume 1. In L. Ellis (ed.), *Social Stratification and Socioeconomic Inequality*. Westport, CT: Praeger.

Hamilton, W.D. (1963). "The Evolution of Altruistic Behavior." *American Naturalist*, 97, 354–56.

Hrdy, S. (1994). In T.A. Bass (ed.), *Reinventing the Future: Coversations with the World's Leading Scientists*. Reading, MA: Addison-Wesley Publishing Company, 7–25.

Lumsden, C.J. and Wilson, E.O. (1981). *Genes, Mind, and Culture*. Cambridge, MA: Harvard University Press.

Symons, D. (1992). "On the Use and Misuse of Darwinism in the Study of Human Behavior." In J.H. Barkow, L. Cosmides and J. Tooby (eds.), *The Adapted Mind*. New York: Oxford University Press, 137–62.

Tooby, J. and Cosmides, L. (1992). "The Psychological Foundations of Culture." In J.H. Barkow, L. Cosmides and J. Tooby (eds.), *The Adapted Mind*. New York: Oxford University Press, 19–136.

Trivers, R. (1972). "Parental Investment and Sexual Selection. In B. Campbell (ed.), *Sexual Selection and the Descent of Man*. New York: Aldine de Gruyter, 136–79.

Wilson, E.O. (1975). *Sociobiology: A New Synthesis*. Cambridge: Harvard University Press.

General References

Dawkins, R. (1976). *The Selfish Gene*. Oxford: Oxford Univeristy Press.
Meisel, J.H. (ed.). (1965). *Pareto and Mosca*. Englewood Cliffs, NJ: Prentice-Hall, Inc.

14

Mining the Depths of the Cultural Gene

*The skylines lit up at dead of night, the air-condition-
ing systems cooling empty hotels in the desert and
artificial light in the middle of the day all have
something both demented and admirable about them.
The mindless luxury of a rich civilization, and yet of a
civilization perhaps as scared to see the lights go out
as was the hunter in his primitive night.*

—Jean Baudrillard

Solitude was not in the book for *Homo sapiens*. Hominids came prewired for culture, evolving devices for rearing children, cooperating in foraging, gathering, and hunting, and protecting against predators and other hominids. These old-fashioned traits were forged during the evolution of the great apes, 15, 20 million years ago. In retrospect it is not surprising that human culture rests on these primate strategies. Those needs transcend time and speciation, remaining the core around which culture flows.

The evolutionary infrastructure of culture reflects common adages: "Look out for number one," "Blood is thicker than water," and "Do unto others as you would have them do unto you." The first adage is the expression of the selfish gene, crying out for recognition and reproduction. The second illuminates the genetic ties with kin that expand interests from "number one" to anyone carrying identical genes. And the third adage is the platform for reciprocal social exchange, where costs and benefits of human interactions are shared for mutual gain. Cognitive rules of the mind that support these evolutionary dictums originated in small families but were applied widely as humans changed from nomads searching for vegetables, fruits, animal flesh, and shelter to farmers and herders, planting, harvesting, processing, and storing foods, and tending domesticated animals.

Small Social Novas

H. sapiens evolved in small groups or bands where kinship was important, where problems were immediate, where cooperation was essential. Years ago the behaviorist John Calhoun argued that the most cohesive mammalian group size was around twelve in number. Populations seemed to expand to that size, after which social strife increased physiological stress and decreased reproduction. At high densities social pathologies appeared, followed by either fission or a population "crash." Many investigators thought that an optimal population size of twelve was fanciful if not foolish, mostly because humans and other species continue to function and survive in populations of hundreds, thousands, and even millions.

Today the idea of "The Golden Twelve" has reappeared. While colonial or otherwise gregarious species function in huge populations, social bonds are generally weak except for small numbers of individuals who share genes in common. Similarly, humans may be surrounded by multitudes but seem to float on small island groups of common interest. Twelve may not be a magic number, but small numbers are critical. Anthropologist Napoleon Chagnon found that the hunter-gatherer villages of South American Yanomamö people reach populations of thirty to fifty individuals before excessive strife and group fission occur. Most individuals within a village are related, but as the average genetic difference increases, political and personal disharmony emerge until a group breaks off to form another village. Social cohesion depends upon small groups with close genetic ties.

As might be expected, the frequency and intensity of communication is related to the degree of genetic relatedness. For example, among the Ye' Kavana people of the Upper Orinoco basis of Venezuela, the number of social interactions between individuals is a function of the genetic distance between them (figure 14.1). It seems that we feel strongly about few relatives, short distances, and brief generations of time.

Things may be little different in our own society today, as evidenced by a recent investigation by Buys and Larson (see Reynolds, Falger, and Vine 1987). These scientists mailed two different survey forms to 500 residents of Victoria, Texas, a town of 50,000 individuals. Of these surveys, 125 were filled out and returned. The surveys were intended to assess the size of "sympathy" groups. One form asked people to list

FIGURE 14.1

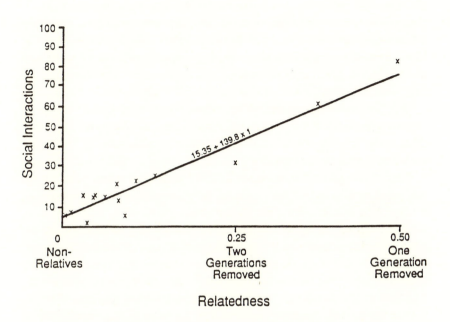

Observed interactions between dyads of Ye'Kwana people of the Upper Orinoco basin of Venezuela. Redrawn from Hames, 1979, p. 246.

those persons by relationship whose death would cause them anguish. The other form asked for a list of persons with whom the respondents had close emotional ties. Invariably, people concentrated their emotions on close relatives and a few close friends. The tabulated results indicate that the "Anguish" form produced a sympathy group size of 12.9, and the "Close Emotional" form yielded a group size of 9.7. The average for the two was 10.9, coincidentally close to The Golden Twelve. Clearly, people tend to concentrate their emotions on relatives and a few close friends.

Given today's importance of close kinship ties, and the kinship solidarity evident in other primates, one can imagine the composition of a group of stone age *H. sapiens.* There would generally be a father and mother, with perhaps two children, an uncle and aunt on both sides of the parents, one living parent, a grandchild, and perhaps two close friends. The exact composition and number would vary with the vicissitudes of life—success with survival skills, availability of resources, climate, and the prevalence of disease. Regardless, in all cases close interacting members would be mostly kin, with a few non-kin involved.

This perspective emphasizes that most of our evolutionary history involved selection for social interactions with kin, with occasional extensions of social ties outside the extended family. Close ties with family members were critical, as they provide an exaggerated genetic fitness through relatives. But contacts with outside members were important as well, as they allow for pools of breeding females and males, stimulation of trade, help with defence, and the exchange of new ideas and techniques.

The distribution of social interactions involving mostly kin established the basic features of our cultural evolution, with "insiders" viewed according to differential needs, and with love, respect, and authority, and "outsiders" viewed with reservation, suspicion, hate, and worthlessness. The common evolutionary adaptations of strong kinship ties were nepotism, ethnocentrism, tribalism, social bonding, obedience to authority, nationalism, patriotism, territorially, enemy thinking, xenophobia, jingoism, and reciprocal social exchange. We carry these traits with us to the market every day.

The Grateful Dead and Kinship Ties

We have no personal immortality. Our self-awareness is a fleeting moment of time—unique, finite, never to reappear. But our genes do survive, changing under environmental pressures, expressing themselves differently, but nevertheless moving across generations. The darkest view is that genes use our bodies and our mental processes to jump from one dead generation to the next—bridges for natural selection, mechanisms of immortality.

Our genes have a number of tricks for reproducing, or, more correctly, reproductive tricks are there because of their association with gene replication. Genes propagate through the bodies of relatives, and ride to the next generation on the goodwill of nonrelatives. The first path is referred to as *nepotism*, where individuals help their relatives reproduce. The second path is through *reciprocal social exchange*, where individuals benefit through interactions with nonrelatives.

Thus, individuals have various sorts of genetic fitness—personal fitness through self-reproduction, with perhaps a little help from their friends, and indirect fitness gained with the spread of genes through relatives. Personal fitness, plus indirect fitness through relatives, are referred to as *inclusive fitness*. Theoretically, a person can have high personal fitness and low inclusive fitness, or the reverse, low personal fitness but high inclusive fitness. The distinction is important because individuals with high inclusive fitness may, on the average, pass their genes to the next generation without reproducing personally. The relatives do it for them. On the other hand, a person with low inclusive fitness may have to work harder for the same genetic benefits, perhaps losing out altogether.

It was W. D. Hamilton who first introduced the notion, providing it with quantitative validity, and suggesting how inclusive fitness serves individuals. The concept is arguably the most important in sociobiology, as it helps explain cooperative and competitive behaviors among relatives, suggests the path of resource distribution, and illuminates how natural selection acts on genes in related individuals.

Reciprocal social exchange is different from the notion of inclusive fitness, in that reciprocity affecting reproduction does not depend on relatedness among individuals. Instead, it hinges on obligations and trust established between individuals. It's a sophisticated version of the old adage, "You scratch my back, and I'll scratch yours." Reciprocal exchange, together with nepotism, weave a pattern of cooperation and goodwill, allowing the selfish gene to reproduce.

A Trip Through the Mind of EGO

Inclusive fitness is best implemented in small groups and along kinship lines, where individuals can easily assess the reproductive fitness of various relatives, and where loyalty and nepotistic exchange are assumed.

We can view the world of inclusive fitness through the mind of EGO, the focal individual oriented toward reproduction. The first lesson that EGO learns is that blood is thicker than water, and that some blood is thicker than other blood. EGO generally has greater inclusive fitness with close kin than with distant kin, as the first share more genes with EGO than the second. For example, EGO shares 50 percent of EGO's genes with a son or daughter, and 25 percent with a nephew or niece. Based on this fact alone, the genetic value of a son or daughter is twice that of a nephew or niece. When it comes down to helping one or another relative reproduce, EGO should favor individuals sharing the greatest number of genes. A look at EGO's family relations (figure 14.2) gives a general picture of EGO's inclusive fitness, suggesting how nepotistic acts should flow. Everything being equal, EGO will be more interested in, and helpful to, close kin. EGO's interest in others diminish in an outward direction from the closest relations to the fringes of distant relatives and strangers.

Another way to conceive of nepotism is to think about the costs and benefits for EGO dispersing cooperation and resources that could affect reproduction. In genetic terms, EGO can help close relatives reproduce with less cost and greater benefit than if the same help were given to distant relatives. That conclusion follows from the fact that close relatives can ultimately reproduce more of EGO's genes: helping genes in close relatives is akin to helping many of one's own genes, a self-grooming in disguise.

Calculating inclusive fitness is complicated by the fact that individuals with the same genetic relatedness to EGO may nevertheless differ in reproductive potential. A mother and a daughter are related equally to EGO, each sharing 50 percent of their genes with EGO, but ordinarily the daughter has greater reproductive potential, or what we may call *reproductive value*. Accordingly, EGO can reduce costs and increase genetic benefits by helping the daughter.

The differential distribution of EGO's resources is evident in probated wills. In a study of a Canadian population, Martin Smith and his colleagues found that EGO listed legal beneficiaries according to relatedness *and* according to the reproductive value of EGO's relatives. Specifically, offspring received willed benefits that were about five times greater than nephews and nieces, and sixty-four times greater than cousins. Reflecting reproductive values, offspring received benefits nearly four times those given to siblings, and nephews and nieces received about 50 percent more than grandchildren. In the latter cases, offspring and siblings are equally related, as are nephews and nieces and grand-

FIGURE 14.2

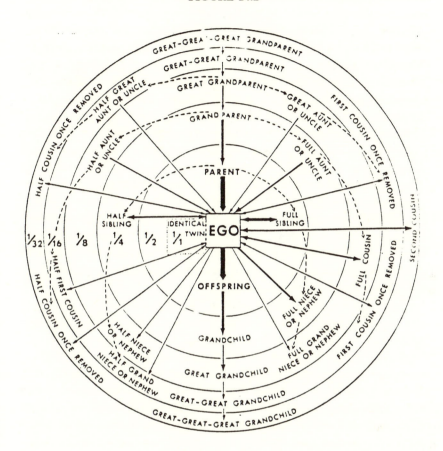

Genetic relatives potentially available to an individual, Ego, for reproductively self-serving nepotism. Arrows indicate likely net flows of benefits. Half the genes of parent and offspring are identical by immediate descent.
Source: Alexander, 1979

children, indicating that reproductive value rather than genetic related-ness determines the flow of resources.

Other behaviors can be explained by similar references to reproduc-tive value. For instance, the common practice of infanticide, the killing of offspring, occurs in accordance with the parents' and infants' probable success. If an infant is killed, it is likely to be because of a high reproductive cost for the parents or a low reproductive value of the infant (the Trivers-Williard hypothesis). In this and other cases of reproductive investment, gene similarity provides the general route for nepotistic and competitive acts, even that of murder, but the specific path of action depends upon differentials in reproductive value.

Thus, there is a matrix of variables which can affect EGO's inclusive fitness, including genetic similarity to others, reproductive value of individuals, and costs versus benefits of doing one thing or another. EGO does not sit around rationalizing the consequences of particular actions, but rather, follows the general dictates of evolution past. Those rules of the mind that *did* result in greater gene duplication are those rules that prevail.

One is not necessarily conscious of the concepts and operations that direct behavior. In fact, inclusive fitness determinations are probably done more efficiently if the genetic tug is silent. Self-deception is the best deception, as it prevents "rational" thought from interfering with genetic influences, does away with a lot of personal guilt, and is the best deceptive strategy in dealing with others.

The implications of inclusive fitness for the structuring of cooperative social units are immense. Nepotism is the social glue that holds small groups together: resources, care, and cooperation flow easily where reproductive gains are possible. Nepotism makes parent-offspring interactions possible and wise; it facilitates cooperation in gathering food, defending against predators, and building political alliances. At the same time, nepotism is the basis for discriminatory acts, conflicts between those with different genetic interests, attempts to deceive about reproductive value, and feelings of enmity toward nonrelatives. Kinship, always kinship, is the defining nature of culture.

Kinship as the Seed of Civilization

Rules of kinship link individuals, determining the specifics of resource allocation, degree of favoritism, marriage arrangements, and political responsibilities. Kinship rules vary somewhat, depending on the attributes of particular societies, but they tend to be universal strategies for increasing genetic fitness. The most common are these.

1. Close relatives are most often favored in social interactions.

2. Benefits from EGO go to those with greater ability to reproduce, when gene similarity is equivalent.
3. Labels that designate kin in non-kinship individuals ("brother" or "sister") are used to ensure reciprocal relations and stabilize political alliances.
4. As nepotistic benefits from older individuals are depleted, younger relatives rely more on reciprocal exchange with these older individuals.
5. Value placed on offspring depends on (1) reproductive potential of offspring; (2) reproductive status of the parents; and (3) number of siblings and other relatives. The higher and closer the degree of genetic relatedness, the more we extol nepotism.
6. Offspring may be abandoned or killed because of parental uncertainty, reduced resources, too many offspring, offspring illness or deviancy, or few prospects for offspring survival or reproduction.
7. While gene similarity is at the basis of cooperation, it also leads to competition for similar resources, especially when resources are scarce. Kinship behaviors strike a balance between benefits and conflicts of close interactions.
8. Incest taboos exist for members of the nuclear family (e.g., father-daughter; son-daughter), where inbreeding is genetically harmful.
9. Men are more powerful than women, hence are more likely to gain in conflicts of interest. They also tend toward multiple matings, as their reproductive costs tend to be lower than those of women.
10. Lowered confidence of paternity among males causes a man's sister's offspring to assume more importance as recipients of nepotistic benefits. The bias reflects the obvious knowledge that EGO and his sister have the same mother, hence are certainly related. Because the male can be fooled about paternity, cues of relatedness, as with facial features, are important.
11. Potential recipients of nepotistic behaviors are in a good position to cheat by (1) deceiving others about their closeness of relationship, and (2) deceiving about the extent of ability to translate benefits into reproduction.
12. In-laws benefit by receiving gifts directed toward biological kin.
13. Larger groups increase the possibility for cheating, hence the groups are typified by reciprocal exchange with fewer members of the group participating. Concerns about cheating and punishment prevail.

Note that all these rules are intended to enhance reproduction, either through nepotism, reciprocal social exchange, or cheating and deception. Nepotism blurs into reciprocal exchange as genetic distance increases between individuals. As that occurs, deception, cheating, and punishment for cheating assume more importance.

The kinship rules represent some of the most universal themes of sociobiology. They, in effect, are statements of genetic intent around which culture must revolve. In turn, kinship rules are set within an even larger network of universal traits that stipulate the characteristics of cultures and civilizations. Let's take a look at the wider network of evolved traits.

Cultural Universals: The Inevitability of Death and Taxes

Within our neural networks are the most complicated features of behavior. The wiring diagrams of the brain specify behavioral strategies, concepts about the world, and operational rules for moving us toward reproduction. These brain networks and traits exist because of their association with successful gene transmission.

The construction of such complexity and specificity over hundreds or thousands of generations ruled out many alternative mental traits—the victims of less successful reproduction. The result was a reduction of response variability—successful traits habitually assume invariant characteristics as alternatives fail. Consequently all surviving individuals tend to share the same traits. Adaptations become "species-specific," appearing wherever *H. sapiens* travels. They are the universals of culture.

Anthropologists often take the position that nonexpression of particular traits means that they are not universal. If war is universal, why are some cultures warless? If aggression is universal, why are some cultures passive? If color sensitivity is universal, why don't all cultures have identifying words for all colors? On the other hand, anthropologists insist that the appearance of universal traits may be deceptive, as traits may go through inevitable stages as cultures progress, a cultural learning process. They need not be genetic.

The anthropological positions are difficult to sustain for several reasons. The first is that there are many traits that do appear in all cultures, regardless of the peculiarities of those cultures. Second, characteristics that do not appear to be present in all cultures still may have the potential for expression; they remain, hidden by other cultural forces, ready to be expressed in a permissive environment. War, for example, may be an exploitive behavior that depends upon resource availability, social and geographical boundaries, and population size. Warlike people of yesterday may be peaceful today. The underlying strategies that involve themselves in war are there, even though they routinely do not show themselves. Similarly, it's been found that individuals in cultures that lack words for sensory events, such as color distinctions, still have the capabilities for discrimination if asked to make them. Last, a comparison of older and newer cultures does not show that there is an inevitable course of cultural learning that could account for universal principles.

Not all anthropologists have embraced the primacy of cultural learning, some recognizing that human culture is structured from species-universals. As early as 1923 Clark Wissler proposed that underlying human universals include language, food habits, weaponry, religious practices, scientific knowledge, family social systems, rules of inheritance, notions of real and personal property, and forms of government. According to him these fundamental traits are the foundation on which the edifice of culture is built. Wissler's perspective was a theoretical down payment on a biological interpretation of human behavior, but was unfortunately overshadowed by trends in anthropology, sociology, and psychology, suggesting that culture is an arbitrary product of man's creativity.

Today the evidence for human universal traits is strong. Many of these are important for kinship ties, as we saw earlier; many are critical for reciprocal social exchange, mating strategies, and the general organization of social systems. The attributes define a wide range of behaviors, none of which seem to be learned as a result of particular and unique aspects of society. They are the general expressions of genetic adaptations that make the expression of culture fairly uniform, even when the specific artifacts of the culture differ. Here is a list, as we know it today.

Human Universals

Reactions to the Environment

- Concepts of space, time, motion, speed, location, dimensions
- Assessments of weather, climate and seasons of the year
- Recognition and naming of flora and fauna
- Building shelters from the elements
- Investigation and use of tools
- Explanations of disease
- Foraging for food, food harvesting, and food preparation

Individual Traits

- Recognition and naming of body parts
- Recognition of individuals, social status, faces
- Knowledge of "not," "same," "equivalent," "opposite"
- Prediction and planning for the future

- Use of drugs: stimulants, narcotics, intoxicants
- Use of clothes and body adornment
- Suicide
- Rape
- Murder

Kinship Relations

- Recognition of two sexes, with possible intermediates and crossovers
- Recognition of degree of relatedness and naming of relatives, such as mother, father, son, daughter.
- Living in families and groups
- Feelings of "ingroup" and "outgroup"
- Socialization of children; ritualization of birth, puberty, death
- Standards of behavior, including sexual modesty
- Rules of kinship relations, involving nepotism, marriage and property rights
- Incest taboo
- Teaching of offspring
- Rules of reciprocity

Emotions and Symbolism

- Expressions of anger, envy, jealousy
- Recognition of facial expressions and emotions
- Lying, empathy, nepotism
- Deceiving; recognition of cheating
- Religious or supernatural beliefs, magic, world view, and soul concepts
- Aesthetic standards, preferences for sexual attraction, decorative art for body and artifacts
- Language, use of nouns, names, pronouns and numbers
- Recognition of consciousness and inner emotional states
- Play and play-fighting
- Dance and music, including melody, rhythm, repetition, redundancy, creation of vocal and other music
- Recognition of reproductive capacity and differential preferences for members of the other sex
- Copulatory behavior and rules of sexual conduct

Social and Governmental Regulations

- Development of leaders, law, rules of membership, and forms of punishment
- Concepts of property, rules of inheritance, and obligations to the "state"
- Division of labor, trade, customs of cooperation

The list of universal traits is an impressive documentation of human specificities, most of which can be traced back to our early ancestors. Pondering these characteristics, it appears that individuals in all societies are much alike—good and bad—oriented toward survival and reproduction.

Of course they differ too. Judgments of reproductive value, mate qualification, nepotistic and reciprocal value, and many other traits related to reproduction, depend upon individual differences. Nevertheless, these differences appear to be small variations surrounding more central themes, and are overwhelmed by general strategies common to all. Similarly, cultural artifacts, no matter how complex, and how much they shape our behaviors, do no more than shadow our basic nature.

The tide of civilization hides a basic truth: we relentlessly pursue the inner drives chiseled by natural selection during our hominid evolution. No new strategies have evolved that we could point to as "civilization strategies." There are no new "rules of the mind" for dealing with unanticipated events and complexity, no novel "cultural cognition" for today's world, no unique "cultural consciousness" relevant for a new morality. It's the same old stuff, doing the same old thing. The evolutionary story of *H. sapiens* is pretty much over; only our tools and toys change their nature.

The Importance of Tools and Toys

The rules and regularities that allow for reproduction are deeply ingrained and common to all societies, yet language, law, and love differ among the aborigines of Australia, the Aleuta of the Unimak Island, the Russians of Siberia, and the Americans of New Mexico. The fundamental drives among humans find their expression in unique and arbitrary ways, but they are expressed. There are many ways "to skin a cat culture." We are haunted by our unchanging nature, even though that nature can flow to the next generation only on the arbitrary stream of culture.

Species-specific universals do not therefore homogenize our lives by creating behavioral clones. They are instead shaped, driven and expressed through habits and social form, linking our universal characters to the latticework of culture. The British author Angela Carter saw the inevitable association between our most basic drives and our clinging culture: "We do not go to bed in single pairs; even if we choose not to refer to them, we still drag there with us the cultural impediments of our social class, our parents' lives, our bank balances, our sexual and emotional expectations, our whole biographies—all the bits and pieces of our unique existences." The culture that we take to bed with us swirls through our actions and dreams, but what we don't immediately understand is that universals must move on the back of culture; we must always take *something* to bed with us.

Our nature is played out within our cultural sum, temporarily tied to the forces of the memes and culturgens that are used as barter for survival and reproduction. The bad is that we sing our genetic songs with arbitrary rhythm; the good is that knowledge of our culture can be used for personal gain—the melody of life plays on. Kinship rules and reciprocal exchange depend on cultural-specific knowledge—determining what sexual unions are prohibited and acceptable, how to identify and name kin, who can be trusted in unwritten contracts, and above all, what is scarce and valuable as commodities in the game of gene propagation. Genes do not fight culture for expression; they use it.

The increasing rise of tribalism around the world may be a sign that predictable norms of behavior are necessary for the expression of human universals. The anthropologist Jack Weatherford comments on the growing pressure to retain traditional cultures against forces that flatten variations and introduce new artifacts and technology. "Neither the classless society of communism nor the global village of capitalism managed to homogenize the world during the twentieth century. Even though economic interdependence increased, and even though an international popular culture of sports and entertainment icons arose and became as known in Tibet and Timbuktu as in Toledo, the emergence of a world culture failed to obliterate local cultures. Instead, ethnic and cultural identities grew stronger, everywhere from the largest cities to the most remote jungle valleys. Rather than blending into a homogenized world culture shared by all, the various tribes, nations, religious, and ethnic groups accentuated their differences to become more varied than ever."

One can debate the reasons for the reassertion of tribalism, but one good bet is that people can best pursue their selfish goals within a clearly structured and well-known culture. Cultural paths toward reproduction are defended for fear that homogenization will disrupt personal advantages and put reproduction out of reach. In the face of uncertainties, ethnic groups, folk traditions, national and racial minorities continue to assert their cultural universals in unique ways.

Social Exchange Theory and Heroism

As the sociobiological theorist Robert Trivers knew, reciprocal social exchange depends on evolved strategies for increasing genetic fitness. Strategies are expressed, nevertheless, within a cultural context. To that extent, reciprocal social exchange is learned. In any case, its importance cannot be exaggerated, as the French poet Jean de La Fontaine understood when he said, "People must help one another; it is nature's law." Reciprocal social exchange, by providing mutual benefits to donors and recipients, allows strangers to interact nearly as closely as kin.

The origin of reciprocal exchange is not known, but it must have appeared early and at the same time that nepotism arose. One sees it in the temporary political alliances of chimpanzees and other primates, and to a lesser degree in other mammals. Although nepotism within kin groups is the primary source of altruistic acts, reciprocal exchange enhance the effectiveness of these behaviors. For example, EGO is more inclined to help a son who is cooperative than one who isn't, thus acting as a selection pressure for reciprocity within families. Nepotism and reciprocity form the strongest of adaptive alliances.

Similarly, as EGO runs out of nepotistic acts, perhaps because of aging or circumstances, family members using reciprocal strategies can still benefit from EGO. Thus, it may be that nepotism was the initial response to natural selection, which was enriched later with reciprocal interactions. Once established, reciprocal social exchange linked individuals sharing nothing more than common interests. Had it not evolved as an adjunct to nepotism civilization would not have emerged.

There are nine possible reciprocal interactions, only a few of which are beneficial to both the "giver" of an act and the "receiver" of that act (table 14.1). The range of outcomes is from cooperation on both sides to pure spite, where both the giver and receiver are hurt. Because exploitation and deception are always possible, reciprocal exchange must be carefully monitored by participants for advantages, disadvantages, and long-term value.

TABLE 14.1
Nine Forms of Social Interaction With Examples
(+ = benefit; – = harm; 0 = no consequences)*

		Consequence for Recipient		
		Positive (+)	Neutral (0)	Negative (–)
	Positive (+)	**Cooperation** I'll find you today if you feed me later	**Minor Selfishness** I'll copy from your exam	**Selfishness** I'll take the promotion
Conse- quences for Actor	Neutral (0)	**Minor Altruism** I'll recommend you for a job	**Minor Cooperation** I'll open the door and let you pass	**Minor Spite** I'll play a dirty trick on you
	Negative (–)	**Altruism** I'll give up my life for any stranger	**Minor Altruism** I'll give up a job that you feel I'm unqual- ified for	**Spite** I'll die, but I'll take you down with me

Pure Cases (Actor/Recipient)
+/+ Reciprocal social exchange
+/– Selfishness
–/+ Sacrificial altruism
–/– Sacrificial spite

We seem to share the attitude of Lord Byron who said, "I detest everything which is not perfectly mutual." The question is always: how can one receive benefits from social interactions and not be exploited?

Chicken or Quail: A Constant Dilemma

Suppose that you are dining out with a small group, where you have the understanding that the total bill will be divided evenly among all of the diners. You are the first to order. Do you order a moderately prized chicken dinner with a small salad and ice tea, or do you go for the pricy stuffed quail and French wine? It probably depends on your social habits, how well off the other diners appear to be, what you think the others will order, and whether or not you intend to interact with this group in the future. Obviously a contingent strategy is involved, but what are the alternatives?

An abstract formulation of the problem is to allow for cooperation and defection (selfish behavior), and associate these with differential rewards. The general representation of the possibilities is seen in a game called the *Prisoner's Dilemma.* There are two players, each with the choice to cooperate or defect, but neither knows what the other will do. Clearly, no matter what the other does, defection has a higher possible payoff, but if both cooperate, both do moderately well.

The dilemma can be pictured in this way. If both players defect, both players are punished (P), receiving only 1 point. If both cooperate the reward (R) is 3 points for each. If one cooperates and the other defects, the cooperator is the sucker (S), getting 0 points, and the defector receives the advantage (A), worth 5 points. It is common in social interactions that defection by one player pays the defector higher than cooperation, and that defection in both results in the lowest payoff. The numbers in the matrix could represent the dollar amounts for ordering differently priced meals, or for many other exchanges requiring decisions.

Prisoner's Dilemma*
Player Two

		Cooperate	Defect
Player	Cooperate	R = 3; R = 3	S = 0; A = 5
One	Defect	A = 5; S = 0	P = 1; P = 1

*Payoffs to Player One is listed first in each cell

If you always cooperate and the other person always defects, you earn nothing and the other person scores an average of 5 points. If your behavior is random, but the other person continues to defect, your respective scores are 1/2 and 3. You lose significantly either way. The only thing you can do if the other person always defects is defect, in which case your averages are both 1. Clearly you both would be better off cooperating, obtaining an average score of 3 for each. Over the long haul cooperation for both parties is the optimal behavior. The question is, how do you teach a person to reciprocate cooperation, when the short-term temptation is always to defect? Enter *Tit for Tat.*

Tit for Tat: The Best of Strategies

The political scientist Robert Axelrod conducted an ingenious study. He invited professionals to submit a computer program that would maximize reinforcements in a prisoner's dilemma game where the opponent would either cooperate or defect. The differential rewards are those described above. Fourteen entries were submitted, including programs that would always defect, always cooperate, or some combination of the two, depending on what the other person might do.

Professor Anatol Rapoport of the University of Toronto submitted the winning, and simplest, program, called *Tit for Tat*. It begins the game with a cooperative act, and thereafter does what the other player did on the previous trial. So, if the other player cooperates, the first player continues to cooperate. However, if the other player defects on the first trial, then the first player defects on the subsequent trial. The strategy is "cooperate, but do unto others as they do unto you." The success of this simple program was astonishing, acquiring an average of 504 points per game, out of a possible 1,000 points. The other programs submitted ranged from a low score of 276 to a high score of 500.

Tit for Tat is considered a "nice" program, in that it intends to cooperate and will only defect if the other player defects. In addition, Tit for Tat "forgives" occasional defects and resumes cooperation when the other person cooperates. Most of the other programs were either "not nice," defecting early and continuing to punish, or were simply too complicated in trying to second-guess what the other player might do. Even when the participants in this study were told about the success of Tit for Tat, and were invited to beat it, no one did. Tit for Tat is simple, robust, and effective. (Recently Axelrod has increased the effectiveness of Tit for Tat by identifying others it can exploit and those it can't. It defects from the former and cooperates with the latter.)

One of its critical characteristics is that it teaches others to cooperate. A defect will always be followed by a defect, but any evidence of cooperation will generate additional cooperation. Thus, over trials it will beat all other programs and will convince others that their best strategy is to cooperate, which in this game is true.

There are difficulties with Tit for Tat. For example, if you interact with another person only once, and your first and only behavior is cooperation, it pays for the other person to defect, a difference of 5 points. Going back to the dinner dilemma, if you are a stranger to the group and will never encounter that group again, if your order chicken and ice tea, the chances are that someone else will order the stuffed quail and French wine. Thus, single interactions make it wise for both persons to order quail and French wine.

The second difficulty is that the value of a decision diminishes over time. Among money investors there is the common saying that a dollar today is worth more than a dollar tomorrow, so take the dollar and run. Thus, when a person orders the stuffed quail, that decision has great value at the moment, but is not likely to be considered important when looking toward the future. What happens today, this minute, this instant, is more important than what happens tomorrow. Thus, cooperation one day does not insure cooperation on another.

Tit for Tat works best in small populations where the same people interact over and over, thus generating predictable sequences—one quickly learns who will cooperate and who will not. It is also an effective strategy when first testing for cooperation, because a single cooperative act may reveal the intent of the other person. To sustain cooperation over a series of events, the rewards must be fairly large and relevant over all events.

Clearly, when people engage in reciprocal social exchange they do not always exchange identical items or services. At one time individual A gives individual B money, expecting B to reciprocate with barter items, child care, or some service, such as drawing up a contract. At other times a favor done by A will not evoke a return favor for weeks, months, or even years. Complex cognitive devices, long-term memory, and consciousness give us the complexity to evaluate reinforcements over time, delaying decisions about others for long periods. Exchanges of exact values may be an unobtainable goal. Nevertheless, people somehow settle on values for different commodities and services, and decide how reinforcements should be distributed over long periods of time. More important than exact and timely reciprocation is the mutual intent to approximate equality of exchange.

There is an additional vagueness about long-term reciprocal interactions, in that the entire cycle of exchange may never occur, even though it may be implicit in the interactions. For example, if individual A's infant falls into a swimming pool and individual B happens along, it is expected that B will jump into the pool to save the infant. This should happen even if B never has a child in similar jeopardy that A can save, or, for that matter, if A and B never meet again. The assumption of exchange makes cooperation possible even if it never actually happens.

If social exchange can be expected for everyone in a group, one person's return of a favor can substitute for another's. Thus, A may help B, but not the reverse, but A can expect B to help C, who someday may return the favor to A. People operate in a network of reciprocity, insuring that on the average all individuals of a group can profit, or at least expect to.

In such a complex network, and especially over long periods of time, deception, defection, and cheating loom large. Individual B may only pretend to repay individual A, or deceive about extending reciprocity to other members of the social network. It's often difficult to judge the cost/benefit consequences of a particular act. Under these circumstances a person's reputation becomes critical. If A observes that B generally does not pay his debts, or if he has that reputation among others, then promises are insufficient. "Reputation, reputation, reputation! O, I ha' lost my reputation, I ha' lost the immortal part of myself, and what remains is bestial," Shakespeare mused. Reputation is that consensus of opinion that pulls a person from opportunism and singleness to cooperation and companionship.

Cultural Morality: Where are the Genes?

Morality and civility crumble around us as civilization plunges through its epileptic seizures. Sociobiologists blame it on the severed lines of nepotism, and the failure of reciprocal social exchange in the surrounds of anonymity. As Aldous Huxley saw it, "The quality of moral behaviors varies in inverse ration to the number of humans involved." Perhaps, but ironically the fragmentation of social standards gives us a focused view of human moral fabric that *seems* to operate independently of nepotism or reciprocal social exchange.

Ascetic Altruism

Sociobiologists have encountered any number of behaviors suggesting that individuals do not always weigh their actions against possible changes in inclusive fitness. There are those who abjure reproduction altogether, sacrificing their genetic future for the sake of strangers or society. Misplaced altruism perhaps, accidental acts occasionally, genetic mutations even, but there are behaviors that occur beyond the obvious "harmony of the genes." Consciousness, with its ability to rationalize and conceive of new relationships, may allow humans to defer and even reject their selfishness. Sociologist Joseph Lopreato refers to an apparent selfless act as *ascetic altruism*, defining it as "*behav-*

ior, conscious or unconscious, which, guided at most partially by in-
nate predispositions, potentially reduces the inclusive fitness of the ac-
tor and potentially increases the fitness of other(s)."

Ascetic altruism, by this definition includes a number of common
behaviors:

1. Christian penitence, where a belief in God leads to an acceptance of self-inflicted pain as a means of self-redemption. It can be as extreme as self-flogging, cutting off fingers, or stultifying vital energies through starvation and other deprivations.
2. Religious flagellations, as with the Christians of the Middle Ages and Shiite Moslem admirers of the Ayatollah Khomeini, sometimes resulting in great pain and debilitation.
3. Masochistic behaviors, often associated with sexual degradations, whippings and inflictions of self-pain with instruments and deprivations.
4. Severe fasting, deprivation of water, sometimes leading to death.
5. Checking of sexual desires with abstinence, sexual taboos, self-mutilation of genitals, and religious virtue.
6. Avoidance of parenthood, including 2.6 percent of sampled women who never reproduce by choice, even when their inclusive fitness is low.
7. Exclusive homosexuality which may include one percent of all men and one-half percent of all women.
8. Heroism, where individuals deliberately give up their lives in order to save strangers.
9. Ritualistic religious chastity, involving perhaps as many as 1,500,000 individuals worldwide, including nuns, priests, and monks.
10. Adopting children who are unrelated to the adopting parents, and who detract from the wealth and viability of the parents.

These behaviors are difficult to account for within the usual dictates of the selfish gene. All seem to involve a loss or a potential loss
in reproductive fitness. If sociobiological principles can account for
them, a more complex level of explanation is necessary. Lopreato's
view pivots on possible relations between selfless acts, self-deception, and notions of personal redemption. If people believe in karma,
or the soul and an afterlife, they can engage in altruism now in exchange for rewards expected later or in the afterlife. Varying degrees
of self-deception are necessary to convince a person of a link between
sacrifice and the belief that good deeds and self-deprivation will automatically reap benefits. According to Lopreato, "once self-deception
was selected, it probably made possible conceptions of a cultural nature that at times thwarted the self-serving thrust of the gene. The soul,

principle among them, may be thought of as the kernel of an internalized morality, reinforced by the will of fictitious forces, whereby some humans are in varying degrees led to subordinate their genetic fitness (and their self-interest in general) to the fitness and interests of others, even strangers who are in no position to reciprocate. Thus, the concept of the soul has to some extent modified the genetic action of natural selection."

Self-deception must play a strong role in ascetic altruism, and in some cases "apparent altruism" may help one to employ the selfish game. For example, a person can consciously or unconsciously deceive in his own best interests. Power, control, and profits can be gained by convincing others to be helpful, concerned for the "larger good," and sacrificial. John Kennedy sent this strong message to the nation in his inaugural address when he said, "Ask not what your country can do for you; ask what you can do for your country." Indeed people are easily led, believe most anything, and cling to the thin thread of salvation. Deception is a two-way street between those who would manipulate and those who would believe, creating an atmosphere of imagined self-understanding, self-worth, righteousness, and comfortable social status. There are those who lead; there are those who conform.

This complementarity between deceivers allows governments to control its people, religious institutions to grow and prosper, politicians and media representatives to control information, extreme environmentalists to tighten their power over individuals and property, and individuals to cheat in nepotistic and reciprocal interactions, all in the name of morality. Antonin Artaud the French theorist would challenge it all: "Ah! How neatly tied, in these people, is the umbilical cord of morality! Since they left their mothers they have never sinned, have they? They are apostles, they are the descendants of priests; one can only wonder from what source they draw their indignation, and above all how much they have pocketed to do this, and in any case what it has done for them."

The truth is that most of us want to believe in moral justice, the belief that allows us to sustain disappointments, adversity, and tragedy. Irrational beliefs may structure our personality, but the very deception that confounds our rationality and causes us to follow others reduces our sadness. If the alternative is self-destruction on the rock of truth, then our self-deception may not only facilitate the goals of others, but potentially increase our own inclusive fitness. Now, that is a dilemma worth looking into.

Morality in the Neuron

We are rarely as bad as we could be, in part because of fear of retaliation, but also because we have evolved brain mechanisms that inhibit potentially self-destructive acts. The exception is the psychopath who has no conscience and suffers no remorse, the psychotic who may explode with destructive rage, and the mentally retarded person who occasionally cannot discern the social limits of behavior. Young children, too, have a deficiency of moral judgment, generally curbed by parents and others.

Psychopathy is especially interesting because of its high frequency in the population. Perhaps 2 percent of the male population is psychopathic, and about one-half of one percent of the female population. In the United States alone, there may be as many as 3,750,000 individuals qualifying as psychopathic.

Characteristically these adult individuals are manipulative, impulsive, antisocial, risk-taking, socially disarming, and without a social conscious. Male psychopaths account for 30 to 40 percent of all felony crimes. They cheat in reciprocal social exchanges, showing a lack of remorse for evil deeds, and are irresponsible in their sexual and reproductive behaviors.

There is evidence that psychopathy has an organic base. It runs in families, and in some instances may be associated with a critical deficiency of the neural enzyme monoamine oxidase. Additionally, psychopaths are relatively unresponsive to fear-producing provocations, suggesting that the normal physiological reactivity to stress is depressed. In short, the psychopath lacks the physiological basis of a moral sense.

There is a neurological deficit that has characteristics like those of psychopaths, suggesting that psychopaths may ultimately show neural dysfunction. In several cases it is known that damage to the ventral, frontal area of the cortex results in a syndrome of socially irresponsible behaviors not unlike the typical psychopath.

The first famous case of this sort was with a twenty-five-year-old railroad foreman Phineas P. Gage, who in 1848 suffered severe brain damage of the frontal areas of the brain. It was his job to set explosives

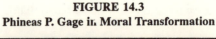

FIGURE 14.3
Phineas P. Gage in Moral Transformation

Source: Damasio, et al., 1994

in holes bored in rocks by tamping in blasting powder with a long metal rod. On a fateful day Gage made a mistake, setting off a premature explosion, driving the metal rod completely through his face and head. The rod destroyed his left eye and exited the top of his skull. A computer image of the damaged skull and brain is shown here.

Amazingly, Gage walked away from the accident and lived for many more years. But his life and the lives of those around him were changed forever. Prior to the incident Phineas was intelligent, hard-working, and socially responsible. In the weeks and months that followed he lost all respect for social conventions, lying, cheating, and acting totally irresponsibly. His friends exclaimed that "Gage was no longer Gage."

This Dr. Jekyll and Mr. Hyde transformation is not uncommon for individuals suffering damage to the ventral, frontal cortex of the brain, as did Gage. Drs. Antonio and Hanna Damasio and their colleagues have examined several cases. When individuals damaged in this region of the brain are compared with other patients who have damage in other regions, the damaged individuals share characteristics with the reports on Phineas Gage, and, as a matter of fact, with some psychopaths and

FIGURE 14.4

A: Frontal Damage

B: Nonspecific Damage

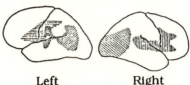

| Left | Right | Left | Right |
| Hemisphere | Hemisphere | Hemisphere | Hemisphere |

Left and Right Hemispheres of the Brain for Ventral, Frontal Lobe Damage (A) and Other Nonspecific Damage (B)
Source: Damasio, et al., 1990

other impulsive and erratic individuals who presumably have no brain damage. A comparison of these brain areas is shown here.

One recent reported case is exemplary of the relation between brain damage and apparent psychopathy. The patient E.V.R. was profoundly affected by brain damage in the ventral frontal cortex. Although of high intelligence, and with full cognitive awareness of right and wrong, E.V.R. manifested an extreme form of "acquired psychopathy." Within a short span of time following the brain injury, E.V.R. was divorced twice, lived six months with a prostitute, his second wife, entered disastrous financial ventures, eventually becoming bankrupt, lost all paying jobs, and ended up in a sheltered environment. Psychiatrically he was diagnosed as "sociopathic," a designation almost identical to that of "psychopathic."

The evidence from these examples supports the idea that the human brain has a built-in morality monitor—the ventral, frontal cortex. This area is disproportionately large in humans; it was elaborated during the course of hominid evolution. That region of the brain does not simply inhibit immoral behavior; it allows an individual to make complex decisions about the social value of behaviors. As many behaviors involving choice are affected—reciprocal exchanges, nepotistic concerns, sex, reproduction, and care-giving, it appears that this brain area is one of the few "domain general" mechanisms we possess: it has the appearance of a synchronizer of a wide range of social behaviors.

These observations put a new spotlight on morality. First, what we call morality is clearly a product of our evolutionary history and a manifestation of localized brain activity. Morality is neither God-given nor learned—its origin is genetic, its importance adaptive. Second, brain studies are beginning to unravel the biochemistry of our moods and dispositions, reducing these qualities to the neural impulse and the chemistry of cellular metabolism. Third, the exploration of the brain is giving us clues as to the evolutionary mechanisms underwriting psychopathy, criminal behavior, and violations of kinship rules and reciprocal social exchange. The conclusion explodes in our face: good and evil lurk in the neural network of the brain.

Too Complex or too Simple?

Culture had its beginnings with nepotism and reciprocal social exchange, fanning outward as populations grew and interactions with strangers multiplied. We had the brain for it, propelling us to create great civilizations. But there was nothing inevitable about civilization. Civilization is not in the genes. The profound truth of this is easily seen with the Tasmanians of Australia who lived in total isolation from the rest of the world until the arrival of Abel Tasman in 1642. The Tasmanian people were even less complex socially than the stone age people of Europe. They usually went naked, decorating themselves with necklaces of kangaroo sinew, kangaroo teeth, and strings of shells. For protection against cold they rubbed themselves with animal fat and charcoal. They lacked the tools for making fire, getting fire from lightning strikes, and keeping the hearth burning at all times. They built thatched huts of branches and grass, lining them with feathers. There were no stone tools, no weapons except clubs and wooden spears.

Yet, all around the Tasmanian culture the world surged toward artifacts, farming, cities, and philosophy. Social complexity continued at an unending pace, but none of that changed the human genotype. Some Tasmanians accepted aspects of the European culture, changing from a pre-stone age society to one of great complexity in a single generation. Likewise, there have been many reported cases where individuals from literate countries were born or lived within preliterate cultures, taking on all the characteristics of that culture. Obviously, individuals and populations do not have to evolve within a developing civilization to accept or reject that civilization.

Through all of civilization, going back only ten or twelve thousand years, humans have not changed in any fundamental way. They retain their universal characteristics regardless of where they are or who they are with. We don't build new genetic or brain mechanisms to cope with expanding civilizations; we use what we have. Rules of the mind for kinship interactions, reciprocal social exchange, cognitive capacities, and consciousness are the evolutionary threads upon which culture hangs. The consequence is that we see the world through the eyes of earlier hominids. Personal, social, and religious morality spring forth from a brain already hewn during our Pleistocene existence.

We must keep our eye on the evolutionary ball, and not be deceived into thinking that somehow we are now superior to our hominid ancestors, or have walked away from our biology. Culture is as biology does.

References

Cited in Chapter 14

Alexander, R.D. (1979). *Darwinism and Human Affairs*. Seattle: University of Washington Press.

Axelrod, R. (1980). *The Evolution of Cooperation*. New York: Basic Books, Inc.

Bechara, A., Damasio, A. R., Damasio, H. and Anderson, S.W. (1994). "Insensitivity to Future Consequences Following Damage to Human Prefrontal Cortex." *Cognition*, 50, 7-15.

Brown. D.E. (1991). *Human Universals*. Philadelphia: Temple University Press.

Chagnon, N.A. (1979). "Mate Competition, Favoring Close Kin, and Village Fissioning among the Yanomamö Indians." In N.A. Chagnon and Irons, W. (eds.). *Evolutionary biology and human social behavior: An anthropological perspective*. North Scituate, MA: Duxbury Press, 86-131.

Cosmides, L. and Tooby, J. (1992). "Cognitive Adaptations for Social Exchange." In J.H. Barkow, L. Cosmides and J. Tooby (eds.), *The Adapted Mind*. New York: Oxford University Press, 163-228.

Damasio, H., Grabowski, T., Frank, R., Galaburda, A.M. and Damasio, A.R. (1994). "The return of Phineas Gage: Clues about the brain from the skull of a famous patient." *Science*, 264, 1102-1105.

Gadagkar, R. (1993). "Can Animals be Spiteful?" *TREE*, 8, 232-34.

Hames, R.B. (1979). "Relatedness and Interaction among the Ye'Kwana: A Preliminary Analysis." In N.A. Chagnon and Irons, W. (eds.). *Evolutionary biology and human social behavior: An anthropological perspective*. North Scituate, MA: Duxbury Press, 238-249.

Lopreato, J. (1984). *Human Nature and Biocultural Evolution*. Boston: Allen and Unwin.
Reynolds, V., Falger, V. and Vine, I. (eds.). (1987). *The sociobiology of ethnocentrism*. London: Croom Helm.
Weatherford, J. (1994). *Savages and Civilization*. New York: Crown Publishers, Inc.

General References

Gamble, C. (1994). *Timewalkers: The Prehistory of Global Colonization*. Cambridge, MA: Harvard University Press.
Harris, M. (1991). *Cannibals and Kings*. New York: Vintage Books.
Rozin, P. (1988). "The Adaptive-Evolutionary Point of View in Experimental Psychology." In R.C. Atkinson, R.J. Herrnstein, G. Lindzey and R. Duncan Luce (eds.), *Steven's Handbook of Experimental Psychology*. New York: John Wiley and Sons, 503–546.
Smith, J.M. (1978). "The Evolution of Behavior." *Scientific American*, 239, 176–92.

15

The Yin and Yang of Sex

*Tis said of love that it sometimes goes, sometimes flies;
runs with one, walks gravely with another; turns a third
into ice, and sets a fourth in flame: it wounds one, another
it kills: like lightning it begins and ends in the same
moment: it makes that fort yield at night which it besieged
but in the morning; for there is no force able to resist it.*

—Miguel de Cervantes

*The Hawaiian beat drifted softly through the palms and over the
moonswept beach. There in the shadows lay a couple, same of heart,
breathless in the tautness of their love, accepting the rhythm of the waves,
each undertaking a fragment of their destiny.*

If Destiny is just a role of dice
And happenstance is nature's main device,
Then love is blind, and mere caprice explains
Why romance comes with all its joys and pains.

But surely there is more to love than this:
When Cupid's wound and Eros' artifice
Unite two hearts with passions set in time
And merge two souls whose dreams are set to rhyme.

If genes turn out to play a vital role
In how we sort in terms of heart and soul,
Indifferent forces shape our destiny
Though how this works is still a mystery.

And yet the sociobiologists
And gene-inspired psychologists
Admit that mental life is just as real,
That how we act will come from how we feel.

321

If feelings that are shaped by ancient force
Compete with feelings pulled by hope's resource,
Then push and pull combine like hand in glove
And past and future merge in deepest love.

—David Cohen

Here on the beach of Maui a man and woman are acting out the history of their evolution, focusing our attention on their differences, their similarities, and their motivations.

Evolutionary Paces

Mating is never random: there is always a place, a time, a person—everything specific, reflecting rules of the mind, adaptations of the past. Sexual reproduction evolved several different times, perhaps under the selection pressures of pathogens, but also in part because fertilization is best accomplished by small, fast moving gametes, sperm, and large, nutritive gametes, ova. The initial causes advanced a way of life where males and females play different roles in sex and reproduction, yet where both must compromise for the good of the next generation.

Gametes, Love, and Self-Interest: First Thoughts

Ova and sperm travel on the hem of emotions, moving or halting according to desire, impulse, repulsion, and consideration. From out of this evolutionary caldron of genetic feelings and cost-benefit analyses came sexual differences in mating strategies. And the differences are substantial.

A female is born with several thousand ova, but she will mature and ovulate only about 400 in her lifetime, on average one ovum every twenty-eight days. An impregnated female gestates the fetus for about nine months. Following parturition the hormonal balance shifts—lactation and extended infant care begins. The costs are high. Approximately 180,000 additional calories, about 16 kg of fat, are needed for nine months of gestation and one year of lactation. The infant's brain at birth is only 23 percent of adult size, requiring additional years of parental involvement before it reaches full capacity. Much of its early growth depends on lipids and lactose in the mother's milk. But if this weren't enough, there are costs of fighting off disease, infant mortality, constant vigilance, work, fatigue, and uncertain paternal contributions.

The entire cycle of female reproduction is so costly that it can be repeated only every three to four years. If the reproductive window of opportunity is between sixteen and twenty-nine years of age, the expected number of children is few. The average worldwide range is from less than two to nearly nine, varying with social conditions and the availability of resources. In all of history, the female tends to have as many children as necessary to rear about two to reproductive age.

The male also has high costs for reproduction, although it is distributed differently from that of the female. A male can produce around 300 million sperm each day, and can reproduce well into the sixth and seventh decade. Theoretically, a single male can produce dozens and even hundreds of offspring, results that have been achieved many times.

For the male, gametic production, gestation, and lactation are obviously not major costs. What does use up time and energy are competition with other males for high social status and resources (things that females prefer), attempts to attract and hold females, and time and energy spent with females and offspring. The shipping magnate Aristotle Onassis clearly understood why males compete: "If women didn't exist, all the money in the world would have no meaning." Many of the costs of male reproduction, including acquisition of status and resources, occur *prior* to copulation; those of the female, concentrated around offspring care, occur primarily *after* copulation.

The male's major postcopulatory cost is investment in the female and offspring. Associated with this "family" cost is possible cuckoldry by the female, where the male is deceived into helping the female perpetuate the genes of another male. Fear of cuckoldry and paternal uncertainty are major issues for the male, as each investment in the female and her offspring detracts from other potential investments. The estimates for female cuckoldry range from 5 to over 40 percent in America and Britain, escalating even higher, depending upon the society. Male jealousy, spousal abuse, and infanticide hang on the evolutionary thread of parental uncertainty.

The greatest potential cost of reproduction for the male is not reproducing at all. In polygynous mating systems, including nearly all human cultures, the female with the heavier direct physiological and behavioral burdens of reproduction, selectively excludes males from the joys of sex and reproduction—ignoring or rejecting those who cannot or will not contribute to her needs. Males also contribute to the

TABLE 15.1
Single, Never-Married, Persons as Percent of United States Population in 1991

Age	Male	Female
18–19	96.6	90.4
20–24	79.7	64.1
25–29	46.7	32.3
30–34	27.3	18.7
35–39	17.6	11.7
40–44	10.0	8.8
45–54	7.4	5.6

nonreproduction of other males, either by monopolizing several females or more directly by intimidation and coercion. The end result is that almost all females have the opportunity to mate, leaving a number of males who never mate or whose mating is limited. The differential reproduction of females and males is reflected by marriage statistics for the ages between eighteen and fifty-four. The numbers indicate that for every age group there is a greater proportion of males who never marry. This "either-or" situation for the male can be catastrophic, sealing his genetic fate.

Typical of other polygynous species, the human female with the heavier postcopulatory investment acts cautiously in her mating goals, acting as a personal selection force on the male to evolve characteristics that are beneficial to her and her offspring. The evolutionary reaction of the male to the female's demands is defined as *sexual selection*. Sexual selection, in contrast to natural selection, can result in traits that reduce general fitness. The long and vividly colored tail of the paradise bird is an example of a trait carved out by sexual selection. The male evolved this extraordinary visual display because it is used as an exemplar of individual fitness by females. But, at the same time, those beautiful tail feathers cut down on mobility and attract predators. Its usefulness as a signal of reproductive fitness must therefore outweigh its disadvantages.

As someone once remarked, if the female preferred males who walk on their hands, sexual selection would soon result in males who compete in the fine art of hand-walking. The comparative psychologist Gordon Gallup bluntly describes sexual selection by saying, "In many respects males are nothing but an evolutionary experiment being run by

TABLE 15.2
Sexual Differences in Optimal Heterosexual Strategies

	Female	Male
Physiological and behavioral commitment	Awesome	Minimal
Pre-copulatory competition for social status and resources	Little	Huge
Reproductive potential	Low & Constant	High & Variable
Assurance of genetic relatedness to offspring	Complete	Uncertain
Best strategy for genetic transmission	Cautious & long-term investment: K strategy	Opportunistic mating: r strategy

females. If there are male traits that some females find objectionable (e.g., domineering) they have no one to blame but themselves and their female predecessors." Yes, but they can also take the credit for male traits that please them, among which may be generosity and the tendency to protect females against harm by others.

As a result of sexual selection reproductive costs arrange themselves differently for females and males. The differences are summarized here. It follows that females and males must differ in attitudes toward sex, courtship, short-term versus long-term relations, parental care, spacing of children, interest in resources, age of mate, sexual jealousy, physical attractiveness, adulterous love, divorce and remarriage, physical and social aggression, rates of crime, rapacious behaviors, and a host of personality correlates. These attributes and behaviors circulate around the primary sex differences in infant investment and sexual selection. If these can be optimized then, like the Yin and Yang of Oriental philosophy, the reproductive interests of both sexes are served.

Wants, Needs, and Ideals

Sexual differences based on genes, development, and evolution, set our sexual and reproductive styles. These sexual differences, the products of eons of natural and sexual selection, should not be referred to as "gender" differences, as this designation implies effects of socialization rather than biology.

TABLE 15.3
Rank Order Preferences for Traits

Rank	Characteristics Preferred by Males	Characteristics Preferred by Females
1	Kindness and understanding	Kindness and understanding
2	Intelligence	Intelligence
3	*Physical attractiveness*	Exciting personality
4	Exciting personality	Good health
5	Good health	Adaptability
6	Adaptability	*Physical attractiveness*
7	Creativity	Creativity
8	Desire for children	*Good earning capacity*
9	College graduate	College graduate
10	Good heredity	Desire for children
11	*Good earning capacity*	Good heredity
12	Good housekeeper	Good housekeeper
13	Religious orientation	Religious orientation

One must not forget, however, that even the evolved differences are embedded in the common weave of life. Males and females are still more similar than different, sharing nearly every gene, enzyme, neuron, physical structure, and motivation. There may be variations in how traits are expressed, but they remain similar, even indistinguishable. For one thing, sexuality is dependent on early ratios of testosterone and estrogen; it can go either way, or get stuck in the middle, as in the case of behavioral reversals and perhaps homosexuality. And, so it is with so many other evolved characteristics—differences in sexual motivation, perceptual acuity, and motor performance. "Tendencies," "inclinations," "statistical variations," "probabilities," "overlaps," "averages," and "uncertainties" are the descriptive terms of most sexual differences.

When we ask males or females what they prefer in the other sex and rank these preferences in importance, the overlap is nearly 100 percent. Within this list of wants, needs and ideals is the evidence for sexual dimorphism (that is, difference)—physical attractiveness, and good earning capacity are weighted differently by the two sexes, but they remain on nearly everyone's list. The common denominator of these traits is the potential for increasing compatibility and facilitating reproduction.

TABLE 15.4
Universal Signs of Beauty

Physical Traits	Behavioral Traits
Youthful	Energetic
Optimal body weight and fat distribution	Neuromuscular coordination
Good muscular tone	Upright stature
Good complexion	Sportily gait
Sound teeth	Firm voice
Lustrous hair	Sound mind
Clear eyes	Lack of deviations
Full lips	Lack of disease

One of the most important marks for both sexes is good health. This feature alone reflects the quality of the genotype—resistance to disease, vitality of the individual—and thus reproductive potential. Signals of health are the universal characteristics that are in demand by both sexes. When individuals meet they quickly assess the physical and psychological health of the other, as though it were a "drive-by" medical examination. As one luckless male put it, "Women look at me, evaluate me, and reject me in a fraction of a second."

The most important clues for assessing health and reproductive potential are shown below. They are so common in our evaluations of others that we tend not to think about them, yet they direct our most important behaviors. The signals have always been important for survival and reproduction; as a result they evolved the attribute that we call beautiful. High reproductive potential *is* beautiful—universal, crucial, an instrument of every female, every male. If a healthy signature were not "beautiful," we would not want it; our fitness would falter.

The biologist Randy Thornhill and his colleagues indicate that both the male and the female prefer others who display symmetrical features of the face and body. Measures of traits that occur in pairs include the ears, wrists, hands, elbows, and ankles. Left-to-right differences do not have to be extreme for individuals to show a differential preferences. Indeed, the judgments may be unconscious. For example, males who are preferred over others tend to be more symmetrical. Amazingly, increased symmetry is associated with the early onset of sexual activity and is related to more sex partners. The importance of symmetry is not as important for the female, probably for the usual reason that the male is less discriminating in his choices.

Symmetry in the male is probably a reflection of a "balanced" genotype and an optimal developmental history—nothing very deviant, everything healthy. The female who is looking for a fit male and "good" DNA is likely to prefer a symmetrical male. If we knew more, it might be that symmetrical males more easily acquire high social status and resources, and will show greater reproduction. In any case, we see the aesthetic equation for successful reproduction: symmetry = beauty = health = fitness.

In another series of related studies the psychologist Judy Langlois and her colleagues find that both sexes prefer facial traits that are constructed to be more average. In this case, photographs of either males or females are digitized and averaged by a computer program. The result of superimposing facial features causes the asymmetries to vanish into the generalized form. But it is not merely asymmetry that individuals avoid, or symmetry that they prefer. This is evident when faces are reconstructed from two right halves or two left halves of the same individuals. The perfectly symmetrical faces are less preferred than the originals. The average, independent of symmetry, is what is preferred. This same preference is found in young infants, suggesting that we come into the world with the ability to assess symmetry, beauty, and reproductive fitness.

Symmetry and averageness are not of course the only critical signals in mate selection or the evaluation of beauty. The anthropologists Victor Johnston and Melissa Franklin find that both the male and the female prefer a female face that is not only symmetrical, but is neotenized—youthful, with roundish face, high forehead, large eyes, small chin, and full lips—babyish in appearance. Johnston has the subject construct specific traits on a computer screen by accepting or rejecting traits from thousands that are available. The most beautiful face, no matter who constructs it, has the juvenile features. When the constructed faces are compared to average traits found in the general population, individuals prefer the constructed faces, and judge them to be younger. We can refer to these idealized faces as "virtual reality" fantasies. For the male, these are the aesthetically pleasing faces that reflect high reproductive value, quite in harmony with the male's pursuit of

FIGURE 15.1

FIGURE 5.   The highest rated facial composite (left) and a composite having the same features but in the proportions of the average face in the population (right).

Source: Johnston and Franklin, 1993

female fertility. For the female, these are the faces that they recognize as attractive to males.

These ground-breaking studies point out that there are multiple aspects of facial and bodily beauty: symmetry, averageness, and neoteny. In addition, there are probably some asymmetrical characteristics—mainly behavioral—that are preferred, especially those that may advance reproductive fitness, as with handedness and perhaps language laterality. All no doubt interact in complex ways: an arresting face, a beauty deep, a harmonious bloom.

For the male, beauty is in the female body as well as the face. Psychologist Devendra Singh has demonstrated that males prefer females who have a waist-to-hip ratio of around 0.7—the "hour-glass" figure. The male also prefers a female of average body weight, but regardless of her weight, he finds the ratio of 0.7 most beautiful. Moderate breast size is also an index of beauty, but in a choice situation the male still focuses on the magic ratio of 0.7. Finally, even asymmetrical breast size

FIGURE 15.2

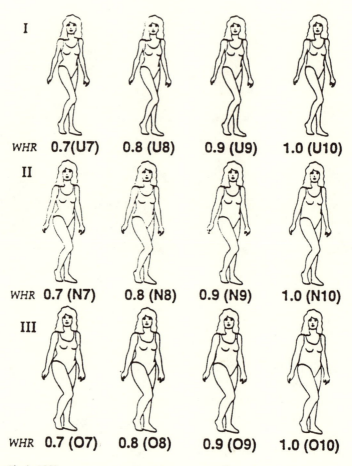

Source: Singh, 1993

that detracts from female beauty will be overlooked if the waist-to-hip ratio is right.

Females show the same preference for the 0.7 ratio in other females, indicating that they are aware of what attracts males. As Singh expresses it, in no culture does the woman try to make her waist-to-hip ratio appear larger, unless she is deliberately trying to disguise her reproductive capacity. On the contrary, in almost every culture the woman strives for a small ratio. The reader can test his or her own preferences from the stimulus figures.

Stimulus figures representing three body weight categories: underweight (I), normal weight (II), and overweight (III). The waist-to-hip ratio (WHR) is under each figure.

Why is female beauty linked to a small waist-to-hip ratio? The answer is that the male prefers a form most closely associated with reproductive fitness. The 0.7 ratio gives him that essential cue. As the waist-to-hip ratio increases, the female is more likely to show reduced reproductive capacity. For a ratio of greater than 0.85 here is what can be expected.

1. Late onset of puberty
2. Increased levels of male-like hormones
3. Elevated plasma triglycerides
4. Resistance to insulin (high risk for diabetes)
5. Risk of gallbladder disease
6. Risk for endometrial, ovarian, and breast cancer
7. About a 30 percent decrease in conception rates
8. Probably a reduced interest in sex

Singh's work gives the most direct evidence so far of evolutionary ties between beauty, health, and reproductive fitness. The male will tell you that he seeks young women, and indeed he does, but what he really wants are the correlates of youth—a waist-to-hip ratio that reflects health, vigor, ovulation, and reproductive value.

Those Differences of Degree

Sigmund Freud once asked the question, "What does a woman want?" He might have asked the same question of man, but perhaps he didn't because the answer is more evident. The point is illustrated by a series of studies done in the United States, spanning fifty years and monumental cultural change. In at least eight published studies females preferred ambitious males who have good earning capacity, high social status, and industriousness. Males, on the other hand, repeatedly sought physical attractiveness in the female, *period*. The sexual difference is obvious in experimental contexts, lonely hearts advertisements, and everyday conversations. Females want resourceful and potentially successful males; males want attractive females—the right waist-to-hip ratio.

TABLE 15.5
What do Women and Men Want of Each Other in 37 Cultures*

	Women > Men	Men > Women
Good Financial Prospects	37	0
Ambition and Industriousness	34	3
Good Looks	0	37
Spouse Older than Self	37	0

*Number of cultures in which women and men show greater interest (>). (after Buss, 1994)

The same sexual dimorphism was found in thirty-seven different cultures around the world by the psychologist David Buss, indicating that the differences are universal and do not depend on the peculiarity of the culture. The cultures studied include those of North and South America, Africa, Great Britain, Western and Eastern Europe, Asia, including China and Japan, Australia, and a few island groups. The summary is seen in table 15.5.

The data not only confirm the investigations done in the United States, but illustrate that sexual dimorphism, at least of these features, is not a product of socialization, culture, language, race, politics, or geography. There is clearly overlap in the distributions of female and male interest, but we are looking at differences that are universal. Females with their heavy postcopulatory investment in offspring want males who can help with their reproductive burden. Males, on the contrary, are interested in young, good-looking females, the very females who have the greatest reproductive value, thus contributing to their fitness. An additional cross-cultural finding, one that has been reported many times before, is that women prefer men older than themselves, whereas men prefer women younger than themselves. These results are congruent with the notion that women are better able to assess health and financial prospects in older men; men target young females who are most likely to be fertile and have reproductive potential.

> Dear Abby: Why do young women come on to older men? I don't consider myself any glamour puss—I am 80 years old—but I have had more young women come on to me in the last few years than I can count. Many are young enough to be my granddaughters. I have never been popular with the opposite sex, even when I was a very young man. And I never was considered good-looking.
> D.C. in Duluth

Dear D.C.: You may be more appealing than you think. On the other hand, please send me your financial statement, and perhaps I can provide you with a better answer.

The universal differences in female and male sexual preferences partly answer Sigmund Freud's question, "What does a woman want?" But, in addition, they address the existence of the global "double standard" of sexual behavior. Females are expected to be more circumspect with regard to their sexual activities, and they are taught this from day one. It may not be fair, but it occurs universally. Instead of asking why all cultures are sexist, perhaps we should ask why every culture finds it important to restrict females more than males in their sexual inclinations. The answer to that question comes down to a consideration of costs and benefits. Females and males have different reproductive agenda and costs, and must therefore surround themselves with different attitudes, behaviors, and moral standards.

When the cloak of sexual morality is parted, the true nature of the selfish gene is exposed. A female who is at risk for reproduction dares not be promiscuous; her genetic success depends on careful considerations of future benefits. The male is less constrained by this dictate; his interests are better served through multiple and indiscriminate mating. Short-term and long-term goals of the female and the male may alter the degree of sexual differences, as when immediate advantage supersedes deferred advantage. But these contingency considerations are simply variations on the more indelible genetic themes.

The Female Tracks the Environment; The Male Tracks the Female

The female is not mandated by her genes to be sexually and reproductively conservative. She does indeed become sexually active later than the male, and is less likely to engage in masturbation, premarital intercourse, homosexual behavior, and extramarital affairs. She avoids sexual stimuli more than the male, and in written surveys, she professes less sexual interest in pictorial, verbal, or written depictions of sexual activity.

But this simplified perception is, based only on average differences between the female and the male. Women can and sometimes do pursue high levels of sexual activity. What's really different is the extreme variability of sex behavior in the female. The French satirist Jean de La

Bruyère said it best when he said, "Women run to extremes; they are either better or worse than men." At one time the female is oblivious to sexual signals, at another time she is highly excited by these same signals and eagerly engages in sexual activities. The male, in particular, is perplexed by these apparent contradictions; the female, by contrast, seems comfortable with her own diversity.

The hypothesis to explain the variability seen with the female was explored by Thiessen: "The female tracks her environment in her reproductive efforts, whereas the male tracks the female. The female, because of her high reproductive investments, must link her sexual appetite and offspring investment to the most propitious environment. That environment will include, but is not limited by, the male and the male's capacity to augment the reproductive goals of the female. The female should defer reproduction and show low sexual motivation in environments that fail to support her efforts, but she should switch into a reproductive mode and show high sexual motivation in environments that can facilitate her reproductive goals. She should also be able to anticipate the quality of the environment and respond accordingly."

There is no adaptive advantage for a female who only cultivates a low and restrictive sexual demeanor; the advantage is in the optimal distribution of sexual responses. Her behaviors are sometimes inexplicable, contradictory, and misunderstood, but in fact when we know more, her actions may prove adaptive. The American writer Sally Kempton expressed the thought with more color: "Women are natural guerrillas. Scheming, we nestle into the enemy's bed, avoiding open warfare, watching the options, playing the odds."

Paradoxically, the female is more variable in her sexual behaviors because she is more specific in her needs. She shifts in behavior, not because she is moving randomly from one behavior to another, but because she is closely tracking the quality of the environment for her reproductive ends, forever making adjustments in her sex behavior. If the environment becomes less supportive of her efforts, she decreases her interest in sex. And in a measure larger than that for the male, she can anticipate the degree to which the future will add or subtract from her reproductive advantage. Her reproductive costs, higher than those of the male, demand that she be able to link her reproduction with the things around her and the roads ahead.

We can only summarize some of the variations that Thiessen believes are exclusive to the female, or appear in the female more frequently than in the male, all of which could affect female reproductive success.

1. Females are highly selective in their interests in the other sex and in response to sexual stimuli.
2. Onset of puberty is delayed in low-quality environments, or is facilitated when reproduction can be more easily supported (e.g., by food supplies, availability of male contributions, institutional supports, etc).
3. Low-quality environments, ill health, loss of body fat, and disease will disrupt ovulation and decrease interest in sex behavior.
4. If the benefits of deferred reproduction outweigh the costs, as with the unavailability of quality mates, or with the pursuit of a career, sexual activities will diminish in importance.
5. Deliberate loss of body weight, as in anorexia, may be an unconscious mechanism for shutting down ovulation and decreasing sexual appetites.
6. Circumstances of living, moral strictures, and chances of pregnancy guide sexuality and provide its rationalizations.
7. A supporting environment or a high-quality male willing to make a commitment to a relationship can stimulate female sexual activity and reproduction.

An example of contingent reproduction is seen among the San who inhabit the Kalahari desert in South Africa. There is a seasonal suppression of ovulation associated with a decrease in available food. The ovulatory inhibition, associated with body fat loss, is reversed under conditions of normal food supplies. Interestingly, male reproductive capacities do not appear to be affected by food cycles. In contrast to this situation, in Western Samoa where food quality is constantly high, women have about 7.8 children on the average, and ovulate even during periods of heavy lactation.

Males vary with regard to many of the same factors that influence females, but are more uniform in their reactions. Onset of puberty is relatively invariant over a range of environments; sexual mating choices are less discriminating, and his reproductive physiology is more constant. To the degree that their success depends more on immediate delivery of sperm and not on infant investment, males are less reactive to environments that might influence female reproductive success. In general, the physiology and behavior of reproductively mature males is keyed more for competition with other males and for constant readiness to mate. Males want more sex; females want good sex.

Extremes Illuminate General Tendencies

Surveys conducted among gays and lesbians in San Francisco and elsewhere do not demonstrate that homosexuals gravitate toward sexual traits of the other sex, or settle at some mid-functional level. Rather, the surveys show that the typical sexually dimorphic behaviors are exaggerated where there is lack of an inhibiting influence by the other sex. The typical characteristics of the male and female still exist; only the sexual orientation is different. Some of the sexual traits of gays and lesbians are indicated here.

Male and female homosexuals differ in ways typical of heterosexuals, except for selective personality traits. The inherent promiscuity of the male and the selectivity of the female are evident in the number and longevity of relations. Gays in San Francisco, for example, admit to having sometimes as many as 1,000 sex partners.

The interactions are brief and rarely lead to long-term commitments. Lesbians, on the other hand, seldom have over three or four sex partners, opting instead for long-term relations. Clearly, the evolved sexual dimorphism continues to be expressed in homosexuals.

The evidence for genetic and biochemical factors underlying homosexuality is growing, but so is the evidence that gays and lesbians are not locked into a homosexual life-style. It is important to underscore that only about two percent of all males and one percent of all females are homosexual at any point in their lives. Although the statistics are blurred, many homosexuals spend part of their lives engaging in heterosexual activities—sometimes switching back and forth, sometimes reproducing before declaring their homosexuality, sometimes marrying and reproducing later in life.

The lesson is important. While homosexuality is a nonreproductive life-style, the natural tendencies to pursue reproduction remains, at least for many. The genes continue to spin out their penchants in novel ways, modified by unique aspects of the culture. Sexual orientation toward others of the same sex, and high levels of gay sexual activity, obscure the basic inclinations to retain reproductive capacities typical of heterosexual males and females.

The free sexual life-style of the male homosexual is duplicated in heterosexual males who have greater than average resources, or who wield significant social power. These males, like homosexuals, are less

TABLE 15.6
Sexual Inclinations of Gays and Lesbians

Gay Male Sexual Tendencies	Lesbian Sexual Tendencies
Promiscuity	Monogamy
Prefer sex in a semi-public spot	Prefer sex at home
Obsessed with beauty	Resent focus on beauty
Avid for pornography	Outraged by pornography
Fantasy and degradation	Less adventurous
Ideal sex partner is young	Looks not too important

inhibited in their sex drive—having greater access to a number of sex partners. The differences are mainly in terms of sexual orientation and reproductive success. Individual stories abound. In 1991 a Stanford University professor, Dr. Norman J. Lewiston, an expert in cystic fibrosis research, died of a coronary, leaving three wives to claim his body or his inheritance. Lewiston married his first wife, Diana, in 1960. In 1985 he married his second wife, Katy, in a public ceremony attended by many of his colleagues. Katy was the wife generally taken to social and professional functions. In 1989 he married Robyn, a person working at the hospital where Lewiston worked. She moved to San Diego where she expected Lewiston to eventually join her. Obviously, life was complicated for Dr. Lewiston. At the end of his workday he usually went home to Katy. Then around 10 p.m. he would leave, telling Katy that he would sleep at the hospital. Instead, he went to the home he shared with Diana, often leaving early in the morning to return to Katy for breakfast. About two weekends each month he visited Robyn in San Diego. Holidays were strenuous times. For example there was one Thanksgiving when he had three dinners. It came as a tremendous shock to all three women when his trigamy was discovered at his death. About ten days before he died, Norman went with Katy to a golf tournament, where by chance he won a weekend trip to San Francisco. Katy was delighted, but Dr. Lewiston didn't look very excited at all. It's unclear by the report how many offspring he had, but the potential was certainly there.

More recently Vernon Pierce, a thirty-three-year-old ex-model, was jailed for bigamy. He married four women, while simultaneously dating other women. He kept track of his dates on three-by-five-inch cards, labeled, "Who to Marry." Pierce told his wives that his job required him to travel, and indeed he was busy moving around from woman to woman. This tangled life unraveled when one of the four wives sent police to Pierce's home to check up on him. The police found another wife knocking on his door.

Then there is the odd case of Dr. Cecil Jacobson, a fertility specialist, who fathered at least seven children for couples who thought they were receiving legitimate donor sperm. It is hard to believe that any woman would have acted like Drs. Lewiston, Pierce, or Jacobson.

Within the law, resourceful men always have reproductive advantages. The late crooner Dick Haymes married seven times, including the actresses Joanne Dru and Rita Hayworth, and singer Fran Jeffries. Just how many of these marriages resulted in offspring is unclear, although the opportunities were there. Rod Stewart, forty-nine, has sired five children: a daughter and son with former wife Alana Hamilton, a daughter from his affair with model Kelly Emberg, and a daughter and son with supermodel Rachel Hunter, his wife since 1990. He has also been involved with such beauties as Britt Ekland, Kelly LeBrock, and Teri Copley. Marlon Brando, seventy, had three wives and eight children. He said that he had an affair with Marilyn Monroe, remarking: "Once she called and invited me for dinner. I already had plans but promised to call the following week. She said fine. Two or three days later, she was dead." Johnny Carson, sixty-eight years of age, married four times, with each wife at least six years younger than her predecessor. Texas oil baron J. Howard Marshall, now eighty-nine, acquired new wives at thirty-year intervals, marrying his first in 1931, his second in 1961 and ex-Guess jeans model Anna Nicole Smith, twenty-six. Nicole Smith, now in a financial dispute with Marshall's son Pierce, made these interesting remarks: "I did not marry my husband for money. I love him so much.... I performed wife duties for Marshall." Billionaire J. Paul Getty was married and divorced five times. At eighty-three he he made the shrewd comment, "A lasting relationship with a woman is only possible if you are a business failure." The real estate tycoon Donald Trump recently had a daughter with Marla Maples. He also has three children with ex-wife Ivana. The popular screen actor Anthony Quinn at seventy-eight years of age recently fathered a baby girl with his secretary. Quinn became a father for the eleventh time. He and his wife have three children; he has four children with his previous wife, Katharine DeMille; he also has three children by other women. Musician Quincy Jones, 61, has a nineteen-month-old daughter with actress and model Nastassja Kinski. Add that to her two children from a previous marriage and Jones' six other children, and the number climbs to nine. The late Burt Lancaster married three times, producing six children: Jim, William, John, Joanna, Susan, and Sighle. Finally, there is "Mark," a University of California student, psychologically stable with "good sperm," who regularly donates sperm at the California Cryobank of Berkeley. Mark expressed his male genotype when he said, "I feel like I'm contributing, in my own small way, my good qualities and hereditary strengths without feeling any possessiveness." These examples could be multiplied many times, illustrating that males prefer multiple matings; the famous and wealthy often translate these matings into viable fertilized ova.

One of the more striking investigations of links between cultural success and mating was conducted by the biologist Daniel Pérusse with a large Canadian male population. Devising what he called a "Number of Potential Conceptions" (NPC) scale (a copulation index), he found a strong relation between occupational status and frequency of sexual encounters. Occupational status accounted for nearly two-thirds of the variation in NPC, indicating that resourceful men are much more likely to have reproductive opportunities with multiple women.

While some well-to-do women have multiple husbands and mates, such as Elizabeth Taylor and Zsa Zsa Gabor, they seldom translate these marriages into increased reproduction. Male reproductive potential is clearly more variable than that of the female, as some males are preferred by several females; others never make the reproductive cut. While almost all females have the opportunity to reproduce, their reproductive potential is limited by the extremely high costs associated with gestation, lactation, and infant care, and the relatively short reproductive life span. Actor Jack Nicholson's slant on this is that "men and women are glandularly different. A woman has a sexual experience and she has to wait to see what happens. A man has one, he has to look for someone else after that. Its not a question of his morality. His glands are all designed to overcome his morality."

The correlation between cultural success for males and infant production has long been evident. The majority of investigations are summarized here. In nearly all of these there is a strong relation between

TABLE 15.7
Relationship Between Male Cultural and Reproductive Success in Human Populations

Study	Population	Economy	Cultural success	Reproductive success	Result	Comments
Borgerhoff Mulder (1987, 1989)	Kipsigis	Agriculture, pastoralism	1. Size of land	a. No. of surviving offspring b. No. of wives c. Offspring survivorship	1a. Yes 1b. Yes 1c. No	Age controlled by grouping into cohorts; independence of CS from RS established
Betzig (1988)	Ifalukese	Agriculture, fishing, paid labour	1. Political status	a. No. of offspring b. No. of wives	1a. No 1b. No	Correlations between RS and CS nonsignificant when controlled for age
Boone (1986, 1988)	15th-16th century Portuguese	Agriculture	1. Status (reflecting title to land)	a. No. of surviving offspring b. No. of serial marriages	1a. Yes 1b. Yes	Precedence of CS over RS established for some tests; age not controlled
Hughes (1986)	17th century England	Agriculture	1. Occupational class	a. No. of offspring b. Offspring survivorship c. No. of offspring surviving to 21 years	1a. No 1b. Yes 1c. Yes	Age not controlled, but independence of CS from RS probable
Voland (1990)	18th century Germany	Agriculture	1. Status (reflecting title to land)	a. Long-term fitness	1a. No	CS associated with RS but not significantly; age not controlled
Low & Clarke (1991)	19th century Sweden	Agriculture, fishing, some industry	1. Occupational status 2. Size of land	a. No. of offspring b. No. offspring surviving to 10 years	1a, 2a. Variable 1b, 2b. Variable	Results not consistent over measures, areas or generations

TABLE 15.7 (continued)
Relationship Between Male Cultural and Reproductive Success in Human Populations

Relationship Between Male Cultural and Reproductive Success in Human Populations
(after Pérusse, 1992)

Author	Society	Subsistence economy	Measures of cultural success (CS)	Measures of reproductive success (RS)	Positive relationship between CS and RS	Comments
Chagnon, et al (1979)	Yanomamo	Hunting & gathering, horticulture	1. Rank of lineage 2. Headmanship	a. No. of offspring b. No. of wives	1a. No 2a. Yes 2b. Yes	CS and RS could result independently from third factor
Irons (1979)	Yomuts	Agriculture, pastoralism	1. Wealth	a. Age-specific fertility b. Age-specific mortality	1a. Yes 1b. Yes (inverse)	Age controlled; partial time precedence of CS over RS established
Mealey (1985)	19th-century Mormons	Agriculture	1. Religious rank 2. Wealth	a. No. of offspring b. No. of wives	1a. 2a. Yes 1b. 2b. Yes	Age controlled; time precedence of CS over RS established
Turke & Betzig (1985)	Ifalukese	Agriculture, fishing, paid labour	1. Earnings 2. Political status	a. No. of offspring	1a. Yes 2a. No for chiefs alone; yes for chiefs, advisors and successors as a group	Age controlled; independence of CS from RS established
Flinn (1986)	Trinidadians	Agriculture	1. Size of land	a. No. of offspring surviving to 1 month b. No. of mates who produced offspring	1a. Yes 1b. Yes	Age not controlled, but CS not correlated with age; independence of CS from RS established

Source: Perusse, 1992

social status and reproductive success. Even where the differences aren't statistically significant, they tend to be in the predicted direction. It seems that males will inseminate as many females as possible, especially when they enjoy high social status and financial security, and when there is no obligation to care for the offspring, a typical r reproductive strategy.

History Sings the Blues

The unequal opportunities for male reproduction is evident in the depths of history—it is not a new enterprise of Western thought or competition—it always was. The biologist Laura Betzig documents the extremes of male reproduction in the best-known civilizations of the last 4,000 years. Her studies include six major civilizations that span four continents—Mesopotamian and Egyptian in the Near East, the Aztex and Inca in the Americas, and the Indian and Chinese in Asia.

These major civilizations were controlled by male emperors, who, in their unrestrained dominion over women and men, mated with hundreds, thousands, and even tens of thousands of women in their harems. Below them on the social structure were other dominant men who in turn controlled females, preventing other males from reproducing. As Betzig summarizes: "Compared to subordinate men, dominant men have had more exclusive access to more women of their own; and they have had more exclusive access to more women. Both kinds of access should have helped them father more children. Across civilizations, the reproductive hierarchy seems to have paralleled the political hierarchy. Emperors' harems numbered in the thousands; noblemen, often emperors' kinsmen, had harems in the hundreds; and heads of progressively lower levels in the political hierarchy kept progressively smaller harems. Sometimes, as in the Incan case, the parallel was mandated by law. In any case, men on the bottom often went without women."

The emperors invariably chose young, attractive women for their harems, tending to withhold semen from everyone except those females who were ovulatory, that is, cycling hormonally. Hundreds of offspring were produced in this manner. However, not all offspring shared in the wealth of the empire. Within this apparent chaos of polygyny, each emperor had a "monogamous" wife, whose children carried on the emperor's name, title, and inheritance. The specificity of inheritance was even greater, in that only the male offspring of the monogamous wife, in fact the first born male, acted as the emperor's genetic conduit to the next generation. In this fashion, the empire remained intact in title, money, and genotype.

By today's standards the emperors' sexual and reproductive activities seem deviant. They may be, in terms of quantity, but not in terms of tendency. Betzig reasonably postulates that men have been exploiting women and men ever since hominids evolved. The exploiters inevitably consume more than other men, implying that they either had to work harder for what they had, or took wealth from others.

Exploitation and extortion continue on a more minor level; in a few Near Eastern cultures harems still exist. The deep-rooted explanation for the continuation of these behaviors is that men are evolved to copulate and sire children whenever and however possible, accounting for the extraordinary levels of sex behavior in gay men, the Anthony Quinns of the world, the Donald Trumps, and nearly every other man who has the chance. Today it is usually not possible to build an empire and maintain harems, accounting for the limited manifestation of this drive. The potential remains.

One wonders why women put up with it all. Why do they often gravitate to men of power, even when they must share the riches with other women? The obvious answer is that a woman often has much to gain by agreeing to a polygynous relation if the male is socially dominant and controls substantial resources. She, in effect, by tracking the environment agrees to share her position with other females in exchange for a privileged status relative to that she might otherwise have. It is better to share a lot than receive little help with her reproductive activities—better a live dog than a dead lion. The argument may sound anachronistic in societies where women can create their own resources, but one must remember that the genetic predispositions have not been eradicated by today's cultural norms. Polygyny evolved under the influence of sexual selection of the female for male social dominance and the ability to acquire resources—traits that can benefit her. We may sing the blues over our history, but the evolutionary tune lingers.

Getting It Together

A couple may be genetically fit, with perfect waist-to-hip ratio, unparalleled health, unsurpassed resources. But if the individuals are not

FIGURE 15.3

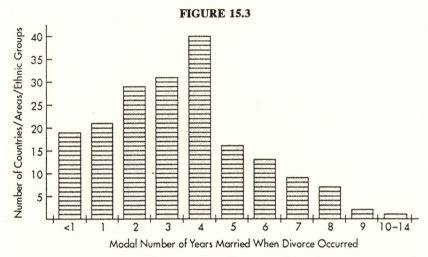

Four year peak in divorce rate, averaged for 62 different societies. U.S. and Finland societies indicate some variation in the average time that divorce occurs.
Source: Fisher, 1994

psychologically compatible, the selection for traits of fitness is a vacuous activity. Obviously relations fail not only because of poor reproductive fitness, but because the male and female simply "do not see eye-to-eye." Mate selection must involve at least two steps, selection for genetic benefits *and* selection for mate compatibility. One may at times substitute for the other, but the optimal choice involves both.

When relationships fail it is usually not because of problems regarding health, beauty, or physiological infertility; it is more because of sexual incompatibility, lack of commitment, general indifference. Anthropologist Helen Fisher has collected data from sixty-two societies around the world, showing a dramatic peak in divorce rate four years after marriage. Here is near universal evidence for a "marital itch," but a "two-to-four-year itch," rather than the mythic "seven-year itch."

Various interpretations for the average four-year peak in divorce are possible, but the fact that many cultures show the same pattern, suggests an underlying feature common to most people. The time involved is perhaps optimal for deciding whether or not the relationship will work, and perhaps whether or not offspring will be produced. If reproduction is at issue, three predictions are possible. The first is that

FIGURE 15.4
Relation Between Number of Children at Time of Divorce and Divorce Rate

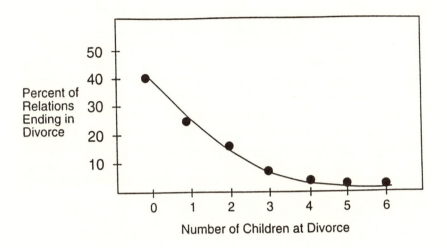

Source: Fisher, 1989

there would be few if any children at the time of divorce. The second prediction is that the probability of divorce would be inversely related to the number of offspring, that is, the fewer the offspring in the relation, the higher the probability of divorce. The third prediction is that people who divorce are likely to remarry faster than those who lose a spouse from death.

The predictions are mostly fulfilled. In the United States the calculated number of children at divorce is 0.89, less than an average of one during a four-year marriage. The average rate of those couples who do not divorce is higher at the same point in time. Second, using data provided by Fisher, there is a relationship between number of offspring and probability of divorce, suggesting that reproductive success is the key to stable relationships.

Finally it is clear that divorced men and women wed at rates far higher than people who have never been married. Divorced individuals marry at almost 2.5 times the rate as never-married people of the same age. Moreover, they don't wait long between marriages. Half of the men remarrying in 1986 did so within just two years; half of the women remarried within just 2.4 years. The rates of remarriage in divorced couples is up to fourteen times that where spouses died. The evidence is compelling that divorce occurs because of incompatibilities and failure to reproduce, not from absence of reproductive capabilities. The fact that people who divorce quickly pop back into a new marriage is in accord with the notion that reproductive success is the goal. The critical confirmation of this hypothesis would be if it is found that remarried couples have offspring more quickly than those who marry at the same age for the first time. The three to four year marriage without offspring may be seen as a loss of time; the second marriage may be an attempt to make up for lost time.

The question remains, what makes individuals compatible? Part of the answer is genetic similarity. How well individuals get along, and how long they stay together, seem to correlate with the degree to which they share genes in common. Like nepotistic interactions among relatives, genetic similarity among mates reduces the costs of cooperative acts. The proposition is that individuals sharing genes actually are helping themselves when they help each other—narcissism in the disguise of true altruism.

The evidence is fairly strong that individuals who are alike in their physical and psychological makeup are also more similar in the genes that they carry. Thus, two individuals who are tall, brown-eyed, and intelligent, probably share more genes for those traits than would individuals who meet by chance. If mate assortment for gene similarity facilitates cooperation, increases the stability of heterosexual relations, and possibly increases reproduction, close mate assortment for trait similarity will prevail in the evolutionary competition of reproductive strategies.

Couples do assort "like-with-like" on a number of characteristics, including race, ethnicity, socioeconomic status, politics, religion, age, height, body weight, eye and hair color, intelligence, attitudes, personality traits, and specific abilities. The list is long and impressive, showing that mate assortment is generally important. Indeed it is, as the stability of relations, and the ultimate reproductive consequences depend on the degree to which the male and female share traits.

An example of the importance of assortment is found among married couples who differed in the degree of similarity on thirty-six physical, cultural, and personality characteristics. Investigators found that those couples who remained married for four years showed greater similarity on twenty-five of the thirty-six traits than those who divorced within that time. It's this sort of similarity that stabilizes relations and leads to greater reproduction.

The correlations between spouses are very high for race, ethnic affiliation, socioeconomic status, religion, and politics (~ 0.90), moderate for intellectual traits, educational achievements, personality variables, and vocational interests (~ 0.40), and lower for most physical measures and specialized abilities (~ 0.20). Of course a great deal of variability is seen within any class of correlations, and a couple may assort highly on some traits, moderately on others, and still not at all on some.

Two additional points should be made. The first is that the evidence is strong that married couples do not become more similar on major traits simply by living together. The correlations between traits are there at the beginning, the criteria by which couples make their initial choices.

The second important point is more complicated. Mating based on gene similarity is low-level inbreeding. Intense inbreeding can be deleterious, in that offspring may be physically disabled and mentally retarded. That's why incest taboos have evolved, and why nuclear family incest occurs relatively infrequently. In any case, the point is that while low levels of gene assortment are adaptive, it can only go so far before it's potentially damaging. Apparently assortative mating must be balanced against any damaging effects of incest. As the old song goes, "I want a girl, just like the girl who married dear old Dad." One doesn't want to marry Mom, but there may be genetic advantages to marrying someone like Mom.

Maui Revisited

We now leave our couple on the beach of Maui with a better understanding of how they got there and what they want from each other. The price of sexual union is unequal for the two sexes, and reminds us why females are more apt to seek relationships, while males are more interested in multiple sexual experiences. Not all is unequal, however, as both males and females seek genetic advantage by insisting on good health in their partners. Facial and body features are signals for health and potential genetic success. In addition, males and females prefer partners who are genetically and phenotypically similar, solidifying relationships and increasing the probability of reproduction. In many ways males and females are unconsicously applying evolutionary adaptations to sexual relationships. Love on the beach should be spelled G-E-N-E.

References

Cited in Chapter 15

Betzig, L. (1993). "Sex, Succession, and Stratification in the First Six Civilizations: How Powerful Men Reproduced, Passed Power on to Their Sons, and Used Power to Defend Their Wealth, Women, and Children." In L. Ellis (ed.), *Social Stratification and Socioeconomic Inequality*. Westport, CT: Praeger, 37-74.

Buss, D.M. (1994). *The Evolution of Desire: Strategies of Human Mating*. New York: Basic Books.

Fisher, H. (1994). "The Nature of Romantic Love." *The Journal of NIH Research*, 6, 59-64.

Fisher, H.E. (1989). "Evolution of Human Serial Pairbonding." *American Journal of Physical Anthropology*, 78, 331-54.

Gallup, G.G., Jr. (1986). "Unique Features of Human Sexuality in the Context of Evolution." In D. Byrne and K. Kelley (eds.), *Alternative Approaches to the Study of Sexual Behavior*. Hillsdale, NJ: Erlbaum.

Gould, J.L. and Gould, C.G. (1989). *Sexual Selection*. New York: Scientific American Library.

Johnston, V. and Franklin, M. (1993). "Is Beauty in the Eye of the Beholder?" *Ethology and Sociobiology*, 14, 183-200.

Langlois, J.H., Roggman, L.A. and Musselman, L. (1994). "What is Average and What is Not Average About Attractive Faces. *Psychological Science*, 5, 214-20.

Lopreato, J. and Yu, M-y. (1988). "Human Fertility and Fitness Optimization." *Ethology and Sociobiology*, 9, 269-89.

Pérusse, D. (1993). "Cultural and Reproductive Success in Industrial Societies: Testing the Relationship at the Proximate and Ultimate Levels." *Behavioral and Brain Sciences*, 16, 267-284.

Rushton, J.P. (1995). *Race, evolution, and behavior*. New Brunswick: Transaction Publishers.

Singh, D. (1993). "Adaptive Significance of Female Physical Attractiveness: Role of Waist-to-Hip Ratio." *Journal of Personality and Social Psychology*, 65, 293-307.

Smith, M.S., Kish, B.J. and Crawford, C.B. (1987). "Inheritance of Wealth as Human Kin Investment." *Ethology and Sociobiology*, 8, 171-82.

Thiessen, D. (1993). "Environmental Tracking by Females: Sexual Lability." *Human Nature*, 5, 167-202.

Thiessen, D. and Gregg, B. (1980). "Human Assortative Mating and Genetic Equilibrium: An Evolutionary Perspective." *Ethology and Sociobiology*, 1, 111-40.
Thornhill, R. (1993). "The Allure of Symmetry." *Natural History*, 9, 31-36.

General References

Diamond, J. (1993). "Sex and the Female Agenda." *Discover*, 14, 86-93.
Goodall, J. (1990). *Through a Window*. Boston: Houghton Mifflin Company.
Nielsen, F. (1994). "Sociobiology and Sociology." *Annual Review of Sociology*, 20,
   267-303.

16

The Dark Lens of Evolution

*If anyone ever believed that we are the chosen
ones—the hope of resurection into a new enlightenment—time has shattered that illusion. Our days are
numbered in blood—the countdown has begun.*

—George E. Marberg

The evolution of the brain's mental complexity brought with it the stamp
of Cain—the out-of-control, species-specific behaviors whose destiny is
hidden in the darkest recesses of time. Irrationality, forces of survival, and
the lust for reproduction are as much parts of us as nepotism, reciprocal
social exchange, love, creativity, and religious devotion. Our natural and
universal traits embrace murder, physical violence, rape, child and spousal abuse, stalking, extortion, robbery, deception, indifference, suicide,
ethnic hatred, social revolution, and war. Though we would deny it, or
wish to believe that evil is a distortion of basic good, the hurtful qualities
of humans are the mosaic of our heritage—always a potential, sometimes
a reality. As the filmmaker John Huston once said, "After all, crime is only
a left-handed form of human endeavor."

Here is what many biologists believe. First, natural selection has
modified our behaviors toward survival and reproduction, regardless of
the consequences for others—the selfish gene always lurking in the
wings. Second, the seeds for the most evil forms of behavior lay buried
within each of us. Third, the manifestation of behaviors harmful to others results from the distortion of Pleistocene social behaviors and the
lack of external restraint associated with contemporary civilization.
Clearly the environment shapes the expression of our genotype, but the
prevailing view that external factors are solely responsible for our behaviors is untenable. The worst is within all of us. With typical insight,

Henry Miller touched the center of the problem: "The study of crime begins with the knowledge of oneself. All that you despise, all that you loathe, all that you reject, all that you condemn and seek to convert by punishment springs from you." We can gain insight into the genetic and evolutionary influences on criminal behavior by looking at the range of crime in the United States.

Crime by the Numbers

The United States crime statistics are numbing. Between 1960 and 1990 the rate of all crimes reported to the police tripled; the rate of violent crime quadrupled. We suffer one homicide every forty-two seconds, one burglary every eleven seconds, one car theft every twenty seconds, one robbery every forty seconds, one rape every five minutes.

The statistics are alarming, calling out for understanding. The usual explanations refer to poverty, drugs, television violence, racism, social tension, and hopelessness. Poverty, in particular, is believed to provoke crime, yet the evidence supporting this notion is weak. In fact, it is more evident that *crime causes poverty*. Criminal behavior of young people often begins before there is evidence of poverty. During the period of time when crime has increased substantially, so has this country's affluence. Similarly, countries are often about equal in crime rates, even when poverty levels differ. Crime, in fact, destroys wealth, with noncriminals acquiring more resources over time. We must look elsewhere for the emergence of a violent street ethic involving gangs, guns, and murders.

Criminologist Ernest van den Haag believes that the most evident root cause of crime is lack of punishment. To the criminal the cost of a crime is the risk of punishment spread over events, much like receiving parking fines. If a single parking fine costs $50, but an individual is caught parking illegally only once in every ten times, the fine per violation is actually $5. If the punishment for burglary is five years of imprisonment, and an individual is convicted and sent to prison every tenth burglary, the actual punishment for burglary is only six months.

According to statistics from the RAND Corporation, the number of crimes committed by the career criminal in the United States is between 187 and 287 per year. Considering the actual cost per crime, a convict serves only six to seven days per burglary, about two years per murder, six months per rape, two months per robbery, eight to nine days per aggravated assault, and only two to three days per car theft. Criminals know that on the average that they will serve no more than 40 percent of their sentence, and in most cases they will not serve at all—62 percent of convicted felons are sentenced to probation, not imprisonment.

The low cost of crime to the criminal is reflected in two major statistics, the number of criminals in prison per crime committed, and in the rate of repeat crimes, that is *recidivism*. In 1960, 738 criminals went to prison for every 1,000 violent crimes. In 1980 that number had dropped to 227, and in 1990 it was down to 90. The prison populations have multiplied, but the crime rate has risen faster than population growth, thus the risk of imprisonment has actually decreased. The state and federal prison populations have increased by 167.7 percent between 1980 and 1993, yet for states, where data are available, the percent of arrests leading to incarceration decreased from 48.2 to 28.5 percent for violent offenses, from 19.1 to 10.0 percent for robbery, and from 41.1 to 31.2 percent for property offenses. The only category of crime showing an increase in imprisonment is drug offenses, increasing from 6.8 percent in 1980 to 30.5 percent in 1992. This is the only crime where state sentencing is mandatory.

Clearly, for most serious crimes there has been a significant decrease in the probability of punishment for crimes. Many believe that this is one of the major reasons crime has increased: decrease the punishment for crime and it becomes less costly for the criminal. But if lack of restraint is a "cause" of crime, then crime itself seems inherent in the species, only dammed up by social mores and fear of prosecution. The view is that the owner's warning and the dog leash have saved many a neighbor's cats.

If individuals at all follow the blueprint of their genetic history, we may be able to recognize the existence of genetic influences on criminal behavior. Genetic variations express themselves through changes in hormones and brain processes, many of which can influence the probability of socially harmful behaviors. Searching for a biological substrate of criminal behavior is not "throwing in the towel," or advocating an Orwellian remedy for crime. Rather, a biological approach opens a new and more promising view of our own behaviors and our relations to each other.

Where is the Biology of Crime?

The crime rate, which can be defined as the number of crimes per 100,000 people, does not reflect how many criminals there are or how many crimes these criminals commit. We have already indicated that career criminals commit between 187 and 287 crimes per year. Overall, 6 to 7 percent of the population commits 70 percent of all criminal acts. Individuals who can be classified as psychopaths, about 2 percent of the male population, account for 30 to 40 percent of all felony crimes.

Males with so-called Attention Deficit Disorder (ADD) are also responsible for a disproportionate number of crimes. ADD is associated with hyperactivity, explosive temper, recklessness, truancy, and pathological lying. This unstable personality syndrome is associated with agitated behaviors and inability to concentrate. Hyperactivity associated with ADD is diagnostic of the probability of criminal behavior. Of the 1/3 of the population that eventually outgrows hyperactivity, about 20 percent commit a serious crime. Of the 2/3 of the population that does not outgrow hyperactivity fully 55 percent commit a crime. Psychopathy and ADD appear to have substantial genetic links, suggesting that genes contribute substantially to high rates of crime.

Just counting the number of crimes gives no hints as to its composition. Clearly, crime rates must take into account the number of criminals involved and the number of crimes that each criminal commits. The crime rate must therefore be parsed into two components: the number of criminals in the population, times the number of crimes per criminal. The first component is the *prevalence* of criminals; the second component is the *incidence* of crimes per criminal.

CRIME RATE =	PREVALENCE ×	INCIDENCE
The total frequency of crime per population (Reflects the total crime within a population, regardless of causation)	Number of potential criminals per population (Reflects biological predisposition toward crime)	Number of crimes per criminal (Reflects the degree to which environment modifies the expression of crime)

If criminal predispositions are genetically influenced, then the *prevalence* of criminals will vary according to individual differences, levels of physiological functioning, and so on. What does change the crime rate are factors that influence the *incidence* of criminal behavior. It is the incidence of crime that is governed by social restraint, cost/benefit outcomes for criminal behaviors, and whether or not the criminals are imprisoned for their behaviors.

Obviously, not all individuals are equally at risk for criminal behaviors, reflecting in part individual inclinations toward antisocial acts and differential sensitivity to social inhibitions. We can construct a hypothetical relation between a decay of social control over behavior and the expression of antisocial behavior. When social inhibitions decline, as with a loss of family values, gang identification, lack of punishment for wrongdoing, and a general attitude that "anything goes," the deep biological drives of individual survival and reproduction express themselves more easily. As this happens more individuals, including young people, are drawn into the network of criminal behavior. Each reduction of social restraint lowers the cost of crime and unveils a deeper physiological and genetic form of selfish behavior. The first dysfunction to appear is a failure to engage in reciprocal social exchange. As more social restraints are lifted psychopathic behaviors appear, physiological predispositions toward crime manifest themselves, ethnic conflicts appear, and nepotism vanishes. The end of the trend can be social chaos.

Although genes do influence criminal behavior, there are no genes that can be defined as "criminal genes." Rather, there are genes for high-risk behaviors, impulsiveness, hyperactivity, poor judgment, mental dullness, hypersecretion of hormones, low enzyme activity, low anxiety, epilepsy, high or low neurotransmitter activity, poor glucose metabolism, and a number of other conditions that predispose individuals toward erratic, careless, and aggressive acts. We can talk about genes for criminal behavior, but what we really mean is that there are genes for particular physiological and behavioral features that bias individuals toward criminal acts, given certain permissive environments.

Evolutionary strategies for social competition, cost/benefit analyses, resource acquisition, and mate choice can also bias individuals toward murder, mayhem, and madness. *Homo sapiens* never evolved adaptive strategies for criminal behaviors *de novo*—only strategies for the preservation and propagation of selfish genes. Thus, there are no genetic and evolutionary determinants for criminal acts, only genetic and adaptive inclinations for survival and reproduction, sometimes expressed in extreme ways. Given these, along with a permissive environment, the likelihood of antisocial acts is substantial.

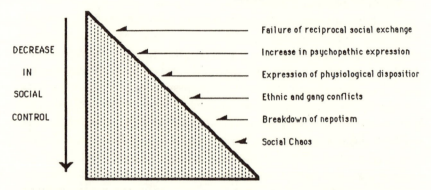

FIGURE 16.1
The Genetic Image of Criminals

*Such things as high testosterone levels, enzymatic variations, neurological conditions. Sociologist Lee Ellis describes the continuum from high to low social control as K to r scale, with K referring to self-controlled behaviors and r referring to impulsive and uncontrolled behaviors. As social control decreases, individuals move from K to r activities, showing an increasing number of genetic and physiological inclinations toward criminal behavior.

Thus, the biological approach to the understanding of crime is to consider the importance of individual differences in physiological dispositions toward criminal acts, and the significant contribution of evolved strategies for individual survival and reproduction. The two in combination, acting within an environment of low restraint, can account for a substantial proportion of crimes. Let's consider some of the data.

Criminality runs in families. According to Justice Department statistics more than half of all juvenile delinquents in state institutions and more than a third of adult criminals in local jails and state prisons have close family members who have also been imprisoned.

Demographer Allen Beck with the Bureau of Justice Statistics indicates that of the 2,621 incarcerated delinquents studies, 25 percent said they had a father who had at sometime been incarcerated; another 25 percent said they had a brother or sister who had been incarcerated; 9 percent indicated they had a mother who had been incarcerated; and 13 percent listed other relatives who had been in prison. Fully 52 percent of the most serious juvenile offenders, confined to long terms in closed or high-security state facilities, implicated relatives who had been incarcerated at some time or another.

Beck found much the same thing among adult inmates. In one study of about 400,000 inmates in city and county jails, 35 percent reported that a close relative had been jailed. In another study of 771,000 inmates in state prisons, fully 37 percent of the inmates admitted to having an immediate family member who had been imprisoned.

These findings have unparalleled implications. Either the crime rate is so high within the criminal subculture that crime involves nearly everyone, or criminal families are overrepresented among imprisoned populations. The data by themselves are silent on the relative contribution of genes and environment. Other findings, however, are more revealing.

Two methods have been used to assess the degree to which criminal behavior is inherited. The first is a comparison between identical twins, monozygotic twins (MZ), derived from the embryological splitting of a single fertilized egg, and nonidentical twins, dizygotic twins (DZ), derived from two separate fertilized eggs. Psychologist David Rowe saw the clear implication of twin research when he said, "Indeed, the best guess we could make about the psychological and physical traits of another person, without interviewing him or her directly, would be based upon the characteristics of the person's [idential] twin (if one could be found). Nothing we might discover about conditions of rearing, schooling, neighborhood, religion, or school yard friends would come close to the usefulness of an [identical] twin in providing information about this person's height, weight, eye color, temperament, mental illness, habits, IQ, values, or nearly any other trait." The twin design depends on the fact that MZ twins share 100 percent of their genes, and DZ twins share on the average 50 percent of their genes. Thus, identical MZ twins should be more similar for traits influenced by genes than nonidentical DZ twins who share only some of their genes.

In one study of juvenile delinquents, MZ twins correlated in their criminal behavior by about 90 percent, whereas DZ twins correlated around 70 percent. Converting these differences into estimates of genetic and environmental influences, behavior geneticists L. DiLalla and I. Gottesman conclude that about a third of the total variation of delinquent behavior is genetic in origin. Similar estimates of genetic influences for adult populations are around 50 percent, indicating that juvenile delinquency is regulated more by environmental effects, whereas adult behaviors are about equally divided between genetic and environmental influences.

The second research design to assess the possible influence of genes on criminal behavior is the adoption design. It takes advantage of the fact that adoptees share genes but not rearing environments with their biological parents. One is therefore able to see the separate contributions to criminal behavior from the biological parents and the adopting parents. A typical question that can be asked is whether a male growing up in the crime-free environment of his adopting parents is more like the adopting parents with whom he is not related, but does share a common environment, or more like his biological parents with whom he does share genes, but does not share a common environment.

Using this approach Sarnoff Mednick and his colleagues showed in a study of 14,427 male adoptees from Denmark that when adoptive and biological fathers were criminal the adoptee was most likely to be criminal (24 percent). The next largest group of criminal adoptees were those where only the biological father was criminal (20 percent). If neither the biological nor the adoptive parents were convicted criminals, the adoptive sons were convicted at a rate that was average for the entire population (13.5 percent). Finally, if the adoptive parents were convicted, but not the biological parents, the rate remained low (14.7 percent). This complex interaction is best seen in diagrammatic form.

The outcome is evidence that genes play a role in criminal behavior, even when criminal environments differ. Without a convicted biological parent, the criminal rate among adoptees is low. An adoptee with only his adoptive parent having a criminal record is no more likely to turn out to be criminal than the population average. This does not mean that the environment is inert in its effects on behavior, but only that when the environmental influences are controlled for, there is still evidence for a significant genetic influence.

High rates of offenses for biological parents are associated with a higher risk of conviction by adoptees, at least for crimes against property. Three or more convictions of biological parents increases the

TABLE 16.1
Percent of Adoptive Adult Offspring Showing Criminal Behavior

		Biological Parent Convicted	
		Yes	No
Nonbiological	Yes	24.0%	14.7%
Parent Convicted	No	20.0%	13.5%

adoptee's risk of conviction to about 25 percent, or more than 10 percentage points above the average conviction rate for the entire population.

Both twin and adoption studies have repeatedly pointed to a substantial genetic influence on criminal behavior. One can hypothesize, however, that as the family environment deteriorates completely, and social restraints become more and more lax, a greater percentage of the criminally inclined will emerge in the population. The environment will push the criminal potential higher under these stressful conditions. Individuals differ in their inclination toward criminal behavior, and evolutionary adaptations play out their destiny in a constantly changing environment. All of these variables interact in complex ways—all deserve our attention.

How do Genes Influence Criminal Behavior?

The march of genes through evolutionary history was possible only because of their association with adaptive traits. Traits, not genes, were selected—only those that facilitated reproduction prevailed. That goes for all behavior and its underlying neural and physiological processes. Behaviors that facilitate reproduction increased in frequency, bringing with them correlated bodily processes.

Let's face it: "criminal-like" behaviors could have been adaptive a million or so years ago, leaving us an ugly legacy. Male competition for social status and access to females were particularly strong selective pressures for any behaviors of "one-upsmanship," including aggression, oppression of others, murder, infanticide, and rape. Deception, cheating, nepotistic biases, paranoia, and conflicts with strangers added to our repertoire of offensive and defensive acts. Those behaviors were not called criminal among our hominid brothers and sisters; they were simply gene-survival devices. Today when these behaviors disrupt our cultural system we call them antisocial or criminal behaviors.

There has been a social transmutation of adaptive acts of the Pleistocene epoch into today's corpus of criminal justice. What was then survival and reproductive behaviors are now subject to approbation and imprisonment. Although a hard pill to swallow, it is probably the case that many deviant behaviors of today are only distortions of adaptive responses of yesterday. They are exaggerated, ill-timed, misused, and socially damaging, but not abnormal in their origin. This in no way suggests that criminal behavior is acceptable or shouldn't be punished. All it means is that the explanations for crime, and eventually its disposition, must be based on our understanding of evolutionary history.

With the exception of brain trauma and genetic mutations that distort some brain processes, we can expect that normal mechanisms of behavior will regulate criminal behavior. There should be no new neurotransmitter chemicals related to crime, no new hormones, and no new brain regions. What we can expect is that the processes that manage "normal" behavior will be the same that manage "abnormal" behavior. The extraordinary savagery of a few, the explosive rage of some, and the insidious knavishness of others, engage the same neurophysiological mechanisms that support survival and reproduction. Individuals differ in levels of transmitters and hormones, and in neural sensitivity to events in the environment, but the neurophysiological principles are those conserved from earlier successes.

Chemicals, Genes, and Criminality

A number of individuals involved in antisocial behaviors show unusual reactions to drug administration or unique profiles of body chemicals. Psychopaths, for example, seem relatively unresponsive to the adrenal hormone epinephrine, showing reduced physiological arousal. The physiological reaction is in keeping with their lower level of anxiety. Others, with high levels of a related hormone, norepinephrine, sometimes show overarousal, rapid heart rate, and increased tendency toward impulsive hot-blooded acts of violence. Some individuals with low levels of the neurotransmitter serotonin are irritable, aggressive, and subject to violent and spontaneous eruptions of criminal behavior. Low serotonin has also been associated with alcoholism, sexual deviations, psychological depression, and suicide. Females with hormone changes associated with certain phases of the menstrual cycle, or males with high blood titers of testosterone, are sometimes predisposed toward exaggerated antisocial behaviors.

The fact is that most individuals with "chemical imbalances" do not react with agonistic behaviors. There is no inevitable association between antisocial reactions and particular chemical activities. Moreover, one cannot tell at first glance if chemical variations cause antisocial behaviors, or if antisocial behaviors cause chemical variations. We are a long way from understanding the complex interaction between chemical activities, genetic variations, neurological processes, and disruptive behaviors.

Currently one of the most promising avenue of research involves the neurologically active enzyme monoamine oxidase (MAO). This genetically controlled enzyme has been connected with criminality, psychopathy, and related behavioral disturbances. MAO is sometimes referred to as a "mop-up" enzyme, because it destroys neural transmitter chemicals that are released at the junctions of brain neurons. If the level of MAO is low, neural transmitter substances linger, overexciting the brain, sometimes leading to socially undesirable behaviors.

There are actually two forms of MAO, MAO-A which works mainly on the neurotransmitters serotonin and norepinephrine, and MAO-B which works on most transmitter chemicals, but especially with dopamine and phenylethylamine. Both forms of MAO may influence antisocial behavior, appearing in areas of the brain implicated in the etiology of criminal behavior, such as the brain stem, hypothalamus, and parts of the limbic system. Most discussions do not distinguish between the two forms.

The potential significance of MAO is indicated by several observations. The first is that MAO activity varies from ten- to twenty-fold among individuals within the population, suggesting a wide range of neurological activity that could affect behavior. Several genes seem to control its level, inducing a range of individual differences in neurological functioning. Whether high or low, MAO levels are fairly constant within individuals. On the average male levels of MAO activity are about 15 percent lower than female levels, suggesting a sexual difference in the impact of MAO on brain and behavior. The hormones estrogen and testosterone both decrease MAO activity, as do the hormones of stress, including corticosterone and epinephrine. MAO may indirectly affect behaviors through its influence on reproductive and stress hormones.

The relations between MAO activity and behavior are widespread. Low MAO activity in infants has been associated with heightened motor activity, high emotional reactivity, and fussiness. In older infants low MAO activity has been related with higher than normal rates of enuresis, thumb sucking, and nail biting.

Sociologist Lee Ellis summarizes an impressive amount of data relating low MAO activity with activities often associated with criminal behavior. These activities include childhood hyperactivity, extraversion, impulsiveness, poor academic performance, drug use, job instability, and rejection of authority. In other words, the MAO profile fits our definition of antisocial personality.

The geneticist H.G. Brunner and his colleagues in the Netherlands have implicated a close association between a gene on the X chromosome, causing a deficiency of MAO-A activity, male aggression, violent activities, and mild mental retardation. In the particular Dutch family investigated the total number of affected males across several generations was fourteen. MAO was assessed in several of these individuals and in other unaffected males and females.

Major behavioral problems were reported for all affected males, including outbursts of rage, forcing sisters to undress, the raping of one sister, stabbing of another individual with a pitchfork, running over a boss, fighting, exhibiting oneself, and starting fires. Of those investigated, only the behaviorally deviant males showed evidence of the abnormal gene on the X chromosome and a depression of MAO activity. For this particular Dutch family there was a close association for the presence of the abnormal gene, antisocial behaviors, and low MAO activity.

The studies are promising bits of evidence that there are proximate processes underlying individual differences in criminal behavior. MAO activity in the central nervous system may be critical. Not all individuals seem to carry the chemical profile of criminal behavior, and those who do may or may not exhibit deviant behavior. The differences in vulnerability, however, may help us predict which individuals are likely to engage in criminal acts as social restraints are removed.

Lurking Within

How can 1,000,000 people be wrong? That's about how many are imprisoned in the United States. Add to that perhaps 3,000,000 more who are on probation, or have yet to be caught for their crimes, and we have statistics difficult to explain. A strong argument is that the bad stuff exposes itself when social restraints are relaxed. Yes, but what is this bad stuff that we talk about, and why is there so much of it?

It's there, and there's so much of it, because crime is in large measure a dark reflection of evolutionary adaptations—the stuff is the stuff of the past, and there's so much of it because we all carry similar baggage. Crime not only comes with opportunity, it is in the chemicals, the neurons, and the muscles; it is also in the essential adaptations of social competition, the battle against an indifferent environment, the reproductive urge of the selfish gene. We still follow the force of testosterone, strive for survival, and push for the ascendency of the selfish gene. Let's look at some of the stuff.

The male hormone testosterone has a reputation of mythical proportions—a killer hormone, according to some, one of irrationality for others. "Down, wanton down! Have you no shame that at the whisper of love's name, or beauty's presto! up you raise your angry head and stand at gaze?" The poet Robert Graves saw the reactivity to testosterone in himself, as others see it too.

Psychologist James Dabbs and his colleagues even relate male testosterone levels to marital discord. The higher the circulating levels of testosterone, the greater the probability of marital disorganization. Consider the data in tables 16.2 and 16.3.

The relations between testosterone and aggressive behaviors are becoming clear; the picture is not altogether pleasant. High levels of testosterone found in prison populations of males are associated with rape, child molestation, assault between inmates, murder, and even armed robbery. These are correlations and do not specify causal relations. Nevertheless, the correlations are consistent and suggest that testosterone is a driving force of antisocial behavior. Some of Dabb's data on the relation between deviant behavior and testosterone indicate that high testosterone increases the risk of all sorts of socially unacceptable behaviors.

But, testosterone also gets a bad rap. This crucial male hormone from the testes does more than stimulate sex and antisocial behaviors. It's

TABLE 16.2
Percent of Males with Differing Marital Status Showing Low,
Medium, or High Circulating Testosterone
(From Booth & Dabbs, 1993)

	Testosterone Level is		
Male Status	**Low**	**Medium**	**High**
Never Married	6	10	15
Ever Divorced	25	36	49
Marriage Separation	22	30	39
Extramarital Sex	18	25	33

TABLE 16.3
Percentage of Normal and High Testosterone Individuals
Reporting High Levels of Anti-Social Behaviors
(After Dabbs & Morris, 1990)

	Group	
Anti-Social Behavior	**Normal T** **(N = 4,016)**	**High T** **(N = 446)**
Childhood delinquency	11.5	17.9
Adult delinquency	10.0	22.6
Hard drug use	9.7	24.7
Marijuana use	22.5	47.6
Alcohol abuse	11.5	16.4
Military AWOL	5.9	13.4
Many sex partners (> 10/yr)	23.1	32.1

anabolic, causing growth of muscles, adding to the strength and stamina of the body. Testosterone differentiates the male brain, increases competitive abilities and influences reproductive success. It has dual functions—some bad, some good.

A wider perspective is that testosterone was the chemical road to civilization, pushing the male into risky behaviors, allowing him to conquer new vistas, opening up new opportunities. Testosterone activates, invigorates, stimulates, and builds. It heightens awareness to potential threats in the environment, increases self-confidence, and makes things happen. For better or worse the feminist critic Camille Paglia may have been correct when she said, "If civilization had been left in female hands we would still be living in grass huts." Mountains, to move, must be pushed.

Grass huts or not, there is a troublesome facet of testosterone that reflects our evolutionary contingencies. Testosterone induced the sexual dimorphism that females preferred—dimorphism that was essential for differing roles and responsibilities. Thus, sexual selection left us with two legacies—the male primed for competition, resource acquisition, and female pursuit, and the male, hair-triggered, paranoic, sometimes violent, and often unpredictable. This notion is modified in figure 16.2 from Dabbs' work. The third column expresses the author's view of the positive qualities of testosterone stimulation, not Professor Dabbs'.

Physical Traits as Predictors of Crime

The physiological substrate for crime, as with testosterone, is sometimes expressed in the morphology of the male. One's body build, one's *somatotype*, expresses an individual's developmental history, and may reflect personality attributes that correlate with behavior. This is an old idea explored in the United States by William Sheldon. Measurements of the male body reveal three major classifications, with a number of intermediate forms. The major types are called *endomorphy, meso-morphy,* and *ectomorphy.* The terms come from embryology where endomorphy describes the inner layer of the embryo—the viscera; mesomorphy describes the muscle and bone layers of the embryo; and ectodermy describes the skin, sense organs, and brain.

Body builds fall naturally into these three types. An endomorphic build tends toward roundness and softness; a mesomorphic build tends to be more muscular and better proportioned; and an ectomorphic build tends to be thin, light, and often tall. Every physique has components of all three types, some more average than others. Each type is scored with 1 as the lowest value, 7 as the highest. Pure cases are scored in this way: endomorphy, 7-1-1; mesomorphy, 1-7-1; and ectomorphy, 1-1-7. The pure average physique is scored 4-4-4. While diet, exercise and other experiences can modify the somatotypes somewhat, generally the predominant features do not change significantly over a number of years.

Below are illustrations of the various body builds among males, and two body-type distributions—the one on the left is of college students, and the one on the right is of inmates of an institution for antisocial youths.

FIGURE 16.2
Testosterone, Misbehavior, and Evolutionary Success

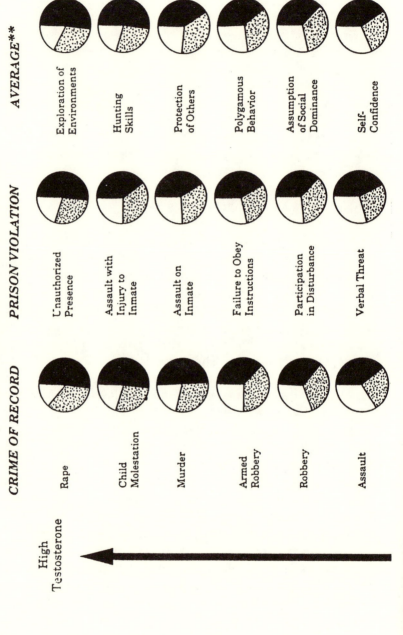

CRIME OF RECORD

Rape

Child Molestation

Murder

Armed Robbery

Robbery

Assault

PRISON VIOLATION

Unauthorized Presence

Assault with Injury to Inmate

Assault on Inmate

Failure to Obey Instructions

Participation in Disturbance

Verbal Threat

AVERAGE**

Exploration of Environments

Hunting Skills

Protection of Others

Polygamous Behavior

Assumption of Social Dominance

Self-Confidence

High Testosterone

FIGURE 16.2 (continued)
Testosterone, Misbehavior, and Evolutionary Success

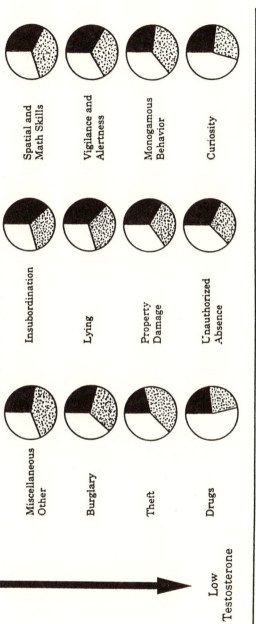

Spatial and Math Skills

Vigilance and Alertness

Monogamous Behavior

Curiosity

Insubordination

Lying

Property Damage

Unauthorized Absence

Miscellaneous Other

Burglary

Theft

Drugs

Low Testosterone

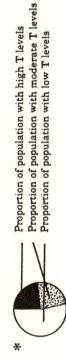

*   Proportion of population with high T levels
     Proportion of population with moderate T levels
     Proportion of population with low T levels

** Testosterone levels for *Evolutionary Success* are hypothetical, representing averages from *Crime Record* and *Prison Violation*.

Source: Dabbs et al., 1994

FIGURE 16.3

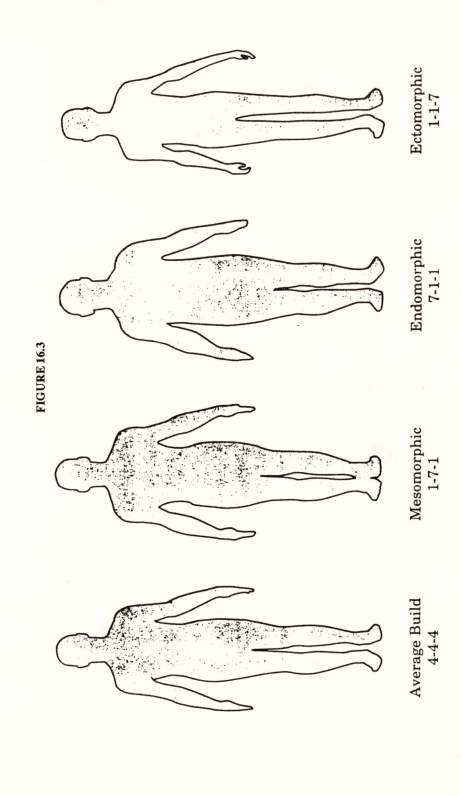

Average Build
4-4-4

Mesomorphic
1-7-1

Endomorphic
7-1-1

Ectomorphic
1-1-7

FIGURE 16.3 (continued)

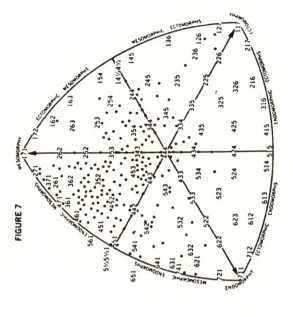

FIGURE 7

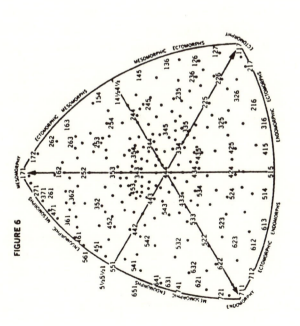

FIGURE 6

Source: Wilson and Hermstein, 1985

The striking feature of these observations is that criminals tend to be mostly mesomorphic, with a deficiency of endomorphy and especially ectomorphy. Follow-up studies have confirmed the original relation between mesomorphy and criminal behavior.

The exact reasons for the fundamental association between mesomorphy and crime are not known. In some obvious sense muscularity may be a useful tool for criminal behavior, allowing for sustained muscle activity and a bullying personality—the idea is "if you've got it, you're likely to flaunt it." Mesomorphy may be the reflection of higher levels of testosterone, acting either developmentally in biasing behaviors toward aggression, or, as an adult, in the expression of psychopathic and violent acts. The issue is not settled, but it is clear that body build can be a contributing feature to criminal behavior. When looking for biological correlates of antisocial behaviors, physique must be considered.

Male and Female in Disharmony

Regardless of the country or continent, males murder more frequently than females. In about 3/4 of the cases males murder other males, and almost always, males are more likely to murder females than the reverse. In 1988, 34 percent of female murder victims in the United States were killed by either a husband or a male romantic partner. In the same year only 11 percent of male victims were murdered by a wife or a female romantic partner. These numbers differ somewhat by year and by ethnicity, but they typically show the male to be more murderous.

The sociobiological explanation is that sexual selection by females for success characteristics in males loaded the dice in favor of male violence. Male competition with other males for prestige, social dominance or resources, elevates his aggression and places him in greater danger, relative to the female. Crime rate statistics indicate that the danger is greatest during the male's reproductive years when competition is most intense.

Sexual selection not only elevates the conflict between males, but increases the conflict between males and females. The male in his quest for control over female mating and his own success, acquired attributes of possessiveness and jealousy. The male is constantly concerned with fidelity of the female and his own paternity—only the female knows that her offspring is hers; the male can only hope and attempt to protect his reproductive investment. The evolutionary biologists Martin Daly and Margo Wilson generalize the point. "Male sexual proprietariness is the dominant issue in marital violence. In studies of 'motives' of spousal homicide, the leading identified substantive issue is invariably 'jealousy.'" Interview studies of North American spouse killers indicate that the husband's proprietary concern with his wife's fidelity or her intention to quit the marriage led him to initiate the violence in an overwhelming majority of cases, regardless of whether it was the husband or wife who ended up dead. Similarly, in other cultures, wherever motives in a sample of spousal homicides have been characterized in detail, male sexual proprietariness has proven relevant to more than half of those homicides. Sexual proprietariness evidently lies behind most nonlethal wife beating, too, suggesting that spousal homicides are not primarily cold-blooded "disposals," but are the tip of the iceberg of coercive violence. Men strive to control women by various means and with variable success, while women strive to resist coercion and maintain their choices. There is a brinkmanship in any such contest, and homicides by spouses of either sex may be considered the slips in this dangerous game."

Females, however, are not passive recipients of male violence. Researchers Murray Straus and R.J. Gelles found in a sample of 8,145 families that the rate of wife-to-husband assault rate is about the same or a little higher than the husband-to-wife assault rate. These statistics are generally ignored, because of the widespread belief that abuse is nearly always initiated by the male. When women do react, it is believed that they respond only in self-defense. Recent studies, however support Straus's findings. Women themselves report higher rates of assault than men, and admit that they are more likely to strike first. According to Rodriguez and Henderson, mate homicides by females occur more frequently in cohabiting relations. Women between the ages of twenty-five and thirty-four kill more than younger or older women.

The apparent differences between the sexes are in the injury and murder rates. Recent reports of The National Family Violence Survey indicate an injury rate of 3 percent for female victims and 0.4 percent for male victims of spousal assault. Males murder their spouses or female partners at the rate of two to three times that of females. Thus, while the sexes are similar in initiating violence, males are ultimately more damaging in their acts.

Female violence is still a real problem and a theoretical issue. A purist sociobiological interpretation would suggest that sexual selection by the female is the major evolutionary pressure moving males toward aggression, and that females are free of this pressure. However, problems of female-to-male violence, offspring abuse, and the increasing crime rate for women, strongly suggest that males and females are more similar than we care to admit. Biological theories must take this into account.

If the problem is recast in terms of inclusive fitness, rather than sexual differences, the similarities in aggressive and violent behaviors are better understood. Both males and females are unconsciously concerned with gene propagation, acting out their genetic history in unique ways. While males guard against cuckoldry, even aggressively, females protect their reproductive choices, sometimes aggressively. Social interactions are conflictual by nature, as individuals and sexes differ in their biological designs and their reproductive inclinations. The path toward reproduction is long and dark for both sexes.

Conflict between males and females extends to offspring investment. Earlier we saw that the dissolution of marriages sometimes occur when reproduction fails—the entire cycle of dating and mating hinges on reproduction, at least for the majority of couples. Robert Trivers was the first biologist to link reproductive drives to parental conflict, indicating that because of differential physiological investment in offspring, males and females have different motivations. The male with his small investment in each reproductive act, is more interested in multiple mates, a greater number of offspring, and a shorter interval between offspring. The female has a heavier reproductive investment and is therefore more conservative on all of these dimensions. Both sexes are reacting to messages of the past that optimize reproduction.

The male and female are tied to their reproductive efforts. If males are uncertain about their paternity, or if males and females find the cost of parental care too high, the reproductive efforts may be terminated or abandoned. One can therefore predict that infanticide, child abuse and child neglect follow cost/benefit considerations.

Martin Daly and Margo Wilson have demonstrated links between evolutionary criteria of reproductive success and family homicide, infant abuse, and infant neglect. In the United States in 1976 the fatal abuse of infants was 100 times more likely where one or more of the parents was a nonbiological parent than where the infants were living

TABLE 16.4
Abuse Cases in the United States for 1976 as a Percentage of
Total Validated Cases in Different Household Compositions

Household Composition	Total Cases of Abuse and/or Neglect	Abuse Cases as % of Total Cases
Two natural parents	35,860	34.4
Natural mother only	31,824	21.2
Natural mother & father substitute	9,137	54.2
Natural father only	3,437	30.4
Natural father & mother substitute	1,786	59.1
Adopting parents	616	59.7
Other relatives	904	30.9

Source: Daly and Wilson, 1981

with biological parents. A similar relation was found more recently in a Canadian population.

Step-relationships lack the deep emotional ties with stepchildren; common interests are lacking and feelings of bonding and commitment are correspondingly shallower. In addition, the burden of care by the stepparent may interfere with other reproductive efforts, thus negatively influencing genetic fitness. Abuse and neglect are reduced to the degree that children share genes with one or both of their parents.

The child, presumably lacking genetic fitness, and thus not contributing to parental fitness, is likely to be subject to neglect, abuse, or even murder. It has been reported that mentally retarded children and children with congenital defects, such as Down's syndrome, spina bifida, fibrocystic disease, cleft palate, and early psychopathologies are at high risk for abuse. Similarly, infants separated from their mothers for the first forty-eight hours postpartum are about seven times more likely to be abused. Separation may occur because of problems associated with prematurity or because of other handicaps. Even children who look different than other family members are more likely to be abused.

It isn't simply the status of the children that provoke abuse in families. In a study by Bland and Orn, fully 69 percent of child abusers and 56 percent of spouse abusers had a lifetime psychiatric diagnosis. The risks for abusers was high among alcoholics and those with antisocial personalities or depression. Biologist Stephen Emlen of Cornell University believes that families are inherently unstable, kept together by necessity. We remain attached to families when our individual interests are served, as when resources are abundant, but bolt when we can better serve our individual genetic fitness outside the family.

Male/female conflicts, murder, spousal abuse, infanticide, infant neglect, and just plain indifference swirl around the evolutionary nodes of survival and reproduction. They are mediated through emotions of lust, hate, suspicion, frustration, and desire, and translated into increments of genetic fitness. From a social perspective the behaviors are abhorrent and deviant, but from an evolutionary perspective they are understandable.

Now or Never

During this last century many cultures have had the luxury of relatively low population growth, a whirlwind growth of technology, a stable social climate, and a system of morality that is almost universal. There have been economic depressions, world wars, and spreading disease, but in every case people have rebounded with greater determination, enthusiasm, and inventiveness. That luxury is rapidly disappearing. Populations press in, wars never cease, economies are faltering, and disease is again on the march. What's worse, people don't seem to want to know the realities. We build barriers, live outside our budgets, deny trends, continue high levels of reproduction, numb ourselves in front of television, and complain about everything.

Crime is the most evident illustration of our failure to adjust. The monster within us is getting larger, yet we have little idea on how to rope it in. But it finally got our attention, and that's a start in the right direction. Mostly we gravitate toward social explanations, and that fits our "can do anything" character quite well. But we must also consider our genetic and physiological inclinations toward crime. Why should that be denied? All behavior has genetic and physiological underpinnings. Genetic diseases are yielding to physiological and environmental manipulation; neurophysiological processes are known to underlay language, intelligence, emotion, and cognitive abilities; we have made our lives happier with medicines, corrective surgery, and better diets and exercise. Crime is no exception to the general principle that a biological understanding can reduce antisocial behavior.

Politicians and special interest groups will not get us very far; every facet of society has an unwavering and unsupported point of view. Science is still one of the best methods for understanding and permanently changing behavior. Suspect as it sometimes is, it is the best thing we have going for us. It may not always be right, but at least it is self-corrective—if the answers can be found, they will be. But time is not on our side, and that is our biggest problem.

References

Cited in Chapter 16

Bland, R.C. and Orn, H. (1986). "Psychiatric Disorders, Spouse Abuse and Child Abuse." *Acta Psychiatry, Belgium*, 86, 444–49.

Booth, A. and Dabbs, J.M., Jr. (1993). "Testosterone and Men's Marriages." *Social Forces*, 72, 463–77.

Brunner, H.G., Nelsen, M.R., van Zandvoort, P., Abeling, N.G.G.M., van Gennip, A.H., Wolters, E.C., Kulper, M.A., Ropers, H.H. and van Oost, B.A. (1993). "X-linked Borderline Mental Retardation with Prominent Behavioral Disturbance: Phenotype, Genetic Localization, and Evidence for Disturbed Monoamine Metabolism. *American Journal of Human Genetics*, 52, 1032–39.

Bureau of Justice Statistics. (1993). U.S. Department of Justice.

Crooks, P. (1994). *Darwinism, War and History*. Cambridge: Cambridge University Press.

Dabbs, J.M. Jr., Carr, T.S., Frady, R.L. and Riad, J.K. (1995). "Testosterone, Crime, and Misbehavior among 692 Male prison inmates. In press.

Dabbs, J.M. Jr. and Morris, R. (1990). "Testosterone, Social Class, and Antisocial Behavior in a Sample of 4,462 Men." *Psychological Science*, 1, 209–11.

DiLalia, L.F. and Gottesman, I.I. (1991). "Biological and Genetic Contributors to Violence—Wisdom's Untold Tale. *Psychological Bulletin*, 109, 125–29.

Daly, M. and Wilson, M. (1981). "Abuse and Neglect of Children in Evolutionary Perspective." In R.D. Alexander and D.W. Tinkle (eds.), *Natural Selection and Social Behavior*. New York: Chiron Press, Inc.

Daly, M. and Wilson, M. (1988). "Evolutionary Social Psychology and Family Homicide." *Science*, 242, 519–24.

Ellis, L. (1991). "Monoamine Oxidase and Criminality: Identifying an Apparent Biological Marker for Antisocial Behavior." *Journal of Research in Crime and Delinquency*, 28, 227–51.

Ellis, L. (1991). "A Biosocial Theory of Social Stratification Derived from the Concepts of Pro/Antisociality and r/K Selection." *Politics and the Life Sciences*, 10, 5–44.

Mednick, S.A., Gabrielli, W.F., Jr., and Hutchings, B. (1984). "Genetic Influences in Criminal Convictions: Evidence from an Adoption Cohort." *Science*, 224, 891–94.

Rodriguez, S.F. and Henderson, V.A. (1995). "Intimate Homicide: Victim-Offender Relationship in Female-Perpetrated Homicide." *Journal of Deviant Behavior*, 16, pp?

Straus, M.A. and Gelles, R.J.(1990). *Physical Violence in American Families: Risk Factors and Adaptations to Violence in 8,145 Families*. New Brunswick, NJ: Transaction Publishers.

Wilson, J.Q. and Herrnstein, R.J. (1985). *Crime and Human Nature*. New York: Simon and Schuster.

General References

Hare, R. (1993). *Without Conscience: The Disturbing World of the Psychopaths Among Us*. New York: Simon and Schuster.

Herrnstein, R.J. and Murray, C. (1994). *The Bell Curve: Intelligence and Class Structure in American Life*. New York: The Free Press.

Reiss, A.J. and Roth, J.A. (eds.). (1993). *Understanding and Preventing Violence*. Washington, DC: National Academy Press.

Thornhill, R. and Thornhill, N.W. (1992). "The Evolutionary Psychology of Men's Coercive Sexuality." *Behavioral and Brain Sciences,* 15, 363–421.

V

Into the Mountains

For in the Market-place, one Dusk of Day,
I watch'd the Potter thumping his wet Clay:
   And with its all obliterated Tongue
It murmur'd— "Gently, Brother, gently, pray!"

   —Omar Khayyám

A strange being, man, creating gods within the mind.

17

The Last Millennium

Destiny is engraved in the human mind, structured on the scaffold of
evolution, running out its course within the shadows of civilization. Our
mind was the single greatest reason we survived on the African grass-
lands and beyond; it was also why we learned of our own beginnings.

Darwin and Wallace lighted our lives with their revelation of natural
selection, a concept of unparalleled magnitude. There it was, the idea
that species change, differentiate, and become new species. Our connection was secured—a deep-plumbed link to our origin, a multifaceted
mirror held up to every organism. Through minds built for survival and
reproduction, the idea of natural selection folded back upon itself to
reveal why we are here. Call it the greatest meme or culturgen in the
world, the theory of natural selection changed our worldview, shattered
our many prejudices, and put religion on trial.

The Emerging Theory of Humanness: A Summary of Survival

Had it not been for the survival of the rare vertebrate *Pikaia* during
the Cambrian period about 525 million years ago, complex vertebrates
could never have evolved. It was a fine stroke of luck that the foundation for our own evolution slipped through the bottleneck of extinction.
It could have been otherwise. Indeed, if the course of evolution were
recreated, the results would be entirely different. Once can easily imag-

379

ine the death of the vertebrate line, leaving invertebrates to rule the earth—perhaps a squid-like cephalopod with a huge brain and a taste for clams and snails.

But chance worked otherwise and vertebrates thrived. The most evident success were the dinosaurs, fleet of foot and wing, large, and in one form or another living over 150 million years. Mammals quietly announced their beginnings during the reign of the dinosaurs, but remained in their shadows, existing in small forms, living mostly by night. Then, as if by fate, a comet crashed into the earth, destroying the dinosaurs and freeing the mammals from their restraint. If not for that, mammals might have remained a minor player: the world would never have been populated by primates. In a nutshell: no vertebrate, no mammals; no death of the dinosaurs, no primates; no primates, no humans.

Chance dogged our heels throughout evolution, the happenstantial loss of the dinosaurs just one of many events that determined the outcome of hominid evolution. At least five global extinctions occurred since the Cambrian period, just one—the Permian extinction about 225 million years ago—eliminating over 90 percent of all species. Time and time again contingencies buffeted all life, destroying over 99 percent of all species that ever lived—the accidental and fortuitous concurrence of atoms, organic life, and environmental imperatives.

The primates did finally appear, but even then our future was not assured. Of the twenty or so great apes that evolved in the rainforests only four survived, one of which had a common ancestor to the first upright hominid, *Australopithecus afarensis*. The hominid road to *Homo sapiens* was rough, initiating monumental increases in brain size and cognitive capabilities. But why did *H. sapiens* make it through the labyrinth, and not *Homo habilus*, *Homo erectus*, or *Homo neanderthal*? Again, it could have been different: one form does not guarantee the next; one hominid is not less capable than another. In its own way each form of life, from single cell bacteria to *H. sapiens*, was perfectly adapted to its habitat. At the same time, each was vulnerable to unpredictable shifts in the environment. The recession of the rainforests and the expansion of grassland changed everything for hominid evolution—eliminating species not capable of coping with new changes, permitting others to multiply.

The battles were not simply with the external world—individuals did more than dodge boulders, complete for food, protect themselves from the cold of night and the heat of the day. Individuals warred with pathogens who, like every other organism, were selected for survival and reproduction. The story is only now unfolding, and if true, indicates that macroscopic and microscopic invaders, set on their own trajectory of reproduction, acted as major selection pressures for the evolution of defense mechanisms in host species. The premier defenses included (1) the immune system that detects and destroys foreign invaders; (2) behaviors that allow organisms to avoid infection and sickness; and (3) sexual reproduction that diversifies traits in offspring, thus confounding pathogenic adaptations. The implications are immense: much of our physiology, our mental sophistication, and even our sexual behaviors are the legacy of millions of years of competition with dangerous pathogens.

Competition was intense between members of the same species as well. Males often competed with other males for access to females, while females accepted only the "best" males. Aggression, acquisitiveness, sexual dimorphism, and love resulted. Social interactions were complicated because offspring had to be protected and groomed for the next generation. Tight bonds evolved between mates and relatives, initiating high levels of kin selection and reciprocal social exchange. Primates, in particular, magnified their own genetic success through individual competition and alliances between relatives and nonrelatives. Our sphere of interest expanded outward.

Throughout the history of our evolution species acquired adaptive strategies to conquer contingencies of their environments. Primates with complex brains turned toward mental solutions of environmental and social problems. Concepts formed; rules of the mind evolved to move behavior toward survival and reproduction, and consciousness multiplied human complexity. Among hominids major habitat changes enlarged the brain, and with it old and new primate strategies emerged. Within the incredibly short time of 150,000 years the hominid potential exploded—language, art, agriculture, animal domestication, trade, travel, nation-states, and all the problems that crowded in.

The short of it is that our nature was shaped by unpredictable demands—ephemeral vertebrate species, environmental catastrophes, punctuational speciations, pathogens, and the flip-flops of climate, food supplies, and shelter. The drying and cooling savannah of Africa dictated the nature of our survival techniques and reproductive strategies, driving the brain to unprecedented complexity—kick-starting the rush toward civilization.

The Two Sides of Destiny

Evolution is sheer destiny, the origins unfolding before our eyes, the future constrained by our past. Contingencies prevailed, alternatives chancy. Yet it was all causal—one thing nudging another—the ecology specifying who lives and reproduces—nothing God-given or directed by unseen forces, no one escaping.

Natural selection left us with an interrelated mesh of adaptations that today we use like a tool kit for benefiting ourselves and society. Our brain is complex, capable of an endless extension into the unknown, and giving us a greater understanding of ourselves and what we are about. The pulsation of our lives lifted us with art, music, literature, science, philosophy, and economic development. Today we are on the edge of understanding our most basic attributes: physics is close to a unified theory of our most elementary structure; astronomy is revealing the nature and destiny of our universe; geology is giving us the fine-structure of our past, present, and future; biology is integrating Darwinian and molecular mechanisms of evolution with punctuational events that drive speciation; and sociobiology is positioning *Homo sapiens* in the mainstream of evolutionary history. The times are revolutionary, creating what before has never been possible, an integrated theory of man and the universe. We can take pride in the fact that *we* are doing it, the unpredicted consequence of biological evolution, the mental complexity emerging from the struggles on the savannah.

Like everything, though, there is the other side—the irrationality of our thinking, the eternal striving of the selfish gene, the inevitability of our march toward reproduction. Biologist William Provine sees the bitter side of our destiny, the implications of the grand theory of natural selection:

- There are no gods or purposive forces in nature. The universe is indifferent to our needs.
- There are no inherent moral or ethical laws to guide human society.
- Human beings are complex machines that become ethical beings by way of heredity and environmental influences.

- There is no free will in the traditional sense of being able to make uncoerced and unpredictable choices.
- When we die, we die—finally and completely and forever.

Our worth is a slender stem, at one time producing fragile flowers, at another transforming into a dried stalk. We bury our parents, our loved ones, our fondest pets; we then are buried by our children, the cycle moving on until there is only a poisoned species, a cold earth, a random universe. This is the bitter knowledge exchanged long ago for the fruit of understanding. In *The Denial of Death* Ernest Becker saw the duality of our existence:

> Man emerged from the instinctive thoughtless action of the lower animals and came to reflect on his condition. He was given a consciousness of his individually and his part-divinity in creation, the beauty and uniqueness of his face and his name. At the same time he was given the consciousness of the terror of the world and of his our destiny and decay. This paradox is the really constant thing about man in all periods of history and society; it is thus the true "essence" of man...

The Land Beyond

At least a dozen prominent writers speak of the "end of a millennium," sometimes with nostalgia, but more often with predictions of worldwide calamity. Anthropologist Jack Weatherford concludes, after a wide view of human behavior, that "The last ten thousand years of history may prove to have been a mistake that nature will force us to rectify in the millennia ahead." Wetherford sees history reversing itself, moving quickly from civilization to savagery. Indeed, terrible events are building; time seems short. There is always something new to be feared—some emerging danger, another extreme—everything balanced on an unraveling tightrope. There may be a "key stone" in the arch of civilization that is loosening, threatening to lay waste to the entire edifice—a basic nature of our lives that can burst forth at any time. Contemporary culture is an artifact of our intellect, revealing our immense capabilities, yet out of synchrony with our fundamental nature. Living in a crowded world of cellular phones, computers, business partnerships, and international agreements requires a constant vigilance, lest we slip back into a savannah mode of daily life. It is far more natural to move swiftly as a small group of related individuals, kill prey and adversaries, and celebrate victory by dancing and eating of the flesh. The prophecy for the future is written in the primate genes.

Our Connection to Savagery

The beginning was inauspicious. The community of chimpanzees in the Gombe region of Africa began to divide into the northern Kasakela tribe and the southern Kahama tribe. The separation was complete in two years, but did not yet portend the future. When males from the two tribes met at the periphery of their territories they hurled insults at each other, but always retreated into their separate territories.

A year went by before the assaults began—the first brutal attack coming from the north, where a patrol of six males encountered the young male, Godi, from the south. Godi was caught unawares, forced to run, and brought down by the combined actions of Figan, Jomeo, Sherry, and Evered. Godi was pummeled and left badly wounded after ten minutes. Godi was never seen again, surely dead.

This incident was the beginning of a four-year war between the chimps of Kasakela and those of Kahana. Jane Goodall, the famed ethologist who studied these chimps for thirty years, was horrified, later telling the world that, "For so many years I had believed that chimpanzees, while showing uncanny similarities to humans in many ways were, by and large, rather 'nicer' than us. Suddenly I found that under certain circumstances they could be just as brutal, that they also had a dark side to their nature. And it hurt."

The attacks continued until nearly an entire tribe was wiped out. In addition to the mayhem and murder that ensued, the nightmare weeks and months included the gruesome feasting on the flesh of the youngest victims. The battles went on, back and forth. Eventually, the northern invaders were forced to retreat. The four-year war was over, and the two tribes settled into routines of probes and threats, but no more ambushes or dramatic chases—the status quo had returned.

War it was, organized, bitter, innate—the evolutionary precursors to hominid tribal disputes, the genetic foundation of war and genocide in *Homo sapiens.* Our connectedness to the great apes speaks loudly about our innate propensity to war. War is in our evolutionary pattern, a male passion to join together in conquest, defense, and acquisition. It is also an individual experience that has no equal, that, in a moment, can hold a person fiercely in its grip. War strategist Martin van Creveld captures the essence of that moment. "Approaching the fighting, we listen to the thunder of cannon and the howl of shot. Soon we discover ourselves trying to guess which one has our number on it. Our nerves are strained, sharpened, focused, until they become impervious to anything else. Our head empties, our mouth dries. Both past and future melt away; at the point of impact the very notions of "because of" and "in order to" vanish as body and mind struggle to achieve the absolute concentration that is essential for survival." Dreaded, yet these moments draw us forward.

It is simplistic to believe that we have specific genes for war, but we do have genes that predispose us to aggression, defensiveness, bonding, acquisition of resources, survival in face of danger, and reproduction. The traits are common to both sexes, but as usual they distribute themselves according to reproductive needs and, probably, testosterone levels. Men, more than women, band together, play the odds, seek the thrill of battle, the stimulating fear of death, and the acknowledgement of survival and victory. Watch the fascination with war in the military, where statesmen, strategists, commanders, and troops swallow their fears and move to the fight. Watch the same motivations work themselves out with the male attachment to gang warfare, rough and tumble play, sports, driving, flying, video games, chess, business competition, and love relations. More than women, men are concentrated, compelled, and competitive in war and their substitutes, forms of behavior entirely compatible with their polygynous style. Polygyny bred male competition, competition bred war. Anthropologist Irvin DeVore was once asked why men go to war? His answer was that the women are watching.

War in Transition

Prior to the seventeenth century wars were fought by republics, principalities, cities, coalitions of cities, religious groups, and independent noblemen, to say nothing of robbers, pirates, and opportunists. Almost tribal and chimp-like, these wars were brutal, protracted, and entirely motivated by self-interest.

The appearance of modern nation-states, beginning around 1600 to 1650, brought with it wars conducted by *governments*, fought by *armies*, encouraged and paid for by *citizens*—trinitarian wars, waged like legal tournaments, with specified rules of conduct. The "how," "where," and "when" of waging war was eventually formalized by the Prussian officer Carl Gotlieb von Clausewitz in the early 1800's. His vision set down in the opus *Von Kriege (On War)* established itself as a classic, setting the conditions of war for Adolph Hitler, as well as Dwight Eisenhower who grappled with it in his early days at the U.S. Army War College. Even today *Von Kriege* is seen as the greatest work on war strategy in the Western world. Its trinitarian theory is based on the concept of the nation-state, appropriate as long as states are tangible realities with real borders and identifiable leaders, appropriate to the degree that citizens are willing to pay for the battles and remain noncombatants.

Trinitarian war became grand theater, played out with great drama and passion, its actors shifting back and forth on life's stage fulfilling their respective roles. The years 1859 (the year of Darwin's great book) to 1937 were the "age of civilized warfare," where wars were waged by *public authority*, with *just intent*, and with *proportional force*. The theory was that a just war resembled the administration of punishment by a benevolent father against a childish transgressor—benefits of the nation-state.

Day of War, Night of Terror

Nation-states represent power, providing greater social and economic opportunities, and increased protection for its citizens. But the entire system is contrived, and inherently unstable. The states' boundaries are arbitrary; ruling parties are not representative of all its members; individuals are only partly responsible for other lives; and diverse ethnic, religious, and political groups are in constant conflict.

The artificiality of nation-states accounts for the revolutions within, where there is a circulation of power, and the natural tendency for their disintegration. Move backward in time and their development is understandable; move forward in time and their demise is certain. States hold together for periods of time, waring with advisories from without and contending with revolutions from within. Eventually, though, the nation-state cracks, the artificial boundaries waver, and its homogeneity fractionates.

We, our parents, and our grandparents have known only nation-states; history glorifying their existence, wars fought in familiar patterns. It's difficult to imagine anything different. Yet, the trinitarian form of war of nation-states, with separation of government, armies, and civilians, is already in transition. World War II ended with civilian populations targeted with nuclear and conventional weapons. The Korean conflict of the early 1950's was perhaps the first war in which the majority of victims was civilian. In Vietnam, not only were civilians targeted for aggression, but they participated directly in the war, often emerging as guerrillas soldiers within the land held by the enemy.

In the collective memory of our family we can see the collapse of the distinction between combatant and noncombatant, the difference between war and murder all but gone. The Soviet empire is no more, replaced by ethnic divisions as old as Eastern Europe; Africa has lost its colonial yoke and is reassembling into ethnic states and religious groups. Similar forces are acting worldwide. Weatherford regards the appearance of new nations with concern: "At the end of the twentieth century, the globe stands divided into roughly two hundred independent countries or states, but these contain somewhere around five thousand different nations or ethnic groups." There is much more fragmentation to come.

War waged by nation-states is costly, unwieldily, and inappropriate for rapidly shifting boundaries and political interests. To maintain a division of troops in the field during the Franco-Prussian war required fifty tons of supplies per day. By World War I the cost rose to 150 tons per day. In World War II Germany required about 300 tons of supplies per day, and by 1945 the Allies' cost had risen to 650 tons per day. The cost for the Persian Gulf War of 1991 was at least double or triple that amount. It took six months to build and supply "Desert Shield" in the Gulf War, and years to disassemble the mission after "Desert Storm." The total cost of the "100 day conflict" is almost incalculable, never, perhaps, to be repeated. Modern armies are expensive, especially when weapon development, deployment, testing, and use are considered.

Modern armies are costly from another perspective. The standard assumption is that an army corp can only respond to two or three orders per twenty-four hours. The larger the military unit the more inflexible it becomes. It is impossible for one person to know everything that is going on, things move slowly, and communication between units are often difficult or contradictory. Bloated militaries are the dinosaurs of our generation, relics with nowhere to go and nothing to do except provide social services to the needy—assemblies that are unresponsive to rapidly shifting events. Nuclear weapons are ineffective in smaller skirmishes—even unthinkable—and conventional warfare with sophisticated weapons is of no use with nimble, mobile insurgents who live within their shifting and unpredictable battlefields.

The United States military is beginning to recognize that the "Clausewitizian Universe" no longer holds, but arguably too late to control the rush of circumstances. The *Wall Street Journal* reports that, "The game, which Navy officials won't discuss, captured the main argument now roiling the Pentagon. It isn't about Bosnia or Haiti or North Korea but about whether the way wars are fought will change fundamentally in coming decades."

The Pentagon strategist Andrew Marshall thinks so, and his views are being listened to at the highest levels. It is his belief that the "information age" will fuel a military revolution, just as the cannon did in the fifteenth century. Among his expectations are:

- Mass armies will be replaced by smaller fighting forces, fighting the enemy from a distance with data and "smart weapons" delivered with satellite precision, and directed by commanders in the field.
- Tanks and aircraft carriers are "sunset" weapons that will lose their technical advantages as missile carriers become more mobile and guidance systems electronically controlled. For example, the best way to destroy a tank may not be with another tank, but with a missile delivered from a submarine 100 miles away. Manned aircraft from carriers will be increasingly supplanted by pilotless drones that are less vulnerable to attack.
- Distinctions between air, land, and sea warfare will naturally disappear as forces are electronically integrated and deployed in different proportions as events require.
- Military commands will become less hierarchical, with middle-management eliminated, and with critical decisions made at the front line by commanders plucking information directly from satellites and other long-range monitoring devices.

It is unlikely that ever again will future Saddam Husseins be stupid enough to allow the United States six months to build up mountains of supplies before war commences. The Persian Gulf War was perhaps the last Clausewitizian war ever to be fought. It was so classic that General George Patton from the tank war of World War II could have been briefed in an hour and taken command from General Norman Schwarzkopf without missing a heart beat.

But those days are over—the book on classic war is closing, the nation-states crumbling. As war and murder become the same, as military costs escalate, and as guerrillas appear and disappear in a moment, war is becoming less grand. The stage lights fade. Even Andrew Marshall seems behind the times. Smart weapons launched toward the enemy by satellite are of no use if the capital is under siege by terrorists who are in Washington, D.C. on Monday, Oklahoma City on Tuesday, and seemingly nowhere on Wednesday. To cite von Creveld: "Armed conflict will be waged by men on earth, not robots in space.... troops may well have more in common with policemen (or with pirates) than with defense analysts. It will be a war of listening devices and of car-bombs, of men killing each other at close quarters, and of women using their purses to carry explosives and the drugs to pay for them. It will be protracted, bloody, and horrible." Like a rotting melon caving in by its own weight, the seeds of destruction spew forth from within—primitive, multiple, and savage. It could just as well be the jungle of Gombe, or the savannah of East Africa. The savage gene is back with a vengeance.

Apocalypse Forever

Clausewitzian wars encompassed only about 300 years, a minute fraction of our history since agriculture began, the casualties amounting to a few million. The greater tragedies were not wars at all, in the classic sense of opposing forces meeting on the battlefield; they were slaughters—genocides, with one group attempting to eliminate another. Here is a list of genocides from 1492 to 1995.

Killers mass-murder for revenge, land, power, religion, ethnicity, and the joy of the hunt. In most instances the victims are considered to be less than human—barbaric, unclean, inferior, animal-like. Physiologist Jared Diamond points out that "modern genocidists routinely compare their victims to animals in order to justify the killings. Nazis considered Jews to be subhuman lice; the French settlers of Algeria referred to local Moslems as *ratons* (rats); "civilized" Paraguayans described the Ache! hunter-gatherers as rabid rats; Boers called Africans *bobbejaan* (baboons); and educated northern Nigerians viewed Ibos as subhuman vermin. The English language is rich with animal names used as: you pig (ape, bitch, cur, dog, ox, rat, swine)."

Denigrating attributes go back as far as the written word. There was always a "us" and "them." The word barbarian comes from the Greek *barbaroi*, meaning non-Greek foreigners. *Ethnic* also comes from the

TABLE 17.1
Some Genocides, 1492–1995
(After Diamond, 1992)

DEATHS	VICTIMS	KILLERS	PLACE	DATE
xx	Aleuts	Russians	Aleutian Islands	1745-1770
x	Beothuk Indians	French, Micmacs	Newfoundland	1497-1829
xxxx	Indians	Americans	U.S.A.	1620-1890
xxxx	Caribbean Indians	Spaniards	West Indies	1492-1600
xxxx	Indians	Spaniards	Central and South America	1498-1824
xx	Araucanian Indians	Argentinians	Argentina	1870s
xx	Protestants	Catholics	France	1572
xx	Bushmen, Hottentots	Boers	South Africa	1652-1795
xxx	Aborigines	Australians	Australia	1788-1928
x	Tasmanians	Australians	Tasmania	1800-1876
x	Morioris	Maoris	Chatham Islands	1835
xxxxx	Jews, Gypsies, Poles, Russians	Nazis	Occupied Europe	1939-1945
xxx	Serbs	Croats	Yugoslavia	1941-1945
xx	Polish officers	Russians	Katyn	1940
xx	Jews	Ukrainians	Ukraine	1917-1920
xxxxx	Political opponents	Russians	Russia	1929-1939
xxx	Ethnic minorities	Russians	Russia	1943-1946
xxxx	Armenians	Turks	Armenia	1915
xx	Hereros	Germans	Southwest Africia	1904
xxx	Hindus, Moslems	Moslems, Hindus	India, Pakistan	1947

TABLE 17.1 (continued)
Some Genocides, 1492–1995

xx	Indians	Brazilians	Brazil	1957-1968
x	Aché Indians	Paraguayans	Paraguay	1970s
xx	Argentine civilians	Argentine army	Argentina	1976-1983
xx	Moslems, Christians	Christians, Moslems	Lebanon	1975-1990
x	Ibos	North Nigerians	Nigeria	1966
xx	Opponents	Dictator	Equatorial Guinea	1977-1979
x	Opponents	Emperor Bokassa	Central African Republic	1978-1979
xxx	South Sudanese	North Sudanese	Sudan	1955-1972
xxx	Ugandans	Idi Amin	Uganda	1971-1979
xx	Tutsi	Hutu	Rwanda	1962-1963
xxx	Hutu	Tutsi	Burundi	1972-1973
x	Arabs	Blacks	Zanzibar	1964
x	Tamils, Sinhalese	Sinhalese, Tamils	Sri Lanka	1985
xxxx	Bengalis	Pakistani army	Bangladesh	1971
xxxx	Cambodians	Khmer Rouge	Cambodia	1975-1979
xxx	Communists and Chinese	Indonesians	Indonesia	1965-1967
xx	Timorese	Indonesians	East Timor	1975-1976
xx	Muslims	Serbs	Bosnia	1990-1995
xxx	Tutsi	Hutu	Rwanda	1993-1995
xxx	Hutu	Tutsi	Rwanda	1994-1995

x = less than 10,000; xx = 10,000 or more; xxx = 100,000 or more; xxxx = 1,000,000 or more;
xxxxx = 10,000,000 or more

Source: Diamond, 1992

Greeks, originally referring to pagan races or nations. Words count and they can kill. In every case they attribute superiority to one group and inferiority to another. The vocabulary surrounding genocide projects fears and hate on others, allays any guilt about unfair treatment, and enhances the feeling of superiority.

Words are important, but they are not the cause of genocide. Without them genocide would still occur, though mediated by grunts, pointing, and chest-pounding. The cause lies more directly in the powerful tendency of individuals to fear and be suspicious of strangers who share neither genes nor common interests. The distinctions between "us" and "them" evolved early, probably to insure that resources and cooperation extended along kinship lines, but also so that advantages could be gained at the expense of nonrelatives. The chimps of Gombe knew the difference between "us" and "them," with hunter-gatherer hominids carrying it forward to the present day. Then and now, "us" was good, exulted, and justified; "them" was bad, lowly, and misguided. Murder, genocide, and war always look different to the aggressor and victim—okay for "us," wrong for "them."

Throughout our history "us" and "them" has been applied to ethnic variations. Ethnic groups often came into conflict over ideologies, land, resources, and opportunities. Tensions tend to build over long periods, until an explosive event sends history along an irreversible course. A prime example comes from Spanish history.

After Spain conquered Mexico it used Acapulco Bay as the seaport linking the New World to the Orient. From 1565 until 1815 a Spanish galleon sailed from Acapulco each April with its cargo, headed directly across the Pacific Ocean to Manila Bay in the Philippines. In October each year the ship left Manila with its wares, returning to Acapulco Bay. Trade on both sides of the Pacific was lucrative.

The Spaniards made the Philippines a colony in 1565, establishing its first governor at the capital of Manila Bay on Luzon, the major island of the Philippines. The bay almost immediately became a trading center of the world, attracting the Dutch, British, Japanese, and Chinese. By the end of the sixteenth century so many Chinese lived in Manila that the Spanish created a special market quarter for them.

Tensions among the various ethnic and nation groups repeatedly flared into violence. The bloodiest episode occurred in 1603 when the Chinese attacked the Filipino community and laid siege to the Spaniards. In the end half of the Spaniards were killed, their heads pinioned on poles throughout Manila. The remaining Spaniards, with the help of Filipinos and Japanese, fought off the Chinese, killing roughly 23,000 in retaliation.

Despite constant tensions and the occasional eruption of violence, the trade links between Mexico, the far East, and Europe grew and prospered. Roughly 10,000 years after the advent of agriculture, the world was unified into a single economic system. The watershed event was the trans-Pacific seafaring from Acapulco to Manila. Mexican merchants sent more silver across the Pacific to Asia than to Spain. In turn, the wealth of Asia streamed into Mexico, quickly moving to Spain and the rest of Europe. The Acapulco-Manila link did perhaps more to bring nations and groups together in business and social commerce than any other single change in history. But it also increased competition among traders and others, setting the stage for ethnic tension and violence. Today ethnic tensions and skirmishes darken our future.

Birds Coming Home to Roost

Ethnic feuds simmer over long periods, flaring up unexpectedly. Hutus battle Tutsi in Rwanda, Bosnians struggle with Serbs, Azerbaijaries fight Armenians, the Irish Republican Army wars with the British, Pakistanis fight Hindus, new ethnic tensions emerging almost weekly. About seventy armed conflicts are now being fought outside of nation-states. Joseph Montville, director of a conflict resolution study at the Center for Strategic and International Studies in Washington, believes that the Cold War was a containing device. With its collapse, groups were freer to act on ancient grievances. "It's as though the cops had gone home, and there's no one to answer at 911." For the biologist, it's more like the veneer of civilization has been stripped away, revealing bare DNA.

Ethnic wars span generations and no one forgets. The Greeks remember the fall of Constantinopole to the Turks in 1453; the Jews remember the Maccabean revolt of 165 B.C. ending the oppression by Antiochus IV. The American blacks remember 300 years of slavery. For the Serbs, the memories of humiliation go back to the 1389 defeat by the Muslim Turks in the Battle of Kosovo. Every Serbian child learns about Kosovo; it was the beginning of 500 years of Turkish occupation. The Muslims of Bosnia have their own ethnic memory. They remember the massacres of Muslins by Serbs in World War II. The Serbs, in turn, remember that half of their numbers was slaughtered by the Nazis, sometimes with Croat help. Their promise of a "Greater Serbia" is a way to revitalize themselves at the expense of the Muslins and Croats who are painted as a threat to their own future. With the collapse of the Eastern Bloc former Yugoslavia became the battleground of old hurts and resentments.

Other hot-spots of ethnic hate are in the East African nations of Rwanda and Burundi. History is deep here too. The pygmy Twa probably settled that area first, followed by Hutu farmers who dominated the foraging Twa. The Tutsi, a cattle-herding people, sometimes called the Watusi, migrated into the same area around the sixteenth century. The Tutsi ruled the other two groups, establishing a three-tier caste system, to which the Europeans added their own when they colonized the area in 1899.

The tensions between the Twa, Hutu, and Tutsi go back at least 400 years. In Rwanda, the Hutu rose up in 1959 and overthrew the Tutsi in a bloody revolution. A plunge in world coffee prices indirectly led to a slaughter of Hutu by Tutsi in 1972. At that time about 85 percent of Rwanda's foreign exchange was from coffee exports, and the drop in price was calamitous. In that struggle the Tutsi came to power. Later that same year a group of Hutu tried to overthrow the Tutsi. In retaliation the Tutsi killed 100,000 Hutu, particularly those who were educated and posed the greatest political threat.

By 1994 the Hutus were again the dominant political power in Rwanda. In April of that year when a plane carrying its president Juvenal Habyarimana mysteriously crashed near the capital, Kigali, Hutu guards went on a rampage, killing as many as 500,000 Tutsi and moderate Hutus. The Tutsi retaliated, killing all Hutu who didn't flee, again assuming national dominance. A million or more Hutus fled into Zaire and neighboring countries, leaving at least 100,000 children without parents and thousands of others dying from famine, malaria, dysentery, and cholera.

There is no telling when the ethnic rampage will cease, if it ever will. Before it does it is likely to spread to Burundi where the ethnic composition is like that of Rawanda. Compounding the problem is a population growth of about 3.2 percent per year, as high as anywhere in the world. As resources diminish even further, and foreign countries are unable to provide for the basic needs of these people, one can expect that the deepest genetic drives for survival will ratchet the slaughter even higher.

The Coming Anarchy

West Africa is becoming the symbol of worldwide demographic chaos—a new and brutal opening of the new millennium. The cities of West Africa at night are some of the most dangerous in the world. Streets are without lights, police nonexistent, the government without power. Armed burglars, carjackers, and muggers roam the streets without opposition.

In Freetown, the capital of Sierra Leone, eight men armed with AK-47s broke into the house of an American man, tying him up and stealing everything of value. In Nigeria direct flights between the United States and Lagos, Nigeria's capital, were suspended by order of the U.S. secretary of transportation because of ineffective security in the area. In Abidjan, the capital of the Ivory Coast, restaurants have stick- and gun-wielding guards who escort their patrons the few yards from their cars to the entrance. Security is sometimes ineffective, for in one of these restaurants robbers gunned down an Italian ambassador. After university students caught bandits plaguing their dorms, they put tires around their necks and set them afire. Ivorian policemen stood by impotently, afraid to interfere.

West Africa is teaming with unwanted men and women—hoards of them—illiterate, poverty-stricken, criminal. Disease, overpopulation, and moral decay are sweeping across West Africa, destroying resources, producing thousands of refugees, and introducing widespread criminal anarchy. Nearly everyone in the interior of West Africa has malaria, about 10 percent are positive for HIV, and the usual diseases prevail: dysentery, hepatitis, tuberculosis, fetal diarrhea, meningitis, and cholera. Zaire has had epidemics of bubonic plague and Ebola in the last two years, and Kenya had a severe outbreak of yellow fever last year. In Sierra Leone, Guinea, the Ivory Coast, and Ghana, the primary rainforest and secondary bush are being destroyed completely. In 1961 as much as 60 percent of Sierra Leone was rainforest; today only 6 percent qualifies. In the Ivory Coast the percent has fallen from 38 percent to 8 percent.

The future of Africa south of the Sahara Desert is almost as certain as night followed by day. In less time than it takes to rear an infant to adulthood, nearly thirty nations will double their population. The population is around 600 millions today, but will be 1.6 *billion* by 2030. Other statistics are just as grim. More than 4 million children born this year will die before the age of five. About one-third of all children are severely malnourished. Of the 14 million individuals with HIV worldwide, 9 million, or 64 percent, are in sub-Sahara Africa. Food production in the 1980s and 1990s was about 20 percent below that in the 1970s, giving strong force to Thomas Malthus's argument that population growth outstrips food production. In fact, population growth in these regions may prevent sufficient organization to produce enough food. Overcrowding and famine in Somalia left the country to feuding warlords, forcing the United States and the United Nations to abandon their efforts to restructure the country. Rebels are fighting in Angola, the Sudan, and Liberia, often for control of food, as well as governments. Rawanda and Burundi are sinking into the chaos of ethnic struggles that ultimately will destroy those nations. Nigeria, already teeming with 90 million people, is facing the destruction of its oil industry and the cataclysm of famine, immigration from surrounding countries, and lawlessness. Famine spreads across the breadth of the country.

Things will get worse. France *will* withdraw from former colonies like Togo, Niger, Benin, and the Ivory Coast. The future of these countries will be more turmoil and bloodshed. In the twenty-first century the conflicts will spread, especially where water is in short supply—Saudi Arabia, Central Asia, Haiti, and the southwestern United States. Ethiopia may soon be fighting Egypt for rights to the Nile River waters. The whole world is involved, not just Africa. Africa is our first major example of near-total social collapse.

The dangers are escalating everywhere that people multiply, resources decrease, and opportunities for individual development disappear. Weatherford sees the world pattern repeating itself in the United States:

> Nowhere in the world had I ever witnessed as much savagery, brutality, crime, and cruelty as I saw on the streets of the capital of the United States. The Tuareg warriors of the Sahara and the Muslim militants of Egypt seemed peaceful compared with the people who ran the sex trade of Washington. Work in the Amazon jungle, among people whose ancestors shrank heads, or among the descendants of cannibals in Melanesia, ranked lower in stress and fear than work among the gangs of Washington. Even research into the cocaine trade in South America, with its coca farms, drug kitchens, and private armies of drug lords' thugs, ranked far lower in danger and capricious violence than research among the drug sellers of Washington.

While the United Nations sponsors population conferences, such as the recent ones in Cairo and Beijing, where the focus was on abortion and women's agendas, the world is literally starving for solutions. The deck chairs are being moved around as the Titanic is going down.

The world is moving toward ethnic and ideological conflicts that re-enact the world's most primitive and savage struggles. But the chaos of the new millennium is different in several unfortunate ways. There are more people competing for fewer things, armed to the teeth with high-tech weapons. Automatic and semi-automatic weapons are only part of the problem. Outlaw groups are acquiring ground-to-air missiles, fast transport, rapid communication, and even nuclear materials.

National boundaries are becoming meaningless as terrorists, orga-nized drug dealers, mercenaries, and refugees move freely and rapidly across borders, plundering as they go, taking no prisoners. Govern-ments posture, threaten, and move armies great distances or against small odds, but their efforts have little impact on guerrilla bands and social degenerates with little more in mind than mayhem, marauding, murder, and madness.

Cinematic Self-Analysis

Glimpses of our future, the reflections of our fears, the terror of the savannah, flicker back at us through our literature, magazines, newspa-pers, and television. Movies, carefully choreographed and set in fatalistic movement by the forces of color, mood, and emotion hit hardest. "Four Horsemen" movies, those that sell apocalyptic recipes, splash the horror of the moment across the silver screen—the wars turned surreal, the devil in punk garb, the cesspool of New York, the garbage dump of the mass-murderer's mind, the failure of any humanity to slip through the cracks of horror, debauchery, degradation, torture, hopelessness, and despair.

The lineup of Four Horsemen movies slices up recent history into the fine-grain of contemporary evil and sin: *Clockwork Orange* (1971), where the number-one "malcheck," Alex, leads his "droogs" through a string of ultraviolent mayhem and murder; *Soylent Green* (1973), the story of hopelessness in New York City in 2022, where a detective stumbles into an explosive government secret that surplus people are being turned into a delicious green delicacy; *Full Metal Jacket* (1987), giving a surrealistic and horrifying view of mindless war in 1968, in which the anti-hero Mathew Modine swaggers, "I wanted to be the first person on my block to get a confirmed kill," and others of the same ilk: *Escape From New York* (1981), *Mad Max 2 (Road Warrior)* (1981), *Blade Runner* (1982), and *Platoon* (1986).

One can almost trace the social downgrading of our civilization through these movies. Sometimes they make their points through exaggeration, science fiction, blunt facts, or satire, but at another level they speak the horrifying truth of what we fear, what the world is becoming. The latest in the series is the demented nightmare *Natural Born Killers*, given to us by Oliver Stone as a warning about where we are headed. One can sense that the mass-murders committed by the two characters Mickey and Mallory are just around the corner, probably in tomorrow's newspaper, maybe in one's own life.

We are not only losing control over mayhem, murder, and guerrilla warfare, we are building up a tolerance to these acts through overexposure, boredom, and the sense that we have no control. Movie critic Roger Ebert sums it up: "We are becoming a society more interested in crime and scandal than in anything else—more than in politics and the arts, certainly, and maybe even more than sports, unless crime IS our new national sport. Once we were shocked that the Romans threw Christians to the lions. Now we figure out a way to recycle the format into a TV show. That's what *Natural Born Killers* is all about." And that is a scary vision of the near future.

The Future

The evolutionary tale of *Homo sapiens* is a lesson in humility. We do not live on Mount Olympus with the gods, sharing their immortality and cosmic knowledge. We are creatures from the dark lagoon of evolution, the only rudder our own, our sparse knowledge squeezed painfully from the universe. What appear to be two faces—one victorious, lined with virtue and creased with justice, the other seared from battles for survival and bloated with ambition—are really the same—the face of worn adaptive processes, the reflection of an indifferent world. We are what we are, the contingent outcome of eons of unpredictable influences.

The transcendent quality of life that we ardently seek eludes us. If we are *nothing but* a biological machine, can we be *anything else*? Our intellectual arrogance tells us one thing, but our heart speaks in a different tongue. However strongly we embrace a mechanistic theory, the ghost is still in the machine, insisting that there is more. But what can that be if not just another reflection of our evolution—a deception, perhaps, that keeps the gears of life turning toward reproduction?

References

Cited in Chapter 17

Asprey, R.B. (1994). *War in the Shadows: The Guerrilla in History*. New York: William Morrow and Company, Inc.
Becker, E. (1973). *The Denial of Death*. New York: The Free Press.
Diamond, J. (1992). *The Third Chimpanzee: The Evolution and Future of the Human Animal*. New York: Harper Perennial.
Goodall, J. (1990). *Through a Window*. Boston: Houghton Mifflin Company.
Green, P.A. (1991). "A Biocultural Analysis of Revolution." *Journal of Social and Biological Structures*, 14, 435-54.
Kaplan, R.D. (1994). "The Coming Anarchy." *The Atlantic Monthly*, February, 44-76.
Kennedy, P. (1993). *Preparing for the Twenty-First Century*. New York: Random House.
Kennedy, P. and Connelly, M. (1994). "Must it be the Rest Against the West?" *The Atlantic Monthly*, December, 61-91.
Liles, G. (1994). "The Faith of an Atheist. *MD* March, 59-64.
Lopreato, J. and Green, F.P.A. (1990). "The Evolutionary Foundations of Revolution." In J. van der Dennen, J. and V. Falger (eds.), *Sociobiology and Conflict*. London: Chapman and Hall, 107-22.
Van Creveld, M. (1991). *The Transformation of War*. New York: The Free Press.
Weatherford, J. (1994). *Savages and Civilization*. New York: Crown Publishers.

General References

Clausewitz, C. (1976). *On War* (M. Howard and P. Paret, eds.). Princeton, NJ: Princeton University Press.

Epilogue

*All my life I believed I knew something. But then
one strange day came when I realized that I knew
nothing, yes, I knew nothing. And so words became
void of meaning.... I have arrived too late at
ultimate uncertainty.*

—Ezra Pound

The idea of human behavior as mechanical is seductive because it places the understanding of human complexity in the same theoretical basket as physics and chemistry. Accordingly, the universe is nothing more than molecules in motion, evolution determining physiology, physiology determining behavior—everything explained within the existing laws of cause and effect. We appear as robotic as plants heliotropically following a ray of sunlight, as ants guarding their queen, as computer programs processing information. Biologist Richard Dawkins devised the relevant Darwinian metaphor, referring to natural selection as the "blind watchmaker," the builder of complexity in incremental steps of trial and error, under the constant supervision of a demanding but indifferent environment.

Bittersweet Destiny attempts to draw the Darwinian argument to its full conclusion, advancing the proposition that cause and effect work their magic on all features of human behavior. Each of our behaviors and cognitive mechanisms, the noble and ignoble, is interpreted as the consequence of natural selection. And to a large extent that may be true. We play out our seven decades obsessed with personal survival and reproductive immortality—our choices limited, our goals specific, our eventuality certain. We appear narrowly constrained by our phylogeny, development, and circumstances—nothing but molecules in motion, supporting Ecclesiastes 1: 7-9, "The thing that hath been, it is that which shall be; and that which is done is that which shall be done: and there is no new thing under the sun." Clearly this is a harsh and deterministic view of reality.

401

At another level, however, the mechanistic model frays at its edges—Darwinian natural selection theory requiring revision. Our evolutionary history was not gradual: our ancestors were no less adapted to their environment than we; we see no evidence for a movement toward perfect adaptation. One thing did not inevitably lead to another. Punctuational events continually broke our connections to earlier species, producing forms with novel adaptations. In many instances new capacities preceded their use—form emerging before function, nothing predictable in advance. Whatever worked remained, many things evolved for one function were coopted for another (exaptation); whatever increased reproductive fitness became the new adaptive strategy.

Chance played out the genetic cards, with large and small extinctions reshuffling the deck, dealing out unexpected combinations of cards, setting the stakes too high for most to complete. The winners were few, never predetermined, no particular advantage for the next hand. Those that survived the many deals were temporary winners, perhaps gaining some chips for the next hand, but hardly aware when the dealer changed the rules of the game.

Still, chance is not randomness, only cause and effect without plan. Looking backward at the fossil record we see the chain of life, but none of these steps was predictable in advance—simply contingencies pounding out the chain one link at a time. While no one can reasonably deny that the steps to *Homo sapiens* were causal—physics and chemistry operating as usual—there was a looseness in the direction and degree of change, inducing unexpected and novel systems of behavior.

The human brain acquired a looseness of another sort, that which was used to deal with contingent ecological events. There was probably never a long period of time during primate evolution when ecologies were stable and predictable. Like our chancy card game, everything was in flux, often short-term and intense—climate, weather, light cycles, forest or grassland, food availability, sexual and social interactions, and pathogens—always changing, a constant challenge. There was little possibility for the evolution of stable long-term adaptations. Instead, hominids evolved multiple short-term strategies that could be variously applied to environmental fluctuations. The multiplicity of adaptive strategies and their inevitable interconnectedness set the stage for novel responses to changing environments, uncertain brain reactions complicit with uncertain ecologies, all causally implemented, but unpredictable before the event.

Surprisingly, "chance" is becoming a central explanatory force in behavioral theorizing. Psychologist Peter Molenaar and his colleagues in Amsterdam speak about a third source of behavioral variance, neither genetic nor environmental, but one of chaotic origin—chancy, nonlinear, highly variable, emerging, and self-organized. Any dynamic system, like the brain, possesses this chaotic nature. "Reiterating, chaotic epigenetic processes are capable of creating variability under constant genetic and environmental conditions. If such a process were simulated twice on a computer, where all starting conditions as well as the genetic and environmental influences are identical between simulation runs, then one would still obtain different outputs."

Thus, our evolutionary legacy is in part one of indeterminacy, both in terms of genetic reactions to changing environments and in terms of dynamic brain processes. Fluctuations in behavior are the expected, not the exceptional: brain activity freed from constraint, novelty of thought and action altogether possible, the sheer complexity of the brain assuring new streams of consciousness—behavior nudged beyond the restraints of our nervous system, unguided by any goal to maximize genetic fitness.

This view of behavior departs from the strict Darwinian model, suggesting that uncertainty of environmental change and indeterminate brain processes enlarge our behavioral potential well beyond our genetic makeup and the influence of the environment. Cause and effect are not abandoned, only delivered in unexpected ways. Consider how the brain probably operates to create diversity. If one could stimulate the same brain twice with a visual pattern, the neural activation swirling throughout the brain would involve different neurons and make different connections each time. As the neurobiologist Gerald Edelman might say, the Darwinian selection of neural pathways is different for each reiteration. On the one hand the outcome seems chaotic, but on the other, the outcome is unique—never seen before, never duplicated again.

Evolution presented us with a variable brain, the kind that physiologist Jared Diamond said gave us the "Great Leap Forward." We used it to walk out of Africa and spread worldwide, we used it to develop language, tool-making, art, music, agriculture, animal domestication, yes, even war and genocide—a brain that had the capability to do more than simply regurgitate old adaptations, a brain that opened a small window to the universe.

From this perspective one could argue that we have almost gone too far in our deterministic attitude about behavior, forsaking the "variable brain" for the rigorous application of natural selection theory. Writer Daniel Seligman hailed our victories in the *National Review*, saying, "Hereditarianism is on the march. Nature is clobbering nurture. A steady drip, drip, drip of scientific studies is cumulatively telling us that more and more human traits are genetically influenced."

The celebration will continue as we explore our evolutionary base, our neurophysiological infrastructure, our DNA imprint. By a twist of fate, though, we are discovering that there are limitations to our deterministic nature, the built-in uncertainty, the irrationality of our thoughts, the stocastic activity of the central nervous system—those things that mostly we try to restrain, but which, in fact, give us unprecedented powers.

If our scientific vision of human behavior moves from natural selection to emergent properties of complexity, we may be able to join the old with the new, retaining a mechanistic view of life, yet augmenting that view to include those qualities that emerge as human.

The Most Human of Qualities

We close the millennium with the soul and heart of man being severely strained by violence, irresponsibility, environmental degradation, and a growing sense of disaster. Populations pulse and surge around the world, oblivious to the needs of civilization, poised for the greatest calamities of all time. Plagues are just around the bend, tribalism everywhere, just a matter of time—total extinction a real possibility.

The Courage to Survive

The aftermath of civilization's crumbling may well be a return to small groups that share common genes or common interests. That's how we evolved; that's how we might survive. There is the sense across the nation that we have lost our way and must thread our way back to our source, much as Dante told of his struggle: "In the middle of the journey of our life I found myself in a dark wood. For I had lost the right path.... And so we came forth, and once again beheld the stars."

The quality that will get many by in the worst of nights is the quality that we talk little of, but which speaks mountains—*personal courage.*

Courage is a human attribute as strong as any—an evolved characteristic that guided us through the bottleneck of human evolution. Strangely, courage has not been investigated to any degree, and its genetic foundation is vague. Yet, it *is* a universal trait that protected our kinship, elevated our ancestors from despair, and led the hominids through the valley of death.

Like any evolved trait, individuals differ in courageousness, and it only shows under environmental challenges. French playwright Jean Anouilh associated courage with death, suggesting that "Until the day of his death, no man can be sure of his courage." Not true; courage is displayed under a wide range of conditions. G.K. Chesterton has a more inclusive definition: "Courage is almost a contradiction in terms. It means a strong desire to live taking the form of a readiness to die."

Witness the raw courage in the face of death of those, Gentiles and Jews, who contributed to the savings of thousands of Jews from Nazi extermination.

- Oskar Schindler of Germany rescued 1,200 Jews by employing them in his munitions factory.
- Berthold Beitz of Poland saved 800 Jews by employing them in the Nazi's petroleum industry.
- Irena Sendler, a Polish social worker, established an underground cell, helping almost 2,500 Jewish children to safety.
- Mary Jayne Gold, an American socialite living in France bankrolled an enterprise to help 2,000 Jews to escape France, while she was hounded by the police.
- Giorgio Perlasca, an Italian, while in Hungry found a set of consular stamps, and without asking Spanish officials, issued more than 3,000 travel permits to Jews for safe travel to Spain.
- Rene Raoul, a French shoemaker and his family, sheltered more than 100 Jews in the small town of Le Malzieu. Other villagers occasionally dressed Jewish children in the uniforms of the fascist Vichy youth organization, mingling them with their own. The local priest hid families in the church belfry. Raoul later said, "My children knew Jews hid among us during the war. But I never spoke to them of my role. Why should I? What I did was natural. I would do it again for anyone."
- Mustafa and Zayneba Hardaga, Muslims from Bosnia, opened up their home to their Jewish friends, urging them, "You are our brothers and sisters. Everything we have is yours; this is your home."
- Then there was Susanna Pechuro, a Russian citizen, who nearly lost her life challenging Stalin's atrocities against the Jews and others. When her group of six activists was caught, three were shot immediately and three were sent off for long terms in the gulag. She alone survived.

Courage is a deep-rooted response to injustices and personal dangers. It doesn't necessarily involve nepotistic acts, although nepotism may be at the bottom of it. If we show courage in protecting our genes expressed in others, our children and their children, we are more likely to show courage with those who do not share our genes, especially those with similar commitments.

The instances of family courage under the shadow of death are legendary. In December of 1992 Army Private James Stolpa, his wife Jennifer, and their five-month-old son Clayton, got stranded in a Nevada snowstorm for five nights with nothing to eat but vitamins. As things worsened James told Jennifer, "We're not doing it for me; we're not doing it for you. We're doing it for the baby." They left a note in case they were never found alive, and walked out of their shelter for twelve miles through waist-high drifts before fashioning a snow cave. James left his family there to seek help, walking another thirty miles before he was found. Jennifer, Clayton, and James made it through that ordeal, even though frostbitten. Said Kevin Mulligan, James Stolpa's stepfather, "For two kids who couldn't keep their rooms clean six years ago, they've performed a miracle."

War has always tapped into the bottom reservoirs of valor and courage. Genetic relatedness is not an issue, just unified commitment. Only recently in Somalia Cliff Wolcott died in an attempt to capture warlord Mohammed Farrah Aidid. He and several Rangers were ambushed by heavily armed Somalians. Turning his Black Hawk attack helicopter broadside in the face of rocket-propelled grenades to give his gunners a clear shot, Wolcott became a perfect target. His last words were, "Super six-one is going down. Six-one is going in."

That day was filled with American heroism. A fifteen-hour pitched battle took place around Wolcott's downed chopper, with an extraordinary display of valor. Karl Maier was one of those heros. Spotting Wolcott's Black Hawk nosing over into the ground he flew his unarmed MH-6 Little Bird helicopter into a space so narrow that his blades barely cleared the houses on both sides. His decision to go in was instantaneous, his radio message to base: "I'm going in." Facing AK-47 assault rifles and grenades, Maier held the chopper steady with his left hand while firing a light submachine gun with his right. His co-pilot Keith Jones loaded two injured Rangers aboard before they left the battle. Not far away Dan Jollota held his chopper steady as rocket propelled grenades whooshed around him until fifteen Rangers "fast-roped" to the ground. Even after two direct hits to the main rotor blade, Jollota held steady.

On the ground Master Sergeant Scott Fales, credited with saving eighty-eight lives during his medical career, worked on several wounded men. A bullet ripped through his leg. Hunkering down next to Wolcott's downed chopper, he bandaged himself and then resumed tending his comrades: "I'd fire a few rounds to push them back, then put my rifle across my lap and turn around to do my medical duties..."

Other Rangers fought their way in to save those pinned down by ricocheting bullets and grenades. Several pilots flew as many as nine missions—their audacity astounding the trapped men below. Sergeant Fales, spotting five grenades coming over a wall in his direction, threw his body over two wounded soldiers to shield them from shrapnel. Meanwhile, Special Forces Medic Tim Wilkinson sprinted forty-five yards through a screen of bullets to respond to a call for help from a comrade. He later said simply, "Once you make the decision to go, you just go." Finally, at dawn the battle was over.

No one can fail to be moved by these deeds of valor, far beyond the call of duty, many others unannounced, all underexaggerated in their emotional and physical grip. Sure, these Rangers were trained for dangerous missions; nevertheless, when the personal choices had to be made, with the only prospect death, "they just went." History is made by such courage.

Many instances of personal courage are never reported or are soon forgotten—police facing murderers, individuals dealing with disease, but one that sticks in the mind is of the student in Tiananmen Square at the 1989 uprising against the Communist Party leadership, who stood firm in front of a moving tank, forcing it to stop. The event, seen on television, was eerie, forcing one to ask the question, "Could I have done that?" The student, like so many others that day, placed his life and principles on the line—his name never revealed, other names quickly forgotten.

There are other heroes too numerous to count, not gory enough for television. Many men and women have stood against the tide, caring more for others than their own lives, walking through death's door, often telling us later that what they did was natural—things they would do again no matter what the outcome. The expression of courage is so obviously innate that it seems mystical—it just happens, unthinking, uninhibited, unreserved. Somehow fashioned within us are those urges to prevail or die, to answer any call, to press survival to the limit—the Mother Teresas of this world, the Albert Schweitzers, the Sergeant Fales, even the Joans of Arc—the "us" verses "them" submerged in something larger. There are no genetic barriers to heroism—nepotism is only one path of courage, for all can transcend prejudices and genetic differences. The Tass news agency even reported last year that a brave dog seized a Siberian tiger by the tail until it let its master escape. Gene similarity means nothing here, only life and loyalty.

This is what's so remarkable about courage. Individuals can give their all for others with whom they share almost nothing—no common ground, no close genetic relatedness, no prospect for success. Loyalty, familiarity, common training, religious fervor, early experiences—whatever proximate mechanisms may be operative—cannot easily account for the depths of courage and the expanse of altruism. It's contradictory, as the samurai Yamamoto Tsunetomo said in the seventeenth century: "I have discovered that the Way of the Samurai is death. There is surely nothing other than the single purpose of the present moment. A man's whole life is a succession of moment after moment. If one fully understands the present moment, there will be nothing else to do, and nothing else to pursue. Live being true to the single purpose of the moment."

It's been said in the press that the glory days of America are over, suggesting that everything has been down hill since 1969 when Neil Armstrong stepped onto the moon with the immortal conjecture, "That's one small step for a man, one giant leap for mankind." Some dismissed Armstrong as too mechanical, all heroics gone, the melancholy spectacle of fallen greatness. Norman Mailer wrote: "Armstrong sitting in the commander's seat, spacesuit on, helmet on, plugged into electrical and environmental umbilicals, is a machine himself." Hardly, Norman Mailer! Heroes are made by their willingness to risk their all, regardless of their surroundings and training. Armstrong and his crew did just that; lesser men can only write about it.

Things have turned bitter, but not because we haven't the capabilities to move mountains; we stepped out of Africa with our eyes on the peaks. And we moved them. We can move many more. Each of us can dig into our biological soul for the courage that is certainly there, and discover the Way of the Samurai. It's not a moment too soon.

The Last Words are for Darwin and Wallace

Many of us have lived through incredible changes in science, technology, and social organizations. Some of us can even remember living with kerosene lamps, hand-operated water pumps, outhouses, and horse-drawn plows. Not long ago radio was an expensive novelty, and there were no televisons, computers, cellular phones, or jet airplanes. Somehow, though, we adapt to change and learn to anticipate it. Yet, think what it would have been like to have fallen asleep on a farm in the 1930's only to awaken in the last half of the 1990's. Would we even believe what we saw, let alone understand the depth of knowledge associate with change?

Now, imagine that Charles Darwin and Alfred Wallace had fallen asleep in the 1860's, finally to awaken today. What would be their impression of today? What would they think of today's notions of hominid evolution, pathogen regulation of sexuality, asteroid-induced extinctions, continental drift and speciation, punctuational equilibrium, molecular biology, the double helix of DNA, and sociobiology? One can only speculate.

Yet the question is important, not only because of the incalculable changes occurring during the past 130 years, but because Darwin and Wallace unwittingly played a crucial role in nearly every idea of biology today. Darwin guessed that our early ancestors would be found in Africa, launching the area of paleobiology; Darwin and Wallace provided the concept of gradual evolutionary change that led to the demonstrations of continental drift and speciation (the longer time the continents have drifted, the greater the differences in fossils and existing species). From their work, too, came the notions of using molecular mutations as a phylogenetic clock. Even the idea of punctuational change, which puts some of Darwin's and Wallace's work in jeopardy, came only as a result of testing their model of natural selection to the limit. Finally, sociobiology, which promises to revolutionize our views of human behavior, emerged only because of these men. Yes, one can argue that all of these ideas may have eventually appeared without them, but the pattern of science would have differed—contingent scientific development, unpredictable at best.

There's no evidence that today's biological world was anticipated by these naturalists. How could it have been? Darwin's and Wallace's agonies in the jungles of South America, Indonesia, and the Galapagos Islands, set sail a wave of scientific discovery far beyond their concerns and hopes. They found a place in history even during their own lives, but they had little inkling of the depth and breadth of their influence. Nor did their contemporaries.

Today we see some of the consequences that flowed from their fertile brains. Some we appreciate, such as the powerful insights of molecular biology, immunology, and evolutionary theory. But other possible impacts are just plain hard to deal with: the crumbling of true altruism and morality, the loss of religious symbolism, the translation of love into parental investment and genetic assortment, the reduction of criminal behavior to genes and biochemistry, and the final loss of free will and self-determination.

Now sociobiology and evolutionary psychology are under siege by those who choose to fight against their most horrifying implications. To some extent the attacks are justified, as much of what we think we know will shatter under the blistering attack aimed at the warriors of biological and social conservatism. These battles will be won by the attackers. But in their stead will come better evidence and more refined theories. The sociobiologists and evolutionary psychologists will then begin to win more battles than they lose, and eventually the war. Be glad or sad, that's our bittersweet destiny. One still wonders, however, how one might feel in 130 years, if sleep comes today.

References

Cited in Epilogue

Dawkins, R. (1986). *The Blind Watchmaker*. Harlow: Longman.
Gleick, J. (1987). *Chaos: Making a New Science*. New York: Viking Penguin, Inc.
Gutzwiller, M.C. (1992). "Quantum Chaos." *Scientific American*, 266, 78–84.
Kauffman, S.A. (1993). *The Origins of Order: Self-organization and selection in evolution*. New York: Oxford University Press.
Lewin, R. (1992). *Complexity: Life at the Edge of Chaos*. New York: Macmillan Publishing Company.
Lykken, D.T., McGue, M., Tellegen, A., and Bouchard, T.J., Jr. (1992). "Emergenesis: Genetic Traits that May Not Run in Families. *American Psychologist*, 47, 1565–77.
Mishima, Y. (1977). *The Way of the Samurai*. New York: Perigee Book.
Molenaar, P.C.M., Boomsma, D.I., and Dolan, C.V. (1993). "A Third Source of Developmental Differences." *Behavior Genetics*, 23, 519–24.
Prigogine, I. and Stengers, O. (1984). *Order Out of Chaos: Man's New Dialogue with Nature*. Toronto: Bantam Books.
Seligman, D. (1994). "A Substantial Inheritance." *National Review,* October, 56–60.
Swinney, H.L. (1993). "Predictability and Chaos." *Discovery*, 13, 27–31.

Index